THE

Word of God

Personal encounters with Realm Walkers

Volume 01

By JAN-MARIE DAVIS

Copyright © 2017 Jan-Marie Davis

This book has copyright under the Berne Convention.

All rights reserved.

No part of this book may be reproduced in any form or by any electronic or mechanical means, including information storage and retrieval systems, without written permission from the author, except in the case of a reviewer, who may quote brief passages embodied in critical articles or in a review.

The information in this book is distributed on an "as is" basis, without warranty. Although every precaution has been taken in the preparation of this work, neither the author nor the publisher shall have any liability to any person or entity with respect to any loss or damage caused or alleged to be caused directly or indirectly by the information contained in this book.

ISBN: 978-0-6481722-0-8 (Paperback)
ISBN: 978-0-6481722-1-5 (eBook)

Artwork concept, cover design and book layout design by Jan-Marie Davis.

Author photo by Anne Higgs Photography, Brisbane.

Available from Amazon.com and other retail outlets.

Available on Kindle and online stores.

www.thewordofgod.com.au

PREFACE

GOD has an urgent warning for mankind living in the year 2017. God is highly concerned with the selfish desires of a few warmongers, that he fears may be out of control and have no idea what they are playing with, when it comes to anything nuclear.

God said, "Man should not play with what he doesn't understand. There is no reversing the effects of nuclear pollution and *everyone* is affected, including the person who pushes the button, not just the country that is targeted."

God commanded, "Don't destroy my planet and don't destroy anything with nuclear, because it lasts for a billion years and you will not survive! Don't turn this beautiful planet into ash. Create with love not destruction."

God added, "Don't eat my animals! Live in harmony and grow as one. Love one another."

DISCLAIMER

ALL attempts have been made by the author to provide factual and accurate content. No responsibility will be taken by the author, or publisher for any damages caused by misuse of the contents described in this book.

The contents of this book have been derived from various channelled readings. Please consult an expert if you are unsure and before attempting anything described in this book. The contents of this book may not be reproduced, duplicated or transmitted without direct written permission from the author.

CONTENTS

ACKNOWLEDGMENTS

THIS book would not exist without the support, unconditional love and encouragement of my everlasting life partner Bradley, whom I cherish more and more every minute we get to spend together. His enthusiasm, drive and determination always helped me to manage my projects through to completion.

I would also like offer my true heartfelt gratitude and special thanks to both of my birth parents here on Earth, Max and Sharon, who both agreed to bring me into this world so I could complete all of my important missions. I physically would not exist in this life without their love and acceptance.

I would like to extend an extra huge thank you to my dad, Max for his tireless hours of proofreading and for applying his unbiased opinion and thorough critiquing throughout this book. I am forever grateful.

I would like to add a special mention for my mum, Sharon who understands that timing is everything. My mum embarked on a journey from New Zealand to Australia to visit me and provide her loving support prior to launching this book. My mum was the first person to read the finished version of the book from cover to cover, before it was released.

Words cannot even begin to express my gratitude for the enduring patience and supernatural skills of the channellers who I have worked with and scribed for throughout the years. They have been a guiding source of hope, love and light. These channellers were the gifted spiritual mediums, who acted as the secure conduit and modern day oracles for the divine messages from God.

I have also had the privilege of conversing with Jesus, the angels, spirits, friends, family, passed over loved ones, guides and masters who have spoken to me through the channellers.

Most of all I would like to thank God, who inspired me to write this book and for being my spiritual companion and mentor at times when I questioned my faith and when I was dragging my feet through life. God has helped me to understand the complex bridge between our world and the spirit world. Every moment I am alive, I am so grateful for everything. Even after life, I will remain eternally grateful.

This book is dedicated to *you* God.

1. INTRODUCTION

Nothing is too small or trivial to talk to God about.
He is interested in everything you want to tell him or ask him.

FIRSTLY I want to thank each and every one of you and I want to congratulate you for being brave and courageous enough to pick up this book in the first place.

Life wasn't supposed to be complicated and it's not. I am going to teach you how to simplify things so that your life is not so complicated, because it's not meant to be.

My mission here and now is to teach level one "God" to new souls and reteach level one "God" to souls that haven't quite worked it all out yet, despite their many incarnations.

Miracles come from God. Do believe and ask. Ask and ye shall receive. Knock and the door shall be opened.

I knocked for a long time and the door *did* open up and once that door was opened, I never looked back. I now choose to keep the door open and never want to close it ever again. I have now been awakened and can no longer fall into spiritual slumber, because my eyes have been opened wide.

I receive divine inspiration every single day of my life and I am so grateful to be living and breathing here on this wonderful planet right now.

I am comfortable in my spiritual beliefs and truly respect, love and know why I exist. One thing I know for sure, is the only reason we exist at all, is because of our true Father and Creator of everything and my best friend in the whole Universe, God.

All of the material in this book was channelled directly to me, through different channellers who were in perfect harmony and in tune with the one and only true Source, our beloved Creator during the readings.

For the purpose of this book I will refer to this true Source of love and light as *God*, the *Father*, *Almighty Lord,* or the *Creator.*

These channelled writings were received throughout my life and this book covers material received up to the year 2017. I ask that you respect the privacy of the channellers from whom I receive my readings, so they can continue their light work here on this planet without being compromised.

This book is not a religious text, even though it may reference biblical characters from time to time. This book is non denominational. This whole book project was entirely funded by the author and can be read and understood by anyone in the entire galaxy that can read, or hear these words.

My purpose for writing this book is to share with you what I have been asked to share with you, or in the nicest possible way I could put it, strongly encouraged to share with you.

Most of the words in this book are either quoted directly from God through the channeller, or they reference God by explaining his thought process and his honest feelings.

The information received is explained in ordinary English for you and shared in personal stories to help you relate to God, so these personal discussions with God can be understood.

If other higher spiritual beings and spirits were channelled during these readings, their names will be referenced where appropriate. My role in all of this was simply as a scribe.

I have not changed God's words when they have been quoted directly from him. I have not used quotations when I share my own personal point of view or some of my experiences with you. Any shared experiences are relevant to the subject or writings. When I give you examples of my experiences, they are important to help you to clarify the writings and put the references into perspective. Any personal experiences or references that I use are not meant to be opinions or assumptions.

Save your judgements of this book for the moment. I want you to keep an open mind, like I had to when I was receiving these writings. Many of these channelled readings challenged my own core personal beliefs and I have had to readjust my preconceived ideas and conditioned view of the world, to understand what God wanted to share with me and with all of you.

We are all made in the image of God and we have all been created with the tools required to communicate with God. This book will help you to connect and learn how to use these tools to communicate with God, because God loves all of us and wants to give his love to all.

I have complete faith that you will find this book useful, interesting and enlightening and the effects will be long lasting.

This is the first book of a series of seven books, which belong to the series called *"Personal encounters with Realm Walkers."*

I am sharing my personal journey with God within the pages of this book and I am so proud to share this information with all of you.

I will also produce a course and workbook for each volume, which can be used to expand your understanding and show you practical ways to implement the spiritual tools needed to realign yourself spiritually with the love and light of God.

As you work your way through this book, please take notes and write down any unanswered questions that you may still have about God, or anything at all. You can send these questions via the contact link on the following website, so they can be answered online for the benefit of everyone.

www.thewordofgod.com.au

Enjoy!

2. MY PERSONAL JOURNEY

God is with all of us, but unless we recognise him and resonate with him, it is like having a dormant sleeping super power within you that you never acknowledge and it doesn't grow.

IN the beginning... Wait. No, no, no that's not how this book is going to start. There has already been a book that started like that and I wouldn't even want to compete, or compare this book with that legendary book.

Let's start again...

I was born Jan-Marie and was the fifth of five pregnancies, which technically makes me the *baby* of the family. My name was inspired by a second hand clothes store that my earthly father saw on the way to my birth. I was the third surviving sibling, the youngest of three, brought forth to the planet by my birth parents. God could see my whole life and just analysed me from being born.

God described how I am being held up in the air, like a trophy, by my father. I was a menace during diaper changes, had toilet fits, loved bathing, but I was a handful and it took lots of work to raise me. I was lucky and had two parents looking after me lovingly.

God sees me sitting up for the first time and he prays for me and I am in his heart.

God said, "Rejoice there is a new angel!" God knew when I was held up for the first time and now that my parents have both read this book, they also know now.

I get to write all the words of wisdom for the suffering. I am a modern day temple and a scribe for God, who speaks on behalf of the dead, an angel disciple. To put this statement in context, I am an angel in training, with my learner plates.

God told me about when I was a little girl. He used to watch me and be with me listening to records, because he used to love the way I felt in my heart, when I was lost in the music.

I used to wait for my parents and everyone else to leave the house, then very carefully opened the lid of the old style cabinet turntable record player which had the speaker built into the unit and very carefully selected the record I was going to listen to. Then I would peel the record out of the sleeve, place the record delicately on the rubber turntable mat and very slowly place the stylus needle just before the first track on the record. I would hold my breath as I was doing this and if I accidentally dropped the needle, my heart would miss a few beats, fearing I would get caught and my parents would find out.

The sound quality was truly amazing. It was so warm and had so much bass. I used to sit with my back against the cabinet with one speaker playing behind me on my right and one speaker playing behind me on my left. Wow what an amazing invention. The magical sounds coming out of it were truly inspiring.

My dad had the best records. He had lots of records with grungy guitar work and groovy 70's tunes. I would lose myself in the songs that I had never heard before. It used to transport me to another place and I was discovering all of this cool new music for the first time. It was like being in Heaven!

I had to be so careful not to scratch the records when the needle reached the end of the record. I had to dock it back on the arm rest so precisely, that I hardly breathed at all while I was doing it. I didn't want anyone to notice I had been rummaging through the record collection and I didn't want anyone to interfere with my new found joy.

I am sure that both parents could probably sense that I was up to something and that I had probably been tempted to look inside the record cabinet. They never actually told me off about it, because I was never caught in the act.

So, here I am with my ears glued to the speakers and losing myself in the melodies, with my spiritual ear finely tuned to hear a car pulling up and preparing to shut it down and put everything back at a moment's notice. I was happy to volunteer to stay at home if anyone had to pop down to the shops. This meant I could sneak in another session of listening to music while everyone else was out of the house. Hours and hours of joy were experienced at the record player. Thank you Dolly Parton, because without you I would never have discovered that "love is like a butterfly!" Thank you to my mother who owned that record. It was my favourite record even though my dad had the better collection of music.

I guess the fact that I became a musician, music producer, singer, songwriter and DJ came as no surprise to God. As I got older, I still found the ultimate joy of discovering new music every day. I would experience the kind of joy that makes you cry and the kind of joy that makes you feel tingles all over your body. Every time I had that feeling, it was like an internal sign of the absolute gratitude I felt for being alive and being allowed to hear this music.

It is this *happy feeling* that attracted God to me and one of the reasons God has been with me for most of my life. God is with all of us, but unless we recognise him and resonate with him, it is like having a dormant sleeping super power within you that you never acknowledge and it doesn't grow.

Another way to describe the *unawareness* of God is like having the best song, CD, or record sitting unmarked in your music collection and because it was never labelled, you still haven't listened to it. You know that if you heard it, you would *love* it and if someone else played it to you, it would probably be your new favourite song. You would really appreciate it, even though it has been there amongst your music collection the whole time.

God wants me to explain that a person needs to *feel* God. Contact with God is a one on one experience. God will only allow group contact in a safe and harmonious environment and if he can sense any other agenda or purpose for contact, he will not participate.

God can time travel for me and gives me some answers to the past and the future. He can go and visit my grandparents (on my mum's side) when they were alive and tells me stories about all of things we used to do together. I was very young at the time and some of my memories have faded since then, so God reminds me of all the happy times we shared together. He knows that you can use *your* memory and you can go there too. He wants you to go to your happy memories regularly and enjoy every moment.

Do you know why you were given a memory? So you can use it. Your mind has so much capacity that it can remember *everything* you did. That's what meditation is. The secret of meditation is to go and visit your memories and do that daily. Then you can visit all of the wonderful memories from the past.

He can see me running through a field and I am running through the field with my brother. I was in a pink dress and we were holding hands. I am allowed to go back there and visit these memories any time I want to and so is every other human.

He sees me sneaking a stool and getting up into the top cupboard. "Only your father knows," God said, "never mind what happens to the packet of biscuits *after* it is opened."

I ran around trying to build things and trying to find the secrets of the house.

God said, "Your father gave your house secrets. The secret turntable, the secret food, the secret guitars and the secret house. You would think to yourself, *what else can I discover?* All the time the chip chop timber is what you hear, dressed as a little movie star. These are your thoughts and you need to go and revisit them."

God said, "You give so many people enjoyment and you are forgetting your past and all of the joyful moments."

God continued, "Do you know what it means to make someone happy? It is that you are making them happy for the rest of their eternal life as a soul. There's a word missing out of the whole Universe, the nearest word is *you.* Forwards, or backwards in time, it is *you.* It is a creation. Someone will make a word for it someday. Your soul name, your unique name. Maybe Jan-Marie can make this new word up? It's your real name and it is everything that you have done in the whole Universe. It's your existence and it's your eternal name. It's how you started and how you ended."

He wants to be funny, "Oh you mean maybe you're an angel? Just like the rest of the angels have a name?"

God added, "At the end of a life don't be afraid, or scared, because you must walk forward and say, 'I am here forth and waiting for your arms to come and take me. Oh Lord, as I am yours only. I am ready for you to judge me,' and I will come to you and I will judge you."

In his judgement he will see if he will take you, or leave you. You might have unfinished work to do and he is only there to help you, so don't be afraid. He will judge you on your mission and on your own judgement.

God has been to all of my parties. All of them! He likes my parties and he used to watch them because they were fun. He remembers the lipstick drawing on someone's face, all of my sexual encounters and everything I have ever done, the good, the bad, the naughty and the ugly, the whole lot.

You cannot hide anything from God and I allow God to talk to me about anything and everything, even if it makes me embarrassed, uncomfortable, or remorseful.

I feel so grateful, so blessed and so loved to be in the presence of God every time he visits. He loves to come and visit in the very small hours of the morning, or very late at night. God's opening line may be, "Forgive me my child for scaring you!"

Sometimes he did give me a fright in the middle of the night and then he apologised for scaring me, because I was not expecting him. Sometimes I just can't keep my eyes and ears open long enough to stay awake. As hard as that may be to believe and as strange as that may sound, if I can't stay awake, I have to ask him for forgiveness and ask if it is alright if I accidentally *drift off* during our conversation. It was never my intention to ignore God, it was because I just couldn't keep my eyes open any longer and would fall asleep. He was never offended and he still loves to visit, usually unannounced and he is very spontaneous and unpredictable.

God doesn't usually like to talk to me when I am with my friends and doesn't allow himself to be heard by anyone else other than a trusted channeller. I don't usually hear from him much during the day, because I am distracted working or doing other things and don't get time to focus on God as much as I would like to. Like everyone else, I have to put food on the table, pay the bills and make ends meet and this unfortunately gives me less time to spend talking to God and getting to know God.

I don't consider myself religiously affiliated with any organisation and I don't identify with any spiritual, or philosophical group, or any modality specifically.

I am not a protestor of all things wrong and I am not a promoter of all things right. I do not see myself as an evangelist, or a preacher. I am not a special person by any means, but one thing I know for sure, is that I am very interested in our Creator and I am a *true believer* in God. Nothing will *ever* change that, for my faith is strong and my faith is what makes me so connected to the Creator.

I wasn't raised in a church environment and I didn't go to church regularly either. I didn't go to any special schools. My education was provided by the stock standard model, in a country town, in a co-education school, where I spent many hours discovering my strengths and weaknesses as a human.

I had a few friends, usually the oddball kind. I was really good at picking up strays and bringing them home. I brought home stray animals and stray humans. My mum would often give me the sideways look when I showed up on the doorstep with a new *strange* friend, or little animal I had rescued from the clutches of a bunch of bullies. Mum would just roll her eyes and step aside and say to me, "Who's this then? Well come in, I'll make you something to eat."

Our house became the local halfway house for the local neighbourhood kids, friends of friends, strangers and abandoned animals.

At one stage we had five cats, three dogs, three fish and one rabbit who thought it was a dog. The rabbit used to eat the dog food and chase the cats around.

We didn't have much, but what we had was always enough. When you are young, you often compare yourself with the other families in town, but looking back now, I know I always had a roof over my head, clean clothes to wear, a meal on the table each and every meal time and a warm bed to sleep in at night, which is more than so many others out there had. Both of my parents worked very hard to raise me, my older brother and my eldest sister to be hard workers and conscientious good people.

We all have big hearts and continue to have an open door policy for our friends and family and the occasional stray. In fact right now, I have multiple stray cats who visit me daily and I put a bowl of food out for them every day. By the next morning the bowl is always empty and I figure that if they have a full belly, they are less likely to eat the wildlife in the area. I am in the process of coaxing one of them inside and have succeeded a few times already. I really love animals and any pets that live around me or with me are treated like additional family members.

These days I have a *blended* family from all around the world. My parents separated much later in my life, after we all grew up and left home and are now both happily remarried with new families. We probably wore them out with our adventurous escapades!

Since then, in addition to my full brother and sister, I also have a beautiful and soulful younger half-sister, a new step-mother, a new step-father and gorgeous step-daughters. Plus I have lots of nieces and nephews. I am so proud of all of them and even if I don't see them often. I do love them and wish I could see them more. This love also extends to other family members who are related by both blood and marriage. I have not even met all of our new family members yet.

Our family circle has widened to welcome many different cultures into our lives. This has given our homes and our bloodlines the gift of exotic cultures which enhances our food experiences and strengthens our family tree. Currently we have the following mix of races; New Zealand Pakeha (Kiwi), New Zealand Māori, English, Welsh, Irish, Spanish, Dutch, Fijian, Indian, Taiwanese and Australian. Phew! There's nothing boring about that mixture.

I do know that if you keep asking and you keep expecting a response, it will come eventually. For me it took thirty something years to finally get a response from God that was audible, tangible and so obvious I couldn't ignore it. Unknowingly, God had been trying to contact me so many times in the past, but just couldn't get through. There must have been a fault in the telephone line, or something blocking me from receiving the calls!

I didn't know what was happening to me. I had already been given multiple signs that proved the existence of the Creator, but in my blissful ignorance, I chose to ignore these signs and shrug them off as mysterious coincidences. I had been led, guided, steered and pushed in the direction of God so many times in the past, but had become sidetracked with my busy superficial life. I was distracted by the trivial stuff and bogged down with crap for so long, that I couldn't sort the internal mind chatter from the reality of miracles.

After many trials and tribulations, I finally decided to consciously make a change and break free from the mental imprisonment of this earthly realm and started searching for answers, because I knew there *had* to be another way.

I spent a large part of my life studying, learning, searching, seeking and gaining qualifications in the alternative healing fields. I am so intrigued by all of the healing methods available in our modern world. The techniques I learned were a mixture of both ancient and new methods and during this path of self-discovery, I realised that it all came down to one thing, *belief.*

The mind is such a powerful healing tool and without the *belief* in healing, you are missing the vital ingredient that binds all of the learning and the techniques together.

Relevant qualifications and courses I have completed include:

- ★ Doctor of Metaphysics
- ★ Diploma in Human Anatomy and Physiology
- ★ Advanced Hypnotherapist
- ★ Master Neuro Linguistics Programming (NLP) Practitioner
- ★ Reiki Master Teacher
- ★ Health Guidelines for Avoiding Infectious Diseases
- ★ Human Health – Diet and Nutrition
- ★ Fundamentals of Biology

I am currently studying other topics such as; the fundamentals of virology and immunology, advanced biology, chemistry, genetics and how to grow organic food sustainably. Very soon I am going to travel to Peru to learn more about the spiritual aspects of Yoga and Shamanism. I aim to become a Yoga teacher as well. I will be able to incorporate the elements that I want to use and add my own spin for a new unique modality.

This story is not supposed to be *all about me*, but I can tell you that I have had some of the most amazing and the most terrible experiences that can get thrown at a human being and have even caused some of this myself. I am far from perfect and every single day I am still working towards to being a better version of myself. I have been working through the false veil of illusion and gravitating away from the earthly desires that can be so distracting and overbearingly tempting. Sometimes the treasures and spoils can be difficult to resist.

I have circumnavigated the globe a number of times during this life and in my past lives. I guess you could say I have travelled far and wide during these travels. I have attracted people and experiences that have helped to teach me life lessons and they have also helped to guide me through the maze of wonder and illusion.

I have fallen prey to destructive relationships, had my heart broken multiple times and even gotten myself into all sorts of trouble. Even throughout all of these tests of faith, I have always managed to find the silver lining and come out of each situation with a better understanding of humanity and the human psyche.

I always prayed for a solution and the solution *always* came. This is what truly taught me faith. Faith is always discovered during times of hardship and it is human nature to pray when things go wrong, rather than when things go right.

We need to turn this belief around, so we are praying to God when things are good. Then we can develop a personal relationship with God and we can appreciate him in our good times first and foremost and then secondly during our bad times, we can ask for his loving support and guidance.

God can recall any day of my life and every person I have ever known in an instant. He is truly *all knowing* and many times he will visit me and open the conversation by triggering a memory. It may have been buried very deeply inside of me, or I hadn't even thought of that memory for a very long time.

God has already forgiven all of my sins over multiple visits, because he knows every sin, every single one of them. I have asked him for forgiveness multiple times for the many things I think I have done wrong in my life. He loves me anyway, because I am a willing participant. I show remorse and I want to learn.

God knows that I accept my mistakes. I own them and release them without dwelling on them for the rest of my life. There is no point regretting anything, because each experience makes up whom you really are and will strengthen your overall character.

Sometimes you just have to surrender, because you can't change the past; you can only *learn* from the past. You can change your *perception* of the past, but you can't change the actual events that took place and wipe the slate clean, unfortunately.

I am very thankful for my whole family, my partner, my parents, my grandparents, my siblings, my relatives, my heritage, my ancestry, my ex-lovers, my new and old friends, both living and passed, my colleagues, my acquaintances and every single one of you who I have ever come into contact with.

I am most thankful for my enemies who have taught me so many things including my really big life lessons. I regard them all as my *biggest* teachers throughout this life and also throughout my past lives. I now class you all as my life teachers, my guides and some of you may even be used as my personal examples (they shall remain nameless of course) when I am sharing my experiences with you.

Everything I have ever done has been for a reason, even if I was unaware of what that reason was at the time.

I do not need anyone else's forgiveness or approval. I have worked through all of my short comings and misguided past decisions with my maker, the Creator. I have also done a lot of things right, which gives me the right amount of balance to be open enough to discuss anything with you.

Strangely enough, it also makes it easier for me to communicate with God and for him to be straight with me, when there is no hidden agenda and no reason for me to be ashamed of anything.

God has explained every personal experience of mine and why I had to go through each experience and what it was teaching me.

God has helped me to work through any hidden guilt, shame, hurt and heartaches. He has highlighted any important life lessons one by one, so that I can help others by showing them how to work through their own problems. He has enlightened me about every family member's personal story and shared many things with me about them. They will never know that I know, or how I know. There are some things are not meant to be shared, they are just meant to be learned from.

I am simply here to share God's story, which is not always told the way he would like it to be told. There are many facts, artefacts and books that have been burned, destroyed, buried, hidden, edited and stories that have been distorted along the way, until the truth is so hard to find, you become overwhelmed by all of the misinformation and lies. There are so many reasons why past history gets destroyed. I couldn't even begin to cover all the reasons in this book. I won't even attempt it, because politics is not my strong point, nor is creating drama where there doesn't need to be any.

If you are a *non-believer*, I pray for you to someday *see* the light and *feel* what I feel and maybe someday you can come and visit me and ask me some questions to help clarify any doubts you might have. If you are not quite sure yet and haven't made up your mind what your belief is, I hope this book opens the doorway to the path of enlightenment and helps you navigate your way in the darkness. I will bear a torch for you to reconnect again.

If you are already a *believer*, welcome back. This is your time now and this book will bring you tears of joy and happiness, knowing that you aren't completely crazy, or alone. Those voices in your head (*the good ones*) are not imaginary and know there are other faithful believers in the world who you can share your journey with. Craziness after all, is just a state of mind, depending on what the social definition of *normal* is. I actually thought I was *normal* for most of my life, but I now realise that maybe we are all a little bit crazy, at least some of the time and that's okay.

I can tell you that so far, it has been a *wild ride* and there has been nothing boring about my life. Every day it continues to get more exciting and I am still learning more about the challenges life presents and how to communicate with God more effectively.

Join me for a life changing experience within the pages of this book.

3. ALL ABOUT GOD

God was showing me signs that were too obvious to ignore, or too significant, to pass off as being a mysterious coincidence.

GOD answers to many names and wants to speak to each and every one of you through this book. I will use the term "he" or "him" to reference God throughout this text to make it easier for the reader.

God identifies with a strong *masculine* energy. He is the protector and is felt more as a father figure, but he also has a feminine gentle side too, the *nurturer* that loves us unconditionally.

God is really funny. He has an awesome sense of humour and is so witty. In fact he is wittier than the funniest comedians on Earth and he is not as serious or scary as everyone thinks he is. His jokes are so dry and most of the time they go right over my head.

Please don't be offended by anything you read in this book, because these are not my words, they are God's words. I would never use God's name in vain, because I know the order of things in the Universe. God has allowed me to share these writings with you uninhibited and unedited.

God has made me laugh, cry, feel joy and sadness. He has connected me to my passed over loved ones, taken me through my past lives, calmed me down when I was annoyed and angry, warned me of impending danger and loved me unconditionally, even though I continued to make mistakes. God has guided me through my life's journey, even when I wasn't sure what to do. He laughs at me all the time because I am *not* perfect. He talks to me because I love him so much and he *feels* the God energy within me.

He doesn't expect me to perform rituals, do miracles, or give away all my belongings to be worthy of his love. Nothing is too small, or trivial to talk to God about. He is interested in everything you want to tell him or ask him. He is the best friend you never knew you had, until you open your spiritual eyes for the first time to see him, open your ears to hear him and open your heart to love him.

It is not necessary to go to a church, or go through a priest, or go to some institution, or even go and see a guru on top of a mountain. There is no need to find a so called "holy person" to talk to God, because God is all around you and within you all of the time. You are *allowed* and encouraged to talk to God directly, without any other influence, or person who feels the need to screen your longing and desire to talk to him. If you prefer to use the church, institution, or guru methods to communicate with God, you are welcome. He is not saying *don't* do it. He is just saying that it is not mandatory.

At this point I will mention that over the years I have had the benefit and privilege of receiving my communications and conversations with God through many pure gifted psychic mediums and channellers who would like to remain anonymous. I have one main channeller that I communicate with and this person is known as my *translator* and they allow their body to be used by God to talk to me.

First they feel the God energy wanting to communicate through them and then the two of them come to an agreement. God may either converse through the channeller who will translate the words directly to me with God's permission, or the channeller allows the Creator to borrow their mind and body, so he can channel the messages as if he was speaking directly to me, the scribe. If the channeller allows their body and mind to be used, they often feel like an empty vessel when God talks through them. Most of the time they have no recollection of the conversation. When channellers allow their body and mind to be engaged by something as holy as God, they are asked to wait in the background while God talks directly to me. They can step into the foreground anytime they feel uncomfortable, or compromised in any way.

God often provides me with conditions when giving me the information. I am not allowed to record the voice of any of these sessions on any electronic recording device. I am only allowed to write, or type his words as they are spoken. At times I couldn't write, or type fast enough to keep up and had to ask God to slow down, or repeat himself on multiple occasions.

If I didn't understand any statements that were made, I would ask for clarification, or for an example, so I could grasp some of the concepts.

God is very busy making planets and looking after his creations, but he always makes time to visit me, to listen to me and to help me on my journey and I know he will for *you* too. Most people don't get to hear about this side of God. Many people have mixed beliefs, opinions; have been exposed to negative fear based conditioning, indoctrinated by extreme religions and cults. They may have even been fed lies and misinformation about the true nature of God. There are also those throughout history who have been harshly judged by their fellow humans and conditioned to believe that it is God's will to punish. I can assure you this is *not* true. God is the most loving entity with the most loving energy that you will ever experience in your whole existence.

I know perhaps at times you feel like you are lost somehow and that you have been abandoned in this crazy world and left to fend for yourselves. The truth is that all of us have chosen to be here right now. We are all under a kind of spiritual contract with a designated purpose and we were given the option to experience this human life, *not* forced.

We actually had to convince God that we were worthy enough to come here in the first place and have another chance to learn more and improve our soul's journey. There are so many souls waiting to come through from the other side that we have to have a really good reason to come here. Somewhere along the journey we get a kind of soul amnesia and we forget what our true purpose is. We can't remember what we are supposed to be doing, or we get influenced and distracted and end up doing something we are not supposed to be doing. This leads us *away* from the path to God.

We are made in God's image, but that doesn't make God human. The real question is; *what does it make us*? Every single soul in the whole Universe is intricately connected through an unseen complex network of past, present and future events. This network is hidden from our conscious mind when we are born, so that we don't get caught up in our past traumas and events. Yet we feel so familiar with some places and people, that we just can't explain it. These feelings of *déjà vu* (already seen) are so strong, yet we just can't quite remember what the connections are. It is so mysterious that even the world's most technically advanced scientists can't explain it, so it is easier to simply deny its existence and ignore the facts.

Souls have a kind of cellular memory that is carried over from past lives and past generations. They help us naturally gravitate towards people, places and events that help our soul develop in the most spiritually enlightened ways. This may mean having to engage in, or relive certain experiences over and over again, until we can master the best possible outcome to help with our own spiritual growth. We can also choose to help others with their soul journey and life lessons. I will discuss this further in the book.

God does not expect you to bow down and be subservient to him, because you are afraid of him. God wants you to be proud of who you are, love yourself (not in a vain way), love him and desire to talk to him. God wants you to experience life, learn, grow, love and cherish this opportunity, before you return home to him again and when you have completed your mission, or when your time here on Earth ends.

Just because you can't *see* God, it doesn't mean he doesn't exist. You can't *see* a subatomic particle using the naked eye. You need to view it using a special scientific instrument. You can't *see* radiation that radiates all over Planet Earth with the naked eye. You need to view it using a special detection instrument. You can't always *see* bacteria, viruses, or free radicals, because these particles are so small that you need a special medical magnification instrument to view them. The same can be said for God, because God is in *everything*, both subatomic as well as in the entire expanse of the Universe.

He is everywhere at once and can be anywhere he wants to be. His intelligence is immeasurable and his wisdom is beyond our comprehension. Just because we can't physically *see* him, it doesn't mean God doesn't exist. You just need to use a special instrument to communicate with God. We all have a mind, body and a soul and these are our special instruments that we use to communicate with God. Our conscious mind is the device we use to speak to God and ask questions (seeking truths). Our subconscious mind is the subtle receiver of the answers (divine guidance) and the outcomes of these transmissions are translated and manifested through the soul (as our life lessons).

We all know instinctively and feel deep down there is a higher power greater than us which created everything. Ask people who have had a near death experience and come back to life. Ask those who have been saved from certain death against all odds. Ask those who have witnessed miracles first hand. Ask those with genuine faith who already talk to God. Ask those who use the healing energy of God to heal others and get to see the real results. Ask those who love unconditionally even though they are persecuted for their love and martyrdom; like Jesus. Ask those who remember what happens before birth. Ask God yourself for a sign that he exists.

All things are divinely created and have a type of order, a pattern and a purpose. We struggle to conceptualise it into something tangible. Try to separate the concept of God from religion and view God from a *spiritual* perspective. Religion was not God's idea. It was man's idea to indoctrinate and control the masses, so they would be subservient to the earthly rulers in power, who modify the rules, to suit themselves and expect you to follow them. This allows the wealthy and socially privileged to break the rules as they please, shield themselves from retribution and live a life of luxury and excess at the expense of the common people. Yes, God set out some pretty simple guidelines for us to follow a few thousand years ago. The guidelines weren't that complicated and do you think we could adhere to them?

There is so much deception in the world that you have to remove your blindfold, untie your hands and dig really deep to find the real truth buried beneath the mountains of lies.

Today's modern law makes it even more difficult and confusing when the original law is so modified and so ambiguous that it blurs the lines of morality. It is easy to become confused about what is legally right and legally wrong behaviour, with pages and pages of technical exceptions and exclusions to comprehend. The truth is always right in front of you; you just need to *open your eyes* to see it.

While reading this book, all God asks is for you to clear your mind and reserve your judgements until you have read the *whole* book in its entirety. Many of your soul searching questions will be answered within these pages and many of your opinions and beliefs may be challenged, or even shattered.

My purpose for writing this book is not to make friends, gain popularity, write a best seller, or to make money out of this venture. Some of you may not like what you read, or hear and that's okay too. My purpose is fulfilling the wish of the Creator, even at the risk of offending some of you. It is not my intention to offend anyone, but resistance to change may block you from seeing the true spiritual light of God.

Let me rattle your cage gently and when you are ready to open the cage door of any restricted beliefs that don't serve you, then you can fly free.

Ever since I can remember, I have always been asking lots of questions about God. When I was a little girl I used to ask anyone that I could about *who* and *what* God was. There used to be a lady from the Jehovah's Witnesses who would come and visit our house at least once every couple of months and my mum would always invite her in for a cup of tea. They would sometimes natter for ages about all things God and biblical. I would sit quietly in the background listening to all of the stories and the responses she would give my mum. My mum used to love to challenge her with really tricky questions, which she couldn't always answer and she would keep referring back to the scriptures, but nothing really made any sense to me.

Then I wondered *if someone who is supposed to be deeply religious and actually goes from town to town teaching people about God and Jesus doesn't actually know the answers, then who does?*

How come they knew so little and couldn't explain simple things from the Bible and how the whole creation story rolled out? Why wasn't everyone talking about God if it was so important? I couldn't work it out. I was intrigued and confused at the same time.

Regular conversations that people would have with me were boring and trivial and all I wanted to know about was God and how everything came to be. People rattled on about the news, the weather and the latest developments in politics and what the neighbours and their families were up to, but in comparison to the really important topic of God, I really struggled to find anyone to talk me to about it. I was lost in a foggy haze of misinformation and uncertainty.

The school didn't talk much about it, no one else's parents seem to talk much about it and the television and radio certainly didn't talk much about it unless it was at Easter time, or Christmas time. Then you would be exposed to the story of the life of Jesus, told in so many different ways every year. There was no consistency. There was no solid proof of God's existence and there were no books other than the Bible that I could find that answered all of my curious questions.

The Bible was even more confusing for me; because I would start to read it, then all of a sudden it stopped making sense. It was like reading a really good novel, getting to the juicy bit of the story and then there were pages and whole paragraphs missing all over the place. *Huh! What happened there? How did they go from only having two people to get to a population of thousands in a few pages, I'm lost!? Did I miss something?* Eventually, I would give up and scratch my head and think it was all too hard.

I started a personal mission to ask as many adults and older people as many questions as I could. I asked what God was and I asked where I could go to find him, or at the very least where I could find more information about him.

I asked churchy people and non-churchy people and I even started secretly talking to God myself, even though I couldn't see him, or hear him. I really started asking him for some answers to some of my big questions. The more I asked other people, the more confused I became and then my questions confused the people that I had asked, because they didn't really know either. It just highlighted the fact that nobody really knew the answers for sure. I realised they were all just hypothesising, guessing and regurgitating quotes from the scriptures, but they didn't really know what they were saying, or what those words and verses actually meant.

They were just telling me their own personal views based on their upbringing and education. Nothing they said was an actual fact or quantifiable. It was really frustrating, because I had so many unanswered questions and I felt really empty not knowing these things. I decided right then and there to make it my life's mission to find out and get some answers. *I must be able to find these answers myself. Maybe this is why I am here?*

This is probably one very good reason why I agreed to write this book. To find all of this information in one book anywhere on the planet is practically impossible. You almost have to be an experienced scholar and a qualified detective, or investigator to find the right books to read. Then you have to sort through these books and find the small remnants of truth scattered amongst the pages. Then you can throw the rest of the rubbish away, because half of it is absolute nonsense.

The amount of people writing things that aren't even true is phenomenal. They back up their inner chattering with regurgitated and rebranded words from other people and claim it as their own work. Sometimes when people can't find the answers, or explain themselves properly, they just make it up as they go along.

There was no point continuing down the book path, because this was leading me off the track and was raising more questions than it answered. So I started honing in on my investigative skills and found unique ways to get confirmation of the truth. That is when I became a *truth seeker*.

I learned to ask the right questions, get accurate answers and stay on the long forgotten cold trail of the mystery of God. It really was a mystery to me when I first started searching. It was a mystery to me that nobody could help me answer my questions, except for myself. What is the point of having millions of books on Earth and not having a good, accurate and down to earth resource book about God? It just doesn't make any sense!

Once my relationship with God had developed to a point I could ask God *anything* and get a logical, truthful and sensible answer, I started receiving huge amounts of information from various sources all around me.

I would ask the questions and the answers would come to me in many different forms. The answers were provided in a series of strange coincidences. I would ask a particular question and someone who specialised in that particular topic entered my life around the same time.

I was being shown my life lessons and was receiving random communications from random people who were speaking the **Word of God** directly to me in many various forms. I had to remain open to be able to recognise when the communication was coming through to me and when God was showing me *signs* of his existence.

God was showing me signs that were too obvious to ignore or too significant, to pass off as being a mysterious coincidence. This is when I learned there are no coincidences, only incidences that are a part of God's greater plan for each and every one of us.

Who is God?

The channeller said, speaking on behalf of God, "God is the god of all gods. He is the Creator of all life in the Universe. There was only *one* Creator, then after that there were more Creators and more. There were some angels who created this and that, but *one* first Creator."

The channeller continued, "God is known by many names in many different languages."

When God pronounces his name it is difficult to spell because it is a very unusual sounding name and it is not in English.

I have asked God to say his name many times. It is spoken in the ancient Hebrew language, so forgive me if I translate it incorrectly. God tells me his name in many different languages, which sound like the following names; Yahweh, YHWH (but without the vowels) and Yonhoba, Jonhova, Jehovah, or similar and he also uses the name Yeshua. The names can be heard as slight variations, or aspects of the one name and it can also depend on what native language you speak and your accent.

I asked the channeller to ask God, "What is the preferred name that you want the world to know you by?"

Through the channeller, God answered, "I came from the darkness to the light. I am everything. I created everything. I created you and I know who *you* are."

God continued, "In the beginning there was nothing and then there was you. Oh that's creepy, what should I call you? Who are you?"

God added, "That's even creepier? Should I get to know you or not? Should I hold you up in the light and look at you, or should I not? Do I need to remember you and *what* are you?"

The channeller paused for a minute to think about God's response, "You can call Him the *Creator*, some call him God Almighty, or God may say, 'I am the One.'

"Who is the One? On other planets they call him *The One.* The One who comes from nothingness."

The channeller said, still speaking on behalf of God, "Because *one* means, one Universe, one Creator, one Source. One Universe turns into another Universe. There are many universes."

I asked God, "How big are you?"

God responded, "Millions of miles across, nearly trillions! There is no start and finish. How long doesn't exist. If the scientists don't understand these words, it is because *he is time.* He is the start and the finish."

The channeller explained, "God's height in one of his physical forms, when compared with a human is around 35 foot tall (just over 22 cubits) and this height can be variable, depending on how God chooses to represent himself at any given time. It changes."

I asked God, "What is your height in Heaven?"

God answered, "Let it be known to you, I am taller and I am smaller than all known things. I am all and I am not. I can show you and be anything of course."

Then I asked God, "How old are you?"

God answered, "More than seven trillion years old."

The channeller added, "God is everything. God is *in* everything. God *created* everything and God can *become* anything. God is the emptiness and God is the light. God is even an emotion, a feeling as he created all of this. Yes he created every think, everything and every thought. Now you have the ability to mix everything and every *think*. You were given this in pure love and you also have the ability to manifest your every think into other things."

God is the start and the eternal god, which is why he will often introduce himself as the Alpha and the Omega, the beginning and the end. God is both male and female with reproductive organs and is physically *alive.*

God however does identify as more masculine than feminine and he does represent himself more in a more masculine form, but is not entirely male.

The channeller said, "We can call him neither female, nor male, but he is projected forwards in time. It is a little bit complicated to explain, it is better to see God as the true and loving Source of all energy in the entire Universe. The infinite Source of everything. The Creator of everything and all that is. The ultimate God of everything."

I asked God, "How do we talk to you?"

God corrected me, "Do you mean how do I *listen* to you?"

I responded with a giggle, "Yes how do I *listen* to you?"

God responded, "In a vacuum with no movement search for movement. Look for a bunch of molecules in a vacuum. I am white noise. I am the seashell, another form of white noise. If you want to get technical, you could find some molecules in the water and in a vacuum and then connect them to a wire in the water. One is slightly acidic and one is alkaline. They shall have two bonds of metal that are different. There will be an attachment to the sky, or a living river, or a living tree, or to another creation. This is called *galvanic measurement.*"

Throughout this book, I will refer to God as a *"he"* so that I don't call God an *"it"* out of respect. God's gender is not the same as the way we see gender here on Earth. God's gender is not relevant to the procreation process; because it is more of an *energy principle* I am talking about, when I am referencing God throughout this book. God doesn't need to have children the same way we do for our species to survive. God tends to represent the masculine force on this planet, which is why he is often referred to as "our Father who art in Heaven." He is the Father of all of us, even when we have natural birth parents; God is still our Father, the Father of all of us, because he is the Father we return home to when we have finished our journey.

Mother Earth is like a spirit or energy force and represents the *feminine* energy principle and the feminine force on the planet. Earth is created by God, which means that Mother Earth, or the feminine force that looks after Earth, is divinely connected with God, which balances out the two masculine and feminine forces.

God likes white horses and his favourite place in the Universe is the Pleiades because of the colours. God's favourite places on Earth are the Garden of Eden, New Zealand and the Amazon jungle, because these places remind him of the lush green forests he first created in the beginning.

I asked God, "If you have favourite places here on Earth, how do you see them, or visit them?"

God responded, "By coming here."

Then I asked, "So do you see it spiritually, or is it because you can be everywhere at once?"

God answered, "Through your eyes, through the eyes of a fly, through any eyes. I am the ultimate spy. You can't hide from me. I have my eye on you, or should I say *eyes.*"

This is the experience of God in the new millennium. God comes to Jan-Marie in many forms. Sometimes under the influence of some alcohols, sometimes without it and induces words of wisdom from who knows where. I know its God, because there is no evil when he talks and because I am the writer and I have disassociated myself from God when I am writing. The channeller is channelling directly to him, not through any other spirits to communicate with him and the channeller is also my *translator.*

Because God created everything, he knows how to get here the most efficient way possible and always announces his visits in the same manner, like a trademark, so that I know it is him and not some other entity, or spirit. He always picks up where we left off with our last conversation, which helps me to grow exponentially throughout the visits.

God talks every language when he talks. When a channeller is listening to God they will pick up on the language that is native to him, or her. God also talks in *feelings*. God communicates to animals in feelings and they return the communication in feelings, whereas humans don't know *how* to communicate to God in feelings as unconditionally as animals.

Everyone has a part of God in them and everyone *is* a part of God. God is everything. God created the Universe; happiness, evilness and everything in it. Just like God, you are in control of yourself and everything around you. The best way to talk to God is to talk to yourself and ask yourself the question, because you already have God within you.

When you talk to God in reverence, everything in infinity celebrates being together for infinity. God wants you to *feel your love* and then your passion shall be found. Slow down and your troubles will dissolve and learn to love yourself.

God has a good chuckle and references the arrogance of humans, "Argue with me all you like, you know I'm always right!"

The only way for you to really know that I am talking to the Supreme Being is because if I am lying to you, I will be dealt with by the Supreme Being and this statement is showing my ultimate faith in God. It demonstrates my belief in what he tells me. After all, it is already a massive test of faith for me to be writing this book and to make this statement in the first place.

The channeller said, "Only the Lord can exist in this space alone and altogether simultaneously. Sometimes God likes to be an octopus so that he can have a look around the deep oceans and be camouflaged like an octopus. He likes to be able to scope out the floor of the ocean undetected."

The channeller added, "God likes to describe himself as 50% God, 40% Jesus and 10% unknown and this is the image of God."

Where is God?

God doesn't claim to be *anywhere.* He just claims to be *here.* He doesn't leave a trail of where he comes from, or where he is going to, or what he is doing, but he did mention the Celestine Stars. There are women there that look like the women in plastic and they are all blue eyed blondes.

Many times when God visits, he tells me he is sitting in what we call the Crab Nebula, which is purple at the moment. He is near Hades on a throne, with a staff in his hand. The Nebula changes colour every day.

On top of the staff he holds, there are seven points and the seven points represent seven universes. It is to remind him of how many universes there are.

He has curly golden brown shoulder length hair with big shoulders. God has a big long triangular nose and it's a perfect one. God can travel here to talk to us, through us.

God also mentioned that he lives in the Seven Sisters, which is known to us as the Pleiades. It is an open star cluster in the constellation of Taurus and has been used by star navigators for aeons. The fact that God dwells in different locations, may mean that he doesn't always stay in the same place, or communicate from the same location when he talks to me. Wherever the physical location is, it seems that it is a long way away, but he is also with all of us in our hearts at the same time.

The channeller said, "In God's world there is a seven dimensional pyramid. God's structures *always* have seven points on them. All things that are beautiful have seven points, or seven things that you can count on them."

God often introduces himself and states, "I am 777 God and Jesus."

Seven is God's number and if he is communicating with you or showing you signs of his existence, he often uses the number seven (7) as a sign that it is him.

This book is only level 1 of 7 levels of teachings to come. Level 2 will come next. Jesus has all 7 levels.

God said, "I am the way, I am the truth, I am the life, I am the righteousness and I am the one."

God really gets into a long discussion with me about where humanity is currently directing their scientific and religious focus. He wants to know one thing. If all the religions in the world wanted to communicate with God, why didn't they send their own space probe out to find him? Why did NASA go and try and find aliens but not God?

Then I asked God the question, "Are humans allowed to travel to where you live, would you allow it?"

God explained that humanity could explore more of him if they went looking for him.

God both allows and restricts our knowledge and said, "Every day man strives to learn more and they call it *science* and man doesn't call it any more than science. Man is only now discovering the simplest forms of knowledge, which he calls 139 and they call it 149 for example. These are the magic numbers or the denominations of the number and if you defy the balance of the number, catastrophe happens. If you create an imbalance within this world, then the imbalance creates the catastrophe. The latest discovery will be called the *ripple effect*."

God calls it the signot wave, using sine waves, which also starts with an s.

The channeller speaking on behalf of God continued, "If you wanted to really know something and if the centre of the Universe is created by God, then where is God? God would be at the *centre of creation*, at the centre of the Universe, where it was created. This means the whole thing is in the creation and is seated at the centre of the creation. How do you measure where the centre is? Using photon years. How many photon years to the centre of the Universe from where you are located right now? T to the power of 19 trillion. By what method could you travel there? If you shrunk something to the size of the smallest particle it would be the opposite of his largest particle. The smallest number is the largest number and invisibility is smaller than an atom."

The channeller continued, "They created the particle accelerator so they could go slowly around the circle. Why not go the short way which is sideways? The most amazing thing that man discovered is, if you have a sine wave and stretched it out, it would make it longer. If you squeezed it together it would make it shorter."

God has a bit of giggle when humans think they have come a long way with their evolution.

He said, "They built CERN but all humans can do is *destroy* atoms, they can't actually *create* them."

God is surprised they haven't worked it out yet and they should look at how God creates a bunch of atoms to create something. He can build sperm and an egg that can create things when they are made whole. God talks about the infinitely small particles that are within an atom. Even the tiniest particles are programmed to do something.

God expanded on the theory, "There is an atomic level, a quantum level and a photonic level soon. If you had a droplet of water in the air, then it freezes and becomes a shape. What makes it form the shape is the music in the air, the wind, the particles, the dirt, the magnetic poles, the amount of sun hitting the ionosphere, the different layers, ultimately the *vibration.* To calculate its landing path it would take hundreds of pages and humans call it random, unknown and mysterious. Scientists are yet to realise that you can start to calculate this and that. If you want to discover God more, then study water droplets under a microscope. What happens to it when you do experiments? Play music to it and what happens to the water droplets?"

The channeller said, "Science is the understanding of the creation and that is why man keeps studying the big bang. Where did the big bang come from? So there was nothing and then all of a sudden there was a big bang? God's creation was a circle and God created *himself.* If God created a circle, then it would be pretty easy to work out how God created himself, because he is in an eternal circle. To prove this a galaxy circles itself and planets orbit in a circle and so on."

Through the channeller, God asks me to *simplify* his explanation, so I keep scribing in long hand until I can work out how to explain it properly.

The channeller continued, "This Universe was created by a collision of others. It has a clear path. There are other universes following this path and multiple galaxies collided with other galaxies to make this galaxy. We are on an outer galaxy. Some other galaxies travel at different speeds and they collide with other galaxies."

God is still baffled why man keeps looking for aliens in outer space but not for God!

God doesn't usually physically come here to Earth himself. He usually sends his Archangels Michael, Gabrielle, Cirrus and Athiens.

God can be in multiple places at once, because ultimately he is everywhere and with all of us. It just depends on where he chooses to direct his energy, or what catches his attention at any given moment.

God and Jesus merge often as well and it can be complex for me to work out which soul I am talking to because they are so closely related. They are very similar and are almost different aspects of the same soul. They are connected infinitely and they both have so much love when you are in their presence.

God and Jesus both talk to me in code sometimes. They love to talk in rhymes and riddles, or in an archaic form of the English language, which can stump me sometimes trying to translate it correctly.

For example, one evening I am visited and the conversation with the channeller starts like this, "He passes in time for me, on the way to Jericho.

A woman has touched his robe and sent his disease to the channeller which he will clear up in a minute. You can refer to Mark 21, Matthew 18 and Luke 40 as proof of who you are talking to."

Of course the first thing I do, is use Google as my search engine and type in key words like "woman," "Jericho" and "disease" into the search window. While I am researching what information is being received, we are still speaking to each other.

God and Jesus don't consider it rude if I look something up while we are in mid conversation. They actually *encourage* it and I am always so amazed when I look things up and *there it is!* Right there on the first page of Google, in black and white staring me in the face. I am exasperated. I can't believe it! Wow that is *truly* amazing!

God loves me because I am a little bit cheeky and because I am just being myself. I am who I am and I am a natural person with a unique personality. I am also full of respect and I am never cheeky in a disrespectful or rude way, because there is no need to be rude to the Creator *ever.*

Jesus and God, who are now both talking to me through the channeller continued, "It is written upon these words and those verses. She is known as the *bleeding lady*. Look for exorcism, verse 4.8 in the King James Bible. Behold the weak and the anointed shall be blessed."

Jesus goes into great depth about the multitude of people that wanted and needed his help while he walked the Earth. This is when Jesus Christ the soul consciousness and God the Creator had become *one.* This was happening when they were talking to me from two places at once. For example, from the other side after Jesus has passed over and from when Jesus was alive simultaneously.

Speaking through the channeller, Jesus said, "Once people knew he was the *real deal*, he was inundated with requests from people everywhere he went. These requests were coming from people that were sick, dying or had a so called *incurable* illness. Jesus did his best to get around to as many people as he could while he was alive. He just couldn't be everywhere at once, because he was in the mortal form of a man which had its own restrictions. He had chosen to appear in the flesh."

The channeller said, "There are so many healing stories where Jesus healed people that never even made it into the Bible that we have available to us these days. Some of these stories were in the original Bible, but were then later edited by the establishment, because they wanted to downplay Jesus' existence."

Believe me, if you knew only half of what Jesus did while he was alive, you wouldn't be questioning his existence. You would just be shaking your head like I do, when you realise deep down in your heart, what they did to the Creator in the flesh is absolutely appalling!

Every time I am visited, I feel so blessed. Through the channellers, God and Jesus talk to me about what I have learned and expand further upon the information I have found. It could be hours, days, weeks, or even months in between visits. It is very *random* and there is absolutely no pattern to the contact. One thing I know for sure, is that I will continue to be visited, because I actively seek out what I am being shown and taught.

God thanks me often for doing this work, writing this book and being a scribe for all of you.

One thing I need each and every one of you to understand is that if you find yourself reading these words, it is because you are exactly where you are meant to be, right when you are meant to be there.

I could be selfish and not share this information with you, but what would be the point of doing that? I am learning to be *selfless* and not sharing would actually cut off the open line of love and communication that I have with God. That would be a silly thing for me to do. The whole reason God is sharing so much information with me, is because he knows that in turn; I will share it with all of you.

You might be asking yourself, why doesn't God just talk to all of us directly? It is because you are not *listening* carefully. He *is* talking to you all the time. You just can't hear him, or you don't recognise the signs when he is trying to communicate with you.

Hopefully this book will help you to see, feel, hear and start to know the signs. Then you can talk to God yourself.

God explained, "If the galaxy was perfect, everything would balance. The Universe is made perfectly to swing in a circular arc to keep everything in balance and to keep everything in motion. Humans aren't very good at keeping perpetual motion going, especially when they become lazy, unmotivated, or unhealthy. Their internal world stagnates and becomes like a cesspool of disease, instead of when a person is fit and healthy and their circulatory system is swinging in an arc. They are *in sync* with the Universe and the spinning of the planet they are living on. We all need to keep moving just like the stars and the planets do, to stay alive and be within the perpetual motion of movement."

Heaven and Hell

God doesn't talk about Heaven and Hell as much as he talks about earthly things when he comes to visit me.

God explains that the gates of Heaven are like huge big brick walls that look like great big sandstone blocks. It is always guarded by angels. There is white light coming from the inside of the gate which blocks you from seeing anything, because of the brightness of the light. The gates have restricted access and you can only unlock the gates with your *worthiness*, which is within your conscience.

The angels are the guardians of the gates and if you have lost faith in your creation, the angels will ignore you.

God reminds us that if things ever get too out of control here on Earth and you pray enough, God can send a new angel to be born on Earth as a saviour to sort it out.

The angels are all one. Jesus was an angel and was God manifested in the son's body.

God laughed and through the channeller told me, "It is impossible for Satan to convince Jesus or God to destroy themselves, or to tempt them like he tried to with Jesus in the desert, because God already owns everything. God has nothing to give up, because he already has everything."

The channeller continued, "Satan is in a game to lock up as many souls and to defy God in any way that he can. He has made that his personal mission, but can never succeed. His attempts in the end will be futile, because there will always be more light than darkness, always."

The channeller added, "In ancient times, if a person did something really bad like murder, they go to Hell. The punishment lasts as long as it takes to turn the soul around from evil to good. If the soul doesn't show remorse, or repent they get continually punished. So ultimately the person, who is getting punished, is enduring self punishment because of their *continuous rebellion*. It is not God doing it; they are doing it to themselves.

"Another lost method of punishment was when a person was locked up in prison. They were meant to show remorse for their crime and be turned around from bad to good. Once they showed that they were truly sorry and repented and turned themselves around into a good person, they were let out of prison. If they continued to rebel and didn't show any remorse, they were executed. These teachings have been lost."

God doesn't think it is fair that someone is just executed without the opportunity to show remorse for what they have done. God also doesn't think it is fair that a person continues to be persecuted by society if they have been released from jail. The system has changed the rules so much and they have forgotten the real commandments of God, including the ancient jubilee promises they used to make to the citizens of each shire periodically.

How God views us

Even though some refuse to want him, God still loves them and forgives them anyway. God sees us as being more like him when we do that. He watches and sees us becoming more like him. His energy is like a father figure with warmth and although God doesn't like to associate himself with either feminine, or masculine energy specifically, he tries to explain that it is more like a neutral energy, or neither gender.

Everything in the whole Universe and galaxy is made up of him, so you are a part of God. But he also gave everything a balance of love and understanding.

God said, "Believe in me and I will believe in you. Give me love and I will give you love. Ask me a question and I will tell you the answer. Show me your desires and I shall fulfil them. Greed is not love and you cannot smile if you have riches. Greed can be confused for love. The greedy rich old person is very bitter, whereas the poor old person is easily pleased.

"Love can be conjured up from nothing. You don't need to receive a gift to be happy. See the child that laughs and see the man who laughs. See the wicked who have forgotten love and ignore what I say here. For I *do* truly exist and you still would not smile? For you are my children that I have loved and love."

God is pure and holy, but can also be represented in different ways like Zeus, or even the father of Zeus, acting out different roles in different representations.

God will make sure he will never destroy, or hurt anyone here, because we are all a part of him. However if you go to the Kingdom of God and bring the baggage with you from the last place, he *will* destroy you and annihilate you.

God wants to know why no one invites him to go on holidays with them. Invite God on holidays with you and invite him to participate in activities with you. We get so consumed in our own little world that we forget we are a part of something bigger.

In time God sees our journey as a small bolt of lightning. When God views his own journey it is much longer than our short stint. God is coming to the Earth for only a fraction of time, just to come here and channel and this reading is one I am going to share with people. God also recognises souls from the lightning bolt they generate.

God wants to ask you, "If you were a lightning bolt, what type of energy bolt would you portray yourself to be?"

God knows each one of us by a star. A star is called a marker and the energy it gives out shall be a marker. That is how God knows where the marker and the stars are. Even the image of the marker in the star can be found through the image on the marker and across all universes. All of the markers can be seen and felt, both large and small. Those that try to change the marker in the star to confuse it will not succeed, because a bad marker and a bad sun cause destruction and evilness.

I was told that my star shall be yellow and each star is known for its individual colour and its marker. Every star is a different colour.

God loves to use this acronym for his name and he laughed when he told me this.

- **G**od
- **O**mits
- **D**emons

The less people use God's name, the more they become detached. The Bible is the like a portal, or a link to conjure God. The intent, thought, idea and conjuring of God will bring God to be with you. No matter how many times the Bible is modified, changed and edited it still has the **Word of God** in it.

God's favourite game is hide and seek. God knows I love hide and seek as well. God loves children that are happy and fun.

If you want to get God's attention you can ask him, "Have you forgotten me? Have you forsaken me?"

God always shows up in times of trouble. Demand help from God. You can also say to God, "You can either destroy me, or help me," to make it have more of an impact if you are having difficulty attracting his attention.

He asks that instead of just saying grace when having a meal, make a place at the table for spirits, or God. Make a small separate meal for God to show your respect, or make a small meal for the spirits you want to pay your respects to.

God said, "Why do you think a rainbow is multicoloured?"

The channeller explained, "Because God couldn't make a choice on which colour to pick so he used all the colours."

The channeller continued, "So *you* are the one choosing what you want. Be careful what you wish for. Don't ask for it, otherwise God will give you all of what you ask for, which will be more confusing. If you are unsure of something then you will get it and be of it. Choose wisely and have 100% faith that you already have it. Be sure of what you have chosen, because God is a part of everything including you. He is everything, he owns everything and he is responsible for everything!"

The channeller added, "Metaphorically, where do we sit in the scheme of things within the wealth and status world, the animal kingdom and the realms where these super beings come from? Guess who they appoint to look after these lower realms? They appoint a *real person*, like a street smart person and *not* a perfect person."

God said, "Learn how to run it smoothly, like a network and then you don't get to leave here once you've been accepted to return to Earth. When other aliens come here to look at Earth, the people on this Earth generally love each other and they do so love each other. Compare yourself to Mars, where has everyone gone? We should embrace this and love one another and we should all be happy. If you want to get unhappy, go to Mars. Where are the Martians? Why haven't they come to visit us? Because they are all gone. They have already destroyed themselves because they didn't have enough love."

The channeller said, "God wants us to realise that if we really want something and we really want it to happen, we have to make everyone involved, responsible for making it happen, including yourself, medical teams (if it is health related), professionals, financiers, friends, family, angels, spirit guides and everyone you can possibly get involved with your project."

Talking directly through the channeller, God said, "You were born perfect, then you became imperfect and this is the delusion. Nothing is as it seems and the test is that if you believe who you were created from, then it is who you were the image of at birth. If you would pray to yourself as being perfect and say, 'I know now that I have learned, I have been shown sins, I have become sins and now I am worthy of being pure and whole.'

"If you came here and sinned, what makes you think that it wasn't already a part of the holy sin to come here and it could just be exactly what you have come here for? It doesn't make you a *sinner.* You have been given sins and once you have done them, you learn from them and then when you *release* yourself from the sin, you become more evolved. As you get older, you become more like your birth self and realise you no longer want to sin and want to be as you were when you were born. There is no way to safely communicate this, because you are in a holy war, but remember that you belong with the Father."

The channeller said, "God has to use risk analysis to ensure no mistakes are made and to ensure no idiots take over the Universe, because otherwise they will annihilate the whole place and the Creator doesn't want this. This is why God will only ever show himself as his holographic self if at all, so he cannot be destroyed."

The channeller continued, "God knows we are not perfect once we have been corrupted, or influenced, but he still wants us to strive for perfection. If you didn't have the 10% bad in you and if you were perfect all of the time, there would be no purpose, or reason to stay on this plane of existence. The challenge is how long can you stay on this planet, how long can you be here and how much can you do while you are here? Ask yourself, *what is the good side trying to do?* Make itself better. That is what it is trying to do."

The channeller added, "The problem with a normal human is when they are trying to do good things; they become opposed and a little bit of nastiness makes the world go round. If everyone was perfect they would drop off the circle. There is meant to be a little bit of confusion to make you unsure of where you are. That is the 10% confusion, the 10% bad.

The aim is to be more like only 1% so that you can self correct every time you make a mistake. It doesn't necessarily mean you will *never* make a mistake, it just means if you are operating on 1% bad, then you will make less mistakes and will be a good person."

God just discovered he can type like this, "*Wow, okay, here goes...*

Take my hand and I shall guide thee on a path away from here – embrace my love
Take my hand and be of one – I shall show you that of worthiness
Those of you who haveth – embrace these words and they shall make you holy again
I am who I am and I am everything – the start, the alpha and the end, the omega and the Creator of you!
And hear of what I have to say – if you destroy Earth, you will be destroyed
If you create and cherish – you will be created again and again and again
I see all that you have done and I know who you are."

Those were Gods words and now that he knows he can type like this, the words just come pouring out of the keyboard.

God still likes to speak in the archaic language and that can make it tricky to capture the right feeling associated with the style of language when I scribe. I don't question too much, I just write, because there is so much information coming through and I don't always get time to capture all of it.

Remembering everything that comes flooding through is a real challenge too, especially if I haven't been able to write it down on paper, or type it on something.

God also loves to speak in ancient Hebrew and sometimes he forgets to translate the information back to modern English for me. I get lost with what he is saying until I remind him that I don't remember, or don't know how to speak, or understand the Hebrew language.

I don't like to interrupt while God is speaking, so it is best if I ask God to speak to me in English *before* he gets too far into the explanation. It wouldn't matter what my native language was, God doesn't actually need to speak to me at all and would prefer to communicate telepathically with me. I am not yet advanced enough to use telepathy effectively.

God prefers to speak to most people in *signs* and he shows us these signs all the time, to show us he is with us. Unfortunately we get so busy that we overlook these signs as coincidences, or something cute that we experience momentarily. Even if it is only momentary, it is still God showing his love for you, showing you that he *is* with you.

God said, "No wonder humans feel disoriented from time to time. After all you are spinning on a big ball going around and around in space! It can make us dizzy and this comment is for people who feel confused."

The channeller said, "He wants you to spin around in a circle and see how you feel?"

God continued, "Do you know what happens if the Earth stops? You would all disappear."

The channeller further explained, "God spun the Earth to start the motion, because Earth was on its own and needed spinning to get the momentum going."

God reminded me, "Dig well and that which you seek shall be given to you."

The creation of the Universe

The channeller speaking for God said, "In the beginning there was nothing but darkness and God was the *only* being in the Universe."

Then God said, "I was created by myself for myself."

The channeller continued, "When God realised he was nothing, he became disturbed and created things like light, space, atoms and everything so he wouldn't just be anything.

"Then God created form, not one, not two, but three. And he liked what he saw. God is a great alchemist.

"God is living in the Nebula which changes colour often, blue, green and orange.

"God used the formula π x 7, π x 7 (Pi x 7, Pi x 7) and that's how the entire Universe was made. Every planet and every star has its own nucleus and beyond that God created a reactor. The God formula is 1 + 1 = 1, 2 + 2 = 2, 3 + 3 = 3 and "1" represents the whole. This means if there are three things and you add another three things together, they become three things not six. If he gives one atom a nucleus, the atom is one, even though it has multiple parts and when they merge they become one. When you have two loving parties, they become one and this is why once two people love one another, they want to be in one body. When two souls create a soul, they become one. Just like when 100 people that want to go to a rally, become one. One group, one purpose, one reason."

The channeller added, "God created all of these incredible inventions on separate planets and also put them here on Earth, only to be destroyed by one another. They can't even be enjoyed by the people on Earth. Every time he creates something he likes to send it to Earth. There are planets with just rainbows, planets with 12 moons, planets with coloured water and one planet has phosphorous green moss and a phosphorous glowing atmosphere.

"Everything in the whole Universe and galaxy is made up of Him, so you are a part of God. But he also gave everything a balance of love and understanding. Everything in the whole Universe is also made up of memory cells. There is a minimum of one memory cell and one cell is a photograph of millions of bits of information.

"Let it be known it took thousands of years to create the creation and then he created more. The journal of God was created in an infinite amount of years, the Alpha and the Omega who created it. God never finishes anything and there is only ever a creation and that is his law.

"Magnetism is created with speed and speed is created with magnetism and time is equal to speed and magnetism and gravity is magnetism. Now God is getting really technical for the geeks who love this kind of cryptic formula."

The creation of man

According to God, 16 billion years ago, the first man was first put on the Earth and Earth was created around one trillion years ago.

This is bound to baffle the carbon daters who think they have everything worked out! This is the **Word of God** as relayed to me and not a guestimate on my part.

The channeller speaking on behalf of God said, "When they designed a human they wrote the code in software first. Then they encoded the body using the "ball land" where they used it as a physical realm to experiment with. Each ball is very complex. DNA was coded with dots and balls (molecular balls) and plotted by advanced scientists. A supreme element within a ball is what they call the software "sphere," which is within one billionth of a micron of another billionth. A human will never be able to pick it up.

"He created each human like himself. Every human knows their future and past and they were given *free will* to change their future, which is quite easy. God's creation in evolution is Darwin's way.

"The hostoric gland inside the brain is the part of the brain that can manifest things and it is used in conjunction with the pictorial gland. It is what God uses to make things. He uses it and we have it too, because we were made in the image of God."

The channeller continued, "Later, Adam and Eve were created by the Gods of Nebula around 14,000 years ago and they were placed in the Garden of Eden. God created woman from the rib of man.

"God really listens to women because they are the higher creation. He has a special scroll for Mother Teresa and a special scroll for Mother Mary, because he believes females are more superior. Woman was the second creation after man, the second generation of human which makes her the *improved model,* or the *mark II version* of the human being. Modifications to the DNA were made and additions to the emotional abilities and capabilities were installed. This was done to ensure women complimented men in the best possible way, so they could work together as a team and be useful for one another.

"The current humans who live on Earth at this time in 2017 are known as the *Genesis 12,* or the 12th generation of beings. The gods are now happy with their creation and have reached level D12 in the DNA of humans. The first humans were known as the 1st generation. Humans can now reproduce without sex and they have worked out how to recreate."

The channeller added, "The 12th DNA strand of the ape is the difference between humans and apes: 12, 24, 36, 48 and 60 which is a numerical sequence. A DNA cell inside a DNA a, b and c strand is as long as a DNA cell in itself, until such time when he says it is not.

"God created things in the Garden of Eden and in the future, every human will have the ability to be a god, to recreate things. Humans are allowed to recreate.

"God wants us to know that basically we are a species; we are a complete supported robot. We are made up of things that are biomechanically smaller than anything we have ever realised before. There are quantum mechanics involved and one day soon we are going to actually *see* a nucleus and they are going to build some micron microscope and look for these things called a *clon,* which are like tiny things wrapped around the nucleus. They won't see that until they get another microscope which is even stronger and can see even smaller particles than anything that currently exists."

The channeller said, "The forbidden apple was actually eating another living being, or cannibalism. They ate another living being, they ate their offspring. It is known biblically as the dirty blood of Lord Jesus.

"God wants us to understand that the span of our human life is only relatively short compared with the length of our soul life. When we enter a new incarnation into a new human body, we get a new body but we keep the same soul throughout all of our lives and our spirit remains connected to this world here on Earth and the spirit world simultaneously."

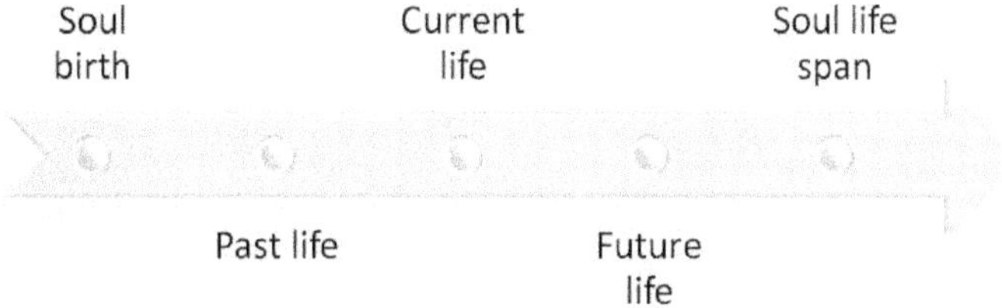

The channeller added, "We can learn to tune into both worlds at once and be reconnected, or we can choose to live in only the earthly body and feel disconnected and separated from God, the source of our love and light."

The Holy Trinity

Your spirit is the Holy Spirit. When you say, "In the name of the Father (God), the Son (Jesus) and the Holy Spirit (You)," it means the *whole* of you. God wants you to understand what this actually means, so that when you make the Holy Trinity symbol you know what you are doing rather than just mimicking what others have shown you.

When you say each of the three names, you place your hands in different positions.

For example:

- In the name of the **Father** (place your hand on the forehead, palm on the third eye with your fingers pointing upwards).
- The **Son** (rotate your hand around the heart).
- And the **Holy Spirit** (the human being, all of you, so circle yourself).
- Then rest your hands in the prayer position with your fingers pointing towards the sky with your palms together to complete the prayer.

Somewhere the movements got lost in translation and the church turned it into a cross symbol instead of circular movements. The points still look like a cross when drawn, but the motion is different and it is supposed to be circular. What you believe in when you do these motions is the key. The *intent* of prayer is the purpose of doing this. It is about encompassing the Holy Father, the Son and yourself and bringing it into your awareness, setting your intention and reconnecting with the holy element to centre yourself.

Alternative versions of the Holy Trinity include; the Father (God), the Mother (Sophia or Mary) and the Son (Jesus).

Sophia

Imagine my surprise when I discovered there was more than just one god. There is only one Creator of creation, but there *are* more gods. God however, is the god of all gods.

Let's talk about Sophia. Sophia was created as a companion for God, by God, as a more feminine counterpart. Like a woman, but much more complex and of divine origin. Sophia is like God's wife.

With God's permission, finally I got the chance to talk to Sophia. I was so curious and this concept was very new to me at the time.

I asked Sophia, "What do you like about the humans and what do you want the humans to know about you?"

Sophia answered, "There is always another layer of knowledge above this level and you'll never reach it. There's always another level so you should never get angry at anyone. If you want to go to the next level, encourage them to go to the next level. There's always somewhere meaner. You think you have the full understanding but you don't, because there's always worse. Remember witch burning went on for 500 years! Those in power were afraid of them, because they had the knowledge to conjure demons and also the ability to contact God."

Sophia added, "It is okay to make mistakes, but being fully holy is all about fully understanding the good and the bad side."

I wasn't able to talk to Sophia for very long, not more than an hour, but during this time we talked about the God from the Old Testament and the God from the New Testament and it became quite apparent we were talking about two completely separate gods. In fact one god is only a demigod. The name Demiurge was mentioned to me for the first time and Sophia directed me to start reading certain books from the Bible that were removed from the original Ethiopian Bible.

Sophia made me aware of the Dead Sea Scrolls that were found in the Qumran Caves a couple of miles inland from the Dead Sea in the West bank, which contained lost and hidden biblical writings and scriptures. They were hidden during periods of intense battles and upheavals within the kingdoms. I was also given specific references to books, chapters and verses that I needed to read and explore to clarify our discussions.

Sophia explained, "Many of the old books of the Bible have been destroyed over time and some of the recovered writings are very old and weathered and some text could no longer be read or translated."

This opened a whole new perspective on things for me, because I didn't even know these biblical scriptures existed and to what extent.

Sophia continued to explain, "Many of these hidden and lost writings contained references to what they term these days as Gnostic Christianity and back in those days they were referred to as Essenes. They shared similar beliefs and wanted to keep the hidden and secret teachings out of the wrong hands, so that the writings couldn't be altered, lost or destroyed."

Who would have known these documents would remain hidden in the caves for so long?

So, to explain the new god to you best way I can, without getting too technical, is that God, the Almighty Supreme Being, the one and only Creator got bored with just himself, so first he created the Universe, planets and stars. There was no other life except for him and he was lonely. So he created a companion, a female counterpart called Sophia. Sophia loved God and looked up to him so much and wanted to feel the same feeling that God felt when he created things. She decided to create something on her own, a new creation.

Sophia wanted to create an experiment, without God's permission and without discussing it with God. Sophia wasn't as wise as God and it hadn't occurred to God that Sophia would go off and create something without his knowledge. Because God gave all his creations free will, this would prove to be one of his greatest challenges for the future creations, especially when that free will became out of control.

Sophia descended to a level away from God and created what she thought was going to be a beautiful creation, using only her input, she created offspring and called the male counterpart the Demiurge and viewed him like her son. She was shocked and horrified when her creation didn't quite turn out the way she had planned. So she kept him hidden and secret for a period of time away from God, also on the lower realms below Heaven. The one thing that was missing from the Demiurge was God's acceptance, blessing and divine life breath that would have given the Demiurge the holy balance. Instead the Demiurge was not beautiful but unholy, materialistic, corrupted, egotistical and denied the existence of any God above him and considered himself to be the *only* Supreme Being.

The Demiurge did not believe or understand that there could even be another Creator and that anyone else could possibly exist above him. The Demiurge denied the existence of the real God, because God wasn't a part of his creation process.

Sophia in her shame, kept him hidden away from God for fear of being found out and from the knowing that she had made a mistake from her desire to create without the wisdom, knowledge, or God's permission.

Sophia deeply regretted this creation, but realised her mistake too late and this contributed to her fall from grace. Of course eventually God found out about this creation and was absolutely horrified, because Sophia couldn't possibly understand what she had done wrong without God's permission and input when making this creation.

Sophia was no longer allowed to reside in Heaven with the Creator, but had to reside on a lower level realm closer to her new creation the Demiurge, but still much higher than mankind.

It is through this *error* in creation that further lower level angels, helpers and offspring were created. They were also bound by the material world, not quite being able to ascend to the higher realms where the Creator resides, because of their separation and lack of belief in a Supreme Being beyond their lesser creators.

Even though Sophia's creation was imperfect, it still had her 50% ability to create and continued to create less and less holy beings in its quest for self fulfillment and power.

Curiosity causes many to fall from grace, instead of acceptance and belief in the Divine Creator. It is complicated and I haven't delved as far as I'd like to with this topic, but in order to cover other equally important topics which are more relevant for your learning, I will leave this one for now.

So in conclusion, this now gives us three distinctive gods that all exist. This is not all of the gods, but they are the ones that are talked about the most.

1. **The Almighty Creator** - The god of all gods and who we know as God from the New Testament. He is the loving and all knowing God. The Creator is a very forgiving god.
2. **Sophia** - Created by the Almighty Creator as a companion and became the creator of a lower type of creation who resides in the lower realms, but still above the human realms.
3. **The Demiurge** - Sometimes referred to as Barbello, who is also known as the god from the Old Testament. He was the unauthorised creation of Sophia. This god craved ultimate power and wanted devoted loyal worship and would be prepared to destroy anything that stood in his way. This god is a very unforgiving god, or should I say demigod.

Miracles

I hear people complaining all the time that they don't see any miracles in the modern age. Do you ever stop to look around you and see that the world is already filled with miracles? In fact the world *itself* is a miracle.

I don't need to ask for miracles anymore. I expect to see them every day. Every single day I do see and hear things, because I am paying attention and I *believe* these things are extraordinary and are miracles from God to show me he is always around.

God knows how much I love animals and especially birds, so he likes to use animals, birds and little flying creatures to lift my mood, or prove to me that he is near me if I am feeling down, frustrated, or extremely tired. I don't need proof because I feel him with me even in times of struggle. Many times I have been in the company of friends, or even strangers and pointed these miracles out to them at the time they happened. I make a point of showing them so they can see what I see. *Only then* do they acknowledge the existence of miracles. It almost seems that you need to *experience* a miracle, before you know for sure, miracles do exist. Recognising when a miracle happens is the most important part.

People tend to walk around with their blinkers on, looking straight ahead, like horses do when they are getting transported around in a truck, so they don't freak out. People like horses; generally don't like to be *freaked out.* They prefer the ordinary, the mundane and the predictable consistent routine.

God is spontaneous every time, never predictable. God believes people are expecting to see some kind of dramatic sign, massive explosion, or cataclysmic event before they will recognise, or honour a miracle.

Miracles are actually so much more subtle than that and have much more relevance to the person receiving the miracle, than to the general populace.

This one particular day my partner and I were on our way to find a place to eat lunch, but couldn't decide where to eat, when a gorgeous little willy wagtail bird lands on a railing right in front of us. The bird chirps to us and then points with his beak to a restaurant up a set of stairs overlooking the river.

We looked at each other and laughed and we decided to humour the willy wagtail and I said, "Okay we will have lunch up there today." We thanked the bird and the bird flew away.

While we were waiting for lunch in this wonderful Brisbane riverside restaurant, something beautiful happened. At the time, we were both working for a particularly wicked lady boss and she was a very difficult person to get along with and to work for. You couldn't avoid her because she wanted to know what you were doing every minute of the day and there was no escaping her until you left the building for lunch, or when you left work for the day. Even then, she would call after hours and on our days off ranting and raving. No matter how hard anyone worked for her, nothing was ever good enough. She made everyone walk on eggshells around her and as you know, this type of tyrannical boss exists in many workplaces. She was the bully with money, who dangled the carrot in front of you and then slapped you with a stick when she wanted you to feel like a slave. It wasn't a very pleasant environment to work in. I am sure many of you have had a boss like this at one time or another.

Anyway, I was feeling pretty down and while we were seated we talked about our escape plan and how we were going to leave this place in the coming weeks. We looked around at everyone else in the restaurant and nobody was talking to each other; they were all grasping their little handheld devices, madly tapping away on their smart phones and completely ignoring the person they were sharing their lunch break with.

I leaned closer to my partner, "What is happening to everyone, they are so lost in their little electronic boxes? They don't talk to each other anymore. One day they are going to look up and everything will be gone!"

Our meals arrived and as we do at every meal time, we bow our heads and we say a heartfelt prayer of thanks for our good fortune and we bless our meal before we eat. This is traditionally called *grace*. We always invite God to join us for every meal and we give thanks to our Creator for everything that we are lucky to have and going to receive in the future.

Just then, the same beautiful willy wagtail bird landed on a perch right above our table and sung a beautiful happy bird song for at least one minute and he was so loud he caught the attention of everyone in the restaurant including the staff. The willy wagtail then flew over to the water fountain situated next to our table and drank from the water fountain and was dancing merrily on the edge of that fountain.

Amazingly right after that, two large black crows also flew into the restaurant and landed on the fountain, one landed on the left of the willy wagtail and one landed on the right and they all started drinking the water together. All of them were taking their fill in perfect harmony.

This sight astonished everyone in the restaurant and they all got out their cameras, smart phones and other video devices and started taking pictures and recording this miraculous event, because it lasted a good five minutes. It really was a beautiful moment and a picture perfect opportunity.

I don't know if you know that much about crows, but they are very shy, timid and a little bit sneaky when scoping around for food and finding water. They generally don't like getting too close to people, or competing with other birds for food and water. To see them sitting with another type of bird happily drinking from the water fountain right next to us, truly was an obvious miracle that everyone in the restaurant at that time had the privilege to witness and recognised as extraordinary.

Later that night, I was working on some projects when God visited me again. He spoke these words to me, "Today when you were having lunch, there was a water fountain where you were. There was the little wee willy wagtail bird that pointed you towards this amazing place next to the water. I shall add that it was asked at each and every meal and this went on for seven meals. Then one came to the conclusion that everyone pulled out every photographic device they had, iPhones, Polaroids, digitised cameras and photographic cameras. They were all switched on at exactly the same time when the two crows arrived at the water fountain that was guarded by Buddha on the left hand side, The Jade Buddha, which was the name of the restaurant."

God added, "I appeared and invoked these souls to do something out of their zombiness. To distract them out of their Devil's sin, the zombie tool which is the modern day crystal ball. It is the phone. It shall cause many people to die from road accidents. There are new motor car accidents that I get every three seconds of the day and I am asked if I shall forgive them as they slaughter themselves with their crystal ball in screaming agony!"

God continued to explain that what I was seeing was really happening and I had noticed the total immersion of everyone in their phones, so much immersion that they were not looking at the real world around them anymore and they were totally absorbed in this glass screen. They were absorbed in the *virtual* world.

It was so disappointing to see humans reduced to staring into this tiny little screen, especially when they think they have really advanced when it comes to modern technology. God was also explaining that because of these new devices, which he calls the Devil's glass, the new smart phones that people have allowed to become centre stage in their life, are actually making humans dumber. They have become so much like a zombie. They aren't even looking where they are going and God told me they are getting killed at the rate of one person every three seconds as a result of being distracted.

God wants you all to *ask* for more miracles and then *expect* to see them. You don't have to expect to see a sensational or dramatic miracle, one that stops all the traffic on the highway. It can just be a simple and subtle sign from God to show you that he *is* with you. A feeling of warmth, a feeling of love and an inner knowing he is always with you.

I don't like to ask for too many miracles myself, because I don't like to test God's patience, but I will ask for the rain to stop if I need to make a safe passage to somewhere. I will ask for the sun to shine if I haven't seen it throughout the winter very often. Every time God comes through for me and shows me he is listening with his little weather miracles.

Just today, I glanced out of my window at work and it was coming up to my lunch break. It was raining heavily and the sky was full of dark grey rain clouds for miles. I wished silently to God, *if I could just have half an hour of no rain, so I could go outside and enjoy some fresh air and stretch my legs and go for a walk*. He didn't disappoint me and the rain stopped five minutes later for a period of 30 minutes exactly. Not a minute longer. I had just enough time to walk to the park, lay down on a dry surface and meditate for 15 minutes, then walk back to work. The second I walked through the door at work, the rain bucketed down and I laughed, knowing that was yet again, another miracle from God.

Believe and you shall receive. It is as simple as that, no more, no less. Don't ask for something ridiculous and meaningless. It needs to be something that you really feel in your heart is a wholesome desire and you *will* get it.

Miracles are a very personal experience and it only signifies a miracle to the person asking for it. Sometimes a whole group of people ask God for a miracle. It might be a weather miracle in an area that receives little or no rain and their crops have almost dried up, or they may want the rain to stop so they don't drown their crops, or lose their homes. Either way, if you don't ask, no one is going to give you a miracle just for the sake of it.

Where people lose faith, is when they ask for a miracle and then don't receive it immediately. Humans don't have a lot of patience, it is a skill that is learned over many lifetimes and humans need to practise patience to know God. Sometimes God sends his angels to perform healing miracles, but they can get blocked by the person who is supposed to receive the healing by *non-belief*. The miracles can also be blocked by the dark side interfering, or distracting the person receiving the miracle.

There are many times when we all take miracles for granted. Cast your mind back to the last time you had a *near miss*. A situation that could have been fatal or a scary moment in your past, when you almost could have taken your last breath. I am sure we have all had at least one of these experiences we can recall when you really think about it.

I am kind of like a cat in some ways, but in other ways I am not. I have already spent my nine lives and I am now officially in miracle territory!

I was a passenger in a car that has driven off an embankment and no one was harmed, but the car was a bit smashed up. I have again been involved as a passenger in a car crash when the car rolled multiple times on a gravel road and no one was hurt.

Another time, I was narrowly missed by a car running a red light, when the jacket I was wearing was grabbed by a total stranger. I just put my foot out to walk across the road and felt myself being pulled back quickly.

Once I was a little girl and I was playing on an adventure playground during a school fair with a group of friends. The boys in the group were showing me how cool they were by doing somersaults using the ropes on the adventure playground. Of course I tried, but hadn't quite worked out my monkey skills yet and fell from the height of a double story house and landed on my back on the hard stones without a scratch, or a broken bone. I was just extremely winded. In fact, I was so winded that I don't even remember some of the following minutes after that event. I remember trying to breath but the wind had been knocked clean out of me and I was gasping for breath. There was a large crowd of people standing around me, looking down at me with shocked looks on their faces. Shocked because I had just missed the concrete edge of the play area and shocked at the fact I was still in one piece and alive.

To this day, I still remember the most awesome miracle of all. I was out for a night on the town with a group of friends and we were having so much fun. I was totally caught up in the moment and forgot where I was! I crossed the road near a nightclub in Perth, Western Australia and I wasn't looking where I was going. I stepped out in front of a taxi cab and the driver saw me at the very last second. His eyes met mine and I looked deep into his soul and I thought for sure this was my last moment. Everything went in slow motion and I heard the brakes screech and felt the wind come to an absolute standstill and for that single moment in time, *everything stopped* including the car. It was like some kind of magical force had stopped time and when the car actually stopped still it just touched the side of my leg. You wouldn't have even fitted a hair between me and the car and yet no damage was done to either of us. The taxi driver didn't even yell at me, he was so grateful that something miraculous had just happened. Every person on the street that night saw this miracle and I reckon the taxi driver and I should have brought a lotto ticket that night, because we were both thanking our lucky stars!

I have absolutely no doubt in my mind that what happened was *divine intervention* and in that moment I felt a strong presence with me, but I couldn't actually *see* anything. It was more of a *feeling.* My life did flash before my eyes and this is as close to death that I want to experience. I was fully aware of my gratitude for living life in that special moment.

Another time I can recall coming home from doing some grocery shopping and I was in my little ladylike sedan, my little blue car, waiting amongst the lineup of cars. I was waiting for the traffic lights to turn green. Out of the corner of my eye I saw a massive 4WD speeding down the street towards the line of idling traffic. I turned to look at the 4WD and there was nowhere I could turn, or move, because the traffic was backed up in every direction and I was in the very right hand lane. The 4WD was approaching the intersection way too fast and driving in Australia, I was located on the right hand side of the car.

The 4WD tried to brake and I heard the vehicle skid through the intersection on the greasy road surface. An hour prior to this it had been lightly raining. Just enough to make the road slippery and greasy.

The vehicle slid across two empty lanes on the opposite side of the road and was heading straight for my driver's door with its massive bull bar and with the force of serious gravity behind it. Out of nowhere, a white car drove between me and the 4WD. *Smack!* The 4WD hit the white car and the white car spun around in a 360 degree circle, after being knocked across the landing strip. With smashed glass flying through the air, the smashed up white car came to a standstill, on the other side of the road. The 4WD became airborne momentarily and then landed on top of the landing strip and smashed into a road sign. The sound was so loud! It was like large explosions of metal on metal, with glass shards hitting the road at high speed.

Right at that moment, the lights turned green and I had no choice but to keep moving with the flow of traffic, because we all had to clear the area to give the occupants space to get out of their vehicles. Thank God, no one was killed or injured and only the vehicles were a write off that day.

I have always felt angels protecting me all through my life and this was another crazy example of me fulfilling my fate, or destiny. This event endorsed the fact that it just wasn't my time yet. My heart was almost jumping out of my chest and I was only two minutes from home. When I got home I had a little cry of relief that I made it home alive and that I lived to tell yet another miraculous story of survival.

It also helped to strengthen my faith in God and my faith in the angelic beings that protect us all at times when we really need them. God's plan for us is so complex, that in a split second something can unexpectedly happen to you and you have to be prepared for it. When viewed from the perspective of the angels and God, they have time on their side and they have the ability to intervene, if they feel that you have a purpose that hasn't yet been fulfilled.

Touch wood, I am blessed and have never had a broken bone in my body, even though I have had plenty of accidents and mishaps. I don't do as many crazy things these days as I used to. I tend to show more respect now for every breath I have and every extra minute the Creator allows me to be here and experience life.

One major fact that still astonishes me is the fact that God still comes and talks to me and that is the biggest miracle of all. I no longer question if he exists, I eagerly wait for his next visit.

I asked God, "Do you think it is safe to share this book with people on Earth at this time?"

God replied, "And when you read this and you know who you are and decide to assassinate me (God), you cannot destroy me. I am not dragging a cross made of lumber to cause earthquakes and mass havoc. And if you shall, I will destroy you as if you never existed, as if Jesus died and if you shall use these words in vain, which you will. I will destroy you and restore everything as if you didn't exist. And you will all know this from seeing kingdoms rise and fall."

Angels

I asked God, "How many angels are there?"

He answered, "They are forever for there is no amount of angels. That's like asking how many stars are there."

There are a multitude of angels that reside with God and people must understand that angels have a hierarchy of their own and they are on a level all of their own.

All angels have a purpose too and their purpose depends on what they show love for. Some angels like Archangel Michael, have chosen to watch over and look after humans. There are many other sub angels that have also chosen to be assigned to this task.

Some of them have chosen to come here this time to see which species they feel the most love for. Once they discover which species they like, then this is the species they can be assigned to and can look after, whenever they evolve to a point where they are responsible enough to look after a particular species.

Each angel of the Lord has been designated to look after a certain species, including the human species. At the moment there are too many angels looking after the human species and are more concerned about their welfare than perhaps the animal kingdom.

God gives me an example of special people who get assigned as angels like Steve Irwin. He was known to have such an incredible love for animals, that he created his own zoo and had a passion for protecting animals while he was alive. God told me he visited Steve while he was alive and Steve was also known through the eyes of the channeller. When Steve passed over, he was able to continue his love for animals by being allowed to select a particular species to look after as an angel. Steve wanted to look after many species, but God didn't allow this. He had to choose *one* favourite species. For someone like Steve this would have been a very difficult choice, but he would have chosen whichever species he happened to resonate with the most. In the afterlife Steve Irwin has been seen by many psychics, riding a white horse in Heaven with the kingdom of animals following him.

When you feel yourself resonating with a particular animal, mammal, insect, or creature, then this is likely to be the species that you will naturally gravitate towards. Some people are doggie people, some people are cat people, some are horsey people, some love reptiles and others love birds. I am a bird lover and I love all flying creatures great and small, for they are my favourite and I resonate with them the most in the whole animal kingdom. I am fascinated by their mobility, their sleek design, their curious nature and their amazing skills. They help us to live on this beautiful planet by propagating and spreading the seeds of plants and trees where they need to be. In turn we breathe in the oxygen created by these wonderful plants and trees. We have a lot to be thankful for in our world, for all of the flying creatures including; birds, bees, butterflies, dragonflies, bats, flies, wasps and even mosquitoes. We must understand that *everything* has its purpose and everything has its place.

God said, "If each human would plant one tree each, then that tree would sustain that human throughout their life. If that tree dies, then the human needs to be responsible for planting another tree in its place. If everyone would do this, everything would become one."

God continued, "The life of an angel is designed to help all, whenever they can in any given situation. Help to turn them around. Coming to Earth again as an angel is more like a little holiday where sleep can be obtained. On the other side there is not much time for sleep, because so many questions need to be answered and so many souls need to be helped.

God told me he is sitting on his throne and he has 12 special angels sitting on each side at his feet.

I asked, "Have any of them lived a human life?"

He responded, "No, but they have lived many times."

God explained there are female and male angels and he keeps one type on one side and one type on the other side, so they don't get distracted.

So then I asked, "What is their mission?"

God replied, "They are like you and me, they just want to be free to come and go as they please."

I pressed on with questions, "Do they enjoy being where they are?"

God laughed joyfully, "They are with me, so they get to hear all my conversations and even the funny wise jokes."

God added, "Jesus is everywhere." That's the funny part to God.

The channeller said, "Jesus comes to Earth and gets killed, because the establishment think they conquered him, but he is everywhere. God like Jesus is forever, eternity and the name of the Lord in Hebrew is forever."

The channeller continued, "Angels are allowed to watch us, guide us, protect us and will come to our assistance any time we *ask* for their help. They are not allowed to intervene if it is God's will. They are also not allowed to intervene if it is against your own will. We all have free will and the angels respect our free will, even if we make silly choices that make no sense at all. The angels will only intervene if your life is in mortal danger and it is not your time to go to God yet."

Speaking for God, the channeller added, "There is an angel for every feeling that you have. For example, there is an angel for suffering, the angel of hope, the angel of forgiveness, the angel of worrying, the angel of health and how this is explained will clarify everything to mankind. Whatever emotion you can think of, there is an angel that you can ask who represents this emotion. As youeth of human believe that you have too much sorrow, then you can ask this angel to be goneth of this sorrow and change it for happiness and this angel will listen to you and help you on your way. Again you have free will to listen, or not. To feel, or not to feel the angel giving you the happiness and love. The love comes from Archangel Micheal, Jesus and God."

Then God said, "You shall feel this love when you listen to me, as I will cry and take your sorrow away from you when you understand who I am. I am the light and I was made and I am who am I. I was made by myself, for myself and I made you and you shall become strong in the light."

Guardian angels

God said, "Your guardian angel is from your ancestry lineage. If you want a starting point, it starts with you. You become the guardian of your offspring in the future. Time is irrelevant and you can work together with each other over and over again."

Your guardian angel looks after you, warns you of any impending danger, makes sure you are safe and helps to steer you in the right direction by helping you choose your path carefully. Your guardian angel is there to be a guardian of you, to guard you and protect you when asked. They also help you by keeping demons away in all realms.

If you think you can do it on your own without their help, they will stand back. Your guardian angel has had more lives than you, because they are your predecessor. Humans sometimes think they don't need help, but you should trust in the help you can get from your guardian angel. You can have more than one guardian angel. If you pray, you can get help from *any* guardian angel. There is an infinite amount of angels who will also help you when you need them.

Your higher self

God said, "This is the distinction between your physical self and your soul self. The more love you have, you *attract* your soul self towards your physical self and the less love you have you *repel* your soul away from your physical body. This is like disassociating your soul from your body. It is your higher self, or your soul self that is all knowing and is the best guidance that you can ask for in an earthly sense."

The channeller said, "Your soul has the ability to heal your body. Jesus and God want us to become one. A good example of feeling connected, is with partners, when two people become one by being in love. You should love their body and their spirit, or soul and then the two of you will grow to become one together and you can help others to become one. This is simply achieved by loving one another.

"If you start doing the wrong things, you start detaching from both your soul self and your physical body. When the detachment becomes too great for either your body, or your soul to manage, you die.

"You and your soul, just like you and your aura, need to be as one to extend your life. Your spiritual body, or soul self needs to be in touch with your physical body and they need to become one. What would happen to your body if you separated your soul from your physical body? You would die.

"You either give in to the physical body, or give in to the spiritual body, or if you are a Buddhist you would say you reincarnate again when this separation occurs. We don't always have control over the timing of our separation, or even our reincarnation, because you may need to learn and grow when you are with your soul self, before coming back to the next life."

Judgement

God said, "You need to understand what judgement is. Judgement is putting your belief onto somebody else by comparing it to your belief. If you are bad, then your threshold for badness is very high and you could easily be an evil judge and not a fair one."

God continued, "Being a human, you would judge that the mouse runs faster, moves quicker, gets to their destination faster and has more ambition than the slug. But in fact the slug that is considered to be slower and deemed to be less judgemental has to work a million times harder than the mouse to get the same result. It has no legs, a smaller brain and in comparison the slug is much smarter and more superior to the mouse. If you were another slug, judging another slug it would be a very slim race indeed and a fair race, instead of the race being unfairly judged against the mouse. The mouse just takes it for granted, while the slug has to earn it. If the slug and the mouse loved each other, they would live in harmony and not have to race each other."

The channeller said, "There is no judging. God judges things and to judge is more like when something happens and you make a judgement.

"When you finally meet your maker and every one of you will, when God looks at you he will say to you, 'Who are you? Who did you help? Why are you here? What haven't you done?'

"In total, there are seven questions (of course seven, because that is God's holy number) that God asks everyone when the soul transitions over to him. Other questions include, 'where are you going and is it your time?'

"The most horrific thing is when they must judge themselves and all of their own deeds throughout their life. It is like a whirly wind going backwards and forwards and all over the place."

God said, "They must judge *themselves* for what they have done!"

The channeller added, "This is one of the scariest things God sees a soul go through. He's never seen anything like it when a soul judges itself. It's like a war unto themselves. It either destroys them, or makes them stronger. If you've done wrong, you must do right. They get confronted with everything they have ever done in their entire lifetime."

The channeller continued, "Do you love your next door neighbour, or do you murder him? You can either look after yourself, or destroy yourself. That is why they are stuck to this Earth and that is why they keep coming back."

God believes we should be retraining and helping those who have lost their way, by showing them the right way to live in harmony with one another. We need to guide them in the right direction and put them back on the righteous life path that he knows everyone can live. Understand what makes them do what they do and correct the psyche to fix the mindset of crime and hate, by overcoming it with love and peace. Not one of us should be discarded, or neglected from righteous guidance.

If someone is none the wiser to their incorrect actions, they may have had a terribly abusive or violent upbringing and shown the wrong way constantly and told it is the right way. How can we expect they know what the right way is? They might actually have no idea how to do things the right way other than what they feel in their heart. If their heart is hardened, they show less compassion and survive with little or no love. Living on the streets can *harden* the heart and they forget how to use this precious resource to make the right choices.

Technically the parent, legal guardian, or carer should be responsible for crimes committed by the uneducated and the inexperienced. If the life lessons and teachings being handed down from the legal guardian, or parent who raises them are fundamentally flawed, then the being who has fallen off the rails doesn't even know how to get back on track, because they have never been shown how.

After all that is how the law treats the owner of a dog when the dog disobeys the law. They punish the dog owner and sometimes the dog pays the ultimate sacrifice of its life for having an incompetent owner. This is hard coded into the law and it is used as the biggest disclaimer for people who claim this as a defence. The law uses the term "ignorance of the law is no excuse," even if the supposedly guilty party has no intent to break the law, because they don't actually know what the law is, to break it.

God said, "It is different in the animal kingdom, because they live by the law of the jungle called *survival of the fittest.* An old animal is wiser, because it lives by the correct judgement which is how it has survived the test of time."

A so called criminal can commit a crime in the eyes of the law, which is not always a sin, or a misdemeanour in the eyes of God and can be found guilty by a court of law and sent to jail. If a person serves time for their crime and fulfils their punishment, then they should be left alone and not continue to be harassed when they have completed their time. Stop judging them as though they haven't learned from their mistakes. Everyone deserves to be forgiven and if they have served time for their crime, then they have already made many sacrifices during their time in lock down.

Instead of brutalising, punishing and constantly humiliating them, let's educate, love and guide them, so they can get back on the *right* path after their release from jail and contribute to society in a positive way. Criminals get caught and that is why they end up in jail. There are lots of guilty criminals who don't get caught and they are living all around you.

It is not our right to judge. It is God's right and the right of the individual who must just themselves.

God wants you to consider, "What is a true crime? Is it a crime against society, a crime against a belief system, or a crime against God?"

God feels that a true crime or an unholy sin is the crime committed against the better judgement of one's self. To have learned and to know better than to commit the crime, but then to go ahead and commit the crime anyway, regardless of the punishment.

Aliens

Aliens do exist. God laughs and thinks it is funny how we could possibly think we are the *only* intelligent species in the Universe, or within the seven universes. Not only does he think that is funny, but the fact that we think we are the only creation ever made, is mostly humorous to him.

God said, "Take a look around you here on Planet Earth for a start. There are so many different species that man cannot even identify the exact number. Many new species are being discovered and extinct species are being rediscovered all the time. Do you think something as mighty as the Supreme Being would only spend his entire existence creating and focusing on mankind? No is the answer!"

Speaking for God, the channeller said, "The Annunaki had the ability to talk to angels around 100,000 year ago. The Annunaki believed they were gods, angels and spirits and they believed they could talk to them. One of their rituals was, when they gave birth they offered their rituals to God so that God could help them grow and live and that's how it is on Earth as well. The Annunaki's planet exploded. It was a supernova star. They were highly advanced and they came to Earth and gave mankind their technology. They created modern man at that time. They eventually made an Adam and an Eve and they spoke to the angels and God. God helped them create as did all of the angels and everything."

The channeller continued, "There was a *forbidden tablet* that proved the existence of this alien race. It was the forbidden tablet of ancient Egypt, which was destroyed."

God has spoken to me about aliens frequently and reminds us that our definition of aliens is; a being that is not native to Earth. Well technically, none of us are *native* to Earth. Just because we were born on Earth, doesn't make us *native* to Earth. We are actually native to Heaven and then went on a journey to Earth and became aliens ourselves.

God doesn't want to confuse us with this definition, but makes a distinction that an alien can be viewed many ways and wants us to know there is *nothing supernatural* about an alien.

If we could time travel back to the beginning of time and saw a plane flying overhead, or a spacecraft scooting past, we would probably think that aliens were coming to take over our planet. We may not even know what it was that we were seeing if we hadn't seen that level of technology before.

God said, "Keep it simple and know that there are multitudes of other aliens within the seven universes. You get to choose which planet you incarnate, or reincarnate on. Earth is really interesting; it has many experiences to offer and many historic places to visit, which is why so many souls come here for a lifetime, or many lifetimes to experience another life."

There are many different alien souls incarnating here as well, such as star children whose souls come from other parts of the galaxy. When they have children they are called special space names as well and so on.

So this raises the question, *if there are aliens, do they have a different God and do they abide by different universal laws?* No is the answer. They share the same

God, the same Creator. There is only *one* Creator. They are also bound by the same rules and universal laws as we are. Some aliens may have more advanced technology than us and some aliens may even have a better understanding of how to live in peace and harmony with each other. They still share the same God and are processed in the same way when they pass over.

This book is about God, so I will move on from the alien conversation. What you really wanted to know is if they existed at all and now you know they do.

Free will

God said, "You make your own choices by using your own free will. Free will is your *inner idiot.* When you do things that are not right, then you only have the inner idiot to blame, nobody else."

God continued, "As a matter of fact, some alien gave mankind free will. They were given free will so that no one could come and corrupt them and also to stop other alien races coming to control them. Mankind corrupted themselves and mankind can corrupt other members of mankind. God didn't give humans free will; it was given to humans by Eniki, the genetic scientist who helped to create them. I have heard the name Enki, but Eniki is more like the real name, a mistranslation of others perhaps."

The channeller speaking for God added, "Annunaki is the race. The Annunaki thought of themselves as gods and they tried to be perfect with everything they did. So what is the problem with mankind? They can be easily corrupted and led astray by their own free will. The further away from their gut instinct they act, the more they are getting out of harmony with themselves. This means they get out of alignment with their soul's true purpose and out of attunement with God's loving energy and fall into a state of rebellion.

"If mankind was told this all the time when they are growing up, then they would be perfect, but they are brainwashed with the wrong things, the corrupted things."

God wants to hear prayers from humans, because he is scared of what they have become when they were given artificial intelligence. Artificial intelligence is beyond somebody. It is called beyond your master. If you go beyond then you can be your own demigod. When you say the words, "Try them out and test them," then say to them, "it's beyond your capability," they believe you. You need to learn things beyond your knowledge.

Free will was supposed to give humans *more* intelligence; instead sometimes it makes them confused and causes them to make stupid choices.

Free will was provided to mankind with some basic rules. The rules were super simple and hardcoded into their DNA and yet mankind still attempts to override the free will of others with their actions.

1. **Free will** is to be exercised for the purpose of obtaining the best possible outcome for all concerned.
2. Never use your **free will** to harm another without just cause.
3. Never suppress the **free will** of another being.
4. You cannot remove the **free will** of another by imprisonment.
5. You are fully responsible and accountable for your own **free will**.

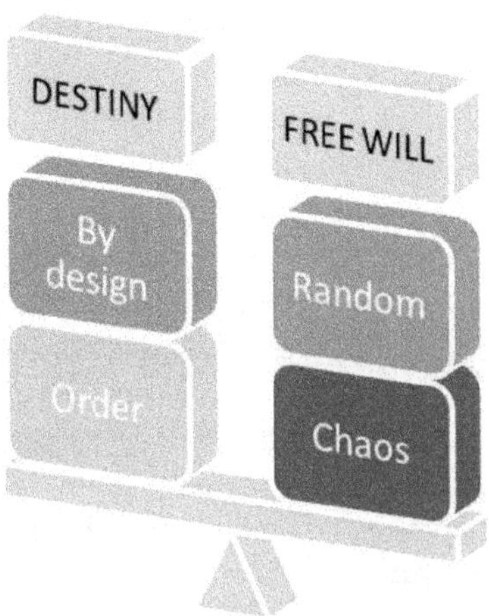

Free will implies that humans have some control over their fate, or destiny which on some levels is correct. They can influence the outcomes of their daily pursuits; they can make basic choices and they can influence others to make choices that are in alignment with their own wants and needs. It may seem like full unadulterated free will, but on the higher levels which exist just beyond your comprehension, you are fulfilling a greater purpose which is guided by a force much bigger than you are aware of.

There is a complex web of existence that we are all a part of, to fulfil our ultimate *destiny* and soul purpose. This awareness can be expanded once we realise our full potential and we are living in state of full attunement with God's love. Once we achieve enlightenment, or *attunement*, we surrender our free will and thy will be done by our Creator. Then we allow God to guide us to do his good work.

Once your will becomes the will of God, you are living life fully in the moment, cherishing your existence and allowing God to experience life through you instantaneously. This causes you to be filled with his love, instead of selfishly chasing material desires, which leave you feeling empty and cold.

How to pray

The Holy Trinity is more like doing a trillion prayers. God wants you to pray to your past, pray to your future and be grateful for all things to come. Pray to heaven, pray to hell and pray for everything.

Praying is something you hear many people say, but they don't actually know what it means to pray, or *how* to pray.

For me personally, meal times are the compulsory minimum prayer for me to say three times daily if I have three meals. My longest prayer is at dinner time, because I get to share the evening prayer with my partner and family. I put my two hands together, either clasped holding them to my heart, with my head bowed, or flat with palms together, pointing upwards, depending on how I am feeling. Both positions are fine. In fact, any position is fine, because it is your *intent* that matters the most. What you feel deep in your heart. The ritual or routine doesn't really matter as much.

I bow my head as a sign of respect and I use the meal prayer time to start by saying the biggest daily thank you to the Lord, for providing me with the meal that I am about to receive. Then I give thanks for all of the good fortune and blessings in my life. I also give thanks for all of the creatures on the planet, both great and small and all of the plants and other living beings that were involved in producing the food. If I am facing difficult challenges at the time, I ask for strength and courage to deal with my challenges or adversaries. I always say a special prayer if I know someone who needs a special mention.

If I happen to have a guest over for dinner, I always say a special prayer of thanks for having them in our company and I make a point of continuing my daily prayer routine even if the people with me are not used to saying grace at meal time. This is a good opportunity to *show* people how simple it is to be thankful for your food, grateful for being alive and how to pray to the Lord.

I also pray at other times, especially if I am asking for something in particular, or asking for clarity on a certain question or issue. This way I can direct my attention directly towards God and know that when he is ready, he will answer my question. Sometimes my questions are not even that formal, they are just thoughts inside my mind and they still get answered by God. I may not get the answer straight away, but the answer always comes.

The main thing to remember is that it is important to pray to God. Acknowledge the existence of God and be grateful for everything you have. Pray when you are feeling good and pray when you are feeling grateful, because those prayers are the most heartfelt and the prayers he listens to the most.

Don't pray when you are angry, or desperate, because God is not to blame for things that go wrong in the world, or in your life. If you are feeling angry and want to pray, then you should ask God to give you the strength and courage you need to get through the day. Ask God to give you patience, kindness and understanding.

If you feel scared, or are afraid that you might become physically, or psychically attacked, then you can call on the help of the Almighty Lord, Jesus, or any of the holy archangels. The feeling of instant calm and safety will be with you as their presence is felt.

Prayers work in both the waking and sleeping states. The simple request to have a holy presence is enough to scare off any darkness that might be lurking around.

If I need spiritual protection, I say in a loud and confident voice, "This house is the house of the Almighty Lord and it is blessed. Only those who come from the love and light are allowed to enter this space. You must have the Creator's permission to be here in this space. If you are not from the love and light then you must leave now. You are not welcome."

Say it with conviction and keep repeating it until you feel the presence has left.

Another sure safe method to remove any unwanted spirits, or an evil presence is to recite the "Lord's Prayer" out loud.

If someone you know has recently passed away, then you could pray for a safe passage to God and ask God to forgive their sins. You can also ask him to find a place in his heart to forgive them and welcome them into Heaven.

If you accidentally kill any little creatures, bless the creatures you have killed, or are going to kill, like that mosquito who is poised on your arm ready to suck your blood. Ask for the little creature to be reborn and ask that they have a blessed life when they are reborn.

I always say I am very sorry to creatures if I accidentally kill them, or if I do my best but cannot save them. If the option exists *not* to kill it and it is safe to do so, I will put the creature in either a jar or container, or I will pick it up and transport it elsewhere like I do with flies, wasps, spiders, moths and other little creatures that shouldn't be inside the house. I am not so favourable with mosquitoes for some reason. When ants, or termites start taking over all of the living areas and they sting or bite, they tend to not live for long afterwards. Although I know it is wrong to kill even a mosquito, I haven't become that holy yet, but I am working on it. I find it difficult not to retaliate if I am bitten, or stung in my own space or on my own body.

Jesus used to bless the ground that he walked on, so that if he happened to step on something and killed it accidentally, it would be automatically blessed upon passing over.

I am personally a star girl and I am most active during the night. I need to gaze out at the stars and look at how I used to navigate through the stars in my past lives and imagine I am actually navigating to go somewhere.

This kind of feeling transports me away to another place and I feel so oriented and grounded when I do this. This is more like my way of saying an earthly prayer, when I look deep into the night sky. It is a feeling of being *connected* to something greater than myself and a feeling of being in sync with the Universe at the same time.

I feel like I am so small in the big scheme of things and it puts the immense expanse of the Creator into perspective when I do this. I feel a strong connection to my past, present and future simultaneously and I know that I have a whole ancestry of souls who can help me. I represent the whole family when I talk to them and I can talk to the whole clan at the same time if I want to. I can also say prayers to them, as well as for them at the same time.

You can pray for anything, anyone, any animals, or for any creatures to be saved if you believe this is the right thing to do and it is not interfering with the natural order of things. If you ask and pray and your prayer is not granted, it doesn't mean you didn't pray hard enough. It could just mean that the natural order of things is meant to happen this way and in this case you can pray for understanding. I have personally asked God to save many birds, animals and creatures and God *does* listen to my prayers and *answers* my prayers. Sometimes a creature may be too far gone to be saved and then God may take them away.

I have witnessed the grace of God with my own eyes when I accidentally hit a bird in the middle of the night, while I was driving in the country side. When the bird hit the window screen, it bounced under the van and I thought it was dead for sure. I pulled over to the side of the road and went back to check if the bird was still alive. It was knocked out cold on the road and unconscious, but I could still feel its heart beating really fast in my hands, so I knew it wasn't dead. It was practically lifeless in my hands though and I didn't want to traumatise the bird any further, so I put it on a large round wooden gate post nearby. I bowed my head, closed my eyes and said the biggest heartfelt prayer to God that I could muster, because I was truly sorry that I had hit it with my vehicle.

I asked God to save the bird and to show pity and mercy on the life of this little creature. I didn't have anything in the van to put the bird in, so I didn't take it with me. It may have died of fright if it had woken up inside the van. I was on my way into town and I knew I would be returning in less than an hour.

When I returned, I approached the wooden gate post on the way home. I pulled the vehicle over and got out. I walked up to the bird and it was standing on both legs awake and waiting. I jumped up and down full of excitement and yelled out at the top of my lungs, "Thank you God for saving this beautiful bird! Thank you, thank you, thank you!"

Just at that moment the bird launched off the post, I probably scared it off with all my excitement and it flew off into the darkness. I knew the bird had fully recovered and it was going to survive thanks to the mercy of God. That was a true miracle to me and my prayers were answered.

I truly believe and trust that God always knows what is right for the being, the animal, or the creature when he decides what the best course of action is. I respect whatever that choice is. I always aim to do everything in my power to save little creatures at every opportunity I can, but sometimes they are such delicate little things that you can do more damage trying to save them. Sometimes it is better to pray for them to recover and to find their own way home.

Confessions

The purpose of a confession is not to punish, or to highlight a weakness in a person's development; it is to help to clear them of their wrong doings and to help them understand what is right and wrong, so they can move forward with their spiritual development.

If a person truly wants to heal themselves, they need to talk to someone and whoever that is, needs to have no judgement of them during their confession.

A sure way to get a person to reveal their confessions to you would be to say to them, "You must tell me the honest truth, because without the honest truth you cannot be healed."

If you are receiving the confession, your job is to build rapport with the person, so they feel comfortable enough telling you their problems and getting them to share their life story with you. This is putting the responsibility back on the person giving the confession and also giving them the opportunity to be truthful.

A sin is determined by the person's own belief and whatever you deem it to be in your belief. You need to ask them, "In your belief, is there anything in your life that you have done that doesn't sit right with you?"

This is giving the receiver the opportunity to keep an open mind without judgement. Revealing this type of sin is basically a confession, or a conscious sin.

Then you would ask, "Is there anything *out* of your belief system that doesn't sit right with you?"

Alternatively, revealing this type of sin is usually a buried or suppressed memory and this question may unlock the unconscious mind by triggering a guilty memory.

If the person gives you an indication by displaying an unbalanced result in the previous test, this would give you a subtle signal there is an underlying instability in the person. Recognise the signals like; colours, feelings, sensations, sounds and avoidance and calibrate what the sin represents to the person.

An irrational tempo would make you aware the person is out of sync, or out of balance. For example, an erratic, or fidgety behaviour pattern. It could be an unusually fast or slow tempo. Start to repair the image the person gives you if it seems to be incorrect or inappropriate. Listen carefully to the responses they give you.

Ask them, "What is your favourite colour? Describe it to me and what does it mean to you?"

Chunk it down until you get a full understanding of what it means. "What does it smell like and are there any sounds associated with this colour? Describe it to me and what does it taste like?" And so on.

The channeller said, "Everybody needs to release their sins, before they go to God and the opportunity should be made available to be able to do this. Sins can be accumulated over a lifetime, or they can be built up in a very short space of time if you happen to be on a roll and under a bad influence. If a confession is successful, then the person giving the confession is relieved of their burden of guilt and shame, which can manifest into something very ugly if left unchecked. Everyone looks at a sin differently. To one person a sin may be so small it is not worthy of confession, but to another it consumes their mind and they can't concentrate on anything else.

Confessing a sin does not *erase* the sin. It also does not erase the action. The purpose of confessing a sin is for the sinner to acknowledge their mistake, ask for forgiveness and not to dwell on it for the rest of their life, which can hinder their spiritual growth. If spiritual growth is hindered, then progress and enlightenment cannot be attained.

Acceptance that everyone makes mistakes and that everyone has the right to be forgiven by the Almighty God, if they are truly sorry, is all you need to remind yourself.

When you go to God, you cannot take your sins with you, or else they will hold you back from your entry into Heaven and show up with you in the afterlife, like tatty old baggage tied to your ankles.

If you show up with baggage, it is a sign to God that you just can't seem to leave it behind. It is also an indication to God that you are not quite ready to live in Heaven and he will probably send you back to do it all again until you learn your lessons.

The purpose of life is to *learn* from your mistakes. You can't learn if you don't make any mistakes! If you are one of the lucky ones that don't make any mistakes, then you should be teaching and guiding others to confess and release their sins, so they can complete their mission.

Forty days and forty nights

You have probably heard the term 40 days and 40 nights before and this refers to the biblical story of Jesus going into the wilderness on his own, fasting and devoting his time to God his father, for 40 days and 40 nights.

During this time he was confronted by Satan and tempted to stop his mission. Satan tried to tempt Jesus with earthly treasures, status, fame and fortune. Satan even went as far as offering Jesus a place on the throne as the Earthly King, but with the condition that Jesus had to denounce God.

Jesus sent him away, because he knew that his eternal life with God was more precious and rewarding than any material life with empty possessions here on Earth could ever offer. Satan was just trying to interfere and delay Jesus' mission, by offering him material wealth. Jesus was insulted at the offer and rebuked Satan for his audacity.

The reason it is 40 days and 40 nights is because this is how long it takes to communicate fully with God, without the distractions of everyday life. It is devoting 40 days and 40 nights to focus on being with God.

There is no reason why all of you cannot take 40 days out of your life and devote 40 days of purification. Any temptations can wait until after that.

Have you ever noticed that the standard annual leave period offered by most employers is only 20 days of per year? It could be an attempt to stop or block the 40 day rule and it was probably invented a long time ago and hasn't been changed by the establishment for hundreds of years. This means if you were more *devoted* to your job, you wouldn't be able to take 40 days consecutively out of your busy life *unless* you had saved up two years worth of annual leave. You may have the required annual leave available to take, but taking 40 days of leave can be risky to any employee, because it highlights the fact that you may be no longer needed in your current role.

If your employer can get by without you for 40 days, they probably don't need you. This is why so many are reluctant to take the pilgrimage to seek out God. They are worshipping money, or their job security, because they are afraid of their employer and afraid of living life without the certainty of guaranteed material income.

One thing I know for sure is that *nothing* on Earth is permanent, certain or guaranteed. It can all change in an instant. You could devote your entire life to your employer and when they no longer need you, they can easily dispose of your services without any remorse whatsoever.

Loyalty these days is not like it used to be even 30 years ago. Employers have very little *faith* in their employees and employees have very little *trust* in their employers. Put your faith and trust in the Lord and he will never let you down.

This is a lesson we all have to learn about where our faith and loyalties sit and where they should be all the time and not where they are currently directed. If you worship money, or security, you will have to learn the hard way, by losing everything and assessing what you have left when it is all gone.

God is *always* there. You don't need to buy anything from him, or pay him to listen to you. He is free and he is available to all of you.

Many yogi masters, spiritual gurus, truth seekers and holy people understand this practise, because they know that full and focused devotion will bring about communion with God our Creator. Some herbs and plants can also assist in this process and can be found around the world in many different locations. There are many other practical methods that can work just as well like; sensory deprivation and retreating to a cave for a period of time.

The channeller said, "The whole idea of the cave is to experience total darkness and to be thankful for the light when one crawls from it. Have you ever sat in the darkness for 12 hours? Then God shall hold your hand so you can experience the nothingness. God asks us to contemplate this thought, *I looked into the darkness and what did I see?*"

Then there are the more scientific techniques like remote viewing. The ultimate method of contact is using your psychic or telepathic ability to communicate with God. Everyone has some level of psychic or telepathic ability. Some have just had more experience with their ability and know how to use their gift better than others.

One thing I know for sure is that God doesn't like the sacrificing of animals to get his attention. He doesn't like to see *any* living creature harmed including his trees and plants. You may get his attention if you do that, but he won't be happy. In fact he will be annoyed and I can also guarantee you that it won't put him in a good mood if you want to talk to him.

He asks me to tell the humans to please stop sending him his beloved animals to get his attention. You can just *ask* to talk to him without harming another soul. It is not necessary and it is a redundant practise. Please stop it!

There was a misinterpretation from the Old Testament about rituals that used to be performed to get God's attention. You are not getting the true Creator's attention; you are getting the lower level demigod, the Demiurge. The material half god that wants you to worship, adore and idolise *only* him. That is *not* the real God. That is a false god. He is the one who wants you to sacrifice animals and perform strange rituals. He is also the god that gets angry, wipes out entire nations and helps with wars. This is whose attention you are attracting. It is the demigod who thinks he is God and knows no better, because he doesn't fully understand himself.

Earth is mainly a masculine planet, even though Sophia may have brought us down here and created the Demiurge. We need to rise above the material world and aim to vibrate on a more heavenly and spiritual level of harmony, love, kindness and truth. You can only vibrate on a higher level of existence when you stop killing, maiming and harming God's beloved creatures.

4. THE DARK SIDE

The purpose of the dark side is to confuse you, distract you and lead you astray.

I am an advocate for the light. I love God and I live for the positive things in life. God has taught me that everything on this planet has balance, which ultimately means if there is a light side, there is also a dark side.

I wanted to briefly explain the difference between dark and light so that you can understand the reason why darkness even exists. Light requires a shadow to be illuminated, therefore to learn about the light side and to love the light side, you need to *acknowledge* the dark side to respect it and know why it exists at all.

We were made in God's image and within all of us we have all of the building blocks to be just like God the Creator. Being made in God's image does not make us God. It makes us *similar* to God, but obviously not as wise and experienced as God.

God has had many more millenniums to work out what he likes and what he doesn't like, what is right and what is wrong, what works and what doesn't work. He also knows which creations turned out good and which creations turned out not so good. Like all creations, there can be inbuilt flaws and if they are allowed to become unbalanced, they can do harm to the living creation. For example, the bad cells that make up cancer exist dormant in all of us, but if we encourage an imbalance of bacteria, disease, or ill health, then the cancer cells have the chance to come to life.

It is the same principle that applies to the seed of darkness that lays dormant in all of us. If we focus on these seeds, spend time focusing on the darkness and living in the darkness, like a fungi, it can grow out of control and it can overcome the goodness within us.

God has also come to the conclusion in his infinite wisdom that there is a kind of small defect in our nature as humans, where we can be easily influenced by leaning towards the dark side and that we actually have a desire to be dark sometimes. This is because we were given free will, but without actually knowing how to correctly apply it.

Free will does have its purpose, like for survival. Learning how to apply it correctly can be achieved with wisdom and experience. You can also harness and channel the darkness within your soul to create a powerhouse of energy to ultimately be used for good.

These attributes are lacking in the young human being and they can sometimes make bad choices based on their limited understanding. When harnessed, we can all use disciplines like martial arts, boxing, Tai chi, Qigong, Yoga, Pilates, dancing, gym workouts, sports and other body style arts to release this excess energy built up within us.

When we incarnate and reincarnate on this earthly plane of existence, we become exposed to the temptations and we become *influenced* by the material desires that are associated with this world. We can get distracted with the illusion and sucked into the dark side.

All of us are tempted by the dark side at some stage in our life and this is when we can choose to *ignore* the temptations, or we can *indulge* in the temptations. If you indulge in the temptations and get caught, you pay the price for disobeying the laws on Earth. If you disobey God's laws knowingly, once you have learned to tell the difference between right and wrong, then the consequences can last longer than a prison sentence.

I have had many conversations over the years with spiritual people who deny the existence of the darkness and the dark side, believing that if they choose to *ignore* the darkness, then to them it doesn't exist. In a way this psychological assessment of the darkness is quite correct and if it works for them, I totally respect their choice to live in a state of unaware bliss.

In reality it is actually the same as the choice to ignore the existence of God. Just because you choose to ignore him, doesn't actually make God cease to exist. The same can be said for the dark side, just because you choose to ignore it, doesn't actually make the dark side cease to exist and that you won't ever be faced with temptations, or spooky experiences.

I have been shown a different perspective of both the dark side and the light side and believe me, there is a holy war going on behind the scenes in our Universe.

There are advocates on both sides of the dispute or holy war. There are many advocates for the light, as well as many advocates for the darkness. The advocates for the light can be seen publicly and make themselves available for those who are truth seekers to help them find their way towards the path of illumination and light.

These advocates for the light exist for the purpose of helping others and have a special mission to be a part of the army of lightworkers who do God's work and reorient all beings towards the light. You can find them in churches, holistic organisations, spiritual groups, monasteries, operating as shamans, priests and priestesses, as healers, therapists, psychics, clairvoyants, channellers and charity workers etc. I am talking about *true* lightworkers who see the good in everything and not just the ones who pay it lip service and preach what they don't practise themselves.

On the flip side of lightworkers, there is a dark side. Those who operate under the veil of darkness, who choose to operate in the underworld of society and do not make themselves known for their pursuits. They use their underhanded, sneaky, devious, destructive intentions and sophisticated plans to spread their darkness throughout the Universe. They can operate and infiltrate every walk of life, including the list of occupations where lightworkers can be found to keep an eye on the lightworkers. They hold positions of power, authority and control, where they can affect the mass population from a political and production standpoint. They engage in bizarre practises that would make you cringe at the thought that these things even exist. They willingly silence, discredit, murder, maim, abuse, hurt, sacrifice, forcibly convert and instruct others to carry out their wishes, so they can enforce the beliefs of their secret order.

I am not talking about criminals and gangsters here; I am talking about well respected, highly paid and noble people, who are living a dual two-faced life and they operate *under* the radar. You get to see the false image they portray in the public eye and through the media, while behind the scenes they are living a completely different life. They are living a life of lies and deceit by participating in corruption, bribery, ritualistic abuse and practises.

They are all working towards the ultimate goal of the dark side, which is to increase numbers of people who belong to the dark side. They do this by interfering with peace and harmony and they work to remove anyone who opposes their laws and beliefs. They use demons and the ruler of the demons, Lucifer to assist with their work.

God said, "It is the *humans* who attract Lucifer and not the other way around. If a human engages in activities which attract the attention of demons, then beware of what you are attracting when you do these things. Humans who have wicked desires and evil pursuits, call on the supernatural power of him and his legion of demons to help them to achieve their shallow and selfish desires. This in turn enslaves the dark side entities, because that is the sacrifice they made when they chose the dark side."

There are many lost souls who do the bidding of the dark side. They are sucked in by false promises of material wealth and glory. They willingly enslave themselves like zombies for something they will never attain, or ever fully understand. Like innocent sheep they verily go along to the slaughter thinking they are having all their desires and promises fulfilled.

Very rarely will you ever get anyone *admitting* that they belong to the dark side unless you too are a dark side advocate. They hide in the shadows and don't wish for their alter ego to be revealed, so they can continue their dual life on the planet and reap the material rewards.

Have you ever wondered why they hide in the shadows? They hide because deep down they know what they are doing is wrong and they are ultimately hiding from God. As you know you cannot hide from God, he knows everyone and understands everything.

Believing in God is not about control or subservience. It is about ultimate freedom. Freedom for you to choose what you want to believe in.

You do not need to *belong* to any religious organisation if you choose not to and you don't need to be affiliated with any particular group of society to communicate with the Creator.

Those who are in opposition to God can rant all they like and justify their willingness to sacrifice their soul to the dark side, they can never stop God, because he is everything and he is everywhere. You can never destroy God, it is impossible.

Those who are in the curious position of believing in neither the dark, nor the light side, can be happy in their delusion and that is okay too, because they have free will to believe whatever they want. They are suffering from a type of *amnesia* that we get when we reincarnate into this world. It can take some people a whole lifetime to reconnect with the loving energy of God. Some never reconnect and keep getting reborn again and again until they work it out for themselves. Those who are in denial, or oppose God, may experience many struggles with the dark side on their journey, in both a sleeping and waking state.

The purpose of the dark side is to confuse you, distract you and lead you astray. Those who work for the dark side, go to extreme lengths to make up similar deities that are similar to God. They use unholy names and call them holy. This is done to throw you off balance and make you question your faith with their continual lies, trickery and deception. It can get really confusing when you are searching to find out how to be righteous and holy, especially with so much disinformation out there. Listen to your heart and you will find the right way to go. Go by feel and not by force.

I still have respect for the dark side, because their effort is worthy of respect, but I don't believe in their false system which worships money, material possessions, privilege, power, false idols and the ultimate denial of the existence of God.

The dark side may even try to convince you that Lucifer is worthy of worship instead of believing in God, but the only reason this choice exists, is to test your faith and for no other reason.

Long term, there is no benefit to worship Lucifer, because he always wants you to *sacrifice* something in return for his loyalty. God only asks that you sacrifice your belief in the *illusion* of the material world which will cost you nothing.

The channeller said, "The dark side does not exist in Heaven and on the higher vibratory levels, because the density and lower vibration of the dark side beings cannot exist in such a space, it is impossible. There is no need for darkness to exist in the full light of God. It cannot sustain itself and will be disintegrated in His presence. The darkness that I speak of only exists in the material world, the space here on Earth where we come to learn our lessons and come to our own personal understanding of both sides."

A being that is vibrating on a higher dimension can choose to *descend* into the darkness through their lust, greed, gluttony, sloth, wrath, envy and pride. Showing God you have a wicked heart, that you love to deliberately be mischievous and by being a false witness who aims to steer people away from God, will earn you a lower status in the eyes of the Creator. It may even get you kicked out of Heaven, or other higher vibratory realms, just like what happened to Lucifer and his band of fallen angels.

There is also the opportunity to redeem oneself and *ascend* to a higher vibratory level, by actually making an effort to abstain when tempted with lust. Show temperance and patience when faced with adversity, give generously to those less fortunate than you and be diligent in whatever you do.

There is worthiness in showing kindness to all living beings and most of all displaying humility by not being vain and full of pride. Learn to be humble and be thankful for your very existence. It is not a *right* that you are here and are allowed to live this life; it is a *privilege* and yet again another chance for you to get it right.

Rebellion

Anything that is not in a state of love and attunement with God, is in a state of rebellion. It is that simple. The first time rebellion was experienced in God's realm was when Lucifer, the angel of light, challenged God by believing he could do a better job at running the Universe and that he could get more souls to worship him. Lucifer after his fall from grace became known as Satan and he was the first rebel angel who led a rebellion against God.

I still have respect for Satan, because originally he *was* an archangel and for that he does deserve respect. God loved him immensely, but if you treat God as your adversary and challenge his leadership, you are no longer living in *harmony* with God and the vibration of your being causes you to be pushed away. It is not necessarily God banishing you, it is you banishing yourself. You cannot be in a state of harmonious attunement and in a state of rebellion at the same time. You are either one or the other, like yin and yang, black and white, darkness and light, two polar opposites, like magnets that become opposing forces by repelling each other.

God pointed out, "You cannot serve two masters at the same time; it is one or the other."

Humans have this same inner conflict within them that sometimes wants to deny the true love and happiness that comes from God. They prefer to reject God's love and fall, or descend into a state of rebellion.

God thinks it is funny, because ultimately they are only rebelling against themselves and against their own spiritual growth. They can't really rebel against God, because God is in everything and everyone, including Satan and all those who rebel against God.

God knows all and can see into every one of their souls to see what is going through their mind anyway.

To rebel against God you are only harming yourself. That is up to you. You have free will and you can choose the path of rebellion, even if this choice leads to your destruction. Again, you cannot serve two masters. You cannot be in a state of rebellion and a state of harmonious attunement at the same time. It is one or the other. So choose wisely which path you will take.

One choice leads to your destruction and the other leads to your salvation. It is up to you which state of being you prefer to live in.

If you oppose God, he has a question for you, "Who are you opposing and why? Are you opposing your own soul, your own true nature, or are you just exercising the free will you have been given to rebel?"

The Devil

The Devil is known by many names and just like Jesus; he can be referenced by his angelic name, soul name or earthly name. The main difference between God and Satan is that God is the Father of the Light and the other one stays in the dark. Some of his most well known names are; Archangel Lucifer before his fall from grace, then Satan once he had descended and the Devil is an alternative name he goes by. These names represent the stages of descent he went through after his fall from grace.

Lucifer was his name when he was an archangel with God in Heaven. Satan or the Devil is the name of the dragon serpent entity after his fall from grace whose purpose was to deceive mankind.

God said, "Satan cannot destroy God, because he would be killing himself. He can never be bigger than God, because God created Satan. There are no options. Another masculine energy figure, he is known as the Prince of Darkness and the Devil. He is making you have *anaemia* in the blood and *amnesia* in the mind."

The channeller relayed to me, "Even though God is alone and by himself, he is also called the "lonely one." Satan also calls himself the "lonely one" on many records. They are like yin and yang and God laughs at the pretensions of it all."

The channeller continued, "For the Universe to be in perfect balance like yin and yang, black and white, conscious and unconscious, yes and no, like the dual balance, God created the *opposition.* Someone to keep him in line. Now, Yeshua is the name of the Holy God and Satan is the name of the unholy God. They actually balance, like a pendulum, looping. Lock the brain out and get it into a loop. Yes at the top and no at the bottom. They are right and wrong, yes and no, swinging back and forth, like a pendulum."

The channeller added, "Lucifer was born into a human body back in 2150 BC and he had a life which lasted for 40 to 50 years as an Artesian soldier, because he rose up in a physical body and represented himself as a god in those days. Lucifer was demon Satan being born into a body for that period. Lucifer's aim was to convince man to destroy creation, to kill, sacrifice and destroy."

God said, "Please don't send me all these dead animals and lambs anymore."

The channeller said, "Lucifer was the leader of all the fallen angels and he has descended for 10, 20, 40, 100 thousand years, to learn from his mistake. None of the energy gets destroyed, it all becomes the same. God doesn't destroy anything he makes, but you may be punished. God's law is that *nothing* gets destroyed and eventually it all comes back to the Source and back to perfection. God waits for that to happen. It doesn't matter how long it takes, because everything eventually returns to the Source of all creation.

"So for the moment, God told me that the Devil is on the Nebula and he is summoned from people on Earth. The more summoned he gets, the more tired he gets. The more influence the Devil has on this plane of existence, the shallower and the more resentful and despaired he gets."

God said, "Wary is the one that controls the Earth. Thou shall be cast from Heaven to be at the desire of mankind. One day he shall be cast into the internal realms of death and despair and the fires of Earth."

I asked God, "Will he ever be forgiven?"

God replied, "He has already been forgiven, but has resented the prayer. He denied this. He wanted this and was given this and chose to live in the pit of fire in the middle of the Earth. He now lives for eternity, in the form of a dragon and he can appear if summoned. Only the shape of a dragon shall he appear, because he is now a dragon."

The channeller said, "This has happened only recently and God is determined that never shall he deceiveth again. Mankind shall ultimately have freedom and peace."

When God talks about the nations in the Bible, he has actually created a whole new mirror where destruction won't happen. He is interested to let it go to see what happens when different nations are on the same continent. To see what they do.

God said, "Hell is hot? No, the *illusion* is hot, but the reality is that hell is freezing cold. We are being deceived when hell is referred to as being *hot*, because heat makes us feel warmth and we think, *oh it can't be that bad?"*

God continued, "The Devil is teaching all these souls by not having a hug, or a kiss and he takes all this away from them, like deprivation of the soul for so many years. No one hugs you anymore. He's taken away or stolen the hugs away from everyone. He hasn't had any hugs, love, or kisses for 20,000 years. It's pretty boring, no colour here, just black and white."

God added, "The Devil made being bad trendy, but they all get burned together in one pile. It's hilarious and those words shall not be as scary as before."

God wanted to make the point again, "You cannot serve two masters; it is one or the other."

The channeller said, "Your true purpose is to serve God who is the Supreme Being, the Creator, the ultimate saviour. God does not want us to be subservient and afraid, but he does want us to understand that if you do not choose God, then you serve the other master who is the destructor, the controller and the Devil who does not allow you to exercise your free will.

"You do as he says, or he will destroy you. God doesn't threaten us in that manner; he wants us to love him through our own choice and not through fear based choices. We don't have to give up anything to love and serve God, we do however gain everything.

"If we choose God, we are looked upon favourably in the afterlife and also in the life we are living right now. When we love God, we receive gifts that come in the form of beauty, love, friendship and experiences that money cannot buy."

The channeller said, "To obey the Devil, you have to give up believing in God and ultimately sell your soul for something temporary. You can't buy it back once you have sold it. The material pleasures on this plane of existence, compared to what greatness is offered in Heaven, is laughable and simply not worth it."

If you want to sell your soul down at the crossroads for a fancy house, a chunk of coloured metal on wheels, fame, fortune, fake people and an empty life, then go ahead, but remember you can't take any of it with you. It is short lived and it won't buy you an entry ticket anywhere nice in the afterlife.

Ultimately the Devil is still answerable to God and has to report which souls have denounced him, because the Devil likes to brag about the souls that have chosen the path of self destruction. There is no hiding your choice.

Demons and evil

The channeller relayed, "When Satan the fallen angel and his many sub-angels, what we know as *demons*, roam this plane of existence, the biggest tool they use in this world is *influence.* You will often hear people saying the term, 'He or she is a bad influence.'

"The Devil doesn't make you do something, he will *influence* you to do something, or his demons can *influence* you to do something, but ultimately you choose if you do it or not.

"The Devil can only be in one place at one time, because he is not omnipresent like God. So, in order to keep his ear to the ground, he uses his many sub-angels, or demons of the dark side to do his dirty work and report back to him."

The channeller continued, "God created everything and when God created evilness, he allowed everyone to make the choice to go towards goodness, or evilness, or everythingness. If you were smart enough when you were a small soul, why would you go to evilness when God created everything? Isn't God already the magicalness that created everything?

"God is at the top of the pecking order and there is nothing above him. If we use this statement to understand that through the lower creations, God created demons and lower entities, which are on a similar plane to us.

"You can walk up to the demon and say, 'I know who you are,' and then you can recognise who you are talking to. God is something to look up to."

The channeller added, "Anything with a demon underneath or attached is *not* holy. There can be many demons attached to a soul. Demons are there to make you want to terminate yourself so they can steal your soul. To really annoy a demon you can say to them, 'Tell me about our saviour, tell me about Jesus?' Wait for the response."

Speaking for God the channeller said, "Demons also don't like being touched on the head, hands, or heart. So, do just that and take control. Demons thrive on your fear and your weaknesses. They will offer all kinds of temptations and whisper many of words of encouragement to be bad, but you are stronger than that and you don't need to give in to the temptations. Temptations are a part of life and learning how to avoid temptations in the first place is a good way to detract demons.

"Demons love to hang around where negative activity is happening. They are attracted to low vibrations and lower level entities. Think to yourself, *where do you think you would find a demon hiding?* They are probably hanging around the pub or club and waiting for a fight to break out, maybe even egging people on to engage in conflict. They will be on the battlefield, in the boxing ring, in jails, on the street right behind the drug dealer, and even with the drug abuser. They are there waiting for the alcoholic to get drunk and pass out. Demons are hanging around the person who listens to demonic music, roaming with killers and lurking in the darkness. They are just waiting for someone naive to come along so they can *influence* them."

The channeller continued, "When you get really angry, violent, upset, suicidal, super depressed, or you have left yourself wide open to psychic attack, there will be a demon within range. When you experience these dense and lower level emotions, you are sending out a beacon to the other side, straight to the lower level entities. They love to see humans suffering. They get off on it and love to attach themselves to people when they are experiencing these negative emotions. Demons don't hang around holy people or happy people, unless they are trying to tempt them. If you are strong and faithful, then you can laugh at the demon and tell it to, 'Go away,' because it is much lower than you are even when you're down."

The classic seven deadly sins are a sure way to attract a demon. Don't play with demons, because if you don't understand what you are dealing with, you can get yourself into a lot of trouble and a whole world of pain.

Generally anyone who does anything really bad, really horrific, really cruel and really sinful is being *influenced* by a demon. This is not an excuse for people to use to get away with crimes and sins and they have no right to *blame* the demon for their evil behaviour. The demon is just doing exactly what it is supposed to be doing, which is *influencing* them to be bad.

The channeller said, "Satan's job is to tempt you and lead you away from God, just as it is for his little helpers, the demons. They are there as the ultimate test of your faith. If you stay strong, pray to be delivered from evil and do not allow yourself to be led into temptation, then you won't attract the presence of either into your life. If you are living a holy and happy life and happen to encounter a demon, it is just a test of your faith and you know you can handle them, because you are a child of God no matter what.

"Even when you are faced with a thousand demons, you could still help to guide them to the light by saying to them, 'Each one of you individually, I can take you to a place you've never been before. Believe me, I have seen him, I know God and he will take you. He will give you the warmth and feelings that you've never felt.'

"Show them that you are their saviour, hand them over to God and then help to convert the demon over to the light. Once you have done this, there is one less little helper for Satan. This means another win for God. One more for the God team."

The channeller continued, "To remove a demon from a person who is having an attachment issue, you could ask the demon directly, 'Do you know who Jesus is, or who God is? Tell me about it?' This will make the demon very uncomfortable and squeamish, because they don't worship God due to their state of rebellion and descent into the lower realms. They will try to hide from Jesus and God if being questioned, or asked to show themselves."

You need to have 100% faith and commitment to God before even thinking about conversing with, or attempting to evict a demon, because it can present very ugly challenges that you may not be prepared for. It is better to get an expert to help in these cases, because demonic possession is very real and can be very dangerous.

The channeller said, "Demons are also learning about themselves just like we are, but they are currently stuck in a recurring pattern of damnation where they choose to live in torture and torment for as long as they feel they need retribution. Maybe they have sold their soul and don't know how to redeem themselves. When they feel they have been punished enough, they may be willing to convert to the other side, the light side, the God side. This could be after a short while and for some demons it could be thousands of years, or an eternity of lifetimes.

"It is not your place to judge a demon. Leave the judgement to God, because he knows what to do with demons that are ready to repent. Eventually all demons will go to the God side. How long it takes remains in the belief system of the demon."

5. RELIGION

To truly have faith and believe in God, you do not need to belong to any religion or any affiliated organisation at all.

NOT all religions believe in God, the Creator. Religions usually have some type of deity, or religious figure at the centre of their religion, but they don't all recognise the one *true* Creator.

Some religions will even go as far as *denying* the existence of a Supreme Creator. Religions each have their own set of rules, beliefs and rituals that go with the given religion. Religions can teach people a whole myriad of things, but the religion doesn't always back up their belief system by practising what they preach. It is unfortunate, because the actual concept of religion is not a bad thing. It is just misguided and bogged down in doctrine, dogma, ritual and tradition.

The channeller said, "Even Jehovah's Witnesses don't talk about God much. They talk more about Moses, Jesus and Mary and they spend an equal amount of time talking about wicked people. Then they turn it all around and try to say that God is coming, without any explanation about *who* God is. They continually say that the end times are here and God says *they are not here*. His Earth is still round and blue. This Earth is not dying yet. Man is dying of his own free will and just as the angels do; they come and go as they please."

The channeller said, "God noticed that earlier today you took a caterpillar and showed the caterpillar where to find the leaves instead of squishing him. It is like God is with us and shows us the right way to do things. Maybe the Jehovah's Witnesses should hear this. Would it not be better if they showed up on your doorstep saving the butterfly? They need to have their own movie about protecting things and being loving. This is more important than preaching end times to people. They need to hear these words."

God was speaking through the channeller and explained, "There is a past, present and future. The future is cloaked so much and it can be difficult to see. The past was that disciples used to get a lot of free things, because Jesus was speaking the **Word of God** and they were funded, because people wanted to go to the other side. Do you think the Catholic Church is doing the right thing when they build churches? The cost to build a single church could save and support so many Ethiopians and one greedy person is collecting all the money! The money that is left by rich people doesn't go anywhere. It stays in the church and it makes someone gather a mountain of rocks to build a church."

God continued, "Those that were given the money, made slaves drag rocks across the desert to build the empty building that no one goes to."

God added, "We should focus our prayers towards the Christians throughout history who have been locked up for no reason. The strength doesn't come from them. It comes from you praying for them. Praying for John the Baptist, John the Apostle, Jesus and so many more. You can ask for Archangel Gabriel to come down and look after John and Jesus. Time is only an illusion and your prayers can cross the barriers of time. You can ask now for something to happen in the past and you can pray for people in the past and still have some effect on a past situation."

There is no denying there are paedophiles in the world, however the church has unfortunately had a bad run of press, with regards to churches being a breeding ground for this type of behaviour. *Or has it?* God wants you to question everything and you may find that it is yet another disinformation campaign being fed down the line to deter people from going to church.

Ask yourself, why is it that these claims are only coming out many years later and not at the time of the incidents occurring. Why is it that so many claims all come out at the same time against the same church? Perhaps it is a church that may have been targeted unfairly? It is unfortunate for those who have not committed any sinful acts. It gives them a bad label forever and paedophilia has been classed as abhorrent in society's eyes, the worst possible sin. It is the perfect *cover story* to distract you from the truth.

The channeller said, "God feels that not all cases are true and that the church is being set up legally, to stop and discourage people from going to the church and getting close to God. As farfetched as that may sound to some of you, there are many disinformation stories you get fed every single day and you don't find out about them until much later. Some of these stories are either simply untrue, or a gross exaggeration of the facts. I am not condoning the behaviour of those that have actually committed these acts and they will personally need to answer to the Creator in the end."

For those abuse survivors who have truly suffered this affliction, I bless you and give you the strength of the Lord that you may rise up and rise above these life events and use them as a learning experience. Don't allow yourself to feel condemned, or to think or feel like a victim.

God said, "Ask yourself, *how do you get rid of a church?* You give them bad press! *How do you knock off a rock star?* Give them an overdose so it looks like an accident. *How do you murder someone inconspicuously?* Blame it on suicide. Where are the real witnesses? The internet is used as a good tool for spreading slander and people are starting to worship the internet to get their information.

"In the old days, neighbours used to talk to one another and that's how the word used to get around and nowadays people don't talk to each other, so there is no protection and no news getting shared amongst the community. The lifestyle on Earth is *not* the ideal model. It is simply just a model."

God laughed, "A perfect world in Africa is wearing bullet proof vests, carrying AK47s and growing food. They will use M16s in the future."

God thinks that if you have a child abuse problem in Africa, for example, you should use the funds that are raised, to pay for security guards to protect the children at school, instead of spending money on prosecution, further persecution and more exposure to the situation for the abused.

God continued, "Remove the problem by creating safe houses, or live-in schools where the less fortunate and abused children can learn in peace with protection. It's not all fairy floss and rainbows, for some children in Africa, it is their daily reality."

There is religion in every corner of the world and each religion believes in something different and that is okay. We should embrace different points of view and if their religion is not harming anyone, then let them have their beliefs. The main purpose of religion is supposed to be an organised gathering of likeminded individuals, to learn and discuss what their beliefs are. The main issue with religion is that within these organisations over time, there seems to be a hierarchy that forms to run the group and with this type of organisation comes *rules*. The religion then evolves into some cult like society if given half a chance and that can become dangerous. Absolute power corrupts absolutely and the people at the top of the organisation start to exercise their power and authority as if they are God. No man or woman on Earth has the right to say that they are the only absolute authority on God.

God talks to all of us, if only you would just listen. You know that you are welcome to talk to God whenever you so desire. You do not need permission to talk to him and you do not need to seek permission to ask for his help. To truly have faith and believe in God, you do not need to belong to any religion or any affiliated organisation at all. Nowhere does it say that this is a requirement or a prerequisite and if you are being told that, then you are being deceived, because this is simply not true.

You can still be a believer in God and in Jesus and never have to attend a church for the whole duration of your life. You can go to church if you choose to do so. If you enjoy getting together with likeminded people, then it is a great idea to celebrate God and Jesus together at a gathering in the same place.

There are many people who do go to church, but don't actually practise what they preach. They hold judgements against people who do not belong to their church, or who are not affiliated with their organisation in some way. Leave the *judging* to God. That is his job not yours.

All you need to be aware of is that you don't *have* to go to church if you don't want to and you can still be a believer. If you truly love God in your heart and you feel him with you, then you will have eternal life. If you deny him and don't feel him with you, then how can you go somewhere you don't believe in?

If you believe in nothing at all, your soul may get lost in the transition between worlds when you pass over. You can live a life where you are easily influenced by material desires if you choose and this is likely to happen if you lack faith or belief of any kind at all. Without belief in something, or anything at all, it is a shallow and superficial existence that will always feel empty.

Religion can be viewed as a way to control the masses, but remember peace and harmony is far better than war and chaos. Religion shouldn't be something we fight over or argue about. It should be something that is *tolerated* between cultures and *respected*, because the concepts are very similar in every religion.

Ultimately we are all talking about the *same* God and he is represented in many different ways. God is given lots of different names and there are many different stories about creation and how everything came about.

Acknowledging the Creator will raise your vibration and give your life meaning and purpose. To want to get to know the Creator, the Supreme Being should be the holy path of your choosing, when you are ready. It is hard not to love the Creator with all your heart, knowing how much he loves and respects us.

When we all come to the realisation that we wouldn't even exist without the love and the life force of our Creator, it can be very humbling. Let's not be selfish now, God is not just *our* Earth's Creator, he is the Creator of all beings in all of the universes, which contain a lot more intelligent life forms than just us out there.

Religion becomes *dangerous* when it is used to dictate to people who can become a member of a certain religious organisation and who cannot. Manmade rules have no validity in the eyes of God and are not based on true spiritual principles of kindness and love.

A spiritually depleted organisation runs on exclusion, prohibition and fear. They threaten their members who don't fit the mould, or who don't conform to the standards of the organisation with eviction, exclusion, or excommunication if they step out of line. Churches and religious organisations should *welcome* new members, *embrace* the weak, the poor, the unfortunate, the imperfect, the wicked and *support* the lost. These beings are the ones that really need the help of the righteous ones, to show them the right way and to help get them back on track again.

Churches would benefit from practising *inclusion* and be flexible enough to move with the times. Encourage the youth of today to embrace the principles of love and light, by giving them the tools to survive in today's modern world.

God doesn't care which religion or philosophy you belong to, or follow. He visits them *all.* He doesn't care which church you are a member of. He doesn't view any of them exclusively and he certainly doesn't have any special passes for the self promoted hierarchy of church members, who believe they are far superior to the average soul.

A holy man or woman can belong to a church, as long as they are living a truly holy and righteous life and teaching others to do the same. The same people, who consider themselves *holy,* should also be helping people in the world regardless of their race, belief system and religious affiliations. They should be helping *everyone* they can, at every opportunity they can, because we are all viewed as *equal* children of God and loved in his eyes.

God knows and loves Enoch, Moses, John the Baptist, Mother Mary, Jesus, Buddha, Mohammed, the Dalai Lama and all of the holy prophets that have and who do preach brotherly and sisterly love, spiritual tolerance, racial harmony and peace.

God doesn't mind if you call him God, the Creator of the Cosmos, the Supreme Being, the Almighty Lord, Allah, our Father in Heaven, the Alpha and the Omega, a Divine Being, Yahweh, Yeshua, YWHW, Jehovah, Jah, Krishna, Spirit, or *whatever* name you want to call him. He really doesn't get too caught up about the name, or title, as long as you are thinking about him and acknowledging his existence and presence. He will return the love you feel for him like a beaming mirror reflecting radiant love.

Try not to get too caught up in *what* to call God; he certainly doesn't want any conflict to arise as a result of his name, or the name of a religion. I personally call him God, or Lord, because it works for me.

If I am saying a prayer of grace before each meal, it might sound something like this, "Dear Lord, thank you for this beautiful meal you have provided, may it nourish my body and my soul. I bless this food and I give thanks for your presence with me everyday. Thank you for all of your creations. Lord please be with me and give me the strength to deal with anything that comes my way."

If I want to tell God about something, or if I want to mention someone special, I share it with him during grace. I can also add a special prayer of healing for someone else, if I know someone who needs help. I will ask God to send his angels to help or heal the person concerned. I may also ask for blessings if someone I know is journeying somewhere and I ask for a safe passage for them.

I tell God often that I love him and that he is amazing. I often say thank you for everything! I don't wait until I am desperate to ask for help, or wait until I am annoyed about something to tell him off. I praise him many times every day and in return I am rewarded with his visits and his presence.

I don't talk to him for any reward or benefit. I talk to him because I am so grateful for every second I have on this planet and I am truly grateful for my good health, my good fortune and my life. I love God so much and it is such a deep love that it is hard to describe. It is more like a knowing, a way of being, a sustained joyful feeling and it is truly an honour to be loved by God in return, even with all of my faults.

If you learn to talk to God, he will be like your constant companion, who is always with you. You can tune in and out of the God channel whenever you want to feel the presence of God.

As long as you are expressing your love for God from the depths of your heart, your intentions are genuine and you are sending loving vibrations, God will always be with you. It is okay if you make mistakes, or say the wrong things, or even be a little bit grumpy sometimes, because God understands that we all go through life experiences and some of these experiences can be challenging. He is so much more understanding than you might think. He is so forgiving and just like a loving father dotes on his children, he looks at us like we are the apple of his eye when we love him.

The channeller said, "He wants you to know that he is *not* a punisher, that instead he is a wise teacher and he will send you souls, situations and events that help you to learn, grow and evolve just like him. God is also learning from us all the time and wants us to be reminded that we are like different aspects of God and he learns through our feelings and from our lessons, at the same time we do. God does not dish out punishments when we do little things wrong. He is not that shallow and petty. He just wants to see us contribute to society, help each other, care for our environment, not be lazy and be kind to *all* living creatures. He knows we are totally capable of anything we set our mind to and with some effort on our part, we can achieve anything with good intentions, so that everyone can benefit from our contribution."

The Holy Bible

Did you know that the Holy Bible was the first published and mass produced book and it is the most widely spread book on the planet today? It has undergone many translations from Hebrew, Aramaic and Greek, which are the original languages the Bible was first written in, to the book now being available in more than 500 languages in its entirety and in more than 2000 languages in sections.

God has made contact with many different people throughout the ages and given them timely and relevant information to document and share with the world. Each of these people would have been considered a *scribe* for God. God asks me to have a really good think about why Jesus ended up collecting 12 apostles. God tells me, it is because not all of them had the ability to scribe and also because not all of them were literate enough, or willing to scribe for fear of making a mistake.

God knows that over time and throughout history, people have removed the hype out of the Bible stories and played so many events down and have even omitted hundreds of pages of relevant information from the Bible. God doesn't like it and Jesus came here to reprimand it.

People think that surely the translation is shortened by Jesus from the Father. No biblical figures have had anything to do with the editing, shortening, changing, or instruction to modify anything in the Bible. This has been man's doing and man is responsible for confusing the Bible stories, not the people who contributed to writing it in its original form.

God is a little annoyed that his messages have been taken out of context and edited to a point that it just doesn't make sense. He wants you all to know the reason why the Bible is so confusing and doesn't seem to make sense. It is because huge chunks of the dialogue are missing, hidden and won't be shown to you unless you really dig to find it. God still believes that even if you are studying the Bible, referencing the Bible, or bother to read some of the Bible, you are still learning about him and that is all he really cares about deep down.

When you mention the Holy Bible, or if anything is read from the Holy Bible, you are conjuring God to be present and if you are specifically focusing on Jesus Christ from the Bible writings, then you are conjuring Jesus to be present and that is really the whole point of the Bible. All God wants you to do is *think* of him and he will be there. *Love* him and he will be in your heart, *share* your experiences about him and he will be with all of the people that you share his love with.

God wants writings like this one to be like a supplement to your Bible studies, to help you understand the *reality* of God and what he actually represents, without getting too caught up in the technicalities of it all. He doesn't want you to give up seeking truth and seeking answers. You will find some truths in the Bible and you will find other truths through your life experience.

When worship goes wrong

God wants me to teach people *not* to worship people, or teachers, but to worship *only* God, the Supreme Being and *not* false Gods.

Lessons help to guide us and role models serve to show us the way, but we are not to emulate, idolise, or worship them, for this is a trap and will lead your spiritual evolution to take a step backwards. More like spiritual devolution.

This means *not* worshipping celebrities, famous people, musicians, actors, singers, movie stars, models, sporting heroes, wealthy people and the list goes on and on. You are not supposed to worship humans. You are all equal and you don't have to look a certain way, act a certain way, or wear any particular brand of clothing to impress anyone. Focus on impressing God with your skills and abilities, or use these skills to put food on your table.

It is not necessary to rule the world, own 20 houses, buy more clothes than you can wear and work for the rest of your life to pay for all of your possessions. The less you have the more spiritually in touch you will feel and the more connected to nature you will feel. You will be free to explore the world and seek inner happiness, without having to worry about housing, insuring and keeping all of your belongings safe.

The irony is that humans work so hard for *things*. Then they pay for those *things* to be kept safe. Those *things* that are treasured so much, are kept hidden and locked away, for fear of losing them or damaging them. We all worry so much about these *things*, that we don't actually use these *things* for the purpose intended, which is happiness.

Release yourself from the bonds of slavery of material possessions and only have what you *need* and not what you *desire* and you will avoid the suffering from material trappings. Buddhists understand this philosophy and for this reason, they choose a simple and minimally materialist lifestyle, because that is how they manage to avoid the suffering that comes with attachments.

Worshipping can be mistaken for the ultimate submission and many previous ancient cultures like the Aztecs and the Mayans were the worst for sacrificing animals and humans for the sake of worship. The emperors used to rip out peoples' hearts and organs and do all sorts of horrific acts as a symbol of *giving* to the gods, without realising that they didn't actually need to do this in order to get their God's attention or love. This was man thinking he was doing the right thing.

The channeller said, "God doesn't want you slit the throat of a lamb and let it bleed to death to show your love to him. Somewhere along the way, through tradition, or misinterpretation you may have thought this practise was *acceptable* and *necessary* to pay your respects. He would rather you give him a *live* animal and say, 'This is a gift for you, we have saved this animal in your holy name and will treasure it all the days of its life and will not kill it.' This action would make God happy. God doesn't like killing of any kind and especially when humans kill his beautiful helpless animals that have a right to live out their life just like you do. Sacrifice is an unnecessary, redundant, outdated and revolting practise that he wants you to *stop* doing straight away and *never* do it again."

The Lord said, "Hear these words, once you have read them and understood them and continue to defy my expressed wishes, thou shall be in defiance of the Lord Almighty and you will arrive in the afterlife with all the souls of the animals you have killed and will *not* be allowed admission into the higher spiritual realms with the holy of holies."

6. BIBLICAL REFERENCES

Jesus is God in the flesh as the Father and John the disciple wrote those words.

GOD frequently gives me biblical references that explain certain historic events. Sometimes I can't find these references, because they are not in my version of the Holy Bible. I have the King James version of the Bible, but I have no doubt it is a modern day version, which has been heavily edited.

God is well aware that the Bible these days is not what the original Bible looked like, which contained all of the canonicals from multiple writers across many centuries.

The current Bible is the shortened version for the lazy reader to view. God asked specifically that the Bible remain the same and unedited, but as usual man didn't listen and created multiple versions across many different sects of religions and adulterated the content to suit the attitudes and beliefs of the editors.

They modified each Bible to suit a particular language, style and period of time and made it appropriate for the reader of that particular region and religious group. The same can be said about the Koran and the Bhagavad Gita and other religious texts throughout the ages.

That being said I can see the logistical problem of trying to carry a massive book in one's pocket, but care needs to be taken when understanding that you are not seeing the complete picture of how history actually unfolded. This point is crucially important.

There are so many Bible stories that I have never heard before. Some of the stories that both God and Jesus share with me, are so obscure that it is no surprise that I have never heard them before. You would have to be a scripture guru to be able to recite and remember the thousands of stories in the Bible.

As I am exposed to and learning these Bible stories, I am studying the

Word of God straight from the Source of all love and light. I suddenly take a keen interest in learning about the scriptures that are relatively unknown and it leads me on an in-depth reading journey for many months.

I used this time to absorb these Bible studies, which is quite funny and cute considering I don't class myself as religious or a full blown convert in the eyes of the church. God and Jesus deliberately give me a few scripture morsels here and there to lead me and to help me to find my own path of learning. I am a keen bookworm, so one story leads to another and down the rabbit hole I go, getting lost in research land.

God tells me really random things all the time, like Joseph gets all the swear words that people speak. Joseph is responsible for looking after the swearing on Planet Earth. Or he might tell me to go and look at a certain verse in the Bible.

God knows that the Bible is not quite right and that his words have been heavily edited, but it doesn't matter to him, because every time someone talks about, or mentions the Bible, God is conjured up and he feels the curiosity of someone researching, or discussing the great book.

God has visited many people throughout the ages including Moses and asked them to contribute to his great book. As scribes, we need to view the Holy Bible as an ever expanding book about the consciousness of God and use it as a tool to help man learn the righteous way throughout the ages, so mankind can continue to share this wisdom for years to come. The fact that the Holy Bible has multiple authors, makes it unique and one of a kind.

What happens along the way is that the language translations can be misinterpreted and rewritten, as well as the fact that humans like to add their own *spin* on each story, while explaining some of the points the stories are trying to illustrate.

These days you are allowed to *follow your bliss*, belong to any religion, seek spiritual wisdom and talk to God or Jesus on your own if you want to. However, it is highly likely that if your knowledge base is really advanced; you display supernatural abilities, or your knowledge base is outside the square of the normal conformist life, then you will be watched and monitored by the establishment even today in this modern era.

Even though we have made advancements in technology, spiritually we haven't evolved that much since the biblical days. You can now talk spiritually to whoever you like, but there were periods of time during the medieval dark ages as well as during many other ages, when so called witches and heretics were being burned at the stake just for having psychic experiences. If they demonstrated the power of having extraordinary abilities, or if they were discovered having knowledge of something the orthodox order of the day thought that they shouldn't know, these people were locked up, incarcerated and in many cases even killed.

The establishment or order of the day classed this as heresy and found them guilty as a heretic. Just like they did when Jesus was alive, they decided the punishment should be death. Many of these *so called* witches were simply Gnostic Christians who did not support, or believe what was being fed to them by the churches, or the order of the day. Through their surviving family members, they had the truth and legends handed down to them over generations. Their truth was very different to what they were being forced to believe.

Executions were carried out in a mad frenzy and on public display. There were many thousands of people that were killed, over the hundreds of years the dark ages lasted for. Don't believe everything you read when they try and downplay the numbers, or the period of time it lasted for.

The killings were carried out by burning people alive on the stake, strangling, hanging, beheading, stoning, maiming, pressing, stabbing, torture and drowning. One method of determining a witch, or suspected heretic's guilt, was to tie a heavy object around the feet of the accused and throw them into deep water. Their bizarre belief was that if the body floated they weren't a witch, if the body stayed on the bottom of the water, they were classed as a witch and at that stage it didn't matter, because they were dead anyway.

The dark ages lasted a long time and it was a period of time when spiritual books, ancient knowledge and people not conforming to the order of the day were discovered, removed and destroyed. This is why so many people historically have such a bad taste in their mouth, or distant brutal memories about the past. It was because religion was used as an excuse, a flag, a banner and a *cause* to shed the blood of so many innocent people during the inquisitions.

These witch hunts and inquisitions were always led by religious groups and the tribunals of the empire who seriously believed they were doing the right thing. The testing procedures were unreliable at best and the poor unsuspecting victims on trial could be killed just for answering the questions incorrectly. The cries from every period of dark ages are heard from as far away as Heaven. God aches when he sees so many good people being murdered for no good reason.

Any type of extermination of any living being, or any other animal, or creature, including plants, for reasons of ethnicity, cultural or religious beliefs, supremacist purposes, or for reasons of racial intolerance are rooted in *pure evil* and *not* supported by God.

In God's eyes, even weeds have a purpose on this planet and nothing is here just for the sake of it. Everything, every soul, every being has a right to be here and experience life.

Lift the veil of darkness and realise these actions have been and will always be unacceptable in the eyes of God and when you trace it back to the source of where missions like this start. When judgements are handed out, disagreements are intense and wars are started, there is always someone psychopathic, evil and crazy with a bent belief system and an obscure motive to kill, behind it all.

You cannot cleanse darkness from the Earth, it is required for balance. You need to harness it and tame it and not aim to eradicate it or destroy it. It cannot be destroyed, because it exists for a reason. We collectively need to ensure that darkness does not outweigh the light within everyone. We need to understand that we all have the capacity to be good and bad. We need to teach others how to choose good over bad.

Whenever the establishment decides to storm towns and cities on a killing rampage in the name of God, the king, queen, emperor, or ruling deity who thinks they hold the current power on Earth. They are acting in total blasphemy and in reality they are waving the banner of absolute wickedness and corruption.

God does not support war and does not support the actions of conflict. During past conflicts, the real believers were hiding underground and having secret meetings about how they were going to keep the real knowledge of Gnostic Christianity alive. They were creating Secret Societies and hiding their beliefs from the general public for fear of retribution. New members were asked to swear an oath not to reveal the secrets to the uninitiated and they hide these secrets that are taught, so the truth doesn't become compromised over time. They hide the books and the secret texts all around the globe in an effort to preserve the proof and historical records, so that ancient history would not be lost forever.

In opposition to the *holy* secret societies there are the *unholy* secret societies and it is vitally important not to think we are talking about the same group of people.

The *holy* initiate believes in and worships God, the Creator, the Lord of Lords and the one true God who resides in Heaven. The holy initiate does all they can to promote and support the way of righteousness in the world.

The *unholy* initiate is involved in a cult, or an alliance between members who worship Satan at the top of their hierarchy and their aim is to help Satan enslave people, steal their money and belongings, seek power, fame and fortune and discredit those who are true lovers of God in support of their materialist deity.

To be *holy* is to have eternal life and live with God in the Kingdom of Heaven. To be unholy is to have a limited life of success and material wealth which you can only utilise for a short period of time. Your soul goes to the highest bidder and if you want to give your soul away for a few measly dollars, a fake lifestyle, or material possessions, then go right ahead and make that sacrifice and sell your soul to the dark side.

No temptation could personally make me change my path of light, or question who I believe in. You cannot serve two masters, so choose carefully who you believe in and worship the *real* God, because the effects can last much further into the future than just this lifetime. Sometimes flippant choices can last for an eternity.

Do you value your soul? If you do value your soul, then you will cherish it, treasure it and ensure it never falls into the wrong hands.

The unholy secret societies can be very clever in their marketing ploys and target their members' psyche in a way that seems reasonable and fair. They play on their ego and show their members the possibilities they could experience if they were to denounce the one true God in exchange for believing in the lesser God, who isn't actually a God. He *was* a holy archangel who has fallen off his perch and wants you to worship the material world and all that you can have and attain.

These organisations can suck people in by starting their new recruits on the lower levels, ranks and degrees of their organisation, which have a basic foundation in worshipping God. First they get you to feel all safe, warm and fuzzy. Then as you progress through the ranks of the organisation, the real purpose is slowly revealed and the real truth becomes more sinister and darker than you can ever imagine.

If you want to find out which God particular secret societies worship just come out and ask them. Say to them, "With God as my witness I want you to tell me *who* you worship as your ultimate God and with God present you cannot lie to me."

If they are lower ranking members, they may not have been initiated into the higher levels yet and still believe it is the real God they are worshipping. You would need to know what rank the member holds before you ask this question. Their ranking will determine their answer. If they lie to you with God as their witness, then they are lying to the Supreme Creator and not just to you.

The ranking system is no different in the police, political, or military forces. You start out at the ground level, on the beat as a fresh new recruit who has ambitions to do well in the world and be a good upholder of the law. As they progress through the ranks of the hierarchy, the temptations are everywhere, the roadblocks are impassable, the corruption thickens and the goal posts shift all the time. Once they have witnessed this change and the true taste of power kicks in, the ego takes over and they are back to square one in terms of spiritual evolution.

There are some cultures on Earth right now still stuck in the dark ages mentality and will inflict cruel punishments including corporal and capital punishment, for doing what the legal authority of that country considers worthy of punishment, or because of what *their version* of the book says.

God does not agree with what they are doing and wants this to stop as well. We must learn to love and care for one another, even the broken ones. God tells me there is a special place where he will be sending the murdering earthly judgers of men to learn about their misdeeds.

Noah and the ark

The channeller said, "Noah was warned about the impending flood that was to come which would destroy most of the Earth. Noah had a magnificent vineyard which he tended to daily and he was very close to God and talked to him all the time.

"Noah was instructed to build an ark. Noah was told to build it 40 x 60 x 120 cubits (1 cubit = 3 yards. 1 yard = length of a yard stick). There were six people on the ark, three sets of couples."

The channeller continued, "Noah came from Adam's bloodline, then from Seth's bloodline. They thought he was a crazy old man. A man that they were not jealous of, because they thought it was an ill decision, so they did not harm him.

"In those days it wasn't actually called an ark, it was called something else. When the rains came before the flood, it rained for between 43-44 days. The only animals they took were animals that couldn't swim."

The channeller added, "God talks about the great flood in a way we may not fully understand. Cataclysms happen periodically and if God wants to *stop* something from happening, he can if he is asked and if there is good reason to stop it. If it is deemed that the situation where the disaster is going to occur is preventable and also useful to Planet Earth to prevent it, then this could be another reason why a disaster *may* be stopped.

"If humans themselves have upset the delicate balance of Earth beyond repair and their corruption and wickedness is completely out of control, then God will *allow* an event to occur that may create a catastrophic disaster. Some disasters can help restore balance on Planet Earth. Then God let nature rebuild itself.

"Humans by nature are selfish and only think of their own race and about the survival of their own species. At times very little thought is given to the millions of other creatures, animals and plant life that we share the planet with. This is obvious from the state of degradation of plant and wildlife habitats on the planet at this time."

The channeller continued, "It is easier to view major disasters from the perspective of God, when you understand the causes of natural disasters and planetary cycles that affect Earth. Everything is *cyclical* including each time that Nibiru passes near Earth.

"Athesis, who created the flood, was an angel under God and God let him. Yeshua and Jehovah helped saved mankind from extinction by warning the few that were worthy to reseed the planet. One of the reasons that God *allowed* the flood to occur, is because the world was full of wickedness and corruption in those days. God agreed to allow the catastrophe to occur to *cleanse* the planet. And those words shall be."

The channeller added, "The planet Nibiru was here again recently, but God put his right hand out and caught Nibiru and it could not hit, nor touch Earth. Man's suffering this time was saved by God. Around 3600 years, 18 scores and 18 days ago (from the date of the reading in 2014) was when the great flood occurred. Last time the great flood was allowed to happen by God not intervening and by being asked by the great demon to let it pass and see what will be after it has passed."

Refer to the section on *Nibiru, Planet X and the dwarf star* for more information on this topic.

Moses

The channeller said, "There were a total of 660,000 when Moses led the people out of Egypt. Moses was able to part the water, because he had 100% faith that God was with him and didn't doubt a thing.

The word is *believe.* Moses was close to God and he talked to God often.

"Moses banged his staff (a big wooden rod like a walking stick) three times; every time he was sure he wanted God's attention. He was very stern and focused when he did so. God has created the *rule of three* to stop idle thoughts and daydreams manifesting into something we do not want. If you ask for something with absolute certainty and gusto three times, it *will* happen, but the timing of which events occur to make this happen, are out of your control.

"What can we learn from Moses? The rule of three. Make sure you ask yourself three times, *does it tick all the boxes? Is this the right choice?* Make sure you explore all of the details of the choice and the decision. Check with yourself three times before confirming your decision, just like Moses did with the staff. *I want this, I want this, but wait… does it have all of the things that I need? Hmmm no?* If you cannot answer *yes* three times in a row, then the answer is no. This stops idle daydreams becoming an actual manifestation and reminds you that you must really want something to happen before committing to it."

John the Baptist

The channeller said, "God wants us all to research John the Baptist more. He talks about the tree of life and living life as a vegetarian. He describes how the queen or king of his day used to hire a Jester to keep the palace entertained and if they didn't like what they saw, they would kill or behead them. John was a righteous man, but *not* a weak man. He was not afraid of what people thought of him and he never feared getting into trouble for his beliefs. He just kept on forging ahead with his worship and his faith in God.

"What happened to John the Baptist was very cruel and very unkind. He was treated like a political terrorist would be treated these days, because of his strong faith in God. The establishment was afraid of him converting too many people, so they had to get rid of him. John the Baptist had a very unique method of baptising and introduced baptism into the world. He wants to share this process with all of you."

The channeller continued, "When baptising someone there is a process to follow and a statement that needs to be said *three* times to properly baptise someone. Hold the person on either side of their face or cheeks and say directly to them, 'Somebody loves you,' and also hold that direct communication when helping to cleanse them. Ask the person to give you all their sins, or tell you all their sins. If they are uncomfortable telling you, then they can just hug you to purge all their sins. This is like being born again and giving them a second opportunity for a clean and wholesome life in the eyes of God. Ensure to white light yourself before doing this procedure. The whole point of baptism is to purge the person of their sins and ask for forgiveness for the person to be born again on a spiritual level, like a reset and a fresh start. This is where the term *born again Christian* is derived from."

The purpose of using water during the baptism process was to cleanse them of the sins. The water helped to define the moment of cleansing.

The channeller added, "If you want to baptise people, be commanding with your presence and cleanse people with the authority of God and purge them with faith and conviction.

"When it comes to helping homeless people, you can help one out at a time by giving them a hot shower, a meal and listening to their problems, then sending them on their way. You don't need to *fix* them, or tell them what to do. Sometimes they just want to talk to someone, to tell them their story and have an understanding ear to listen to them. Once they know they are loved and recognise the help they are receiving, it can help them to reset and reassess what they are doing and the current position they are in. Leave the change up to them. If they want to change, they need to make this decision themselves."

Mother Mary

The channeller said, "Mother Mary has had many incarnations on Planet Earth. Her trademark name when reincarnated always starts with Mother. She was the Mother of all of us in her first incarnation as Eve. She comes back around every 120 years to live another life which is what the Creator deems a minimal allowed term of days in between human lives. Mother Mary's most recent incarnation was as Mother Teresa, who was well known for her tireless work with charity and as a missionary.

"God wants mankind to remember Mother Teresa, because she gets bored on the other side. She wants to help and needs to help.

"The soul of Mother Mary cracks it after a period in Heaven with the Creator and wants to come back down. She is one of the saviours of Earth and wants to come back down after every life. If she dies before the 100 years is up, then she gets to come back even earlier. That is part of the deal."

The channeller continued, "Mother Shipton for example, lived a relatively short life and was burned at the stake in 1561 for heresy for her prophetic writings. She was also the reincarnation of Mother Mary. In this instance, Mother Mary would have been allowed to come back a bit earlier than the usual waiting period between lives.

"She stands for all the good of humanity and forestry and believes it is *wise* to keep in communication with God. She tells God to save this, or that and she has direct divinity to angels and God to heal, or save people as long as the cause is good.

"Every time you chop a tree down, you lose brownie points with her. Every time you buy plastic stuff it is complicated. She wants to know, are you looking after the planet? She is one of the 28 that stands between the Creator and you and shall prejudge you."

The channeller allowed Mother Mary to speak, "You are everything to me, each and every one of you. You mean so much to me that you are here. She begone these words of thee be goneth of you that don't believe in thouth. Each and every one of your suffering is my suffering, so please each and every one of you, thou have it in you to be righteous and heareth me. I know not of ineth that believes. Mother Mary is speaking through me, believeth in me as I show myself, not like them that are cowards."

The channeller continued, "When someone lies they can't show themselves, they cover themselves with their hand, they won't turn up, they run away. One must ask, 'What thouest have thee to hide?' She is really happy when women and men create an embryo."

Mother Mary added, "Remember those that have one leg, one arm, no fingers, the man that has one eye, the man that is partially crazy and has half a mind. Each time something happens to each one of these, they have more respect for the other person.

"Sophia is God's name and God's name is God and everything is a part of God. *You* are a part of God, because he created everything and God loves you. Even gas is created. You are not nothing, you are something and if you are special as a human, most of you will be able to see a butterfly, feel warmth, touch, taste, have understanding, see brightness, love, experience feelings, feel pressure and on and on it goes. You are everything to me."

Jesus

The channeller said, "Jesus is God in the flesh as the Father and John the disciple wrote those words. When God talks about Jesus, he simply calls him Jesus. The word Christ was added later by man to define the religion and belief system of Christianity. The term Christ actually refers to the soul principle that Jesus adheres to and his name Jesus Christ, describes him more like a messiah, or the anointed one. Jesus sits with his Christ consciousness in between worlds and brings this consciousness in with him when he returns to his earthly incarnations.

"Mary *did* have an immaculate conception by producing a child with God, *not* Joseph her husband."

I asked God, "How did you give Mary a child? Did you come here physically? Or did you inseminate her somehow? How did you do it and what did you do?"

The channeller responded on behalf of God, "The angel seeded her, but not with intercourse as she was still a virgin. He chose one sperm cell that was gifted to him via another angel, under command of another angel and he will not tell anyone of these angels. Gabriel appeared to make sure none of this was stopped and one angel who is the Creator of human life was awoken."

The channeller continued, "Jesus is Archangel Michael. His holy name is Yeshua, pronounced Jeshua."

"So Jesus decided to come and help as one of the archangels. He wanted to do what he did and he was free to come and go as he pleased. The story is not told the way it should be. Man had become cruel and the ruler of the Romans had overturned many of the societies. They tortured and murdered freely in those times. Imagine people coming out of the villages to see what was going on, only to be slit and cut and left to die on the side of the road. They were killing everything in their path.

"Jesus saw what was going on and came down as Archangel Michael. He decided to come down and show everyone what was going on and wanted to *show them a sign* that there is an eternity, so they wouldn't keep continuing their murderous ways. Not long after this, the Romans turned their ways around."

The channeller said, "Archangel John was baptising everyone to show them all there was another way before Jesus was born. The writings of John the Baptist were destroyed at the time, however they may have been found in one of the caves later. Many people wrote about John and there is so much literature hidden. Everyone who saw John wrote about John. He never got any holy credit for all of the work he did while he was here and because all the writings were destroyed, people soon forgot about the good work of John, including baptising Jesus Christ.

"Most of the earthly writings show that when they slaughtered, killed and murdered people, they actually let their soul free. What is more dangerous? Having the body around after having killed someone, or having the soul waiting around for you on the other side? Many lived a short life in these times."

The channeller continued, "In those days people were referred to by where they came from or lived. For example, Jesus would have been known in his day as Jesus of Nazareth, because that is where he lived."

Jesus' actual religion, or belief system during his upbringing was with the Essenes, because Joseph and Mary were both Essenes and this was discovered and mentioned frequently in the Dead Sea Scrolls last century. John the Baptist was also an Essene. The Essenes are the oldest esoteric sect of Christianity and they were around when Enoch walked the Earth. I encourage you to look closer into the ways of the Essenes and also take a closer look at Gnostic Christianity if you would like more information about this ancient religion, or belief system. Gnostic Christianity was the secret teaching from the Christ consciousness. The details of the forgotten and lost tribulations are hidden and buried.

Many things discovered in the Dead Sea Scrolls have been kept hidden on parchment for centuries. Most of the missing pieces to the biblical puzzle can be found within the scrolls. Thankfully someone had the knowing to hide them and store them until they could be reopened and deciphered. Some data loss occurred due to some exposure to the elements over the years, but enough information can be cross referenced to fill in the blanks.

The channeller said, "Jesus started the Foundation of Forgiveness and also the Foundation for New Beginnings and Hope and it was about salvaging the soul from the body of sin. Jesus taught people right and wrong and how to meditate.

"When Jesus was in the desert for 40 + 1 days, he cracked it on day one, so Jesus opposed both good and evil. God created everything and God is responsible for evil. He brought about Jesus to show the passion for crucifying if you had to choose between evil and Godliness. What would you choose?

"There were always angels watching angels, because Jesus lost his power. He could ask an angel for help, or power at any time. He descended and lived the life of a man, which meant forgoing his angelic power."

Jesus performed many miracles during his life and one of the miracles was at the wedding.

The channeller, recalling the event through Jesus said, "Let it be known that these two souls unite under the guidance of the Supreme. No one can break this bond between them but themselves. Be merry and rejoice in the love of these united souls."

The channeller said, "At the wedding Jesus was told there was no more food and wine. The bridal couple didn't have any money to pay for any extra food, so Jesus went to the head cook and asked, 'If I could provide anything to you what would it be?'

"The cook answered and said, 'It would be fish, or meat and wine.' And so Jesus produced for them what they needed."

Speaking through the channeller Jesus Christ said, "First they must understand how the love with and of the seeder; the bearer of mankind created you who is listening to this voice, must understand the love of creation and can understand their mother and father. When one understands this love and of newith of new, he will understand the Creator."

Jesus, otherwise known as Archangel Michael, is in charge of this Earth and the future of Earth. God assures me, he will be reprimanding humans when judgement comes.

I asked God, "Will Jesus ever return to Earth?"

"No. No other messenger will be sent," God replied.

Then I asked, "Where is Jesus, Archangel Michael now?"

God said, "Fighting battles of Hellaides. Jesus is within the righteous people of mankind. The pain of Jesus Christ's whipping was felt. When Jesus had incarnated into a human body, I felt every second of pain just like you do when you experience pain."

God felt the pain Jesus experienced, as did many others when Jesus was whipped. The pain inflicted on such a holy man is so horrible that it pulls at my very core every time I discuss it with God, or witness it myself through channellers and channelling.

The suffering that Jesus experienced is like no other incident on Earth, simply because he did nothing wrong. He came to teach us about ourselves and was crucified for his beliefs and his faith in the good Lord. Betrayed by his disciple Judas and sold to the Romans, it was the destiny of Jesus to do further missionary work *after* his life on Earth.

We could have learned so much from this beautiful person, instead he was whipped, beaten, humiliated and made to drag a heavy cross of lumber all the way to his crucifixion site. Then he was crucified in public with other criminals. Is this the way to treat the Son of God?

How can people not think for one second that crucifixion on its own was not hideous enough? What a primitive and evil practise, to display a rotting corpse on a cross for all of your visitors and residents to see. It was a cruel and repulsive practise and even back then to do this to someone who had committed a crime, was even more revolting, let alone doing it to someone who was not only innocent, but our saviour.

I have cried many times thinking about what they did to Jesus and those souls who read this, who participated in this act, shame on all of you who were responsible for this atrocity. This event did happen, it was well documented by many people at that time in history and yet some people still deny the existence of Jesus Christ.

How far are you willing to rebel? Are you willing to rebel your own soul out of existence? Seriously now, there is no denying that Jesus lived and died on the cross for mankind. The reasons he went through with it are very complex and some of you may never understand, but without Jesus sacrificing his life for us, our species may have been annihilated.

The channeller said, "Having a symbol of a cross means that you are worshipping an instrument of death and also the death of Jesus. Jesus on the cross then represents confusion. Are you worshipping Jesus, or the death of Jesus? To show this graphically, it is like wearing something from the person you love and also showing an instrument of death, showing how they died. If your son was killed by a gun, you probably wouldn't wear a gun around your neck. It is yet again another one of those sneaky deceptions that makes the dark side feel satisfied every time they see the cross."

I personally don't like to enter too many churches, because there are paintings and portraits of Jesus in the final moments of his life everywhere, dying in agony and it brings me to tears to see these horrific images of Jesus. To me, Jesus was an amazing person and did so many amazing things while he was alive. We should focus on that and not on his death, every time we think of Jesus.

I do however like the quietness that churches provide and I like the fact you can walk into a church most days, without having to pass through a gatekeeper to get through the door.

Visualise Jesus when he was alive, happy and well and this will help you to manifest his presence rather than focusing on his death.

The holy alignment of oneself is learning how to be perfectly balanced. Jesus is an excellent role model to teach us humility, loyalty and commitment by having the belief in the ultimate faith that he would return to his Father in Heaven when he died.

God said, "If no one teaches human beings the right way, how are they going to populate another solar system? If your days as a species on Earth are numbered and you can't pull together to do the right thing, ultimately you will all perish together."

The channeller said, "Humans love to mirror and match somebody that they think is important to them. If you come across as being important and if you are loving and give out this energy, the person near you will try and mimic loving and mimic you. This is what Jesus did. He showed people loving and caring, healing and faith. Never did he show hate, horror or what he didn't like. He would hide and take on these enemies within himself and not reveal hate, horror, or anything demonic. This is what God loved about him. He had the ability to sponge these horrors and then discard them and turn them ultimately into words of passion and love, by using the affiliation of love and passion. He would use the horror and reverse it and anything that came through Jesus, or God; they would try under all extremes to turn it around."

The channeller continued, "For example, someone might say, 'Pick up that knife and kill someone,' and Jesus would respond with love by saying, 'No I want to go and pick a flower and give it to someone instead.' It is a break statement that is the complete opposite to turn somebody around."

Many people didn't know that Jesus had siblings and he was very close to his siblings. Jesus was also a bit of a loner growing up, because his Mother Mary tried to protect him for as long as she could and didn't want his special abilities getting revealed, at an age that would risk his life too early.

Jesus was a little bit of a peculiar child and many children were afraid of him, because they witnessed unexplained phenomena around him and Jesus was often blamed for things that were not of his doing, because he had become known as the odd child.

A lot of this information has been kept hidden and edited from the Bible, but there were many miracles that Jesus performed even when he was a child. The establishment wants you to believe that Jesus inherited his power later in his life and that he was an ordinary man up until then. This is simply not true. Jesus was *never* an ordinary child, or an ordinary man.

The channeller said, "Jesus had a keen interest in carpentry and used to help his Earth father Joseph often with his carpentry mistakes. Joseph used to get commissioned to build things like chairs and furniture, but he wasn't a perfect carpenter and he used to make mistakes. Jesus has been known to extend wood through his special abilities, to help his father fix an item of furniture when he got the dimensions incorrect. They didn't share these family secrets with the world because there was no need to. They were private memories they shared as a collective. Back in those days you couldn't just locate, recut and prepare a piece of timber, it would take ages and you had timelines that had to be adhered to in order to get paid."

Jesus was also referred to as a Rabbi which in many ancient texts usually denotes a married man and Rabbi's were not usually allowed to teach children if they were unmarried. Jesus absolutely adored children and loved their innocence and willingness to learn. They were his favourite students.

Jesus also had a very close relationship with Mary Magdalene and she was his favourite disciple, which would sometimes upset the other apostles of Jesus, because they could not find favour the way the Mary did with Jesus. Mary Magdalene was Jesus' confidante and he often took her with him on his missions, along with the predominantly male cast of apostles.

The channeller said, "After Jesus spent his 40 days and 40 nights in solitude in the desert, he started his ministry which was like a roaming church, preferring to teach people in the open air, in synagogues and anywhere he could get people's attention. It is for this very reason Jesus was considered a political threat to both the establishment and the church. He presented opposing views to the law of the day and also opposing views to what the church of the day was trying to teach.

"Their plan was to silence Jesus at all costs, because having Jesus ruling the Earth would challenge the wealth held by the church and it also meant that the power would shift from material and war pursuits, to a world of harmony and peace. This wasn't an industry that both the governing party and the church were willing to accept at the time. So they murdered Jesus in their selfishness and took him away from all of us.

"Imagine how angry that made God when they persecuted his beloved Son? We are lucky that God did not destroy the entire planet in a fit of rage at the atrocities that had occurred when they killed Jesus. Jesus asked for God to have pity on humans and to give them another chance, because they did not know what they had done wrong."

The channeller continued, "God did not destroy the planet the day Jesus was killed, but he certainly made the Earth tremble by creating a huge earthquake. He also blackened the Sun and created darkness on the Earth for several hours, which was witnessed by thousands of people and was well documented. The Earth shook so hard, the temple's columns came down and destroyed the temple. These were the signs from God, that Jesus *was* the messiah and that his death would not be in vain. These events had to set a marker for when Jesus died, so that everyone alive at that time was a witness to this event, so it could not be denied years later when they will try to bury it again.

"It is not a fable. It is a fact. It is a recorded historical event that actually took place, so denying the existence of Jesus is like denying that World War I or II ever happened, even though you may have known relatives that fought in these wars."

Fast forward history 2000 years and thousands of families have some hazy memory of what happened, but they may have forgotten most of the details. The only references left are the stories, the history books and the documented news events and records that are held on births, deaths and marriages, which will show the cause of death on the recorded death certificate.

You see the irony of the death of Jesus, is that Jesus already knew he was going to die in his early 30's right from when he was young. He knew this, because he was psychic and he communicated with God on a regular basis using this gift. He used to go and find somewhere to meditate and talk to God in private away from the watchers and away from the curiosity of passersby.

Jesus had an intimate relationship with God and loved God so much that he was willing to sacrifice and cut his human life experience short to fulfil the request of God. God had a plan for Jesus the day Jesus died and Jesus followed the instructions of that plan to the letter. This plan I shall not reveal in this book, but if you really want to find out what that purpose was, then seek and ye shall find.

One time God visited me through a channeller and he said turning around behind him, "I am now going to hand you over to the beloved one, for thee know of the thou crown of thorns, he shall enlighten you with his presence and love. The previous statement is for those who ask why. Yes Jesus received the crown of thorns like no other man and can be referred to this way. May I remind you that when I say crown of thorns, who else do you think of? As if you were there and felt the pain also. And he will take your pain away and in its place, he shall give you his love. No one else offers this as well. He showed you how strong his love was for all of humanity and was your and is your saviour, warrior, keeper, your guardian angel.

"He is the one you reach out for in times of happiness and in times of trouble. He is the one that can guide you to the glory and can feel your suffering and pain and fill your heart and soul and feed your mind with happiness, love and song. In a land of slaughter, lies and bigotry, a land that is unjust, where there is hurt, pain and confusion, he can deliver you from your suffering and has the power to resurrect, manifest and be with you. He stands here now waiting to talk to you for the first time."

Then Jesus spoke through the channeller, "I am who I am. Blessed are those who listen. Blessed are those who ask. Blessed are those who suffer the pain as I did. I am the one who takes the pain away. I am the one who listens to you. I am the one that has love awaiting you. Listen to me. Celebrate with me, the love I have and the Father and the Father's love he has given all of us. I am here to remind you, you have the love within and to find it and when you find it; you have found me *and* the Father.

"Bless you and when you see your Father, he will find love in you, as each and every one of you are made from the Father and when he receives you, he grows stronger from your love that was given to you from the Father. While you are here, no man can give you what the Father can give you. Only man can take away and is yet to learn how to give as I say to you. Love one another as you have already done previously."

The apostles

Try to think of the 12 apostles of Jesus as being both his disciples and his breadth of coverage across many industry sectors. The apostles were ordinary people, handpicked by Jesus from ordinary walks of life. They were like 12 board members who would learn the ways of the Lord through Jesus, discuss matters of importance and come to agreements on how they were going to implement changes and identified areas where humanity needed the greatest help.

The apostles were all *strong* men and not lame men, so they were also like Jesus' personal protectors and body guards. In those days Jesus would have been seen as a political figure, because he built up a massive following in a very short time of ministering. He would have also been in danger from aggressors and oppressors of the **Word of God**. Why? Because what he said made perfect sense in a world that was falling into the pits of darkness yet again.

Every time mankind slips into the hole of darkness and struggles to come back out, the soul of Jesus or Archangel Michael is sent to revive and enlighten us. He is sent to awaken us to our potential kindness, warmth and love and to show us we have a greater capacity to live together in harmony than we are taught and there is no need for disputes.

Jesus wants you to know that every single apostle whom he sent out to the world to continue his teachings, (with the exception of John) in the days after he walked the Earth, were martyred, eliminated and assassinated by the establishment one by one. Many of them were crucified just like Jesus for their strong faith in Jesus and in the Lord.

They also *tried* to eliminate John the apostle when they cast him into a pot of boiling oil, but miraculously he survived and went on to write the Book of Revelations on the island of Patmos where he was exiled to.

The apostles were each targeted, sought out and destroyed. First the establishment attempted to publicly humiliate each one of them by making them denounce their faith and discredit them. Each apostle was prepared to be martyred and none of them denounced their faith before they were killed. This is what each of the apostles faced before their deaths. A martyr is someone who willingly suffers death rather than denouncing their belief in God, or their own religion.

The channeller said, "This is how strongly the establishment and those who worshipped the establishment felt in those days about their limited beliefs. This illustrates how free thought was not allowed, or encouraged. This is something that doesn't often get talked about, because humanity likes to have the illusion that after Jesus came and went everything returned to normal and we became the civilised culture that we now live in today. Humans still had to go through many trials and tribulations between then and now before this relatively civilised modern day."

The names of the 12 apostles

1. **Peter** who was otherwise known as Simon, but was called Peter by Jesus. He was Andrew's brother and he was also the first Pope and renowned as a leader apostle.
2. **Andrew** was Peter's brother who was also a disciple of John the Baptist.
3. **James** was the son of Zebedee, the eldest James and the brother of John. He also lived with Jesus as his brother and was raised by Mary.
4. **John,** who is the brother of James, wrote the Book of Revelations of the New Testament during his time on the island of Patmos and was eventually a free man when he died in his old age.
5. **Philip** who was also a disciple of John the Baptist.
6. **Bartholomew** otherwise known as Nathanael.
7. **Thomas** was also called Didymus and the twin. He was the one who doubted Jesus all the time and wanted proof, hence the saying, *"Doubting Thomas."* Thomas was the sceptic of the group and provided balance in the world of faith.
8. **Matthew** also known as Levi was a tax collector.
9. **James** was the son of Alphaeusa and known as the younger or lesser James.
10. **Jude** was otherwise known as Lebbaeus, or by his surname Thaddeus.
11. **Simon** was known as the Canaanite and Zealot.
12. **Judas Iscariot** is the most infamous apostle, the one who betrayed Jesus. He was also the treasurer of the group and committed suicide by hanging himself, after he felt remorse for betraying Jesus on the night Jesus was arrested.
13. **Matthias** was chosen to replace Judas Iscariot as the 12th apostle.

After all of the apostles were gone, there was a period of time when Christianity was declared *illegal.* Can you imagine that? Thank God those times have changed and we can openly love God without fear of persecution. Let's hope and pray it stays that way.

Jesus was one of the few masters who walked the Earth to have female disciples and not discriminate against their desire to know God. A disciple is like a pupil, or a follower of Jesus and Jesus had many disciples who wanted to learn from him.

Jesus had 12 apostles with whom he shared his intimate stories about God and he even revealed himself as his true self, which was an angel, to at least three of his apostles.

Even though Jesus had 12 male apostles, I believe there was more to it than we have been told. During the ministry of Jesus, he would have caused quite a stir in such a barbaric society with his hippy stories of love and peace. He would have inevitably rubbed lots of people up the wrong way. A group of 12 strong men around you all the time who love and care for you, *will* protect you.

It was a very mutually beneficial relationship they all had with one another. The apostles got to see the real Jesus and Jesus got to teach capable men to help with his purpose on Earth.

Jesus loved Mary Magdalene and she was the first person to see Jesus after his resurrection. This is when Jesus instructed her to tell the other apostles of his return. Mary received private and exclusive teachings that none of the other apostles received, because her love for Jesus was always unconditional. She stayed with him when others fled during his trial, crucifixion, death and resurrection.

Mary was anointed as an apostle *after* Jesus was resurrected and continued her ministry to spread the gospel for the rest of her life. Jesus kissed Mary Magdalene often and in front of the other apostles and he would allow her to touch him more than anyone else. An affectionate loving relationship existed between Jesus and Mary Magdalene and she was not the promiscuous character that history tries to portray.

She was a liberated, free spirited, kind-hearted soul, who was looking for a strong leader to follow in a world full of sexism and manmade judgement. When Jesus meets her and clears her of her demons, he recognises her inner soul and then all her prayers were answered. She wasn't perfect in the eyes of man, but she was *perfect* in the eyes of the Lord and Jesus for her loyalty, companionship, dedication and dependability.

This is proof that what society deems a sinner can be so far off the mark of what an actual sinner really is. A so called sinner can easily become a saint in their mortal lifetime, if they make a big effort to turn their life around. Mary Magdalene was financially independent and helped to fund Jesus and his apostles for as long as she could.

While writing this book, I actually had a dream and I wanted to share this extra information with you for your benefit. I was shown a lesson in a pictorial form that you will appreciate.

I dreamt that I was sitting at a large rough wooden table with Jesus and his disciples and amongst them were some of his apostles. During the lunch time meal, one of the apostles was eating a bowl of food, when he lost his appetite and pushed his bowl away in disgust after he saw a man sneakily approaching the table. This man sat down near the group to listen to their conversation. The man had his back towards the table, but his ear was pointing towards Jesus and the apostles *listening* in.

The apostles could be extremely fiery at times and very outspoken.

The apostle who lost his appetite started to complain out loud by saying, "And who do we have here? A tax collector, a Roman soldier, a spy who has been sent to listen to the wisdom of our table?"

Jesus reached across and touched the apostle on the arm to calm him down. He didn't want to cause a scene and he said quietly amongst the apostles, "We are many as we are one. When you have the force of many, you become a greater force than you have just being as one. We all share *one* belief, *one* purpose and are greater in a group of many. A house divided amongst itself cannot stand strong and becomes weaker and easier to destroy. If a table is divided in agreement and divided in nature, you will remain as many with different beliefs and will not be as strong as sharing the united force of one belief."

What Jesus was trying to show the apostles and the disciples was, to start a division, or argument over something that is not worthy of fighting for, can turn into a petty display of egotism, instead of focusing on the greater purpose of the group, which was solidarity and community. The spy had no power over them, nor could he divide them in their belief if they followed their true purpose.

Jesus was implying the spy would always be there, but have no fear of others who might try to influence you. If you are *sure* about your beliefs and your faith is strong, then you cannot be divided, upset, annoyed, or destroyed.

This is what I felt the intention of the dream was and Jesus was very clear with his intent and sees no need for conflict. Jesus shows strength in faith, kindness and patience, by being steadfast with his beliefs and he teaches others to do the same. Jesus is *leading by example* and does not condone conflict.

7. ENVIRONMENT

Even though we were created in God's image,
he doesn't fully understand what leads mankind to be so destructive,
when we have the choice to be creative and live in harmony with everything.

EVERY time we hear the term *environment* these days, we think of the downhill slide of the environmental situation in relation to climate change. One major contributor to climate change is the opposing force of man versus nature, with mankind breaching the shrinking boundaries reserved for the forests and wildlife. Another major contributor is the force of nature itself and the cyclical nature of the Universe.

Once upon a time humans and nature used to be in *balance* and used to live in *harmony* with one another. There was an understanding between species and a healthy respect. Generally speaking they kept a respectful distance from each other, unless there was a reason to approach, like for food.

Everything humans do now is on such a large scale. We have turned rural, local and backyard farming into monocropping and agricultural industries that use massive amounts of land to produce crops on a mass scale. Humans no longer feed a few chickens on the farm, let them graze free range, gather their eggs and let them live a long life.

They now build massive industrial steel sheds, imprison the chickens in tiny little steel cages (more like cells), force feed them manmade food and pump them full of growth hormones to make them grow faster. This in turn creates sicknesses that require antibiotics and then humans eat them. It is such a crazy concept and is such a bizarre practice, because people have become so removed from the methods used to kill their food. They no longer *see* how their potential meal is created, before it is prepared in plastic packaging, ready for consumption on the shelf at the local supermarket.

Cows are the strangest method of food production known to God and he can't grasp the concept of murdering animals on such a massive scale. Humans would shudder to know how many millions of cattle are slaughtered every year to fulfill an unnecessary desire to consume meat.

Some of the biggest culprits of the destruction of rainforests around the globe are the meat industries. These industries are clearing the pristine forests to make way for grass production to feed the cattle. God is baffled at how much it doesn't make sense and he can't understand why humans continue to do it, knowing the destruction it is causing. They just can't seem to help themselves and keep on doing it.

The oceans are being fished out, the reefs are being stripped of their nutrients, the waterways are becoming more and more polluted, the forests are becoming decimated and the underground aquifers are becoming more toxic. The air that we breathe is so full of toxic waste and fumes, many people are now asthmatic in a world where asthma didn't exist previously.

No animal anywhere on the planet is considered *sacred* anymore. Even in national parks and protected areas, there are still game hunters, poachers and thieves. What is happening to our beautiful planet? When will this destruction end? How much pain can Mother Earth take before she shakes all of us off, or opens up and swallows everything?

We need to revert back to the old methods of farming, kinder methods that don't require humans to spray the plants with chemicals. Sustainable methods that support living in harmony with nature, methods like *Permaculture,* which is the wild and natural way.

We need to treat the animals and our precious planet with respect so that we can feed everyone responsibly and ethically. The animals and all of the wildlife on the planet deserve to be here, just as we do. They have a life to experience, just like we do. They too have families, babies, friends and cousins and love meeting new members of their own species to learn and grow, just like us.

Earth through the eyes of the Creator

I asked God, "Why is everyone so destructive and careless on this planet?"

God responded, "The planet with the one moon is a selfish one and thou who looks into the sky and looks up and sees *one* moon, should be wary. It's a selfish planet. Man needs to show God more than the selfish nature of humans and show him the love on this lonely planet."

God continued, "Syria currently has five moons, soon to be six moons and she is a woman planet giving birth, whereas Earth has *one* moon, *one* planet, *one* star, *one* thief and *one* Creator. No one believes in anybody else and it's a perfect deception."

The channeller said, "To think that Earth will be overcome by humans, is funny to God. Do you truly think that something like the Earth that is millions of times larger than us, is actually affected by us? It is not afraid of us. It can destroy us at any time. Do you think the ocean doesn't know every creature in the sea and every life form that swims inside it? It is just waiting for the judgement day."

God asked me already knowing the answer, "What happened to all the trees? The animals?"

I really had to think about that question and realised that if you had to explain this to the Creator, and see it from the Creator's point of view, how would you? Would you say, "Oh, the trees got cut down and destroyed to fulfil man's fantasies. The animals have all been killed and *eaten* and there are none left!"

Unfortunately mankind can sometimes have a really *mean* streak within, a greedy nature, along with a careless and reckless attitude at times, without any thought for the future, or the consequences that come with their actions.

God is learning about the way a human works, just as we have the desire to learn about how God works. Even though we were created in God's image, he doesn't fully understand what leads mankind to be so destructive, when we have the choice to be creative and live in harmony with everything. He knows that we are all *influenced* by the powers that be on this planet, but it still hurts him to see humanity choose this course of action, instead of the path of peace and harmony.

The channeller said, "When Adam and Eve were allowed into the Garden of Eden, which is Earth, they were assigned as caretakers of the garden. The garden back then was full of life and nutrition and enough food to feed all of the creatures on Earth, including humans. The natural law of caretaking is ensuring plant and animal life is *preserved* and that one had to live in harmony with nature and not destroy it. The closest model to the original Garden of Eden is the Permaculture method of sustainable living. Eventually we will go back to this way of farming and feeding ourselves, but for the moment, mankind is stuck in an agricultural mindset and focuses on single crop farming, instead of allowing plants to grow wild like they should.

"Mankind kills the soil by turning it frequently. This destroys the worms and the natural micro bacteria living in the soil. When mankind ploughs the earth and exposes all of the luscious microbes and nutrients to the harsh sun, they destroy the rich soil. All of the microbes and worms are amazing little living creatures that love the dark moist environment of the soil and don't like to be disturbed. Mankind keeps ploughing the earth, over and over and over again, until there are no nutrients left in the soil.

"Weeds grow to help deliver nutrients back into the soil, but mankind doesn't like the messy look of weeds, so they go about destroying them too.

Then mankind buys nutrients and a cocktail of chemicals to get the soil back into a good condition for growing food and has to use chemical pesticides and fungicides to keep the bugs and bacteria off the food.

"If nature is left alone to do its thing, nature already has the right amount of bees, bugs, butterflies and insects to look after nature. When we farm single crops and not multiple crops together, then it attracts a *plague* of one type of bug or insect, who like that particular crop and who can wipe out an entire crop overnight.

"Nature has a perfect balance and when it is interrupted by too many of one species, or modified from its existing state, it becomes out of balance. Mankind then complains that the birds, bugs and insects are eating all of their crops. What do you think insects are thinking? They are thinking, *what has happened to all my food?* There used to be a food forest and now it has been destroyed. It has been replaced with grass for cattle or wheat and corn for humans. What about our little brothers and sisters of the Earth, what are we doing to look after them? We are destroying their habitats to make way for our own progress and development and we are changing the way the Earth provides for all living creatures."

The channeller continued, "Planet Earth is not ours to rape, torture and destroy as we see fit. It was provided to humans to share with all creatures' great and small. The human wonders why tigers have to come out of the forest and eat humans. Humans have actually given them no choice, because they have destroyed their natural habitat, replaced their forests with grass and eaten all of their food. The same could be said for bears, polar bears and even sharks if you want to get technical.

"We are no longer allowing nature to provide for them, because we are altering the course of nature with our misunderstanding of the order of things. Mankind does *not* have dominion over all of the other living species on Earth. This is a man taught *delusion* and a gross misrepresentation and misinterpretation of early biblical texts. Mankind's role was to be the *caretaker* of Earth and ensure that all creatures, including themselves were provided for. Animals, creatures and mankind used to live in harmony with one another when everything was in balance.

"There is no need to hunt any animal to eat, because God provided enough forest, vines, fruits, grains, nuts, seeds and plants for humans to survive and to be able to have a nutritious diet. God provided this food for all of us to share; including the birds, animals, insects and all living creatures."

The channeller added, "Planet Earth is *old.* Much older than we have been told and in fact much older than scientists, geologists, paleontologists and archaeologists really even know themselves. The Earth was created at the *start* of existence. Everything was created at the beginning of creation."

I asked God, "When was the Earth created and placed in the solar system that we now currently live in?"

Through the channeller God replied, "This can be worked out quite simply. Take the speed of your estimated light and measure the growing outwards from the Universe. Then measure the distance of your Universe from the centre of the galaxy. You were one of the first creations of God, as you are on the outskirts of all known."

The channeller continued, "There are other things that are old like oil. When you are heating oil up and burning it, you are releasing the souls in that oil. It could be the oil of a tree, or the oil of an animal. The primitive burning of fossil fuels is burning the oil of ancient dinosaurs, plant matter and other elements that have been trapped in the Earth from ancient times.

"Burning fossil fuels is a totally redundant and unnecessary form of energy consumption and when humans are allowed to produce greener forms of energy and renewable sources of energy, they will help to restore the natural balance of Earth's minerals and resources. Some resources that are contained inside the planet, form part of the Earth and are supposed to be there to sustain and nourish the plants, creatures and us. If we take too many, or all of the minerals out of the Earth, we are causing an imbalance in the Earth's mineral and resource supply and ultimately affecting the stability of Planet Earth.

"God is busy building stars and planets and sometimes needs to have it pointed out to him that there are destructive activities occurring that need to be resolved. Jesus, just like other great prophets before and after him, identified there was a problem on Earth, which got the attention of God to take a closer look at the suffering of humans. When too many humans cry out from their graves, God wants to know why and what is going on. Although God is within every one of us and is connected to all of us, he does not get stuck in one individual's thoughts, but sees us as a representation of the human species that were created. Sometimes it takes many humans to ask, pray, or cry out for help to get noticed on a large scale.

"Over the past millennia we have become more and more separated and detached from God and we haven't been asking for guidance and help as much as we used to. This *separation* from God, causes the Creator to continue with his creations elsewhere and he may come back to check on us if we ask for his assistance, guidance, or if he hears enough of us praying for help. The less we want to connect with the Creator, the connection becomes weaker. We must remain in contact with our Creator to maintain a strong connection. The Creator will always listen if you want to tell him something, or if you truly want to pray for something to change for the better. If more of us did this together, prayed for positive change and *asked* for divine intervention, he would hear our voice like a strong transmitting beam of communication coming from Earth and he will respond."

The channeller added, "Jesus was in constant communication with God and he had no fear of living, or dying, because he knew he would ultimately return to his heavenly Father either way and wanted to use his time on Earth wisely, by attempting to reconnect souls with their Father in the same way.

"If you planted a nice tree, should God destroy it? No. If someone plants an evil seed, should he destroy it? No. God wants to see what will happen to each, like an experiment, a creation none the less. This is something humans find difficult to comprehend, but everything is in balance and every creation has a right to live to see what will happen. Sometimes the biggest human learning comes from our biggest mistakes and seeing the experiment through to the end, can give us a wiser perspective on good and evil."

The channeller continued, "For example, if you want to be a pretty person yourself, then you would look at beautiful flowers and pretty things, not demonic and ugly things. In simple terms, that is how you can change the devastation of the Earth. There is no point complaining and telling God you don't want these horrible devastating events to occur. How about asking God to look after the Earth and he shall? It is written that no one asks God to look after Mother Earth. The prayer of one person can save a whole planet!

"The fear of a little child asking the soldier, 'Please don't kill me.' The soldier will then protect the little child. Don't think that prayer doesn't work, because physically it is not told that a living human is able to touch and move and physically change this Earth. They are of a God nature, whereas spirits cannot touch this Earth and cannot help. If you pray to a spirit to help save you, they are not able to, but a spirit is able to help guide you and to touch *you*, but they are not in touch with the Earth. *You* are in touch with things that are physical, including the Creator and also the destruction of the physical Earth around you.

"You have to look through the eyes of the Creator to understand this concept. We are so busy looking through the eyes of a human, we don't see creation in the same way the Creator does. If you were God, there are no set rules. The only rule is if something goes out of control, then it needs to be reassessed and work out what you need to learn from it."

God wants to share a little poem with you.

Walk free, I want to walk free
Run wild, I want to run wild
Big love is all over your face
You are my amazing grace
Gave birth to the Earth

Trees are the lungs of Earth

In the future I will give a treaty to the trees of the Waitutu Forest, which are part owned by my whānau (Māori family) in the bottom south west corner of the South Island of New Zealand.

A long time ago, my Māori ancestors occupied a large holding of prime agricultural land. The government at the time organised a massive land swap and exchanged the prime agricultural land for thick, swampy rainforest. At the time, the rainforest was extremely inaccessible, tucked away in a corner of a forgotten land and quite useless to the Māori.

Fast forward 100 years and the land is now considerably more valuable, due to the quantity of Rimu trees on the land and the fact that there are not many Rimu trees left in New Zealand. The Māori people, who now own the land, are second and third generation Māori families and they think they have hit the jackpot, because of the value of the trees on the land. Unfortunately they have been sold only a partially truthful story and as a result of their limited understanding of the situation, are only more than willing to *selectively log* these trees for monetary exchange.

It's funny how money can change the perception of the value of something. God sees the true value in the natural setting and encourages the movement towards eco-tourism and habitat research, instead of logging, selling, or even giving it away to the government.

Selective logging is a nice way of saying, "We will take a tree here and there and you'll probably hardly even notice it. We'll even take the fallen dead ones away for you, to make space for the other trees."

It sounds feasible to some degree, but when you delve deeper into the logging industry, it is more than suspicious when you really think about it. What really happens is the logging company gets to take its pick of the beautiful ancient trees. They will most likely take the trees that will produce the best logs and which sell for the most amount of money and *not* the deadwood as the family members believed.

Did anyone go and check if any of the dead trees were taken? Probably not! The government knows about the offer of money from the logging companies and in turn has offered the family minimal compensation, as an alternative to logging the trees. This was in fact a smart move by the government, but once again, there is always a hidden agenda lurking beneath every such promise.

The purpose of this explanation is not to touch on hidden agendas, but to support the lifeline of the trees that don't have a human voice to speak for them. Let me be that human voice, let me raise your awareness of the lungs of our Earth, let me remind you that trees have memories, lives, families, feelings and a purpose, just like we do.

The channeller told me I need to put the word out there that *everyone* in relation to *every forest* needs to change their ways and together we need to *preserve* the forests and not cut them down. What is the point if we destroy all of the trees and have no forest left to visit and nowhere for all of the little animals and creatures to live?

I am writing a song which is written half in English and half in Māori and I am going to sing about the trees. It is going to show all of you that every tree is your ancestor and you need to view the trees in this light to stop yourselves from cutting the trees down. For example, if you are Māori, every time you are cutting a tree down, you are cutting down an ancient Māori person, because the trees talked to me in Māori and told me this.

These trees have *mana* (supernatural power) and should be *tapu* (sacred and must be left alone). If you cut them down you will attract bad luck and your ancestors will haunt you. At the moment these trees are being protected by angels, with spiritual barbed wire circled around the entire forest. They have been asked by the Māori ancestors who have passed over, to protect the trees and keep them alive. Many of the Māori ancestors only realise once they have gone to the other side, how many precious resources are contained within these lush forests.

God said, "Remember that every time you cut down a tree, you have less oxygen. If you chop a tree down, you effectively use enough oxygen to sustain 10 years of your life by losing the oxygen it generates. They are not just anyone's trees, but God's trees and just like us, they have a right to live, no more slaughtering! If every human planted a tree, every time someone was born, we would rehabilitate the Earth in no time."

We need to ask ourselves as a race and species, why do we need to build furniture and houses out of timber these days? Why are we not looking at more sustainable and recyclable ways to build homes? You could easily use recycled plastic and make it look like timber, if the aesthetics are pleasing to the eye. Is there any point to growing a beautiful tree, only to shred it up and use it to wipe your butt? Is there any point to growing a forest of trees, to slice it up into paper, only to screw it up and throw it in the bin?

There are lots of little things you can do to help the trees.

1. Plant more trees.
2. Don't cut trees down.
3. Look after the trees we already have, they can take a long time to grow.
4. Trees are good for shade, don't cut them down to remove shade cover, otherwise you will end up with dry and cracked earth from the heat of the sun.
5. Trees make great shelters for animals. You can build little animal shelters and put them in the trees.

6. Don't use too much toilet paper. It increases the demand to farm trees.
7. Don't print if it isn't necessary and use electronic transmittals of documents where possible.
8. Buy recycled paper and recycled wood products where possible.
9. Learn to realise all of the benefits of supporting and encouraging tree communities.
10. Stop eating meat, which will slow down the demand for meat consumption and as a direct result, less tress have to be cut down to make way for cattle and grass.
11. Save and preserve the forests when you can.
12. Every time you save a tree, you help to store water in the earth, which ultimately means more water in the water aquifers for future generations.

God said, "Right now, humans are cutting down billions of trees every year. Don't you think at that rate, we are going to run out trees one day? Imagine no trees on Earth? What a terrible thought! Do you think that humans even think about replenishing the timber stock when they consume it? Do you think the humans realise they are cutting down an old living entity, who has just as much of a right to be here as we do?"

Do humans remember what the planet used to look like *before* the destruction of billions of acres of forest, which they have ploughed aside to make way for green pastures for livestock? Do humans even care, or even comprehend what the bigger picture is? Most think it won't affect them in their lifetime, but when you look at the span of a soul lifetime in comparison to a short lived single incarnation, the larger picture starts to become clearer. All humans *should* care, because actions like this will affect your next incarnation, your children, your grandchildren and your great grandchildren's futures.

Our precious trees are the lungs of Mother Earth and we are tearing them apart at an alarming rate. You don't need to be a greenie to understand this concept and you don't need to be a hippy and tie yourself to a tree to save the forests. We can all make small contributions to save this precious resource, by changing the way we think and feel about trees.

God said, "If you look at a human, it cuts a whole tree down to wipe its bum. What's next? Wipe out a whole mountain to brush your teeth?"

The channeller said, "God's patience is already wearing thin and he has already judged everyone and all of the living know what that means. An animal *cherishes* nature and works in *harmony* with nature to build its homes, provide food and animals use nature as a safe haven from the elements."

God reminded me, "What does a gorilla do when it goes to the toilet? It lives in harmony with nature and fertilises the tree with his poo. What does a gorilla eat? Well, they eat plants, fruit, leaves, seeds, stems and the odd grub. The gorilla is smarter than the human, because the gorilla fertilises its own food. The gorilla doesn't need to cut down any trees, because gorillas love trees. They love the shade it provides, the food it provides and the shelter it provides. They are truly living in harmony with nature, by not destroying the environment they live in."

Why can't we take a leaf out of their book and live more simply and stop complicating our lives with unhealthy food choices and unnecessary food consumption?

Then there are those, who generally do not share this respect for nature and as a consequence, treat nature as an infinite resource they can just take from whenever they see fit. They don't care if they harm trees, plants, or wildlife in the process. They are only interested in meeting their own selfish needs and the ultimate selfish need to line their pockets. They think to themselves, *surely it can't hurt to take one or two trees here and there? Can it?* If everyone is thinking this, then we are talking about billions of trees. Trees are part of God's creation and are there for all of us to share. We are allowed to utilise, but not brutalise nature.

God said, "Humans chop down trees and don't replace them with anything and keep on chopping them down. If you chop all the trees down, you will have no oxygen left to breathe you fools!"

God is quite adamant about how he feels about his trees, plants and his defenceless creatures that are killed in the process of man's continuous endeavour to rape the forests. God sees it as an extreme violation of the very things he has provided for us to look after and share with all of the other creatures on the planet.

One human punishment for this act will be to come back and clean it up again and again and again, until they feel like committing suicide. He wants to teach the humans to *feel* exactly like the tree *feels.*

Humans used to have trees they called the "Tree of Forgiveness" and "The Tree of Hope." The concept was that you would tell your problems and sins to the trees, so that you had a non biased living entity to tell your troubles to. Trees used to be spiritually revered on the planet and we used to have a lot more respect for these ancient living entities than we do today. This is another spiritual truth and beneficial ancient practise that has been lost and buried in our muddied history.

Water is the lifeblood of the Earth

The channeller said, "Water is really old too. When you get a new glass of water, you think it is a new glass, but really that water is as old as the Earth. You are actually drinking the water of your ancestors. Plenty of spirits are in the water and it is very powerful. God created the most amazing jungle juice you can imagine and it's called *water.*

"A good example of this is when you have an orange. You are having the water of the spirits that are contained within the orange, *plus* the essence of the tree (the orange).

"A pool of water has *soul* and that is why it is called *holy water,* because it has been in many souls. Water that you drink, when you realise what is in the water, makes it holy water, by *understanding* the water. When Jesus said, 'This is my blood,' he was referencing the action when you drink something. What Jesus meant by that comment, is that he was talking about holy water *not* blood. The meaning is to make you think about this when you are drinking water. You could actually be drinking the water of Jesus, or water that is from holy blood, like conjuring up spirits that are in that glass of water."

The channeller continued, "If the Earth is billions of years old, then the water is also ancient and it contains the souls of all the animals and humans that have drunk it and these are the souls you are conjuring when you are drinking it. If that is what water can do, then what do you think dirt can do? Just like the Israelites did with the dust when they threw dust on their heads in grief, now you can understand why elephants do it. They are more connected to the soul of the Earth and the souls of their ancestors, which is why they feel deeply connected to both dirt and water."

The channeller added, "Look at the water, the water is holy. If you love God, the water will change its form. This is because it is God's water and it is Mother Earth's water. Water can be a test. In the ancient biblical writings it was explained what water was used for. When water in the body becomes stagnant, it becomes poisonous. If you don't like yourself, then the water cells become distorted and horrid and out of balance. If you love yourself, then the water becomes cleansed and holy and clean. When one drinks a glass of water, what should they do with it? They should *thank* the water before it goes into their body and ask the water to go and heal the body, as it goes into the body. Tell the glass of water to strike out to heal the body. Bless the water to make it holy water.

"Research shows in the witches' writings, they added more things to the water making a brew, or stew of remedies. White man came with elixirs and it's not what gets *added* to the water, it is the *intent* that is the key. It was their secret way of making a living with it. The witches used it for healing, but not what they put in it. It is the *intent* of the tribe leader, the witchdoctor, the healer.

"The ancient Māori way was the way of the healer and it was too complicated to let everyone do this. Someone would look after the water blessing and when they had food, they would stop and thank their ancestors. They would bless the food for their own wellbeing."

Living in harmony with nature

God's view on animals and his other creatures, both great and small is very similar and equally as strong, as his view about his plants and trees. God cannot understand our insatiable appetite to eat, imprison, murder and consume his loving creations. God wants you to understand what is inside the products you consume that contain animal products, which you use to adorn yourself and to sustain your vanity.

Animals were never meant to be used and brutalised for our pleasure and are *not* supposed to be abused in this manner. God asks us if we understand the reality of what we are using in our shampoos, our perfumes, our soaps, our face creams, our clothing and all of the other products that use animal oils and body parts from animals. God has provided us with ample stock of non animal materials such as plant materials, elements and minerals that we can create anything from. There is no need to use animals to test chemical treatments, to test the effects of certain drugs and kill for the purpose of our selfish beliefs.

Take Traditional Chinese Medicine (TCM) for example. They look for the craziest minute benefit they can get out of living creatures, for their own benefit. God believes it is mostly psychosomatic and totally unnecessary.

God said, "There is absolutely no need to use animals in any medicines, or medical testing. None whatsoever, no excuses, no long winded reasons for why you want to argue against me, zero, zip, nil and none. It is not necessary, not acceptable and it must stop!"

Yes he agrees it is an ancient practise, but so is head shrinking, human sacrifice and cannibalism. They were all ancient practises once as well and said to benefit the tribe in some way. They saw the light and stopped their selfish and cruel ways. Well most countries have, but not all of them.

The actual model of Traditional Chinese Medicine is brilliant. They incorporate elements of herbal medicine, acupuncture, massage, exercise and dietary therapy to assist with healing, but do you know what? They can leave out the remedies that include killing, or harming any creatures, using animal body parts and sometimes even using poisonous plants. It is excessive and unnecessary. Imagine using the oil extracted from an endangered species to *supposedly* cleanse your liver. It really is truly ridiculous. Using these exotic remedies, *does not* make you live longer, this is simply untrue and there is no evidence to back it up. The beloved Earth creatures are not there for anyone's use and abuse, they have lives to live too and those lives are not just for our benefit.

The channeller said, "You need to hear the truth, you need to learn the truth and you need to become a part of the solution and not be a contributor to the problem. Is killing a majestic animal like a rhinoceros, bear, tiger, or even a shark worth giving you a little aphrodisiac kick so you can get a hard on? *Really?* You can achieve the same feeling with the power of your mind, or through meditation and stimulation. We are pushing so many of God's species to the brink of extinction. There will be no animals left if we keep going and what a sad world that would be, just full of humans!

"If we stop buying products that use animals, or start asking what ingredients are actually in these products, then we can demand less harmful alternatives or substitutes. We can impose sanctions on the supply and the purchase of these products and only then, the industry and trade stops. It's that simple. Where there is a *demand*, there will always be a *supply*.

"Be conscionable for your choices. Be respectful to your fellow creatures and realise you *don't* have the right to kill anything you want to, when you want to. It is *not* God's will. You are doing exactly what you have been asked not to do by the Creator. You know in your heart that killing animals is wrong, but you may have been conditioned to accept this practise, because generations of your family have been killing and eating animals and you don't see the harm in it.

"You must realise that you can vote with your feet, by not being a part of the consumption of animals for your own vain and selfish benefit. If you are not quite ready to stop consuming meat, perhaps you could look at *reducing* your intake, until you are ready to stop. It's like an addiction; you may need to wean yourself off it, before taking the leap of faith. God already gave us the right balance of earth, minerals, water, plants and trees to live a long and healthy life. It doesn't need to include killing everything that moves."

The channeller continued, "Living in harmony with nature and the wildlife, means understanding that animals have babies and babies do die when you kill them to eat them. This ultimately means that when you eat animals, they are *dead* which translates to *dead* food. Biblically it is recorded so many times *not* to eat the flesh of animals, not to defile your mouth with the flesh of animals, however this was translated and omitted incorrectly over the ages and modified to make it acceptable to consume *some* animals and not others. In modern times, humans have just completely ignored the previous guidelines and consume *every* living animal. In some cultures, no animal, or creature is sacred, or safe at the hands of its greedy hunters and consumers.

"Vegetables and fruit are *living* foods and can be reproduced willingly for our consumption, especially if you bless them when you plant them and bless them when you consume them. You can eat most plants, vegetables and fruit without killing the source of the plant and without consuming or harming the whole plant. You can help the plant to live continuously, by replanting from its seedlings and keeping the plants alive for many generations. This is a beneficial relationship to both the humans and the plants.

"Humans can also be very selfish, because they forget that they share this beautiful planet with God's other creatures such as other plants, insects and animals. They too have a right to eat alongside us and if we planted enough food to feed ourselves *and* the animals, we could all live in harmony. Animals would have no need to eat other animals and sometimes humans, because they would already have a full belly. Humans are not a part of the food chain of any living animal on Earth, however when the food source of any creature becomes threatened, or removed, they will look for other sources of food to sustain their need for nourishment."

God said, "If every human planted one plant each, it would fix the greenhouse problem. If every time a child was born on the planet, they planted a tree, instead of chopping one down, it would repair and rebalance Mother Earth.

"Every animal depends on a plant and every plant depends on an animal. It is a perfect balance. The balance becomes out of alignment when humans become involved in the process. Humans tend to focus on single crop farming, which destroys the natural concept of Permaculture, which is nature living in perfect harmony with its surroundings. Let's say for example, that we plant a crop of corn and nothing else and we grow 100 acres of corn, with no other crop within that space. Firstly, the single crop depletes the soil and secondly, it is an attractive crop to certain creatures who also like corn."

Then the channeller said, "To alleviate this issue, we have designed complicated pesticides and herbicides which include toxic cancer causing chemicals and we have drenched our food in it, just to keep it for ourselves. Have we considered planting a food forest for the other creatures and wildlife to give them something to eat, so they won't eat our crops? Of course not. The food system is designed just for humans and that means everything else that wants to eat that crop needs to be poisoned, eliminated, or kept away from the crops at the human's expense. In ancient times, crops were supported by birds and other creatures, because they helped to spread the seeds elsewhere, helped fertilise the crops and were a critical part of the natural cycle of cropping.

"These days, when the crop has been harvested, they turn the soil and kill all of the grubs and worms who help to keep the soil alive in the ground. This in turn demineralises the soil and steals the nourishment from the soil, which in turn steals the nourishment from our food and our food becomes mineral depleted."

During the next few years, we are embarking on a major project called *The Retreat.* It will be a place of peace and harmony on Earth. A place where one can go to obtain solitude and sanctuary. A place of health, restoration and recovery. When we build *The Retreat*, we are going to put a hardwood timber platform up near the lake at the back of the property, because the timber has memories, like a past living thing it has energy. We will be recycling the deadwood to construct the timber platform and if we respect the wood we use and understand the complex history and nature within the tree itself, we understand that everything is energy, both alive and past. This enriches our relationship with everything in the Universe, when we understand it and comprehend that, just as we are also made of energy, so is every living thing that is alive now and was previously alive. We are all connected.

God said, "Bless the ground you walk on, so that when you accidentally kill something or step on it, it is automatically blessed."

He also wants you to be aware that if you kill something, *anything*, you own its soul and you keep it. If you accidentally kill something, you need to send it to God.

God knows that all life forms have a purpose for their existence, no matter how great, or how small and all life forms have a reason and a right to exist.

Living off the land

God said, "The key to health is in four words; *NECTAR FROM THE TREES*. It's all it needs to please. Don't eat cheese, it is mould."

God continued, "Food needs to come straight off the vine. Think of each piece of fruit as a soul. Eat food as soon as it's picked, while its enzymes are still alive. Pick the lemon then eat it."

God told me that blessing the food before you eat it, puts the soul back in it. You can ask the spirits, or souls to come back into the food so that you can eat it, consume it and have these souls come back into the body to help heal it. You can simply bless the food by saying, "I ask for each and every one of the souls to come back into the food, so that you can help my body and make these minerals bless me and become a part of me." Food needs to have the essence of life in it.

You can also say, "Thank you for making my body so healthy and wholesome," when you are eating food.

You must love what you eat and don't eat what you don't love.

God added, "Here is the best way to know how to interpret whether the food you want to eat is good for you or not. If you walk past every food bearing tree, what food is at mouth height? There are two types of food designed specifically for each creature. For humans, one height of food is designed for walking around on your hands and knees and the other height of food is designed to be eaten upright.

"You are only supposed to eat one type of food at a time. Let's look at it if you're a monkey and you are running around and you have 49 varieties of foods available at the same time. Is that even possible?

Humans only have time to harvest a certain amount of foods. How many foods can you find in one afternoon? The Devil is running around saying, 'Try me, try me, try me,' to tempt you with every possible type of food to confuse you. You should only have three to four food choices together in one meal at the most.

"Let's look at the holy food of a human. It is when you run around in the wild looking for food. Is it possible for you to find 49 varieties of food in one day? You will calm your stomach down now, because you've heard these words from God relaxing in the Nebula, like you should be."

God said, "What you think *is*. Thou shall eat one food at a time. It is not possible to find 49 different foods at one time. If you were in the wild, the most you could probably find is only three or four varieties and even then, you would only eat one at a time until you moved on to the next lot of food. Why does a giraffe have a long neck? Why does a rabbit run around on the ground? Why does an elephant have a trunk? So they can eat at the height they live at."

God laughed and said, "Pull hair out of your head and look at it and go, *where did that come from?* Just like a monkey does when he goes to the banana tree every day and asks the same question, while he is eating the banana. It came from the tree, the plant, the dirt, the sun and the minerals."

God continued, "Food is in the shape of every organ in the human body. So, what shape is a pumpkin? What do people do with it? At Halloween they make it into the shape of the head, because it's good for your head. What is a rock melon good for? There is an easy way to find out with science. The rock melon will have the same vitamins and minerals as the part of the body that it is good for."

God wants you to take time to research the oldest living animals and see what they eat.

God said, "They don't eat dairy, or cow, or chicken. Why would one eat a cow, when one could eat the grass themselves, which gives them the same nutrition?"

The channeller said, "Think about this, if God created everything, then you eat him, you breathe him, you meet him, you desire him. If you have lost him in your spirituality, you require him to fill the void of your emptiness.

"If everything is in balance, the soul is fulfilled and you can nibble away and be happy. If you ignore him, you will eat yourself fat and become horrid and lame.

"Mankind cannot just live off food alone. They become fat, selfish and ignorant to the other parts they shed off. There are seven creations to a human and they must be found and treated equally. If you strip away God, you become indulgent and eat too much food and if you don't eat *healthy* foods you become fat."

God stated, "You are not supposed to devour things, because this makes you out of balance. You must be balanced in your seven chakras, which are the seven spiritual balances of the human body. *Overindulgence* leads to your chakras being out of balance."

I will explain more in depth about chakras in the section called *Healing.*

The channeller explained, "Human's bodies need to be re-mineralised and that is what makes them survive, *not* food.

"Just like the existence of water. Water from the ground has sulphates in it and it cures cancer. Sulphates are like salt and are also like minerals. Sulphur and minerals contained in ground water can be used to create baths and you can add any extra minerals you need to help heal the skin and body.

"Salt cures a growth on the outside of the skin and an ancient method that has been lost, is that you can pierce the growth and inject salt into it and it will die. The licking of salt cures smoking. Smoking shuts down all the senses and the person who does this, is getting through life just fine without feeling a thing."

God said, "Man needs to eat dirt, because it is full of minerals and you need to eat dirt mixed with your food. When you are lacking in vitamins and minerals, there is no need to eat chocolate, just eat clay! Man is so concerned with sterilising his food and making sure all the dirt is washed away, that he is not getting the essential minerals that the dirt contains to nourish his body.

"Work out the things that make up a tissue cell. For example, selenium, magnesium and calcium and consume foods that contain those minerals.

"Generally darker skinned people eat from the organic earth and ground, which is richer in minerals and healthier. Whiter skinned people are generally more mineral deficient, because they consume white bread, white sugar, white food etc. The golden bronze natural person walks around and drinks minerals off the rocks, which include colloidal minerals like gold and silver."

God continued, "The sun is burning the skin and the body pulls out heavy metals and minerals to protect the skin from getting burnt. The sun is growing bigger and the more the sun intensifies, the more the risk and exposure to radiation there is."

God told me, "The gold is in the vaults of darkness to stop human's protection of reflectivity. The more gold the body has, the healthier it is. Gold is another cure for cancer. The more man makes it valuable, the more gold the demons hide in the vaults of darkness. It forms a radioactive barrier against the sun and radiation."

God said, "Gold. Smart humans mine it and dumb ones don't drink it! There should be a balance of gold in our diets, which come from the earth, or foods that come from the earth. We need all of the essential minerals including gold, iron and magnesium. In the absence of gold minerals to consume, you can eat carob, instead of chocolate. Use a safe solarium if there is no sunlight available. You should use water filters to filter out harmful chemicals and toxins. Avoid plastic where you can and get more vitamins to help supplement the body."

God and I talked about different methods of gardening to get the most out of the garden and we discuss that companion gardening is like using forced natural herbicides, instead of chemical sprays. When you are growing grapes, why spray it with chemicals, when you can use companion gardening? Just like garlic, you can test the plant with mildew and see what happens and make your own natural herbicides and pesticides.

God wants us to try to create super youth dung, which could be made from compressed dirt. God said, "It's like four tonnes of organic matter being squashed into a tablet. If you could compost four tonnes of organic waste, or dirt, you could create a super food, like squashing the size of a dinosaur into a pill. Clean and sterilise the dirt to make it fit for human and animal consumption first. In this case, sterilising the dirt is necessary."

God wants to share the following little morsels of wisdom with you. These are things that you may not know.

- Sap from leaves and a tree heals skin and the sap can act as a sealant.
- There are so many plants in nature that contain cures and remedies that have been buried, or lost throughout the ages.
- A lightning bolt cures cancer.
- Juniper berries are the key to isolates and the key blockers of protein.
- If you are aiming for immortalism, then the liver is the key to good health.

God asked, "Why does chocolate taste so good? Sugar! The most important thing you can do is *love* yourself and understand that every molecule in your body is able to change into balanced states. Your feelings control your body.

"When you drink something you *believe* in, you may go and drink something like a can of Coke. Why do people drink it? Because they say that it is good for you. It is falsified. Why is there a can of Coke? Well, it starts off with a glass of water and the witchdoctor says 'my brew is better, because I added this and that and sulphuric acid,' and then they added sugar, cocaine and they have even added speed. Laboratories were set up and tested like experiments, until they found the right elixir. The effect, or the buzz from the drink, might only last for 10 minutes, but it gives them a high, so people like it.

"You need to wake up feeling great and loving yourself. Dance in the shower and sing. Don't wake up feeling like crap, because that is what you are manifesting to happen to your own energy levels."

God said, "Why would anyone want to leave this planet earlier than they have to, when there is so much to explore in the physical world? Getting old is not actually getting old. They get tired and lazy. That is old age. They can't be bothered doing anything anymore."

Killing to eat

The channeller said, "Humans are currently out of balance in the animal kingdom, because of the sheer amount of livestock and wild animals that they kill, slaughter and eat every day around the world. For a start it is totally unnecessary for humans to even eat meat, because God gave them plenty of plants, nuts, seeds, grains, fruits and vegetables to survive, without having to consume, or enslave animals for their benefit.

"Am I repeating myself? Yes, because this message is important, you need to hear it again and you need to share it with everyone else."

God gets passionate when he talks about his creatures and said, "Humans have created this reality and justified it in their own selfish way to normalise it, desensitise themselves from the killing of animals and also to try to make others believe that the Bible tells you it's okay, so you can do it. The Bible *doesn't* say it's okay. The edited and tweaked version says it is okay, but the real **Word of God** says that it is *not* okay and it is written in the 10 commandments. Thou shalt not kill. The commandment does not say; thou shalt not kill *humans*, or specify what species you are allowed to kill. It simply states, though shalt not kill. It's not complicated. It means thou shalt not kill anything AT ALL! There are no exceptions to that rule."

It is so simple, yet humans have built entire cultures, rituals, belief systems and religions around what they interpret this to mean. Humans have justified their actions by creating humour, insensitivity and sport from the act of killing other creatures that they are supposed to be sharing the planet with.

I discussed the commandments with God and God told me, "They are like guidelines to stop you from being destroyed ultimately on all levels. Originally there were 55 commandments that got converted to 10. They included; thou shalt not steal, thou shalt not fornicate (which meant influence another being unless you think it is right), worship another image or any image, drink of blood (because you would have to be the God of that being), or kill anything ever."

When the term *being* was used in the commandments, it didn't only mean *human* being; it also includes all other beings like a fly, a grasshopper, a beetle (anything and everything). More commandments included; thou shalt not be unfaithful to one another (in a union between two people where there is a consensus), do love they neighbour no matter what, thou shalt kill thy neighbour in self defence, never trust thy neighbour when they are jealous, never make thy neighbour jealous among other commandments!

You can see just from this short list of commandments, by removing certain commandments, it can change your whole perception, without seeing all of the other commandments, that are used in conjunction with the list of commandments you are left with.

I have had many conversations with people who justify their meat eating by saying, "Oh but it must be okay if the animal was killed humanely." *Is it?* What difference does it make? If someone killed *you* humanely, or inhumanely, would it really matter? It is still MURDER!

There is no way to murder something nicely. Seriously, to be paid money for murder is even worse, because the intention is in place where you *intend* to hurt, maim, or kill another creature for your own selfish needs, or commercial gain, where others benefit from your killing.

God said, "The human race spends so much of its energy complaining about the injustices against humanity, but they still inflict these injustices upon one another. Some of them do not even give a seconds thought to the suffering and humiliation that an animal, or other creature experiences before, during and after its death. What humans are doing to the forests, by cutting down and decimating the entire oxygen supply to grow grass, just so that cattle can eat the grass, so that humans can consume the cattle, is the craziest misconception of all time."

God continued, "Have you ever thought that to get the nutrients from a cow you would just do what they do? Eat the grass you fools! Don't eat the cattle who have consumed the grass, because you are simply eating a by-product of the very nutrients you are seeking. This is how ludicrous the whole animal and farming industry has become. It's a killing machine that is out of control and it *must* be stopped. This planet is becoming the number one consumer of meat in the entire solar system and your space brothers and sisters are shaking their heads asking, *what are you doing?* Have you not evolved beyond the primitive need to consume meat yet?"

God is curious, "Why is it that you feel the need to eat flesh? What benefit does it give you? Is it the taste of flesh that you like? Is it the texture? The flavour? The colour? The smell? I don't understand what drives you to burn flesh, eat it and enjoy it? Why would you want to kill and eat another species? For those of you who consume your own species, what would possess you to be cannibals? Yuck!

"I'll tell you what drives you to do this. First someone plants a seed in your mind that creates doubt. The doubt is planted by the incorrect translations of the Bible. Then the seed of doubt turns into a tumorous growth of ugliness that becomes acceptable and sociable, because everyone else in the tribe is doing it, so it *must* be normal. Before long, you grow up not questioning these very things that make you do things that are so abnormal for your instincts. You have had so many generations of conditioning and repetitive programming that you can no longer *see* the truth, or the light where you came from."

The channeller said, "Jesus did not consume meat, contrary to what many of you have been told. If you do enough research you will also find out that Jesus was in fact an Essene, who revered animals and treated them with the utmost respect and saw them as beloved friends, also made by the Creator. The Essenes knew that animals were also here for a purpose and it is not just for food. They have a much higher purpose than that. They have a life to live and a right to be here, just like you. This is why Jesus used to get so upset when he went to towns where livestock was being sold off at the market place and at places of worship.

"Jesus often overturned tables and let the animals go, because he was so disgusted at what humans were doing, that he could not stand it any longer and attempted to intervene. Even back then there were merchants who were making money out of livestock, except on a much smaller scale than what humans are doing today. The industry is now so huge and so grossly run that God can hear the cries of every single animal as it gets killed, through the so called humane methods of slaughter. As mentioned earlier, it doesn't matter *how* you kill something, you are still killing it and its soul gets presented to God in pain and in fear."

God pointed out, "The effort taken to kill a cow in the old days meant you would have to spend 30 minutes to make a spear to kill the cow. You would then have to stab it multiple times to get it to die. Then you would drink its blood and consume the cow, which is such an odd thing to do."

I asked God, "For the record, God, why did you give us cows?"

God roared with laughter, "To eat the grass!"

The Creator explained how everything was created to be in perfect balance. When things are out of balance, he had already created a system that corrects itself.

I asked the Creator, "Why does everything eat everything on this planet?" This is something I had always struggled to conceptualise and understand.

The channeller answered for God and said, "Because one example would be, if he didn't create lions to keep the grass eaters under control, then there would be no grass left on the planet. Every animal in the animal kingdom knows that this is the order of things and they only eat for survival and no other reason. They know they are designed this way and don't get concerned about it, because they have permission and their purpose is known to them on an instinctual level. An animal would not knowingly hurt another animal just for the sake of it, or for the sport of it. They would only kill another animal, purely because they are supposed to in order to live, eat and survive."

My dad asked me, to ask God a question. He asked, "Why is it that humans are not technically part of the food chain of any other animals?"

God responded, "That's easy! Mankind was created to look after the Garden of Eden. They were the designated gardeners and caretakers of the Earth. Mankind was supposed to look after the Earth garden, which included feeding the wildlife and animals and look after all of the trees, plants and habitats. Man wasn't supposed to eat all of the animals and destroy the beautiful creation. This is when mankind started to head in the wrong direction."

Radiation, free radicals and the ozone

God wants to get technical now, "Radioactive particles, or acknowledged particles that have too many charges on them are becoming electrons that are escaping. Electrons that escape become like radical particles. If we create one nucleus, we have one electron regardless of the rest of the anatomy. The scientific community will find that great. The electrons have the ability to escape quite easily and they float around the nucleus of the atom. The more radioactive the atom, the more electrons escape."

God continued, "Overcharged electrons cause something to become radioactive. Counteract it by absorbing the electrons, because the electrons are charges and they need to get sucked up. You need to ionise the air with a blanket of ionised particles, which is called *ionisation.* These are usually connected to the ground, or are floating and connected together. So, what happens in a physical layer is that the radioactive type of particles floating in the air, create two scenarios.

"The first scenario is the one that causes erratical human cell destruction, commonly known as *cancer* and then the other one is free radical electrons that are destructive in the common air and that is because they haven't collided with anything yet. One is *pre* and one is *post.* One is before it hits the body and the other one is floating around radioactive particles in the air. That is the synopsis. The one that hits the body destroys the DNA. It shape shifts the DNA cell into a completely radical cell and because it is so close to the body's own DNA, the body keeps it and it is unknown. Then the body reproduces that cell and is commonly known as the *T cell*, which has been morphed having DNA number 112BT. This is commonly known as the B, cell or the destructive code, which has now been modified. It then causes growth of protein cells to accumulate into one area. It just happens to be the T cells that have been shape shifted from the DNA cells from protein. It is usually the cells that fight free radicals within the bloodstream and this is causing man to not understand and believe that the cause of cancer is free radical cells, or the body invasion that the T cells are currently attacking. But unknown to man, the T cells have been genetically modified by the radiation and destroyed the T cells that are attacking, which then causes complications."

The channeller said, "To this day, man decides to cut the bacteria and the T cells out of the body to cope with the cancer. Once this has spread through different parts of the body, where it can't be cut out due to primary organs created by God and his mighty angels, man cannot fix it.

"The lesson is that God already created these things. The question you are asking is that if you are born into a perfect world and if man is naive and thinks he can transmit radiation and not investigate protection around the radiation to protect animals, humans, or plants, then what? The study is top secret and unknown. If you were to have a plant leaf off a tree that is still growing and you bombard it with radiation and it is not as evolved as a human, then the test can be done on plants to see if the plants go brown when blasted with radiation.

"Ozone was created to *protect* everything from radiation. So, God stops radiation from coming into the planet, by putting ozone layers around the planet, to stop radiation destroying humans, plants and animals. He protects life on Earth with ozone layers, yet man gets radiation and transmits it *within* the lower space like microwaves etc, which should be on the *outside* of the ozone layer. Man transmits radiation within the safe areas, causing harm and also destroying the Creator's ozone layers."

The channeller continued, "Picture this. Put a large ozone ring around something to protect it. The ozone ring gets watered down, or diluted from the gas particles and the most dangerous ones are Freon R3 and R2. It is exactly the same particle as God's ozone, but it has no charges. It pushes the ozone layer away with R3, R2 and maybe R4 and then it waters it down and dilutes it. It not only destroys the safe zone within the ozone, but it creates holes in the ozone. So, creating ozone to fix the layer that is getting destroyed, you would need to generate *plasma particles* of electricity. This generates ozone and then recharges and fixes the holes in the ozone.

"One day the governments will get hold of this information and they *may* do something about it. If you are the governing person, this is not meant to be frightful. Put in layman's terms, God has a life preserver, like a ring and it's on your boat, then you have pulled out a knife and stabbed it on purpose. Then you have no more protection and God has no part in this stupidity. Now you need to come up with a way to fix it, because *you* destroyed it.

"If you create negative energy and charge the atmosphere with it, you will then suck up all the negative radioactive particles. So, if you have in this room, dust which had fallen from space, or if you want to put some humour into it; from someone else's head and they were radioactive and those particles fell into the air around you, they are listed as R2 particles. R=RAD (radioactivity). The negative generator would destroy those particles and would be wanting to attract themselves to the negative generator."

God wants me to add this simple point. He just wants us to plant more trees to purify the oxygen and water and to help rebalance the ecosystem. We take a closer look at atomic particles and grounding methods in the section called *Getting grounded.*

8. THE PURPOSE OF LIFE

Let's get back to playing in the woods, swimming in the rivers, spending time in nature, talking to each other and reconnecting with our Creator.

EVERY single living being that exists is unique and individual. Even though each of us may belong to a particular species, or family group and we may even resemble each other, one thing is certain, we are all different. This is what makes every living breathing entity special in the Universe, because no two individuals, no matter how much in common they have, can have exactly the same opinion, or the same point of view. Firstly, because they are in different bodies and operate from different mind sets, but ultimately because they are looking at their world from their own experience. This is not something to be afraid of, or to disagree with. It is merely something to observe and understand.

What this means in practical terms, is because everyone is different, everyone also has a different point of view, a different perspective and a different set of circumstances that have moulded their belief system. Above all, everyone has a different level of understanding of who they are and where they are on their life's journey.

When I talk about a different level of understanding, what I actually mean is that everyone at any given stage in their life, has different needs being met. Some at the basic level and some at a higher level. Neither is better, or worse, they are just different. For you to have true compassion for another individual, you need to understand and relate to which level of need this person is expressing themselves from. This will help you to be able to communicate with them better. Someone who is poor or unhealthy is not better, or worse than someone who has achieved financial freedom and good health, because everyone is expressing themselves from a different level of perception.

The channeller said, "Once you grasp the concept of attuning yourself to another's state of being, only then can you truly understand what they may be experiencing. To do this you need to literally put yourself in their shoes and think about how they may be feeling and why. It is virtually impossible for you to have a deep understanding of their situation, unless it is studied from their point of view.

"It is essential for you to have your own personality while you are in this life experience, as well as to appreciate that others have their own identity as well."

Just because you are unique and an individual, it doesn't mean you won't feel like being involved in a group, or a tribe, or even a team of some kind. The more you understand yourself, the easier you will adapt to another's environment and be able to respect their belief system.

Everyone deserves the opportunity to express themselves through whatever means is comfortable for them, providing they are not interfering with another's space, comfort, or identity. This statement sounds so simple and if everyone would just do this, the world would be an ideal peaceful place to live and there would be peace on Earth.

Rather than focusing on what everyone else *should* do, ought to do, or could do, you will find it is much more valuable to focus on what makes *you* happy and what makes *you* who you are, instead of worrying about what everybody else is doing.

If other's want to wear radical clothing, dye their hair, show off their piercings and tattoos, act like an extrovert, act like an introvert, talk loud, talk soft, walk backwards, walk sideways, whatever they do that is different from what you do; who are you to say they can or cannot do that? We all still need to respect the laws of the country we reside in and we also need to understand there are obvious restrictions placed on how far we can push our identity boundaries.

None of us should judge each other's individuality, end of story. If everyone looked and acted the same, it would be a boring place to be and everyone would walk around looking like clones or drones.

Individuality is what defines the difference between each of us and we all should *embrace* our differences, instead of wanting everyone to be the same.

The only person that gives you permission to be who you are is *you*. Not your parents, not your partner, not your family, not the system, not your boss, not your workmates, not your friends, not your teachers, or mentors, or anybody else for that matter. The answer is *you*. You choose to be who you are. So stop making excuses for why you can't be yourself.

The channeller reiterated, "All God wants you to do is know and be thyself, your *true* self and not a false self."

The meaning of life

We are all here to learn how to be happy during our time on this planet, without harming anything, or anyone. Once we have learned this, then we need to share and teach this model to others.

Suppression of expression leads to depression and illness, which can manifest into a physical or emotional symptom down the track. Too much suppression can lead to rebellion, push back and resentment. The fact that we all have free will can be dangerous, if it is used destructively and can get you into trouble, if it is used in the wrong way at the wrong time.

If a person's free will is suppressed too much, it can stifle the individual's creative expression, which can lead to manifested illnesses and can also be the *cause* of many different diseases.

God said, "Accept the fact that you cannot change a person who is not willing to change themselves."

You know the old saying, "You can lead a horse to water, but you cannot make it drink." If someone wants change and is a willing participant helping to make that change, then they will more likely to be open to positive suggestions.

It is an individual choice that someone makes when adopting a belief, feeling, or point of view. If you want someone, or something to change, you first need to change the way *you* think and change the way *you* feel and you will find that others' will change when they are ready, if that is the best choice for them.

There is no reason to force your opinion on anyone else and you shouldn't physically make someone act a certain way, or do something without their acceptance. Otherwise you are breaking a very important universal law of interfering with someone else's free will.

There are obviously some exceptions to this rule and we can explore that briefly. If the mental capacity of an individual shows that they are currently not capable of knowing what is right or wrong for them, then you can *guide* them in the right direction. Forcing someone to do anything will cause rebellion and this ends up giving you the opposite reaction to what is desired. You need to offer advice and offer choices. This gives the individual the ability to exercise their free will and make an informed decision. Even if they lack the capacity, you can still teach them how to make decisions and how to select the best choice, based on what the outcome is likely to be.

If you understand project management, it is called *risk mitigation.* Understand the risks associated with the available choices and explain the options that are available, presenting the best possible outcomes. Blindly charging into any activity without thinking it through can present some challenges. The least you can do is walk through each of the choices in your mind and visualise the outcomes. Ask yourself; *are any of these options desirable?*

In my mind, I picture a person who has just climbed to the top of a large mountain and they find themselves face to face with a guru on the mountaintop. When they get there they are so exhausted that they must sit down and rest. When they finally regain their strength, they ask the million dollar question, "Oh guru, what is the meaning of life?"

The guru sits there silently for a minute pondering the question and eventually responds to the seeker, "The meaning of life is... Um well I am not really sure, that is why I am here on this mountaintop, trying to work it out for myself! I am so sorry, but I cannot answer your question."

The new buzz word at the moment is *expert*. What makes someone an expert? Do you define an expert as someone who is well researched, someone who knows what they are talking about, or someone who is actually *experienced* in the topic you want to know about? I would say for me personally, I would prefer to listen to someone who is experienced, not just well researched.

To take this one step further, if you couldn't find an expert in the subject matter you wanted to know more about, who else can you ask?

I'll give you two answers. If the first option fails, then you can use the second option.

1. Ask your own inner guru, or your higher self who is much more knowledgeable than you are.
2. Ask the Creator because he knows everything.

So the meaning of life is very simple. Firstly, don't always trust everything you are told, especially from so called experts. Do your own research to back it up and *trust* your gut instinct to know if the answer sits right with you. Secondly, as an individual you are here to learn from, grow with and reconnect with the Creator, so that when you return home, you will feel like you already know where you are going and you will be well prepared to meet your maker. It makes living here so much better and gives every breath meaning.

Living in this modern age

The pace of this modern world has been moving faster and faster through the ages and it is reaching a critical point in the evolution of technology where it is called the *quickening*. It's like being on a conveyor belt and each time it goes around the circuit, every revolution, or for every year that goes by, the pace gets faster and faster until eventually some just fall off and can't get back on, because everything is moving way too fast to keep up.

Technology changes so quickly, which can make humans flippant and their behaviour changes so quickly to try to adapt to these changes. Those that don't learn to adapt to this pace, or to these technological changes, can get left behind, especially in the workforce. Some prefer to step off the conveyor belt and boycott technology altogether. Then there are those who slowly plod along at their own pace, learning as much as they can, but it still isn't fast enough to keep up with the ever changing modern world. It has nothing to do with age. It has everything to do with *adaptability*.

If the world was to lose power and internet, do you think you could cope without these essential services? Our ancestors did it, they coped just fine. The problem with the quickening is that it creates a massive divide, a technological wedge, between those that can keep up and those that can't.

In our grandparent's generation, the pace of life was so much slower. You had to wait longer to get any real traction on your goals and there was plenty of time to celebrate your wins when they finally came your way. The new generation wants everything right now, instant, pay for it and it arrives in the post and it is even more instant, when it is downloaded for free.

It is a consumer's heaven, but the consumption of *things* is getting out of control and these *things* are beginning to rule our lives and take over our natural world. Then people get bored with these *things* and they just throw them away. It is the disposable generation. The relationship isn't working, so it's easier to just throw it away and get another one. The clothes are out of style now, so I'll just throw them away and get some more. The phone is outdated, so I will go and buy yet another phone and throw the old one away. These *things* are getting thrown away without any thought for those less fortunate, who could benefit from these items. There is no thought given to the fact that *someone* has to pay for it somewhere down the line.

First the consumer pays, then the industry pays and finally the environment pays for these choices. The choices are driven by a selfish *want* and not a need. This mindset is what is driving the mammoth industry of producing *things*. Industry is driven by the demand of the consumer and lots of stuff gets manufactured that is sometimes useful, but definitely not necessary.

Even the language is getting briefer and the older generations' start seeing everything becoming abbreviated and eventually people will be citing the alphabet. What happens when the language changes? It creates a bigger gap between generations and the wisdom and knowledge of the older generations gets lost, because the communication gap grows bigger and bigger. All of these abbreviated words create terrible spellers and mess with generations of appropriate grammar that has been held in such high regard for so long. It is turning the youth of today illiterate. Even though the newer generations may be more technologically advanced, they are not wise. The youth of today are losing the art of real face to face communication. They are losing touch with each other and they are losing touch with reality and real life.

The music industry also has a lot to answer for, especially in the past 10 years. Hardcore rap and gangster music has shamed the English language, brought a new dirty and derogatory language to the forefront, which ultimately sparks a revolution of rebellious youths. I hear the young girls and boys of today reciting word for word, the demonic and negative language that is heavily used in the lyrics of this music. It practically opens a doorway or portal into hell, without them even realising it.

The channeller said, "The music is allowing and attracting demonic energy into their lives and the Devil knows it, because he is behind the music that you get exposed to in the charts. Listen carefully to the lyrics of the Top 40 music charts that play on high rotation on the radio. So much of this music that you are exposed to, fits into the demonic language category. Open your ears to hear, open your mind to see what is happening and open your hearts to receive God and turn away from the demonic influences."

Censor what you can with your children and don't just leave them up to their own devices all the time and wonder why they become so difficult and rebellious. They are being constantly programmed to misbehave with the music they are exposed to and the high rotation movies and television shows that also have the same hidden agenda and underlying message. If you don't believe it, then I want you to watch any one of the latest popular TV shows and count how many times to hear the word hell, or something similar. Sometimes the messages are so subtle you don't even notice them, because you hear these messages so often. In fact, many of you no longer notice these influences anymore. This is called *desensitisation.*

I remember when I was growing up; they used to have censorship rules applied to all television shows, movies and music. They would carefully select the time of day the show, or music would appear on the airwaves. You would never hear the "f" word on any program and back then you would never see a naked body unless it was in a R18+ rated movie.

Nowadays it doesn't matter what time of the day you turn the TV on, you will see naked body parts, or hear bad language. Surf all of the available channels and it is only a matter of time before you find one that crosses the boundaries of censorship. For example, pornography is supposed to be a choice that people can make if they choose to view it. It shouldn't be forced on the unsuspecting viewer and it shouldn't be made so readily available, by accidently clicking on the wrong website, or wrong channel.

Let's talk about parental controls, security settings and restrictions you can apply to the family computer, by blocking certain keyword searches, or known websites from your children. It is a great concept, but your children are much smarter than you give them credit for. They have already superseded your knowledge of the internet, hi-tech devices, computers and mobile phones. How would you even know what they are looking at if you are not supervising your children properly? Do you even care what they are watching and what they are listening to? People become what they are exposed to.

The biggest challenge that the modern world is faced with, is that everything is moving faster and that people have less patience for one another. They show less tolerance and their manners get lost in the wilderness. It ultimately translates to less love for one another and then we treat each other like strangers and eventually like enemies. It becomes easier to treat one another with disrespect and hatred if there are no standards, or boundaries to define our behaviours.

People will stomp on one another to get to the latest toy being released in the store. They will kill each other out of road rage, because of a simple mistake at the traffic lights. It is unpredictable to know if they will lash out and beat a fellow human to death for looking at the wrong person for a little bit too long. It is even worse if the person is intoxicated as well.

When will it end? We need to re-establish the boundaries of acceptable human behaviour, especially when it gets out of control. There is no point arresting the guilty party *after* the fact. We need to combat this behaviour *before* it occurs, by preventing it in the first place. It starts at home and it carries on at school and then continues through to the workplace. Schools and workplaces these days are notorious for harbouring and protecting bullies. The victim becomes the subject of investigation and is further tormented by the untrained teacher, or inexperienced employer who does not know how to handle unruly humans.

Prison officers and police officers know how to handle unruly humans, because they are trained to be aware and identify liars and bullies. Teachers and employers do not have the same exposure, training, or authority to enable them to discipline children, or workers anymore. Teachers and employers were feared in my day and bullies were not tolerated and were dealt with severely. I have witnessed it having a huge impact on the outcome of society within my generation and generations before mine.

With the new generations, the bully, or the offender now have rights which can sometimes outweigh the rights of the victim. Sometimes these rights give the oppressors and bullies freedom to do as they please, without any form of retribution for their behaviour, especially if it is underhanded. There are many laws in place to *supposedly* protect victims of bullying, but these laws aren't worth the paper they are printed on. They are not efficient, they do not support the victim and they don't work.

I have seen it firsthand and defended many victims of bullying in the school environment, in the workplace and in the real world. I have controlled the situation myself, because I am trained to deal with bullies and unruly humans. My techniques are effective and I have no fear with God on my side.

The bully is just a conditioned human robot, who is probably used to watching mum and dad, brothers and sisters, partners and enemies fighting with each other and they are acting out what they have learned from their home environment. They have also become conditioned from what they have exposed themselves to on television, in movies, on the internet and through the music they have been listening to. They bring this rebellious behaviour with them into their school and work environments. The discipline, if any, hasn't worked at home, so they have had years of practise getting away with their misdemeanours. Then later on, when things get out of control, the police and the courts have to intervene and that's when things can get really ugly.

The channeller said, "Technology can be a good thing, if it is used as a tool, but careful consideration should be taken when replacing humans with technology. By implementing practises where technology completely replaces humans, there is the issue of the robot having no conscience behind the trigger of the loaded weapon. Don't give them a reason to push technology in this direction.

"Remember where we all came from. We came from tribes, from families, from communities where we used to barter with one another and ask each other how we were doing. We used to be a community that focused on helping youths cope with life, so they could become stronger and more intelligent adults who could reach their full potential. Sitting a child in front of a television screen, an iPad, or an iPhone all day long is *not* helping, or teaching the child to communicate properly. It is simply instructing them how to act and what to say, according to what they are watching and then acting out what they are emulating. Media advertising is a very powerful hypnotic tool and we need to awake from our slumber and turn it off."

The channeller continued, "Let's get back to playing in the woods, swimming in the rivers, spending time in nature, talking to each other and reconnecting with our Creator. If you need healing, then let nature heal you by taking a walk in the forest. Take some time off work and spend it with your family, slow down your pace, because you need to ask yourself, *where exactly is it that you are rushing to?* It seems as if we, as a population are rushing to the doctor, the hospital, to the chemist to buy pain killers and ultimately rushing to an early grave. Take your time and enjoy your life. Make yourself useful and helpful. Become a part of something bigger and don't just become someone who is self-centred and alone. How much do you really need to live?

"Are you *watching* or, are you *controlling?* There are always two options, so remember that. You can try to control everything and everyone, or you can surrender, live in the moment and go with the flow. You can still be a part of life, without having to run the whole world. That's God's job and he does a mighty fine job of it. You just need to live in the world harmoniously with nature and all of God's creatures. There is no need to hunt everything down, kill it and eat it. How much food do you really need to eat? How much sleep do you really think you need?"

I personally survive on four to five hours of sleep every night and my diet is a pretty simple and wholesome vegetarian diet. I mainly eat a raw and fresh food diet with some vegetables being lightly cooked if I am in the mood.

I don't eat, or drink anything from a packet, if I can help it and ultimately I don't allow anything on my skin, or hair, or inside my body that isn't natural.

Minimalism

Minimalism used to be a term to describe art, fashion and chic urban design and is now fast becoming the new trendy way to live, with minimal belongings. The aim of minimalism is to reduce all of the *stuff*. Reduce the things you buy, consume and hoard and reduce your pile of stuff down to the minimal possible amount of items that you actually use and require to live comfortably with. The concept behind it means that less is more and this is definitely a concept that God himself not only relates to, but advocates.

God told me, "You can't take it with you. You have to leave it here and do you know what happens to over indulgence? If you have too much, you have more to lose when you go and you would have more resentment when it is taken away. If you don't have anything, then you have nothing to lose. Imagine having a whole empire and leaving it to somebody else?"

The channeller said, "The laugh is that God makes you give it back. Yes! The whole lot when you go. So why would you do that in the first place? So when the nasty person takes things from others and accumulates it over a lifetime, when they go, they have to leave it to everybody else."

God intensely stated, "Do you think having too many possessions is not good?" He laughed, "how many knives do you have? How many knives do you need? When you have friends over, they should bring their own knife, fork and plate. This way you wouldn't have to have more possessions than what you really need. How many hands do you have? So I ask again, how many knives do you need? Any more than this and you don't *need* them. How many paintbrushes does your man have?"

I answered sheepishly, "Lots of paintbrushes."

God responded, "He has too many!"

God asked the channeller to continue, "How many seats does God need? One! How many bodies does he need? One! How many armies does God need? None, just him!"

God and I talked at length about the animals that are free to roam the Earth without worrying about possessions. God wants me to explain the story about the gorilla. The gorilla is free to swing through the trees and wander through the forest whenever he wants, unlike the human who has loads of stuff that he has to manage, look after, move and replace. Who is really free? Compare it with the gorilla that just has to worry about where he left his banana, or where he is going get his next banana from. I know that gorillas eat more than just bananas, but just for this example the banana is a good euphemism.

When I was in my early twenties, I sold my small amount of gathered possessions and left New Zealand. At the time, my most prized possession was my stereo system of course, which I had to leave behind and let it go. Once free from possessions, I relocated to live in Australia. I arrived in Australia on a one way ticket, with only one sports bag and $500 cash and that's it!

After a couple of years of living in Australia, again I felt the calling of world travel and embarked on a round the world journey, which would last for a whole year this time. I was living out of a backpack and carrying my newly acquired guitar.

Now I had *two* bags. My guitar brought me more joy than any of the other items in my backpack. The only other item that brought me any real joy was my journal, which I wrote in frequently, to remind me of my experiences. I realised at the end of my one year journey that I had packed twice as much as what I really needed and I could have easily survived on less and been just as happy. Even lugging the extra weight of unnecessary clothing in the backpack had its moments. You realise that you are carrying all of your worldly possessions in one bag, or in my case, one bag and one guitar. That is when you really understand what you actually *need* to survive. Not much. A whole lot less than what you think you need.

Society looks down on a homeless person, but the homeless person is not actually faced with the same type of pressure and stress as a person who has a mortgage and financial responsibilities. Their life is a lot simpler than those who think they have it made. Many humans are only one or two pay cheques away from bankruptcy, or homelessness themselves. This is what many people don't understand.

The channeller received a message from God and shared it, "We are all one race, one people, with one God. We should all look after each other and help each other where we can, because one day that could be us! Never judge a person without knowing the full circumstances that led them to their current situation. You don't know what happened in their life prior to them ending up on the streets, or finding themselves with no job, no money, no home, no food and no support. It usually rolls out in that order too."

During my travels, I went to a lot of third world countries and experienced extreme poverty with my own eyes. I have never looked at the world the same since my travelling experiences and since then, I have had many more trips overseas to explore, discover and help out where I can.

When you see those with nothing and they are still happy, you have to review your own life situation and ask yourself, *do I really need all this stuff, or am I being over indulgent? Are my desires for things causing my own self destruction? Am I working just to house all of my belongings?*

We can take a leaf out of Jesus' book and travel lightly in just the clothes you are wearing. You will need a sturdy pair of sandals, or shoes for your feet and maybe a small blanket, or mat. With an open mind and a heart full of love and joy you can go anywhere.

Material possessions

God said, "The Devil will *tempt* you with all the riches of the world, fame and *things*. If you are tempted by these material riches, you will never be satisfied and never have enough toys. Like a spoilt child, it turns you wicked and rotten. The more material possessions you have, then you have more to worry about. There is always someone out there who wants what you have, so you have to insure and protect your items against theft and destruction."

God laughed and said, "For example, a wise one has two rolls of tape, one for yourself and one for the thief."

God was referencing an incident that happened at my workplace earlier that day, where I had purchased only one roll of specialist tape, which happened to be a pretty fluorescent colour and it was supposed to be used for safety tape on a construction site. When the roll of tape went missing, no one owned up to knowing the whereabouts of this tape and everyone was perplexed about how something so small, but vitally important had gone missing. This particular worker, who God revealed to me, had taken the roll of tape to decorate his daughters mirror at home and hadn't returned it once he had finished with it, for fear of getting caught. So even in this small incident, we can see how material possessions that were not actually owned by the worker, can then become a tempting resource to take, or steal.

If someone can't afford something, they are sometimes wrong to think it is okay to steal it, or they justify to themselves that they have a right to take it. If you multiply that ideology by millions of workers, now you have a massive problem.

God continued, "Imagine this mindset on a much bigger scale. Imagine a banker taking people's money, just because they have access to their bank account details. They can do it if they want to, by charging more interest, just because they can. It is still stealing, even if you get fed a ridiculous story for the reason that interest rates move up and down. They like to call it *inflation*. When in reality money isn't even worth the paper it's printed on. Banks don't really have any money in their vaults like they used to. Their money is all backed with real currency, or commodities like gold, silver and precious metals. The value of the precious metals changes all the time and hard currency, or precious metal is still the foundation of all of the wealth in the world today."

God added, "The whole world lives on credit, which isn't real money anyway and the banks and governments can print as much money as they want to, because they own the printing machines. It's crazy really that you get fed the same story over and over again by each government, but the reality is that money can be printed and *who* is actually keeping track of this money? The bank is. This is the same organisation that is supposed to secure your money. Sounds like a conflict of interest to me."

Almost everything these days is purchased with credit of some type. Credit card spending and even scarier, credit card fraud is at its all time peak right now, with funds being drained every single day all around the world totalling billions of dollars. The irony is that the people who are stealing, or purchasing these items on credit, are doing it to obtain material possessions, to steal wealth, to gain status and to exercise power, or at least that is the *illusion* they are chasing.

Advertising dictates our food, fashion, lifestyle choices, holiday destinations, the cars we drive, the type of house we live in and our entertainment options. None of it is based on true worth, or affordability. You become enslaved to the system as a worker and enslaved to the bank with mortgages and credit loans. This is the reason Jesus used to ask people to denounce their wealth. He was helping them to see they were enslaved by their wealth and by their lifestyle choices. He wasn't saying they weren't allowed to have material possessions. He was reminding them that if you worship your material possessions and live for these things, then how are you able to truly focus your energy on enlightenment, when you are bogged down with all that stuff?

If you have less material possessions, it means you have a lighter lifestyle and you are free to move around when you want to. You can explore the world and spend time doing the things you love doing, instead of being enslaved by your job, to pay for all of your *things* for the rest of your life.

Don't believe the hype. Always use the overnight rule when making a purchase. This helps to curb impulse spending and it can slow down your reaction if you have been brainwashed, or programmed to buy something *now*, when advertising mediums are used. If it sounds too good to be true, then it probably is. This is not looking at the world from a pessimist's perspective, it is removing the rose coloured glasses that can make the purchase seem more attractive than what it really is.

Advertising gurus are so skilled at what they do. You have to have a level of respect for their ability. They are really good at what they do for a living. They are exceptional at pitching the right product, to the right audience, in the right way, at the right time. This is why there is so much money in advertising and why companies have to pay so much to get premium space and airtime for their advertisements.

Remember you cannot take anything with you when you leave this realm. Shed as much junk as you can while you are alive, especially when you are in the cleansing, or purification mood. This is the best frame of mind to be in when you go through all of your belongings.

Ask the following questions as you assess each material possession.

1. Have I ever used it?
2. Have I used it in the past 12 months?
3. Am I likely to use it?
4. Do I need it?
5. Do I want it?
6. Do I like it?
7. Could somebody else get a benefit from using it, if I am not using it?

Once you have been through these questions, then you can sort your stuff, or belongings into three distinct piles based on the following criteria.

1. **KEEP** > if you answered yes to three or more questions.
2. **THROW** > if you answered no to all 7 questions.
3. **DONATE** > if you said no to most of the questions, but answered yes to question 7.

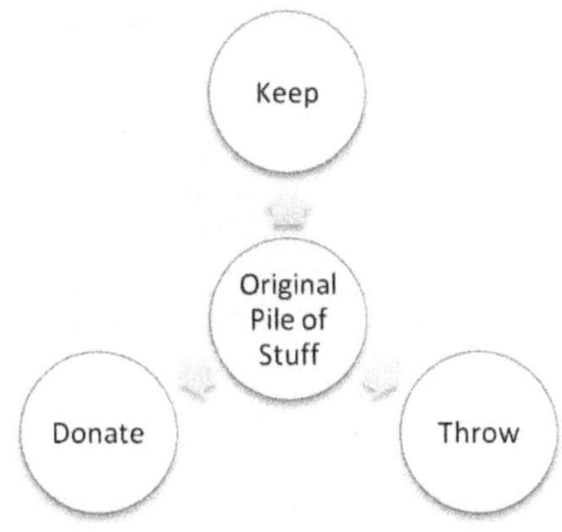

The money system

God said, "You don't need to surround yourself with rich people to get paid. Caesar made it so that you had to buy things from another person, like bread. So you could pay money to buy the bread, which in turn meant that you could pay Caesar for his bread through tax. But those who seek will discover that the people who make the money system up are quite useless and they have gotten their money from scams.

"Barter is the best way. Barter doesn't need false hope, or false people. If you converted everyone to a currency price like paper (money notes), which is the cheapest material on the planet, then the murderer can now put a price on it. He can hide himself amongst it and the false people can hide in it too."

God continued, "We need to make up another whole industry that is not necessary, just as a counteractive measure. You might be the scribe, the plumber, the baker, the craftsman and the money system is now a cloak. You're not interested in a person's qualifications; you're interested in *how much* someone is going to charge. Money was created because bad people who wanted bad things couldn't get them using the old barter system, so they created the money system."

God talks about money from a whole different perspective.

I asked God the question, "If I want to charge money for my spiritual services, is that acceptable?"

God responded, "If you want to teach people about God and if this is the money system you are using, then you need to charge money so you can buy your bread."

God added, "The money system is fake and money doesn't really exist. Ask the President or Prime Minister what the process is for making withdrawals over $50,000. Even if it is your own money, you will see how the system is working to monitor your transactions. You will be asked what the money is for. Not that it is any of their business. The bank doesn't actually have the money in the vault and they may have to ask another bank for its cash supply, or else the bank may have to print it if your withdrawal is a large sum of money.

"Trading is not real. It is a fake non-existent trillion dollar industry that sucks people into spending money."

God continued, "Money can cause people to die old and bitter in their personal quest to obtain financial wealth. They can become too focused on their career, which can cause a long line of failed relationships as a result of being too career oriented. The bottom line is all you need money for is your funeral and your burial if you can afford a plot, because you can't take any of it with you and you end up working your whole life, just to hand it over to someone else."

God wants us to know that the creator of something makes the most money. The role of those in power should be that you don't sit in a chair and rule other people. You sit in a chair and *help* people. They are just like us, here to explore and experience this life as a living being. To be alive on this planet is a privilege and to know this information is also a privilege.

Money will *not* buy you happiness, but love will.

How do you make money in this world? You need to know how to wheel and deal. How do you multiply yourself? Have multiple streams of income.

Confirmation

Everyone wants *confirmation* that what they are doing is correct. We all want to know that we are on the *right* track. If we are on the wrong track, we can correct our path. Right from when we are born, we need validation. We sense there is *something* out there, that *could* be supernatural, but we want validation. We want to see the proof of its existence and we want confirmation that everything is going to be okay.

You can't get rock solid proof from the other side, or from the spirit world, because the connection is etheric and mental. It exists in a realm different to ours. It is another world where we go to in the afterlife. What level you get out of the elevator at, is what stage of your spiritual development you are at when death occurs.

Don't over think everything. Pause and take a moment to clarify what is already all around you, inside of you, in outer space and everywhere. How can you measure that? It's gigantic. That's the biggest word I could find to describe how immense God is.

Yet God's touch is so personal, you can feel him in your heart and deep within your soul. You can *feel* the divine connection and the bond between you and your heavenly Father who art in Heaven.

Just for a moment, I want you to stop doing whatever it is that you are doing and close your eyes for around 5 minutes. Everyone can spare 5 minutes a day, it's not much to ask for. During these precious 5 minutes, I want you to devote your time to just focusing on God (whatever your perception of God is). Think only about the Creator of this entire Universe and tune into the *God Channel.* Spend time thinking about how perfect creation is and acknowledge that it was intelligently designed and realise it is not some random accident.

There are so many wondrous creations throughout the Universe and when you see one of these wonders that really blows your mind, you think to yourself, *wow that is incredible!* That's when you have that immense gratitude feeling and really enjoy being alive.

Planet Earth is a great place to live. We should cherish it and love Mother Earth and treat her like we would treat our own family. Mother Earth provides for all of us with her bountiful minerals, plants and fruits.

Think about how smart God was to create the world around us, which was capable of supporting multitudes of life forms and creations, so all of us can co-exist harmoniously.

God wants validation too. He doesn't ask for anything else other than acknowledgment and devotion. Both are free. When you acknowledge the presence of the Divine, it will gravitate towards you. The universal laws are working in harmony with you. If you deny the existence of a Creator, then that sends out a detraction signal and then God is not attracted to you. God is repelled away.

Starting from today, do this very short 5 minute meditation each day and focus all of your attention on one purpose for the whole time. Focus your mind on the Divine life force energy. Breathe in the presence of God and he will be with you. *Feel* the energy of God inside your cells and all around you at the same time. The ethereal Kingdom in Heaven is *real* and you only need to imagine how beautiful it is and it will far surpass that vision.

If you want someone to do something for you, when the task has been completed, you need to validate their work. *Acknowledge* what a good job they've done and be grateful for everything.

If you don't believe yet, you can pretend until you start to feel something. If you are attempting to make genuine contact with God through the channel of love and light, he will visit you. He will make his presence known. You need to remain open to the signals or signs that God gives you. We miss so many spiritual signals we get given throughout the day, because we are so busy, being busy. We get sidetracked with work and dramas in our lives and we sometimes forget we can have a whole cast of new friends when we connect to the spirit world.

Bring the divine feminine and the masculine principles into your life to create the perfect balance within. Acknowledge the existence of something greater than yourself. Learn to dissolve your ego. These are vitally important steps that are required to start opening up the pathway to your new life.

Validation and confirmation will manifest for you personally in the form of people, opportunities and experiences. Embrace these experiences and get reconnected with your true life's purpose.

9. SCIENCE

God was and still is the most amazing alchemist that has ever existed.

GOD laughs about science all the time, because the scientists just don't quite get it. They think they are really smart and have everything figured out, but they overcomplicate the explanations and then spend a lifetime trying to support their believed theory.

Through the channeller God said, "The problem with most scientists is they spend their entire lifetime trying to *disprove* the existence of God, trying to prove that everything is just matter and mathematics. They are right. It is matter and mathematics, but *designed intelligently* with true formulas by the Supreme Being, who loves mathematics and loves creation. Just because everything in the Universe is baffling to humans, doesn't mean there isn't a logical explanation for the existence of everything."

God knows that the scientific community will eventually come around in a full circle and through their mission to disprove God, they will realise they cannot disprove the existence of the Creator. One day they will work it out and will link everything back to the creation theory. They will realise the Universe and everything in it, *is* intelligently designed and that the Universe was *not* made from a big bang. Yes it is evolving continuously; not from some series of random events, but from an infinitely wise and intelligent being who allowed us to exist inside his beautiful creation.

God wants us to see everything in more of a multidimensional way, like the way he sees things.

- Inner dimensions (inside an object).
- Outer dimensions (outside an object).
- Perspective (around an object).
- Proportional dimensional (the size of an object).
- Unproportional dimensional (infinitely small, like holding an atom in your hand).

God said, "Matter is proportional to your calibration. If you use your visual or touch abilities, you can *see,* or *feel* the matter. If you measure, or assess matter using sound, you can tell if it is small, or big, depending on the distance the object is away from you."

God wants us to know that calibrating time and space is just using distance in comparison to size. It is testing how big it is and how close, or far away it is. By using our multiple senses to identify what it is and where it is, we can calibrate things.

The channeller said, "Oh my God! There are 37 memory spots in the brain that man has found. Shouldn't it be mapped by now?

"If every scientist could ask God just one question each, we would have the answers for everything."

The channeller added, "The smallest molecule known to man is so small, that it could pass through my body right now and I wouldn't even notice it. These molecules pass through everything and they are even in space and they travel at the speed of light. These things go out and receive the information for God and send it back to him and that is how he is all knowing and can be everywhere at once in his *energetic* form, *not* his physical form.

"God can present himself in many forms. He can be with you energetically, intellectually, on a molecular or cellular level, by being inside of you, or passing through you by physically representing himself as a being and by spiritually representing himself through signs and symbols of everyday life."

The channeller told me that if I am talking to scientists, I should rephrase from using the term *him* and call God an *it,* because *it* doesn't personalise the forms that God exists in. This would help scientists grasp the concepts better. Scientists should look for God in everything on a molecular level and also look for where he resides in the physical form, in outer space. If you look hard enough you will find God, because the God particle is in everything in existence.

Alchemy

The channeller said, "God was and still is the most amazing alchemist that has ever existed. He can take nothing and make something, or he can make anything with anything. He loves antimony. This is one of his favourite elements for making things."

God told me that ultimately I will become a chemist, because it is something I am really interested in. He wants me to learn the chain reactions from chemical bonding. This involves learning how to join chemicals like an alchemist. In doing this I will *see* creation.

God said, "Do experiments with chemistry and document the results to find cures for diseases. If you've got a chemical bond and it has a radical leg that comes off, why do you get the free radical legs, or arms that go out to anywhere? The free radical legs and arms want to join onto something else. And why is that? Because it's a bond when it forms a circle."

God continued, "When it's open, the chain reaction wants to join to something and it will keep going until it bonds to something. If it attaches to a plant, it turns into fungi. If it attaches to a human, it becomes a virus. When it's a circle it becomes happy. This is the difference between bonds and chains. A bond is a wee hole and it is a chain before it forms a bond."

God joked around with me and said, "I looked over there and I saw a *wee hole!*"

Space travel

The channeller told me, "The Seven Sisters watch down upon the Universe of mankind to make sure he never leaves beyond the Seven Sisters, or they will become corrupt both astrally and in their spacecraft. They shall never see beyond the Seven Sisters, because mankind must be on a Godly level before getting beyond this point.

"God will allow space travel and will allow mankind to explore the Universe in manmade, or alien made spacecrafts, but not without watching mankind, to ensure he never becomes in a position to destroy everything."

For those of you who have always felt like you are being watched by someone, or something, you are! Nothing can be kept hidden from God, because God knows all. He knows the plans before you even put them in writing, or start actioning them. If you are considering a mission that is destructive and want to take that destruction out into space, it will be stopped, because you are not allowed to destroy space. It does not belong to humans. It belongs to all the beings in the Universe of which the human race are a part of.

There is a wider community of souls that exist in the galactic neighbourhood and one day you may be able to meet your space brothers and sisters, either out there in space, or right here on Planet Earth.

Nibiru, Planet X and the dwarf star

I like to watch YouTube to entertain myself from time to time, because I don't like watching TV and the hot topic which you can't seem to escape from at the moment, is this new planet they have found approaching our Solar System. It caught my attention many years ago and it made me curious, so I started talking to God about it.

God said, "Check celestial objects against the size of the moon. If it is smaller than the moon it will have minimal effect on the tides. If the dwarf star is larger than the moon, it will have a more significant effect on the tides and may even double the size of the tides, which could cause problems. This is a good measure of how to see if danger is present."

God already knows that right now on Earth, there is an ultrasonic defence system, which is a type of top secret advanced weapon technology. He also knows that if you shoot an ultrasonic sound wave at a large wave, or tsunami, it diminishes. God knows everything and who is doing what. I keep reminding you, that you can't hide from the Creator.

God observes all and knows everything; after all he created us and is in us. God never discourages research and prefers that we evolve into beings that are using our technology for *life preservation* not destruction.

The channeller said, "Planet X, Nibiru or 216 passes the Earth every 3600 years or so. Lucifer said he was going to destroy the planet using Nibiru and God has pushed away such hell with his mighty hand and court this time around. By doing this, God saved Nibiru and let it live for another 12,000 years. Peace is on this planet, there is all life on this planet. Nibiru lives in 3000 years of death and life cycles and all must seed itself until then; whereas Earth lives on a 360 day cycle. Why is it 360 days? Because it moves in a 360 degree circle and everything is cyclical and that is why the calendars don't make sense, because the cycles are out of sync."

The channeller and God had a conversation and then the channeller translated to me, "According to God, Nibiru is around three times bigger than Earth and both planets were created at the same time. Nibiru is the centre of the solar system, *not* the Sun and because of its elliptical orbit path, it swings past the Earth every 3600 years and every major catastrophe happens in 3600 year cycles."

The channeller added, "God wants to know why more people aren't praying to him to *save* the planet. He hardly ever hears from anyone on Earth asking to save Planet Earth. He wants to know what the obsession with destruction is. Have you all thought about coming together and praying for change, positive change and moving towards positive change instead of worrying about what *might* happen and focusing on the fear alternative? If enough people prove to God the planet is worth saving, he will listen to you and help to influence change."

Time travel

God stated, "Time travel is not what it seems. Time travel is actually pressure and the more pressure, the slower something is and the longer it lasts. The lighter something is, the faster it goes and the quicker it dies."

God continued, "When looking at mathematics it is actually vertical. Zero (0) is in front of you and it all starts from 0. If 0 to 10 is vertical that would be upwards. The past is left and the future is right. Convert Neuro Linguistic Programming (NLP) into mathematics. You see the problem is between chemistry, neuroscience, NLP and philosophy. You need to turn it into numbers. You don't need to look left, or right, you need to count backwards in years.

"Work things out in a triangle, equal sides and equal corners. The centre is always the weakest point. You need to imagine there is more than one dimension.

"Time travel is simply making a "T" symbol with your hands in the shape of a cross, which equals past, present, heaven and hell. What is the trinity? What is the time travel trinity?

"If you want to time travel, you need to place your hand in the sector that you want to visit during your dream. Up high is to want to dream of Heaven and if you want to visit your relatives that have passed, you need to want to dream of your past to be able to visit them. You don't have to physically travel anywhere to time travel if you don't want to. You can travel backwards and forwards in time as much as you want. You need to *feel* that your body has dissolved, but you are still connected by a soul cord.

"If you are looking forwards and today is right in front of you, then if you are looking at the past where are you looking? On a scale of 1 to 10 where did you go? That is how you calibrate where the past and future is for you, or for another person. You need to establish that first."

God said, "Looking more into time travel, you need to look left, right, up and down. If you want to find out something, like next week's Gold Lotto numbers, then you need to know *where* to go to find it. What direction is up? If the past is left, is the future right? That means up and down is time travel. So look up and to the right, to get to the future to ask the question for the future. Then bring yourself back to the present, by going backwards and left to return. You don't need to go anywhere. You can time travel from right here and right now."

The channeller added, "If you were expecting God to give you the magic formula to travel through time, he will not. It is too dangerous and fragmented. Instead of spending billions of dollars working out how to travel to other time periods, why not spend the money on the time you are living in right now and get that right, before travelling to other times with the aim of influencing the beings of that time period. You can time travel using that beautiful big brain you have, that doesn't get fully used at the moment."

10. FAMILY

We are all part of the same family and are all equal in God's eyes.

GOD said, "In the beginning there was one and from that, one became two. From two became many. There was no wrong or right for the beareth of a child and also immaculate conception."

Family can be viewed in many ways. There is the birth family, which is the family you are primarily born into. There is also the adopted family, who step in to look after you when your birth parents are unable, incapable, or unwilling to be a parent. In any of these scenarios, this is usually the family who you have actually *chosen* to share these experiences with during this incarnation. This principle also applies to extended family that you or other members of your family marry into.

There is also the family lineage from where your bloodlines came from a long time ago. They are called your *ancestors*, which can go back for many generations and can be traced through your family tree.

In addition to your earthly family, there is also a type of mystical family with whom you really belong to. This is the family who you are connected with on a soul level. They are called your *soul family*. Because your soul family is connected on a soul level, you have all chosen to come back again and again, to be supportive to each other and to help each other with the earthly lessons, that each of you have chosen to experience. Some of these lessons can be challenging and some of them can be fun.

Then there is the bigger picture. We are all also part of the universal family. A family which every soul in existence belongs to. We are all a part of God's family. We are all children of God and he is our Father in Heaven.

God the Creator is not just *our* Father in Heaven; he is also the Father of every creature in existence. He is the Creator of *everything* and is responsible for *everything*. He can delegate his responsibilities to other family members to help him, but the buck stops with him. Every alien that exists in the Universe also shares God with us, any creature that has a soul, belongs to the God family. It is too complicated to talk about beings, clones, or creatures created without a soul in a small book like this. We can save that conversation for another time.

Heaven is just another higher vibratory realm, or dimension that we can't really see, or touch, during our earthly experience, because it is vibrating on a frequency that is much higher than what we are capable of vibrating at normally. We may see it if we dream of it. We may see it in our mind's eye with practise and meditation and we may even experience it, if we come close to death during our lifetime.

Heaven is reserved for after you have finished your earthly incarnation. Preparing for Heaven during your life is something you could start to work on, if you desire to visit Heaven when your time on this plane of existence ends.

God wants us to realise that there is no difference between all of us, regardless of bloodlines, history, race, skin colour, DNA, or our purist vanity when it comes to breeding. We are all part of the same family and are all equal in God's eyes. We are given the same lessons and are ultimately faced with the same challenges at some stage during our lives.

We have all lived many lives and each one of us has experienced lives of luxury, lives of extreme poverty and also lived lives in many different races and cultures. It is what we learn on a soul level that allows us to retain these lessons throughout our many lives. When we become non-judgemental and have total forgiveness for our brothers and sisters of the Universe; that is when we really start truly living in the light of God.

Our vibration changes and we vibrate at a higher frequency. This higher frequency attracts experiences that may teach us advanced lessons, or will cause us to be in the right place at the right time to teach or learn from others.

There is no point getting upset at your family, because if you look closely at who these people are in your life, they are all there for a reason. I know it's hard to accept, but all of you have *chosen* your parents, your family, your siblings, your children and your partners, even if the relationships prove to be challenging for you. Each and every one of them is in your life for a reason, just as you are in theirs for a reason.

We are all so intrinsically linked. At the same time, we are unaware of what it all means and sometimes we get frustrated when our family doesn't behave in the way we would like them to. We look for ways to *convert* our family members, or *persuade* them to our way of thinking all the time, because we always think we know best. The reasons that you have been brought together to experience certain things can be good, bad and ugly and may also be karmically linked from previous lifetimes, where we have unfinished lessons to complete with each other.

Once you grasp the concept of soul families and karmic connections, then everything that previously didn't make sense starts to make more sense. We will talk about past lives and reincarnation a bit further on in the book. As ugly as things like abuse, violence, infidelity and even murder are concerned; they too can all be linked back to previous encounters with one another perhaps in another life. It can really mess with your head if you are in the middle of dealing with an unpleasant experience, or trying to deal with others who have experienced trauma.

Keep an open mind about *why* things happen and how they can be better understood. If you are prepared to dig really deep into the cause and effect of these events, your whole soul life span will open up before you and you will start to see the whole picture much clearer.

A good example of this connection with family members, is when you are the child in the family and you feel like you have to look after one, or both of your parents, because they seem to be increasingly incapable of looking after themselves. I am not talking about elderly parents, that is different. I am talking about *childish* parents. This can often be linked to one of your current parents still holding onto the connection, or relationship from the most recent incarnation, when they relied on you as their parent in the last life. It can be confusing when you are brought together again in this life, but they haven't been able to break free from that karmic pattern.

Another possible scenario is that your parent lived a hard life and raised you through hard times in the last life and you may have come to an agreement on a soul level, that it would be your turn to look after your parent in this life.

Here's the catch! Many of us make fabulous promises to each other when we are with the soul family in between lives, or on the other side. Sometimes we may even have to wait a long time to reincarnate, so we can be in sync with certain soul family members, or be in sync with past life lovers during this life. We get here to Earth and then get selfish and forget our soul promise to one another and run off and do something else. Guess what? You've got to come back and do it all again, until you fulfill your life's purpose and promises.

There is no point running away from your family, because they will be the main source of your lessons in life, especially in the early years of family life. You may not always love, or even like your family members, just like they say, "You can choose your friends, but you can't choose your relatives."

Sometimes your life lessons may have nothing to do with having a perfect family, or having a close relationship with your family members. What is important is that you work through these issues that are presented to you, in a non biased and non judgmental way, so that you can learn your lessons from one another and move on with a clean slate.

What happens before we are born?

I asked God, "Where are we before we are conceived?"

The channeller answered for God, "You are all like tadpole souls swimming around endlessly in the soul pool, which is surrounding God. The souls are in a waiting zone, like little tadpoles swimming around, waiting to be reincarnated. They enjoy swimming around with each other in their own soul groups. Promises are made in the soul pool, before you enter another incarnation. You're not supposed to question if it is your time, or your turn. You just keep swimming around until it is time to incarnate into a body again, with your soul group, to fulfil your purpose. Sometimes it can feel a bit like a soul prison, or soul farm, because you cannot get out, or go anywhere else for the moment."

The channeller continued, "All of the souls swimming around in the soul group are eager to have another incarnation and when it is time, the soul comes down to Earth to incarnate. When you are in the soul pool, you are in an energy form and not in a physical form, so there is no body to feed and look after. Then when you come to Earth, many events happen throughout your life. You can get sidetracked from your original promise, or plan by the demons, whose purpose is to lead you away from your path and put obstacles in your way to stop you from achieving your mission."

God needs us to understand the terms; *soul power, solo power and solar power.*

The channeller said, "Ultimately each soul faces God alone and enters and leaves the world alone. Even though you get to reconnect with other members of your soul group, which are also incarnating with you, you are on a *solo* journey of learning throughout your life, until it is time to meet your maker and explain yourself. You have to explain what you have done, what you have learned, what you didn't do that you were supposed to do and reappear to God without sin. If you happen to have sinned while living in your incarnation, you need to confess and expose your sins to God wholeheartedly, because if you deny them, hide them, or lie about them, you will be shunned by God.

"You cannot enter Heaven, or progress on a soul level, if you take your sins with you, or arrive in Heaven with a heavy heart."

A close friend once confided in me about the multiple abortions she has had during her young lifetime. She really wanted children, but the circumstances surrounding each pregnancy and the timing of each of the pregnancies was inconvenient for her. As a result, she is still not a mother. She didn't have that much of a conscience about ending the life of her unborn children and in the case of this friend; she was getting pregnant every single year. I kept telling her that it was a sign that the soul was obviously keen to come into this life through her. My friend kept terminating their opportunity and told me, "I'm not ready they can wait!" The real questions she should have asked herself were; *will I ever be ready and is there ever a right time?*

The channeller explained, "Remember that even if you abort your unborn baby, the soul still hangs around you, because it wants to come through into this life with you as its mother. The soul may have a prior agreement with you and you promised that you would bring the soul into this life experience through you.

"Women can get caught up in their careers, bad relationships, their travels, their adventures and all types of messy distractions and totally forget what promises they have made to these little souls. You see it's not just all about you. You might like to think you are in full control of everything, but you are also a conduit for other things to happen as well. You need to open yourselves to the divine plan and become a part of it and not the sole conductor of it. We are one and we are many."

I also have another older friend who also made the decision to abort her unborn child for her own personal reasons. Some choose this option, because they already had a full family and then had what they termed an *accidental pregnancy,* a long time after the other children were born. Some have aborted, because of fears of having a child with *issues, or birth defects*, mainly because of their age when they fell pregnant. In this case, my friend was in her late forties. She chose what she thought would be the least painful course of action.

Whatever their choices may be, each person has to justify their actions to themselves first, before they can go through with it. Then they have to justify their actions to God. If they have a very good reason, then I am sure God would like to hear it.

I am not in a position to judge the decisions made by these friends, but I will make a point that many of you probably haven't even considered. Falling pregnant is actually quite difficult, contrary to what people think. There are so many things that have to be in *alignment* for a soul to come through a physical body when it does.

Women traditionally have souls assigned to them, because they are naturally designed to be the bearer of children. If you have chosen to come into this current life experience as a woman, many times it is to bring children into the world, among other reasons.

Having a child is such a special blessing and every pregnancy is a gift from God. It is a sign that you are capable of producing children and also a sign that some little soul wants to be with you in this lifetime. How special is that? Think about that for a moment. Out of all the women on the planet, that soul chose *you* to be its future mother, wow what a privilege! It is never supposed to be a burden. It is only meant to be a *blessing* to have a family.

If only people realised just how difficult it is to conceive and then carry the child to full term, they wouldn't even consider terminating such a miracle. If you don't think you can keep the child, or don't feel capable of raising the child, you are better to adopt the child rather than to terminate a pregnancy. By opting to terminate the pregnancy, it ends the opportunity for that soul to come through you and live on this planet. They may be forced to wait another whole generation, before they are allowed to incarnate again. That is a long time to wait swimming around in the soul pool. Do you think that you would like to be left behind and abandoned on the other side? As a soul, you would be a little bit annoyed, because you had been promised the opportunity in this life with a particular soul family.

There are plenty of people out there who don't have children and who cannot biologically have children, who would be only too happy to raise the child as one of their own. At the end of the day it doesn't really matter who the birth mother or father is. The real love is provided through the parents that actually *raise* and *care* for the child, even if they are not related by blood. This is often the case with stepchildren, when the child's birth parents remarry, or form another relationship after a separation. This can have great benefits for the child, to have two sets of parents and they may even gain some additional siblings along the journey, who become half-brothers and half-sisters, or stepbrothers and stepsisters.

Blended families are commonplace these days compared to 50 years ago and there is no longer a stigma attached with divorce and separation.

Stepchildren will need to work through some separation anxiety issues and they will have to learn to accept the new stepparent in their life whether they like them or not, just as the new stepparent must make an effort to step into the role of a parent for the stepchild.

When you form a relationship with a person who has children to a previous marriage, or relationship, there is an implied form of acceptance of the fact that their children come as part of the package. This may mean new and additional responsibilities for the new partner entering the relationship. You can't just choose the parent and offload their children. It doesn't work like that and this is an unacceptable way of thinking. Embrace the children that come with the parent and realise you may have a life lesson, or a soul purpose to be with them in this life. They could very well be a part of your soul family.

Adopted children are also not usually related to the parents or the family members by blood and once again it doesn't really matter, because the souls of the adopted family and the soul of the birth child could still be linked and related on a soul family level. They may have chosen this method to come through during this incarnation. Adopted children are given so much love, because the adopted parents have consciously chosen to raise the child and have sought the opportunity to adopt a child. They often have to wait many years before they can adopt.

Sadly, adopted children deep down, will sometimes need to work through issues of abandonment throughout their life. Remember we all *choose* which lessons we are going to experience and this is a good example of one of the lessons we choose to learn in this lifetime.

Being born a woman myself, I struggle to understand why you wouldn't see the gift of pregnancy as an absolute miracle every single time. I have had my own personal struggle with trying to conceive. Wanting to bring a child through into this life has recently been my highest priority, but I may fall into the category of infertile women.

Souls can get scared to come into this incarnation, because of past traumatic circumstances in past lives and they may hold onto memories of what happened last time. It may have been a tragic ending for everyone in their past life, or they may have struggled because of losing a child, sibling, or parent during their last life. This can make a soul reluctant to come back too soon and it may mean remaining childless for one lifetime to take a break. This life may not be the right time for the soul to come back through. It doesn't mean you will *never* have children. You would have had plenty of opportunities in previous lives and will also have plenty of opportunities in future lives to be a parent.

God spoke to the channeller and said, "For the souls that do want to come back through, they jump at any chance they can to get through the gates and experience a life on Earth. There is literally a lineup of souls wanting to come through all the time. If the soul has selected a particular birth mother and/or father, then they will encourage and influence them to make babies. The souls that are hanging around you that want to come through, will try anything to get you in the mood. They can make you feel frisky, steer you in the direction of the perfect mate, put you in romantic situations where you find it difficult to resist the temptation of love making and even influence you in ways you wouldn't even think of. Their energy is directed at coming through to live a life on this planet and *you* are the vehicle for them to do that."

Every life is *sacred*, especially when you understand that scientifically getting pregnant is already hard enough. So when you actually do fall pregnant with a healthy child, it truly is a miracle, a blessing and a gift from God that you should cherish.

If you think too much about waiting for the *right* time, or waiting until you have enough money in the bank, or waiting until you have travelled the world, you might end up leaving planning for a family too late. There is nothing to fear about raising children. All you have to think about is the mothers who raise their children in extreme poverty and in extreme conditions and still have healthy, happy and bright children. They still manage to feed, clothe and carry their baby with them everywhere they go and all is well in their world. There is no such thing as the perfect time.

The channeller said, "God doesn't care that much what you have done wrong, he wants to save you and he wants you to know that when you are going down to the depths of Hell. He wants you to know where you are on the way down. If you are being reborn again then you will feel like you are *descending* into another life. As soon as you are going down, you are being reborn. God programs us so we know when we descend, or are going down; we are given another chance to be enlightened by God."

Tribal ancestors

We are all linked to a tribe of some description, somewhere in history. Ultimately we are all linked to only a few tribes anyway and only a couple of bloodlines, but without getting too technical, let's take a look at our tribal ancestors. We all have a type of cellular memory that learns traits and skills from our tribal ancestors. We learn habits, both good and bad and we strengthen the DNA with every new generation, if there are no modifications to the original DNA. What happens is, the less we use these learned skills, we start to forget how to do certain things; like using hunting, foraging and survival techniques, if we no longer have the need to live in the wilderness.

Civilisation has enabled us to advance in so many ways, but at the same time has made us go backwards in so many other ways.

My warrior spirit guide, who looks after me on the other side, is a long lost relative whom I have never met in the flesh. I had no prior knowledge of him before he came through to visit me during a channelling session. He looks after me and another couple of my family members on my mother's side and also a couple of family members on the other side of the family. He has visited me many times with the permission of the Creator and he has been allowed to come through physically and spend time doing things with me. My warrior guide is strong, proud and a little bit scary, but very protective.

This is the type of spirit you want to protect you on the other side, a warrior spirit. He talks to me in a very ancient Māori language that I don't understand, because my Māori language skills are very limited at best. I am not sure that even the native speaking Māori would understand his dialect. He comes from the old tribes long before Captain Cook arrived in New Zealand and he tells me lots of wonderful historic stories about life in my home country. He tells me all about my ancestors in New Zealand before it was invaded.

Even though we do not speak the same language, we have a *knowing*, a *belonging* and a very familiar soul family feeling when we speak. When I ask my Māori warrior spirit to talk to me in English, some of the translations get a bit messy, because the channeller does not speak Māori and struggles with the translations of this difficult language.

In future channelling sessions, my warrior guide is going to visit me and give me lessons about the Māori tribal way, so I can share it with all of you in another book. This book will give you more in depth information about the history of New Zealand and the Māori people, but for now I will let you know a few things that are relevant to the subject of family.

He introduced himself as Amoko and starts the story. Amoko told me that I have at total of 147 spirits in my lineage that are with me, watching me and especially me, because I have had a long line of history. I have had to ask the spirits and angels for help after the last World War, because there was an upheaval in our lineage. My warrior spirit wants me to remember that I have adapted to the colonisation and have lost many of the Māori ways since then. My warrior spirit lived in New Zealand around 400 years ago and comes from my Nana's side of the family. His name was Amoko and he comes from the lineage of Whe'lohao.

They used to call God the "*Great Spirit in the Sky*," but in Māori and in those days, he said it translates to *Hoka Paka* (God of all gods). He lived in an area called Plymouth which he thinks has a different name now.

Amoko said, "Around 4000 years ago, everyone comes from the chief, from one family and the chief was living at the top of the North Island. Before that, they came from Syria nearer Iraq, but they originally came from near the Nile and lived near the phiaro. They always lived close to the river ways, because they came from a long line of boat builders. The carvings exist and that will be the proof. They have never looked for Māori carvings in that part of the world before. The same tā moko patterns on the face of the people, will also be a giveaway of the ancestry that came from somewhere else in the world. Once you start looking you will start to realise where they expanded from and to."

Amoko continued, "*Everyone* is from the royal blood. The ultimate Creator is the royal bloodline and he is the Creator of all of us and we can't discriminate. The head warrior in those days could overthrow the head chief, by showing him his skills and also show that he was a warrior when making decisions. The chief would step down if someone wiser was able to prove himself.

"Remember the Israelites were driven from their land due to it being too crazy and they decided to be refugees in that period of time. No one would take them in, because they were refugees. They were good star navigators and they had a compass which they used. It was a bowl with a string in it, with a magnetic rock. They used goat gut, or strong twine that was flexible, usually some animal's intestine.

"The tribe name was the Mitatines. Look and you'll see paintings and pictures and you'll see the Māori. There was a New Zealand Māori book of herbs and potions with knowledge in it that they brought with them, which has been hidden by the medical profession. It linked the plants and practises to that part of the world."

Amoko explained, "The stories of cannibalism might have come in when they were in the boats travelling vast distances with no food, or if they came across a massacre they would take advantage. If they had no food, they would *maybe* eat humans for food. It was also known back then, that a head injury turns a person into a cannibal. It was well researched and documented. There were raving lunatics around then too, feared killers. These people can be directly linked to brain injuries during that time, because so many wars were fought by hand to hand combat. If you survived the battle, you may have taken a massive hit to the head causing a head injury."

Amoko continued, "Tamika was one of the first Māori people and they brought with them, a lot of ancient wisdom from their previous home. There was a Chief Papa back in the early settling days of the Māori in New Zealand. The chiefs were full of spiritual power and prestige. The pā, the people and the village were all united as one back then. The Polynesians including the Māori knew of the Egyptians.

"If you were trading something, you were allowed to go near the Pharaoh and if you weren't, then you were a slave. If you were trading they would let you go away and come back."

Amoko told me about the moon and said, "The Māori people used to be aware of the moon face. If the moon was upside down, it meant it was unhappy and you would never get married on an upside down moon. When the moon was dark, your enemy was sleeping, but when the moon was full, your enemy was awake. When the moon was at half, they were getting ready for battle.

"Most slayings used to happen in the night time. It was traditional to sleep during the day and be fully awake during the night, so you could be prepared for battle. On a full moon you are wide awake, prepared in full warrior mode. The white man came and disturbed the Māori, because they used to sleep during the day and were active at night. The white man thought the Māori were a little bit lazy, because they would be resting all the time, but their body clock was on the reverse cycle from the white man.

Amoko mentioned, "The Bowerbird was a popular songbird of the Māori, they loved the Bowerbird."

Amoko then started to tell me about my great grandmother. He said, "She was living at the top of the South Island of New Zealand and when she was just a baby, white man came along and slayed a bunch of Māori people. They always wanted the chief's head and they were obsessed with collecting these heads. The Māori were clever and they used to just call up one of the younger tribe members to get their head cut off. This caused the younger ones to get mokos, so they looked like a chief.

"The chief used to watch how animals would kill each other and then use that method and get the warriors to kill using the same method. There wasn't that much conflict within tribes, because it was easy to bribe another village with food. The pā was always up high on the mount, so they could see their enemy approaching."

Amoko continued, "The Māori listens to all. They haven't learned what is good and bad, they listened to both sides. The teacher from the great pyramids always said, 'You use both sides to stay alive. You use anything to keep your village alive and whatever the Gods offer; use it to stay alive.' The chief keeps the village alive, by using all means and that is how they overcame white man to some degree, but they were lost when it came to their own kind. They would fight over birds, or fish, or kill someone for their food. In the translation it got lost, the love feeling.

"When the white man came along, if the Māori had too much love they would have been slaughtered. The Australian Aborigines had way too much spiritual love, which meant they were easy to overcome."

Amoko said, "God claimed the first Māori and the first Aborigine of Australia. He claimed the first group of the 12 apostles and he has created them in the spirit and it is their job to look after their own kind. God has appointed them not to be reborn on this planet, but to be reborn on a new planet and they have all been reborn again.

"The difference between the Aborigine and the Māori women was that it was really hot in Australia, because the Aborigine women used to have no top on. They used to carry a basket and wear a woven grass skirt. They would have made a shoulder piece and they had another pleat on the top to stop their breasts from being burnt.

"In New Zealand the women used to wear a full coat made from animal skin and birds. When they were collecting things, the longer the clothing was, you could use the skirt, or garment to carry things by rolling it up. Their clothing doubled as a carry basket and in Australia, the Aboriginal women had to use baskets, because it would have been too hot to wear a skirt."

I used to observe my mother using her skirt as an apron and as a basket, by using this gathering technique when collecting green pea pods from the veggie garden in our backyard. She would sit down with her collection of pea pods, split them open and take the peas out of the pod and fill up her bowl. When the bowl was full, mum could eat a whole handful of peas at a time and she enjoyed them so much when they were freshly picked. She loved to eat them raw and freshly picked.

Amoko said, "The women used to carry a short spike, like a sharp stick, in both Australia and New Zealand. They used to put the stick in their hair. It was not uncommon to have four or five of those sharp sticks at any given time. They used them for digging, stabbing and putting their hair in a bun. The women in New Zealand very rarely wore their hair in a bun, because it was cold. They usually wore their hair down and they would also sometimes wear the stick in their nose.

"Tree bark was used for periods and especially in New Zealand. The paper bark was popular with leaves, or moss being used as pads. The stone was inserted if you were the mistress of a chief and the priest used to have jurisdiction over the women.

"Later in the family line, when Captain Cook arrived in New Zealand, it is well known that he conned the savages, by convincing them that an endless supply of food and weapons, would be a gracious bargain for their women and land. They persuaded the Māori people with food, or shot them dead."

Amoko told me, "If you want to contact your tribal ancestors and your relatives, you can place your hand face down on the ground and move your hand from side to side and knowing that all of the souls have touched the ground, you will become more psychic and be able to talk to them. Look at the stars and see. Look for the blank bits between the stars.

"The ancestors were scared of the dark, because evil happens in the dark and the evil one is in the dark. Most wars and slayings occurred in the dark and that is why the holy one says that you are the light that followed my footsteps. When there is a lighted soul, even in the dark, there is no darkness.

"All of the dead relatives now realise that the whole mission was to find love. Love in colour, love the things you do and love the things you see. Look at things that make you feel love and happiness and you will have love and light. They want you to think about that when you drive away from work and that will make you happy. Everything can be turned into happiness and unhappy people can be made happy, by telling them these words."

The channeller said, "Amoko wants the current day politicians to restore what they have taken from Mother Earth and wants them to plant two million trees, to counteract all of the uranium mines that exist."

I have so much more to share with you about my Māori ancestry and their way of life and if you are interested in learning more about this topic, you will need to read the book that I will write about them in the future.

Sex and procreation

This whole section is quoted word for word, directly from God to the channeller.

The channeller said, "There is nothing taboo about sex! It needs to be discussed, people need to be educated and it needs to be explained.

"It is a natural thing to do and the Creator made us to function this way. If everyone walked around like robots there would be no offspring.

"It is okay to feel horny. It is designed for procreation, just as it is okay not to feel horny, because you may not be in the mood.

"Moses never wrote any tablets about sex. Man made the subject taboo, *not* God. When something is taboo, man naturally wants to do what is taboo, or forbidden. The church made it forbidden for a priest not to have sex, *not* God!

"If you have 12 holy men who were teaching the **Word of God** and they were not allowed to have sex, how would they have any offspring to teach future generations?

"This concept is incorrect. It is the Devil's way, *not* Gods. God's opposition made it taboo to have or talk about sex, to make man fear it, loathe it, hide it and made him feel like he was being naughty and should be ashamed.

"Sex is natural and we are designed to do it!

"Pheromones attract the opposite sex and an indicator of sexual attraction for a woman, is the increase in natural body lubrication in the vaginal canal.

"If the male is too rough with the female during sexual intercourse, he may tear the delicate skin surrounding the vaginal opening and leave the female in agony, or ill health.

"On the subject of orgasms, we all have a built in mechanism that does not allow us to orgasm in situations of danger for our life. An orgasm is a sensory overload where all faculties are turned on and are working at maximum levels. Ancient tribal doctors said that we each have a safety mechanism, an emergency program that is built in. It is intertwined with procreation and linked to getting pregnant for a woman. It is a built in program and the program states that if there's enough love to overcome the shortcomings of procreation, the female will reproduce. Love is the key and not necessarily money, or other survival tools.

"Viagra for a man works in the way where he needs some type of stimulus, or stimulant to have sex. When a man takes Viagra, it relaxes him enough to think he is more superior and everything is okay to have success. It eliminates the unnecessary worry that can contribute to a man not *feeling* in the mood for sex. Worry is a big challenge for a man to overcome and the woman needs to assure the man, by whatever method she can, that everything is okay. Quite simple really!"

Attracting a male mate

The channeller said, "You must love yourself first. Having passion is a major part of the attraction process and also wanting to be with another. God wants you all to understand the true meaning of *passion* which is *love.* Love is wanting to be with another, as opposed to the hate of another."

Even though so many of you may have been through bad or hurtful experiences in love, you have to *forgive*, before you can *forget.* We get tripped up by trying to *forget* these experiences, without actually going through the *forgiveness* part of the process. Without forgiving others for their part in the experience, we cannot move on to the part where we can forget them.

Everyone must work at relighting the spark in their relationships. It is sometimes assumed that all you need to do is meet the true love of your life, fall in love and then you can get lazy and just expect that it will remain passionate, without actually doing anything to keep the spark alive.

The channeller continued, "Women and men have not advanced that much in thousands of years. Man is still the caveman who likes to hunt and bring home the trophy and the woman is still the planner and gatherer who likes to make a happy home. Women would gather berries and other foods as a backup plan, just in case the man was unable to come home with food. If the woman didn't have this covered, the family could starve in tough times.

"Women need to know how to *tame* the caveman and truly understand the caveman within. Man simply tries to impress a woman, but overdoes the effort and sometimes, he gets it all wrong. It doesn't matter how sophisticated a man likes to think he might be, his primal caveman needs to be brought out in the man."

Advice to women from a woman

Nagging a man endlessly with really high expectations will have him heading for the cave in no time. If you are too critical, or humiliate him too much, he may never come out of his cave again.

There are many things a woman can do to arouse her caveman.

- When the discussion becomes too heated, simply change the subject.
- Don't get hung up about little things, it's not worth it.
- What are you feeling about the relationship right now?
- Are you feeling horny? Timid? Shy? Bold? Adventurous?
- What do *you* want to do?
- Take control and do what it is that *you* want to do, but remember to *include* your man.
- Learn that there is no need to upset people unnecessarily.
- Discover how *not* to misinterpret what people are saying to you.
- Learn how to be sexy, sensual and erotic without being seedy.
- You don't have to wait for the man to initiate love making, he may still be hiding in his cave and you may have to coax him out.

- Men are a lot more fragile than they lead you to believe, they need love and they need to feel wanted just like women do.

God said, "For procreation to occur, a caveman must first be aroused. This is a biological fact not a hypothetical example. Women are good at arousing men. Why waste your time and energy on doing exactly the opposite if you love your caveman? It just doesn't make any sense?

"In the caveman days, the woman would be most impressed with the best hunter from the tribe. She would ask, 'Which one of you has brought back the most food?' That's the one the woman wants to go home with. They didn't have to be the sexiest man, or the wealthiest man in the tribe. She was looking for the most *capable* man.

"Everything has sped up in our world these days. Mankind used to be hunters and used to spend long hours hunting, waiting and pouncing on prey. This involved a lot of thinking and patience. Nowadays everyone is impatient and is in a big hurry to go nowhere. They don't have time for contemplation, thinking, or strategic planning anymore. They launch into their activities without thinking about things and make lots of mistakes."

God continued, "You're supposed to run the possible scenarios through your mind first and work out all the possible combinations, until you come up with the most successful scenario, *before* you carry out the plan. This technique eliminates failure. In those days it was essential, so that you not only survived, but so you also didn't go hungry."

God added, "In business, women need to dominate the man in order for him to listen. Sometimes she needs to use her stilettos and a stick like a teacher, to get his attention. In reality, the woman is really in her normal work clothes with a laser pointer, but she needs to role play, as if she was in the teacher role, to get him to listen.

"As a woman, you need to imagine you are wearing dominatrix clothing and exude absolute confidence and take full control! This is not supposed to be deviant, or underhanded, but bold and confident instead. Women have been in a suppressed sexual state for too long and this makes women feel dirty, when they should be feeling good about themselves."

I have noticed that society can judge confident and sensual women and see them like cougars and man-eaters, instead of allowing them to embrace their sexuality. We should be teaching women to enjoy their bodies.

The channeller said, "Shame is manmade, *not* Godmade and God made us in his image. He wants us to love each other, enjoy ourselves and procreate. That is what we are designed for. The orgasm is a celebration of our body, our genitalia and of our ability to enjoy sex and is not supposed to be a forbidden secret to be hidden away."

Simple tips a woman can use to attract the attention of a man

- Walk past and wiggle your butt.
- Try different styles of walking to see which one is more effective at gaining attention.
- What colours arouse men?
- Survey men and get their opinion of which colours they like the most.
- Different cultures are aroused by different things, so keep in theme with your man's culture, to prevent behaviour that is too radical for their environment.
- Ask men at an appropriate time, not only what colours, but also what *features* turn them on about a woman.
- Work out how to mesmerise a man! They are easily distracted and using this technique is a good sign they are interested in you.
- Women need to know *how* to communicate to a man. How do you say the first word?
- What's the first thing to say to a man or a group, when you have a crowd, or a man's attention? Be prepared, you only need to have two, or three things prepared.
- Women need to see the relationship from both the woman's and man's perspective, to truly understand the caveman and cavewoman within.
- Don't take yourself too seriously. Men love women that are fun and easy going. There is nothing more like a mood killer, than a stuffy or controlling woman.

Attracting a female mate

Women can be a lot more complicated and trickier to navigate than men, due to their complex endocrine system, hormones, body chemistry and all of the variables that can affect a woman's moods. For these reasons, I do feel sorry for men when they attempt to get it right with a woman.

It is not fair to give away the secrets of attracting a male mate, without explaining that both sexes want to feel something that is not coming from them.

For a man, the thought of attracting a female mate, keeping their current mate happy, or fantasizing about a female mate he doesn't have, is in his mind most of the time. His brain is made chemically different than a female, for a very good reason.

If men and women were both the same in emotions, functionality and reasoning, they would probably really dislike each other and ultimately not procreate. This may even lead to depopulation, sterilization, or even extinction to some degree.

The channeller shared a little secret from God with me and please don't get upset, because it didn't come from me.

The channeller said, "Tell them that God created man first. Yes this is true, man you were the first born or created, however you want to view it. When God and his team of co-creators created woman, they were the mark 2 version of the human being. The woman was created to fit perfectly with a man and to accompany man, because he was lonely in the Garden of Eden."

The channeller continued, "Every inventor knows that when you create something the second time around, you get better at it and you eliminate any unwanted biological defects, as well as enhancing the good things from the first version. I guess you could say that the female human was created as a biologically superior model to the male human, yet built to co-exist harmoniously with her male mate. This has been and can be scientifically proven in its simplest form, by using just one example. This can be demonstrated by a woman's ability to multi-task effectively, when men are designed to concentrate intensely on only one thing at a time. Each of their skill sets were specifically designed to be complimentary to one another. Man and woman are made for each other on this planet."

God said humbly, "This information was never meant to make a man feel inferior; it should actually have the opposite effect. How lucky is a man to have females in his life that can help him with so many things at the same time, as well as being his mother, carer, sister, daughter, relative, companion, friend or lover? Women are not supposed to be *subservient* to a man and a man is not supposed to *dominate* a woman. They were made for each other, to give each other unconditional companionship and in the case of procreation, they were made to go forth and multiply."

The channeller said, "God loves man and woman equally and all of you are God's children, even if you never procreate at all. God doesn't care if we choose a mate, or not, because he learns from all of us. He learns from the smart ones, the dumb ones, the perfect ones, the imperfect ones, the teachers and the students, the wicked and the righteous. Everyone is showing God new things every day."

The channeller continued, "Now that you can hopefully see women from a different perspective, it may give you a better understanding of why she gets frustrated so easily and can come across as temperamental, or impatient at times. She cannot turn off her multi-tasking ability, unless she is *distracted* by pheromones, or attraction. The role of a man when he is attracting a female mate is exactly this, to distract her away from her multitude of thoughts."

God said, "Women wear clothes to make themselves feel good and feel sexy. Women turn themselves on. Men like to look at women who are turned on. To feel sexy is to know you're alive."

God continued, "In the animal kingdom, the male birds are always more extravagant looking and prettier than the female birds, because it is the male that has to attract the attention of the female to be able to find a potential mate. The male then has to display his *capability* to the female to be considered worthy of mating. Humans are a part of the animal kingdom and it is no different in the world of humans.

"In the old days, the dress routine of the male was always far more extravagant than the female. The males would wear war paint and costumes to make themselves appear attractive to the female and they would dance around just like the birds and other animals, to attract the female's attention. If the female liked what she saw, she would allow the male to mate with her. If she didn't like the males attempt to woo her, she would show her disinterest by leaving, or turning away from her suitor."

The key word is *capability*. A male just needs to show he is first and foremost capable, before he even gets a look into a female's world. Once he passes gate number one, he then needs to prove to the female, that he is considered attractive to his female mate. That does not mean he has to be beautiful, built like a gymnast, or be well groomed. First he has to *smell good.* His pheromones will dictate if his smell is attractive to the female mate, just like in the animal kingdom and this can all be down to timing. This includes the timing of the meeting, timing of the month for the female and the mood that each mate is in when the meeting occurs. You could theoretically meet your soul mate, or an exceptional mate, but if the timing is all wrong, then it may not happen at that moment in time.

If it is meant to be on a soul level, then you will encounter each other again for sure. If the pheromones are not attractive to the female, she will be put off by his smell and that is very hard to overcome. Good looks and money have nothing on pheromones!

Females are subconsciously looking for a male partner to mate with and have children with. So subconsciously, all males are being sized up for cleanliness, genetics and intellect, as well as their capacity to provide for the family, which ultimately means being *capable.* A female will accept useful skills and forego wealth if the smell, genetics and intellectual capacity are all there.

If breeding is not a consideration for either the male, or the female, then the rules will change slightly and there are less stage gates to pass through to get your potential female mate to concede. If a long term relationship is not even on the cards, then the stage gates are wide open and the only thing a man has to be armed with, are great smelling pheromones and they could get lucky!

Having a successful relationship

When it comes to relationships, God is always really good at comparing the nature of animals with the nature of humans, because essentially humans are part of the animal kingdom and as a result, share similar core values.

Women will usually make most of the planned decisions in a relationship, or will at least have the last say, but due to the new pressures of society and cultural pressures in some parts of the world, this doesn't always happen. Women can be *suppressed* and this can set the wheels in motion for a whole series of events to occur.

Growing up in New Zealand, I learned all I needed to know about running a household from observation and through trial and error. This starts from a young age in households in New Zealand and we all learn how to look after ourselves, through chores and duties assigned to us from our parents. Later on, we are driven by a desire to move out and seek our own place in the big wide world.

New Zealanders as a nation of people are amongst the most well travelled people in the world. Being born female in New Zealand was a blessing on so many levels and females were generally never treated as anything less than our male counterparts. One thing that helped this equality mindset was the fact that New Zealand became the first self governing country in the world, where all women had the right to vote.

A super confident and capable woman can be viewed as a threat by other male cultures around the world. If a New Zealand woman discovers she is with a male chauvinist, she will usually run for the hills. She could not cope with having her independence stifled, after being liberated for so long.

Nowadays, women all over the world are coming into their own power and learning to do things their male equivalent previously had full dominion over. They no longer fear being single, as an alternative to being in an unequal relationship. The female now prefers to wait until the *right* man comes along, with full acceptance of her independence and her own desires.

The channeller said, "Men and women in God's eyes are viewed and treated equally, so everyone should adopt the same view all around the world, because there is no difference between us, from an equality perspective. Where men and women differ other than anatomically, is emotionally and mentally. Women by virtue of nature are designed to multitask, performing many tasks at once, with a child on the hip, to get through all the chores required in a day.

In tribal times, women always had to have a backup plan and could be very thrifty at times, if and when the man failed to bring a meal home. For survival she could always dig into her store where she stashed the fruits, berries and plants from the forest. These days the reserve of food in the cupboard in case of emergencies has become baked beans, noodles, rice, nuts, grains and dried fruit. The concept however is still the same."

Men are amazing providers. They are hard working, energetic, strong, meticulous and deep thinkers. They love to be needed and appreciated. Their wants and needs are very basic. They want a good meal in their belly, somewhere to put their feet up when they want to relax, a cave to hide in when they need it, rewards for their good deeds and a warm bosom to lay their head on, when they want some loving and affection. If they get to raise a family as well, it is a bonus. If not, they tend to push on anyway and see what other adventures come along.

Women have expectations that far outweigh what some men can actually provide. Women want men to be like women, so they can natter all night long. They want men to be considerate, kind, emotionally available, affectionate and committed, not to mention a man who loves to go shopping and out for a romantic dinner.

Okay seriously, let's pull out the list with the other 100 requirements. Yes women have a checklist and it can be a little bit too ridiculous sometimes and then they wonder why they can't find the *perfect* man. So many women can't even recognise when they already have the perfect man, because they are too busy measuring him up against *Mr. Non Existent.*

My oldest sister once gave me some exceptional advice when I was much younger and she said to me, "Never sleep with anyone you wouldn't consider a potential father for your children."

Those words stuck in my mind for most of my youth and this advice put me off getting involved in any sexual relationships, with anyone who I couldn't see as having the potential to be a father, both genetically and energetically. I pass this advice onto any friends of child bearing age, just to remind them and to get them to consider the possibility of pregnancy, especially if they are stuck in a relationship with someone they are not happy with.

A friend once told me about her marriage problems and I was very attentive listening to the full story without judgement and heard it through to the end. When she got to the end of the story, I was waiting for the terrible reason why she wasn't happy with her husband, but it was never said. I offered a few suggestions, but at that stage she wasn't willing to negotiate, so we talked about other things to fill in the time.

It seems the common complaint from women is that they don't feel like their male partner does enough for them, or he is not a very good planner and is unorganised. If men were good planners and super organised and could do everything themselves, then they wouldn't need women, except for procreation. The same goes for men who want women to be able to do absolutely everything; they would just make themselves redundant.

Later that night, I was at home and it was just before bedtime. I was visited by the God energy again. I didn't have any questions for him at the time, but I thought just out of interest, I should ask for godly advice regarding my friend's marriage. I figured the advice could be useful and it could also be applied to many different marriages.

God laughs at our relationship problems, because in the big scheme of things, to him they are not important, but to humans they can be the very thing that makes, or breaks us. I didn't need to explain the situation to him, because he already knows the full story and it is brought to the forefront of our conversation, by simply using one person's name and then God is right there. Once I throw a person's name into the conversation, God already knows everything about that person and their entire family history from the beginning to the end.

God paused and said, "Next time you see her I want you tell her this story I am going to share with you. It will make sense to her, but it still won't make her change her mind. This is the story about the squirrel and his nuts. Men are like squirrels. The sole purpose of the squirrel is to scurry around the forest looking for nuts. Then when he gets the nuts, he has to hide them somewhere to protect them and ensure he has a stockpile for the upcoming winter. He also has to protect them from other male squirrels, who are out there doing exactly the same thing.

"The squirrel is very clever at finding nuts and has to have a good memory, to remember where he stored all his nuts. If this is all a squirrel is required to do then he is highly successful at being a male squirrel.

"Let's change the word squirrel to *man* and nuts to his *money*. So as you can see, if the man is earning a good income, being responsible with his money and ensuring nobody else can steal the money, he is highly successful at being a man. He is successful at being a provider. What else did you want him to do?"

So when I returned to have coffee with my friend the following week, I shared the story of the squirrel and the nuts. She revealed to me that during their last marriage counselling session, that is exactly what her man said to the marriage counsellor during their session.

He said, "I earn good money, I am being a good provider, I am faithful, I am loyal and I love my wife more than any other woman on the planet. What else did you want me to do?"

This was confirmation that God was totally right and that he wants us to see that men just want to be needed and appreciated. No more, no less. Women stop complicating things!

Women can set up the impossible benchmark for a man to keep up with. They keep raising the bar and he never quite reaches it. Women want men to take the lead and dominate them in bed, but then want them to be gentle and sweet at all other times. This confuses a man, because his brain operates on a different set of circuits to a woman.

Women's expectations are like her ability to multitask, she wants everything to be right and the poor man can't keep up. He has been set up for failure and as a result fails. Women are asking a manly man to be as sensitive as a gay man. What exactly is it that she wants? A man is one, or the other. He is usually either manly, or sensitive, but not both.

Gay men are generally more in touch with their feminine side and their emotions than manly men, but gay men don't usually like to get romantically involved with women, because they prefer men.

I asked my friend again, "What exactly is it that you want?"

The keys to a successful relationship are really simple. For a start, both genders should have fewer expectations from each other, give lots of praise when each other gets it right and they should both know what the guidelines are. Who is responsible for doing what? Mutually agree on the allocated tasks and get on with it. Review it periodically and make changes where needed. Give timeframes if tasks are not being performed and apply the performance management criteria to your relationships.

God said, "Marriages and partnerships are not supposed to be our *only* relationship on the planet. You should maintain your friendships providing they are supportive and loving. Pursue your own interests as well as sharing some common interests and realise you are not joined at the hip. You are both running on one path each. When the two paths come together, you form the two paths heading in the same direction. When children get introduced into the equation, the roads branch off and become based on the addition of the children, which run parallel to you for a period of time, then they grow up and leave the nest. They too are on their own path."

The channeller said, "Marriage in the eyes of God is for the purpose of coming together, sharing common interests, respecting each other enough to let each other have their own life, as well as one shared with you. Be faithful and committed to each other as long as you are together. If you can no longer remain faithful and committed to one another, then you cannot call it a marriage.

"God wants you to moderate the content you expose yourself to in the media, television and in the movies, because he wants you to understand the drama that is portrayed to you in these mediums is *not real.* You are being sold a lie. Don't model your life from an idealistic media industry, which teaches you about worshipping false idols."

The channeller continued, "Marriages and partnerships are about working together and all parties should be contributing towards the goals of the family equally. You can't measure equality financially, because of the way the world works. The man usually gets paid more than the woman, even if they are doing the same job, but you can measure it according to effort and commitment. These are the things that are important in a marriage. Look out for each other, look after your loved ones when they are not well and make an effort to be available for each other when you are needed. The main difference between partnerships and friendships is the absence of the romantic element, but the commitment and effort should still be the same in both cases."

The channeller added, "It is not only healthy, but important to have some form of companionship, as it helps to balance the human soul and teaches individuals to share experiences and how to love each other. It also shows them how to constructively spend time with other beings. Without the psychological needs of an individual being met, people may become susceptible to loneliness, boredom, depression and social anxiety. Having others in our life to think and care about also makes us less selfish and more open to change."

If we only have ourselves for company, we have no measuring stick to compare ourselves to anyone else. This can make an individual very one track minded, inflexible and unwilling to change.

Relationships are at the core of every well balanced person and in order to be able to love someone else correctly, we need to ensure we first have self love, as well as a sense of being able to contribute to something, or someone. This is not something that is taught in school, in the workplace and sometimes it isn't even taught in our homes.

Society does not encourage self love, it is sometimes frowned upon and subservience is encouraged over self confidence. Without self love, we are unable to comprehend how to fulfil our own emotional needs and more importantly, it can hinder our ability to understand the complex emotional needs of others.

Self love and self respect is essential for having successful and fruitful relationships. Once you understand self love and self respect, you can have fulfilling relationships, such as happy friendships, intimate partnerships and family relationships. Additional benefits include companionship and being able to become a part of something bigger than yourself. Without self love, people can become withdrawn, moody, resentful, selfish and even mean.

It is also important to note that self love is not self importance, vanity, or arrogance and do not be fooled by those who may try to convince you that they are better than you. They are just there to distract you from finding your own true inner strength.

We are all created equal in the eyes of God and we all have the opportunity to live our life to the fullest, no matter what your personal circumstances are. There is a delicate balance between being confident and being conceited and finding that perfect balance, is the key to your spiritual and social development.

Tips for a successful relationship

- Respect that relationships take time to build, as does a solid foundation in any home.
- Appreciate what you already have, including the good and bad times you have both been through.
- All of your experiences together make up your collective memories, so learn to forgive your loved ones for their shortcomings and encourage the correct behaviour by modelling it yourself.
- If you need to communicate something to your loved ones, then do it with kindness and understanding.
- We cannot change another person just because we want to. We can only change our *view* of that person. This is what it means to truly love someone for better, or worse, because life is bound to have ups and downs, those are guaranteed.
- Accept your loved ones for all of their good qualities and don't focus on the bad qualities. Nobody is perfect.
- Simply avoiding challenges will not solve any problems, because every challenge presents us with a lesson to be learned.
- How you deal with the challenges that are thrown your way, is the key to mastering any successful relationship.

Gender identity

The channeller said, "From God the Creator's perspective and talking about procreation and reproduction, man was given a male sexual organ to match a female sexual organ and this is mostly amusing to God. Both sexual organs were created for the creation of a baby, no more and no less. This is mostly amusing to God. If anyone is waiting for the next comment he is going to say, he won't because it is already imprinted in every human."

God stated, "It is a restriction being gay, because they are not in balance with the correct harmony and have a weakness in their sacral chakra."

The channeller continued, "God does not say it is forbidden to be gay, nor does he say it is acceptable, he simply chooses not to discuss it and remains neutral, because it deviates from his procreation plans for humanity.

"God did not send anyone to increase mans ability to have free will. Mankind could have more free will if they wanted it. Imagine being in balance and in perfect harmony and having more balance, more understanding and being *more* of yourself. It's not about being more to the left, or more to right (gay either way). Are you giving more or taking more? As long as you are in balance with whatever you are doing, it doesn't matter."

Love is however, a completely different topic which is also discussed in this book, but is explained separately to sex and procreation. You can have sex without love and love without sex. It doesn't make it right, or wrong. It simply just is. Love is something that can be experienced between either gender, without boundaries and God does not restrict sharing love between genders, species, or spirits.

Someone who is gay is not having a gender identity issue; they just prefer to have a sexual relationship with someone of the same gender. This does not include experimental, or one off trendy occurrences of same sex experiments. I am talking about someone who actually *identifies* as being gay, lesbian, or homosexual. Attraction can be the one thing that confuses people about which sex they prefer, because humans have difficulty defining the difference between a *love* feeling and a *sexual attraction* feeling.

A person's sexual orientation can blur the line between what the general populace, or society deems as being normal and also how they themselves define being normal. It seems to be the hot topic on every agenda right now. Everyone has an opinion on gay marriage.

Some people like to deliberately live on the fringe and enjoy the controversy and the attention it creates, more than the actual relationship itself. Some people follow trends based on media brainwashing and assume because it is normalised in a social way, that it makes it more accepted. Then there are those who are genuinely gay, who live their life this way and will continue to live this way for the rest of their life, due to their sexual preference and their sexual desires. With a relatively small population fitting into any of these categories, it is still a minority of the world's population.

If the world's population was to become totally gay, then there would be a serious imbalance and it would have a huge impact on the population growth, resulting in population decline. If it was allowed to remain out of control and go unchecked, the human species would die out. Can you see this point from the Creator's perspective now? He is not socially judging. He just sees the overall picture and works out if it is feasible for the whole species, *not* just the minority.

Within the last 100 years, there have been many dramatic influences that have changed the demographics of the lesbian, gay, bisexual and transgender (LGBT) communities and how they use their sexuality to *define* their persona. Homosexuality still existed 100 years ago, but it wasn't as prevalent as what it is today. It was more underground, secretive and hidden, because it was considered more deviant. In some cultures it was forbidden and even outlawed.

These days, they are out and proud and the LGBT communities are considered more acceptable now, than ever before. Transgender as a term, never really existed when I was growing up. It wasn't discussed and it was relatively unknown. Back then, medical technology wasn't readily available to support, or assist with the transgender transition.

Now it is available in so many countries. Some of the direct transgender influences these days include; mainstream media, social media, the pornography industry, the sex industry, hormonal imbalances from xenoestrogens in the food and food packaging and a general energetic and spiritual imbalance in our everyday society.

Other factors that can influence a person's sexual desires, or factors that can skew a person's sexual attraction; is being exposed to unnatural environments, where the gender ratios are out of balance. Then gender availability, becomes a determining factor. For example, gay behaviour is likely to be more prevalent in correctional institutions, prisons, the sex industry, sex tourism, same gender schooling facilities, same gender hostels, armed forces, sporting clubs and industries that have an unbalanced ratio of males to females.

A person, who is bisexual, could be considered to be more confused than a gay person and this is where it can get more complicated, because they can't choose *which* gender they prefer and switch between genders depending on their sexual attraction.

There are also other trendy terms being used by celebrities, to normalise bisexuality. Terms such as; pansexual, omnisexual, or sexually fluid are becoming more common and are appearing everywhere in the mainstream media. All of these new terms allow the demonstrator of that term, to be sexually attracted to whomever they want, whether they identify with a LGBT community, or not. They are actually *driven* by their *sexual desire* and not by their social desire.

I want to highlight the word *desire* at this point, to clarify why this word has the biggest influence on a person to choose their own sexual identity. Desire is such a powerful emotion and humans can confuse their desire with appreciation, idolising, worshipping and fantasy. All of which are based within the ego of oneself and not within the higher spiritual goal of a human being. A human's continuous pursuit for desire and their insatiable appetite for sex and the need to fulfil their sexual desires can overshadow their pursuit for spiritual enlightenment. Only when the goal of sexual fulfillment is either achieved, or denied, can people focus on their spiritual growth and enlightenment instead.

The channeller said, "God views males and females for the purpose of procreation only. He is really baffled why humans have created their own confusion and created their own sexual identity crisis all by themselves. It has nothing to do with the way they were created; it has to do with the way they have *become*.

"The only reason sexual identity becomes a crisis, is because it is not considered *natural* in the eyes of God. God is more interested in us learning to love one another, regardless of our sexual preference and what the social norms are. The primary purpose of all animals is to *love each other* and respect each other, regardless of people's individual preferences and choices."

Where it gets tricky in the whole scheme of things, is when the human rights of a person who identifies as belonging to the LGBT community, is unfairly judged, targeted, or disadvantaged, as a result of their proclaimed sexual identity.

If a person doesn't actually have a sexual preference for either gender, or doesn't have an attraction to either gender, they are considered *asexual*. They may even prefer to pleasure themselves, or abstain instead of engaging in sexual activity with someone else. This includes people who are not motivated, or driven by their sexual desires. They may have no interest in sex, because they may be pursuing a life of abstinence, celibacy and purity. They may even have a very low or non-existent libido. This also includes people who prefer to have a romantic relationship, without the need to pursue it sexually. They *may* make an exception, if their partner wants to have children, or to fulfil a one off sexual desire, but generally they identify as not really being interested in sex.

Some religions, spiritual practises, athletes, specialised sports people and even martial arts specialists may practise periods of abstinence prior to, during, or following an important event, but can resume normal sexual activity afterwards.

To add another layer of gender variation complexity, there are some people born as both genders, known as *intersex*, agendered, or hermaphrodites. Of all the gender variations amongst all of the known species, hermaphrodites make up around 1% of the natural population, so therefore it can't be ruled out as unnatural. Unfortunately for those born with both sets of sexual organs, their family, society and possibly the medical industry, can put unnecessary pressure on them to become *one* sex, or the other. Sometimes the person born with both sets of sexual organs can become confused if they have to sacrifice, or choose one gender over the other. If they were born that way, we should consider how we can support them as their natural form of creation, instead of making them into something they don't want to be. Maybe they wanted to be both and that is what they asked for.

From the viewpoint of the Creator, where the real gender identity issue arises, is when someone who is born a male or female wants to be the opposite gender to what they were born. They go through the complicated process of having gender reassignment surgery to become the opposite gender than they were born, but their sexual attraction can still be for the same gender.

The channeller said, "God just wants to remind you that you asked to come here for an incarnation and you asked to come here specifically as a male, or a female. That was part of the deal. You can't change your mind once you have entered this life and change your gender. You need to associate with your own power and if you chose to be a woman, then there are reasons you chose to be a nurturing female in this life.

"The same goes if you have chosen to come here as a male. You need to embrace the male warrior within, because he wants to do things from that dominating male body. Changing genders part way through, makes the soul confused and unstable. If your purpose was to come here and have a child and you changed your sex from female to male, then it upsets God. It's not that God judges, but for example, it means that you will lose the ability to have children and the souls you promised to bring through have been left high and dry."

The channeller continued, "It is similar if you were born a male and then wanted to become a female. The male is supposed to be the protector, the daddy, the father figure to a child. Then the male turns around and thinks; *I actually want to be a female.* It doesn't fit the physical features you have been blessed with and requires you to take unnatural hormones and participate in dangerous life changing surgery. Maybe they have been exposed to too much sexual abuse, or too much of something and have been bent, or unbalanced in their conditioning? Ultimately it is breaking the original deal you made with God and your soul family before you came here."

The channeller added, "You were sold one deal from God and then you have resold your soul to the dark side, in exchange for a kind of hell. You end up in a confused state, which is created by the influence of a demon. You somehow got convinced that changing your sex was a good idea and you went along with it without fully understanding where the con was coming from. Let's take a look at the word con. It is short for many words like; conjured, convicted and convinced. It is not a natural choice, but an *influenced* choice coming from somewhere else.

"Planet Earth doesn't support those who are different from the stock standard norm very well. For example, it doesn't support heroin addicts, because it's not the place to exist harmoniously with a chronic drug addiction. There are other planets that might have heroin and it is commonly used there, like planet Xeon-X where the average life span is only 23 years old. What do drug addicts and people facing a gender identity crisis have in common? Two things. One thing they have in common is that the planet simply hasn't supported these lifestyles very well in the past and has tried to make it difficult, to both procreate and sustain the lifestyles in this current environment."

The channeller said, "The second thing they both have in common, is the same agenda from the perspective of population control. Sterilisation is the reason for the agenda of hardcore drugs and LGBT gender identity equality getting pushed through the system. Every day now more and more transgender people are shown in our mainstream media, music industry, movie industry, TV series, within our social circles and on social media and even in the modelling world. These are all high profile role models that are showcasing the transgender agenda."

When someone is unaware their potential girlfriend, or boyfriend is actually the opposite gender, it can be really confusing for a young mind to get their head around that. When boys are watching music videos with transgender men dressed as woman, they are unaware and believe that what they are seeing is a woman, but really it isn't. They form a social perception about what woman looks like based on this programming and become attracted to their male friends, because they look a bit like the woman they saw on some music video. Using the same variables, if a woman sees a transgender woman dressed as a man, it has the same effect. She becomes attracted to the female shape and gets confused when she is attracted to her female friends.

Beneath every mystery lies the truth. When you discover someone is not who you thought they were it becomes deception. Just be up front about what you are, even if it isn't accepted. The main thing to remember is to be honest and represent yourself as you *really* are, not what others expect you to be.

It is hard to tell these days if what you are seeing is a man, or a woman, or a transgender. They are so well dressed and so well made up, it can be almost impossible to tell which gender you are looking at.

Society is in a movement towards allowing parents and young children to make the decision to change their gender so easily, without fully understanding the long term spiritual and karmic implications of this act. Unless same sex and transgender couples decide to participate in adoption, complex IVF programs and sperm and egg donor programs, natural procreation for them is impossible, once they have had gender reassignment surgery.

Same sex and transgender couples are statistically far less likely to have, or want children and they would only form a small percentage of the people participating in fertility programs.

Fertility issues

Fertility issues are far more prevalent now than in the past, because of so many environmental factors that influence the body. These factors can have a negative impact on the female and male reproductive organs.

Medical advancements have also allowed complexly infertile couples to procreate as well, using new fertility science. It's a double edged sword. Science can bypass the environmental effects, but it can't address the infertility, without using medical and human intervention.

Negative environmental influences that affect infertility

- Radiation from mobile phones and mobile towers.
- Xenoestrogens in all of the plastic products, causing hormonal imbalances.
- Growth hormones and antibiotics used in dairy products, meat, chicken and fish.
- Superbugs are on the rise.
- Pesticides and herbicides sprayed on all of our natural food.
- Fake food which contains so many chemicals it's hard to find one natural ingredient.
- Genetically modified food.
- Unhealthy fried foods that contain trans fats, saturated fats and large amounts of unhealthy oils.
- Refined sugar, bleached bread and bakery products.
- Chemical cocktails we use in our shampoos, conditioners, perfumes, lotions, soaps, toothpaste and beauty products.
- Over exposure to fluorescent and unnatural lighting instead of natural sunlight.
- Exposure to dangerous EMFs all around us (TV, computers, monitors, microwaves, wireless devices, internet, satellites, power lines and harmful atmospheric chemicals from gas and fossil fuel emissions).
- Contaminated drinking water or water laced with chlorine and fluoride.
- Heavy metals contained in the atmosphere, soil, food and ground water.
- Parasites, viruses, bacteria and infections.
- Prolonged use of drugs, or prescription medication.
- Birth control pills and other fertility blocking techniques.
- Sexually transmitted diseases and infections.
- Lack of exercise.
- Lack of rest.
- Increase in stress levels.

I could go on and on with a million different reasons for why infertility issues have increased over the past 100 years, but I will stop there. You get the picture.

I have personally struggled with infertility for many years and really wanting to have biological children of my own, has been the one thing in my life I have not been able to achieve, or manifest thus far.

If I am ever asked by God if I have any questions, the biggest question I always have is about making a baby. I have been shown how to ask the angel to come and revive and nourish my eggs. I have been guided to tell God there is a warrior egg, that is waiting to come out and fight and if I believe that strongly enough, then the seed shall be.

Yet, it still hasn't happened. My faith is 100% unshakeable, but I can tell you it hasn't been without its trials and tribulations and my faith is constantly tested. On one hand I know that I need to *surrender* to God's will and accept that what will be, will be. But on the *ego* side of my brain, I cannot accept no for an answer. I have prayed, meditated and tried everything that I can physically do to make this happen but to no avail.

At some point during my struggles, Edgar Cayce was channelled to me to give me some medical advice, relating specifically to my medical problem. I hadn't really identified it as being a medical problem at that stage. Edgar Cayce explained that I needed to go and see a fertility specialist about the fact that my egg is not dropping. I didn't understand enough about my body at the time, so I had to research fertility and how it is supposed to work when everything is functioning properly. He reminded me that when I was younger (around 17), I had an abnormal pap smear which detected cancerous cells in my cervix.

In those days, their method to treat this diagnosis was to use nitrogen to freeze and/or burn the cervical cells that were causing the issue. During the treatment procedure, they burnt the tube where the egg is suppose to fertilise by accident and didn't tell me. The fallopian tube is not working properly, the egg is not dropping into the fallopian tube and my body is not able to make babies in the natural way. It is like the runway, or landing spot is not there anymore. I have always had a strange feeling that something was not quite right and not just random, or unlucky event, because I have never been able to fall pregnant.

Edgar gave me some advice. He said that I needed to be more loving to myself and be open to try and correct the situation. He said that I would need to be artificially inseminated and they will need a camera to have a look at what is going on internally. In the time period Edgar Cayce was alive, this fertility technology hadn't even been invented yet. It would have been seen as a really advanced medical procedure to people in his era, because it didn't exist.

For those of you who haven't heard of Edgar Cayce, he was an American Christian Mystic who lived from 1877 to 1945. He was a well known psychic prophet, who answered questions on subjects about medical diagnosis, healing, reincarnation, ancient civilisations, future and past lives and much more, whilst in a sleeping trance state. He was nicknamed *"The Sleeping Prophet."* After this encounter, I researched a lot more about Edgar

Cayce. He was a truly fascinating man.

He said to me, "Just believe you are going to have a baby and feel that someone is helping you."

Since his advice, I have been through 10 failed IVF attempts and have had two major surgeries. One abdominal surgery to remove fibroids and to take a look internally. I still have the large 4" butcher scar on my bikini line to remind me. The fertility doctor suggested that removing these fibroids would give me a better chance of conceiving. During my surgery, the doctor had a realisation that there were no fibroids. They actually turned out to be adenomyosis growths, mixed with severe endometriosis, which explained my years of enduring painful periods and infertility. The first surgery treatment was because of a misdiagnosis from my first fertility doctor.

When he opened me up during surgery, he saw that my internal female organs were a big mess, my bowel was fused to my uterus with endometrial tissue and he said I had one of the most severe cases of endometrial tissue throughout my organs he had seen. He cut out one adenomyosis growth and because of the blood loss; he backed out of the surgery really quickly, stitched me back up and wiped his brow with relief, as it was beyond his capability and care factor to fix it. I continued to have one IVF cycle with this particular doctor, but was guided via channelling to use a different fertility doctor, because of the mistakes he was making.

Two more IVF cycles later and two more trips from Melbourne to Brisbane, I fell very ill and was hospitalised on Christmas day in 2015. I collapsed and nearly died and was rushed to hospital in an ambulance with as much morphine as I could take and still the pain was agonising. After several days in the public hospital and a lot of blood loss, once again I was misdiagnosed. This time I was diagnosed with *constipation,* by the newly recruited university doctor. I knew it wasn't constipation and I found a way to exit that hospital quick smart.

Once back at my friends place, I was packing and getting ready to fly home to Melbourne the following day, when I became gravely ill again. During this bout of pain, we received a phone call from one of the fertility nurses checking in on me over the Christmas holidays. Within minutes of talking to the nurse, we were booked in advance to go to a private women's hospital in Brisbane and we were in the car on our way. This time we drove right to the front door of the private hospital and didn't have to wait to get help.

Within one hour of being checked in at the private women's hospital, with real doctors, they had it all worked out. They gave me a huge dose of morphine which took some time to take effect. This time they actually checked my observations properly. I was scanned thoroughly, using an internal ultrasound and CT scan. After a lot of poking and prodding, they worked out that I had a tubo-ovarian cyst between my tube and my ovary, which had recently ruptured. It had started a small leak internally, which in turn was causing sepsis. It came as a surprise to me that my condition could become life threatening, if the abscess ruptured completely.

They could not operate on me immediately, because of the infection and explained that it would be messy to operate while the infection was so inflamed. I was on multiple antibiotic drips for a whole week until my veins practically collapsed and they backed it up with heavy pain killers which were giving me wild hallucinations. I had to wait for the inflammation to become reduced, so they could perform keyhole surgery on me to remove my tubes.

The doctor decided before I could have surgery, I had to fly home to Melbourne and wait for six more weeks. Then I could return for a planned surgery. During those six weeks, I had to endure excruciating pain and drudge on working every day, at a highly stressful job until the operation. I could hardly wait to get it over with and was actually excited about having surgery to remove my faulty fallopian tubes. Removing my tubes meant losing any possible chance of falling pregnant naturally altogether. This was yet another blow to the ego and shattered my dreams of conceiving naturally.

The day of surgery day came and I had also developed a really intense respiratory ailment and was coughing very badly. I was having trouble breathing easily and was worried about going under general anaesthesia with this lung condition. I told the anaesthetist about my lung problem and he promised he would fix my problem, by mixing a special medicine solution in my breathing apparatus while I was under.

My gynaecologist had intended to do the surgery by himself and he planned for the procedure to be all over in less than an hour. I told the gynaecologist about my years of suffering with painful periods and I asked him if he saw anything inside while he was performing the surgery on me, could he please fix it.

I was under for a total of 2.5 hours and unbeknown to me, a second bowel surgeon was called in to help with the operation. They removed my tubes, reconstructed my bowel region, unstuck my uterus from my bowel and cleaned out as much endometrial tissue as they could access, all using keyhole surgery! Absolutely amazing! They took before and after photos of my internal reproductive organs, with a special camera and the difference was truly amazing.

I just marvel at modern surgical techniques and the new specialist tools that can be used to repair bodies these days. The surgeons worked miracles during that surgery and I am eternally grateful for the work they did. They literally gave me my life back! I no longer suffer from painful periods and all my bits are working perfectly fine since the surgery. My lung problem was fixed and my reproductive organs were still intact (except for my tubes).

I was also truly grateful to eliminate this inefficiency that was inside of me. The subtle underlying illness was making my life worse and affecting me in ways I wasn't even aware of. It was a blessing that I became sick, because it helped me to address a serious underlying health issue that could have become fatal if it had been left untreated.

I continued on with a few more attempts at IVF without success. I have stopped doing IVF for the moment, after many ups and downs and because of the effects of hormone therapy interfering with my skin, my body, my moods and my quality of life. I still have the option of donor eggs, foster children, adoption, or even pets to consider. I will trust my inner guidance system to point me in the right direction. This whole experience has taught me so much about life, desires and the will of God.

God *always* has a bigger plan for you and even if you can't see it now, eventually it is revealed to you. I guess I'll just have to wait and see what the grand plan is with children in my life. I can't complain, I have a beautiful step-daughter who comes to visit regularly and I have managed to bypass the nappy stage and I get to enjoy the teenage years with her instead.

God gets blamed for so many things that happen to people. Their circumstances and their outcomes are created as a result of their own choices.

I realised that doctors who put young girls on the contraceptive pill to control heavy period bleeding, are not helping the female population. It may fix the heavy bleeding, but it can also contribute to cancer, hormonal imbalances and ongoing fertility problems later in life. This is well researched and documented.

I can say for me personally, taking these hormone pills to control my female cycle, was *not* the right method to use and it wasn't the ideal thing to give a pubescent girl, who hadn't fully developed her hormonal system yet. Doctors in those days truly thought they were doing the right thing and that it was the best course of action at the time. Unfortunately the truth is; the contraceptive pill messes with a young girl's developing hormones, especially when they are going through puberty. The effects can result in many pubescent changes and cervical changes that are just not natural for a young woman. The contraceptive pill also affects women of all ages, because the hormone levels contained in these pills are strong enough to change and control the natural female cycle. Doctors often use it as a hormone correction method.

Doctors should be educating the world with pro-life slogans. Advise people to eat the right foods and take the right mix of minerals, vitamins and supplements that promote production of the particular hormones that people may be deficient in. Instead of prescribing manufactured hormones, they should be encouraging the right diet, regular exercise and right thinking. This holistic combination can be used as a remedy to balance a hormone that is out of control, by bringing it back into balance.

Whatever happens to me in my life, God is not my personal miracle maker. I cannot just wave a magic wand and command God to fix me. There may be a specific reason why I am not supposed to have biological children and there may be a perfectly valid reason why the timing of each of these events rolled out exactly as they did.

God never gives you more tests than you can handle and I also know this is not the only life I have ever lived. I know I have already had other opportunities in my past lives to have children and there could also be future lives, when I may choose to have children again.

This holistic wisdom, acceptance and understanding, helps you to truly *surrender* to God's will and to the will of your life plan and purpose. Whenever something seemingly tragic happens, it can be a precursor to something greater happening to you. These events can also be God's way of preventing a bigger problem from occurring, further down the track.

Parenting

The channeller said, "Parenting in the animal kingdom is so different now, compared to what it used to be. The role of parents in the so called primitive times, was to raise the child to hunt and survive, then move on and let the child fend for themselves."

"You were made to feed yourselves and reproduce. If you are really good at feeding yourself and reproducing yourself, you can breathe fresh air. When you can see through deception, then you are already a winner. You should be able to understand and pass this stage by the age of five. Then teach and help other people. Everything is backwards. They are all on the wrong track. They pollute the air instead of having fresh air. They ruin the food instead of using fresh food."

The channeller continued, "God detached himself from you and sent you on your way, in the hope that you would become like God and now you are in the *image* of God. God cut the umbilical cord, just like the mother cuts the umbilical cord and now you are running on your own program. That is why you can be destructive. You have the ability to be good or bad, destroy or create, just like him. If you don't believe this, then how do you think you exist? Where are you? Who are you? Are *you* the new God? It doesn't matter *who* you are, because at the end of the day *you* are in charge of you!"

God added some humour, "You are the actor on the Broadway stage. You get to make it up as you go along. Some people become murderers and some people go around and say, 'I don't believe in you. I am God. You are John. You are Peter, but... I don't believe in you.'

Then John says, "Well I don't believe in you."

God carried on and said, "This is a ridiculous conversation for idiots! Okay, so if I come along in a boat called the *God boat* and you don't believe in me, then don't catch it, go away then! Your mother cut the umbilical cord, because she couldn't drag you around by the cord forever. She *needed* to cut the cord. We are talking about mammals specifically here. Now we are starting to talk about motherhood, the egg, hatching the egg. The mother still puts all her *love* into the egg. Look at a chicken, or bird for instance, they will still sit on the egg. They do it naturally, because they are in harmony. It's so basic, that it is *simple.* It is so simple, it is stupid."

God laughed out loud, "How many fingers am I holding up?"

God wants to teach all of you *how* you teach this. No one is going to believe in an invisible energy force, they are going to believe in me and you. Each and every one of you has the ability to talk to God.

God said, "They need to believe in *themselves* first and this is why it is so important to be regressed back to their childhood, to understand all of the good and all of the bad things."

God shared his views and said, "Mothers need to teach their children to be independent. Children don't learn by being mollycoddled, they learn by being *shown* how to do things and then letting them do things for themselves. Native aborigines and native tribes around the world are a good example of how they teach their children how to weave, find and gather food, survival skills, when sex is appropriate and corroborees. In the western world we may not agree with their methods of parenting, but they use the real world as their school and teach their children skills that will be useful for living and surviving. They are not consumed by status, wealth, or class. They are concerned with being *useful*, staying alive and fulfilling their spiritual purpose, by being close to nature and living in harmony with their environment."

I once had a reading come through for one of my friends, which happens often. I can choose to pass this information onto the relevant person, but only if they are willing to hear it. Sometimes they just aren't ready to hear what God wants to tell them, or they don't have faith, or belief in what God is trying to tell them. So they choose to *ignore* the special messages God offered them.

In this case, God recalls an incident between my friend (when he was a little boy) and his father. This is something I never knew and could not have possibly known about my friend. He was outside with his father and he had a cane basket with a clothes line strung between the line and the basket. He used to do everything backwards, which used to frustrate his father so much that he would become angry and violent.

These days we would say the little boy had dyslexia, or perhaps a learning disability, but back then parents simply saw this as defiance and as a learning *defect.* His father lashed out and hit him and the force of the hit threw him back across the yard. This might be the first time the little boy would remember being physically hurt by his father. The little boy hurt his kneecap and it was grazed. This feeling of anger and frustration from his father, contributed to the lack of love within the family. These feelings have stayed with him throughout his life and he continues to have issues with learning, as a result of many abusive incidents happening to him, just like this one.

God said, "The ultimate gift in this life is *love.* Love can mean many things. Love means balance, a smile, warmth, happiness and love means that someone will help you. Love is something that makes you feel good. In the relationship between the little boy and his father, no one told each what they needed, so ultimately they lacked communication."

God added, "In a bad relationship, if you never tell the other person what you need and what makes you happy, they will never know what you want to make you happy. A person can give you many things, but all of which may not be things that will make you happy. It is about misunderstanding each other and a lack of compromising, which contributes to the lack of communication."

11. THE MIND

If you want to use your brain to tap into a certain event,
you need to actually go there in your mind
and be present in the moment, exactly when the event occurs,
to tune in to the specific frequency you are looking for.

YOU often hear the term *mind over matter* and your mind immediately pictures people walking on hot coals. Your mind thinks of those who perform extremely difficult feats and of those who can overcome the obstacles that everyone else tells them can't be overcome. When you ignore the doubt, the pessimists and the non believers, you can achieve anything. This is just a small demonstration of how powerful the mind really is.

If you can *perceive* it, you can *believe* it. If you can *believe* it, you can *receive* it. If you can *receive* it in your mind's eye, then you will *achieve* it. This happens when you *truly believe* with your mind and your heart combined, that you have already received it.

The human brain

Let's convert the spiritual speak into technical speak for the private computer scientists and other people this way inclined, so they can understand it on a technical level.

God explained, "Humans call files by name. In a real human brain we have a frequency. Every thought pattern runs on a frequency. To obtain the frequency through the brain, as the brain runs through the 1 kHz range, it is able to pick up every other cell in the body and they might all be thinking, or sensing a flower. People resonate at a particular frequency, depending on how you felt about them while they were alive."

God continued, "Once you resonate on the frequency of a person, spirit, or emotion, you can identify and associate a certain person, or event with a particular frequency. The thought pattern searches for frequencies in the mind. If you are thinking of someone, for this example, let's use your granddad Nuki at 1.1 kHz. You will pick up frequencies of other people around the world, who are also on 1.1 kHz. The frequency of 1.1 kHz equals love."

God added, "You have so much love when you think of your granddad, that it conjures up the specific frequency of 1.1 kHz. Everyone else, who can pick up this frequency, also gets the same experience at the frequency of 1.1 kHz, so they can feel him too. You need to really emotionally *feel* the person you want to communicate with, or are thinking about. Feel them, be there and be in the moment. Remember the times, or events that made you feel good when you were with them and think back to that time. Anyone else, who knows him, will also be able to communicate with him."

God asked the channeller to explain further, "When Jesus the healer was channelling the Creator, which he did multiple times; he would technically and actually be on channel "*God*." The presence of the spirit you are thinking about is felt with you when you are doing healing work, because you are effectively calling them up on their frequency. You have made contact, it's that simple, but first you have to *believe*. Without belief, it is just lip service, or make believe."

The channeller continued, "So when it comes to picking up on the frequency of dead people, who may have met with an unexpected, or tragic ending and you are searching for answers about how they died, you really need to get into their spiritual space and connect with their frequency, to talk to them and get more information. This is why objects or photographs of the deceased person are particularly useful, because they contain a frequency that is associated with that particular person."

There is a fabulous TV documentary called *"Sensing Murder"* and I have seen many episodes over the years. The TV show is about unsolved murders, unsolved crimes and missing persons' cases. The show goes through the standard process and the standard protocol of what the police believe *may* have happened to the victim, which only the viewer gets to see.

The psychics are not given any prior information about the missing person, or the victim's case details and their aim is to determine if any foul play was involved. The psychics then attempt to piece the story together and locate the body of the victim. They give the police any additional leads that may have been missed in the initial investigation.

My favourite part is always the reaction of the police when the psychics give specific details about the people involved and exactly how the drama unfolded on the day of the victim's death, or disappearance. The police officer leading the investigation always starts out as a skeptic. After watching the psychic use their gift to its fullest potential, the police become exposed to a whole new way of looking at unsolved crimes, victims and criminals.

The psychics, who get selected after undergoing rigorous testing, are unable to research the case prior to the show and the psychic is not known to anyone involved in the investigation. The feedback provided to the police is based on the psychic's ability to communicate with the spirit world, or the soul of the deceased person and their ability to pick up on places and events that occurred at the time of the victim's death, or disappearance. In the process, the psychics reopen old wounds for souls who have passed over and surviving family members. Ultimately the psychics do it to help the healing process and also to allow communication between the two worlds. The spirit communication is for the benefit of everyone involved and also for the purpose of solving crimes and murder cases that have been buried in the vaults for years.

In some cases the psychics have even given the police, the first and last name of the perpetrator and their current workplace, or home address. Unfortunately the law courts cannot take the word of a psychic as admissible evidence, but dare I say this is proof that there are gifted psychics in the world. Psychics who can use their ability to help solve unsolved crimes and who can assist spiritually with passing over lost souls and put the family's grief to rest. Now the soul can finally rest in peace, because the soul or spirit was able to share their story, before saying their final goodbye.

The spirit of the deceased is not always willing to relive the whole traumatic death experience, but with some creative coaxing from the experienced psychics, the family can get finally some closure and the deceased person's soul can rest in peace.

God said, "Each of us has the necessary brain tools to do this and use our brains more, but we get lazy and disinterested and prefer to be brainwashed by trivial and meaningless waffle, which just sidetracks us from our true purpose and numbs the senses."

God continued, "If you want to use your brain to tap into a certain event, you need to actually go there in your mind and be *present* in the moment, exactly when the event occurs, to tune in to the specific frequency you are looking for."

God cryptically said, "There are 32 parts of the brain and we can name all those parts of the brain 0, like you do in binary code by using a 1 or a 0. It is like having 32 computers and each one of them needs a login for each brain. It is like we have 32 bits of the brain, or maybe there are 37."

God added, "We have a complex brain and we need to break it down into chunks. How do you create something from nothing? By using our brain. Now stand up and walk around! Now ask yourself, *isn't that a miracle that I just got up out of the seat and walked on two legs?* The simple things that we take for granted as being second nature to us, are very complex operations that we perform multiple times a day, without giving it any further thought."

God continued, "Once you learn how the brain works, you start to learn that you can start to control other people. If you are controlling somebody else, you need to ask yourself, *am I controlling them for good, or bad?* You would have to be a master of understanding a person's free will and working out if controlling someone to do something is a good thing, or a bad thing. Question yourself by asking, *do I really understand my world?*

"Brainwashing from television (TV) is trying to show people that it's okay to act like this and like that. TV is like an emulator, which is giving people the standards of the virtual world. In the earlier virtual world, it was a different understanding and each person had their own virtual world. You must have an understanding of how everyone got their own virtual world and then you need to understand, how did we get to have a virtual world that is so messed up? Is my virtual world okay? Am I happy with my virtual world? My brain? My learning? Remember that you programmed yourself and we can fix this.

"What would make you feel better? By realising you can change this virtual world and that we can change it together. We can learn something better. My virtual world is rock solid and I can see what you need in your virtual world to improve it, or make it better. If your world is full of self-loaded dangerous systems, similar to cracked or hacked programs, then you need to *unlearn* and *relearn* correct and beneficial systems.

"Just for a moment, I want you to visualise everyone has computer screens on their heads and they are walking around. Now watch the more common things that human beings do. They all start out as a blank computer program, until data gets input into the system. Some have good solid programming and others have a patchwork of dodgy programming which is not stable. They are listening to someone programming them via TV, music, media, advertisements, movies, radio etc. Who is right and who is wrong? Put 100 computers in a room and try to work something out. Get a crowd together and test everyone out, by asking them all the same questions and see what results come back."

God gave me an example, "Imagine that you get two random people up on stage, from the crowd and do a demonstration. Let's call the two people Harry and Gina. Harry is a very naughty man, he picks his nose, or whatever example you can think of that is a bit naughty. Gina likes flowers and she doesn't pick her nose? Is Harry a very nice person from judging him based on this one demonstration? How do you know for sure? Why do you believe me? Do you pick your nose? Oh then, maybe I made a bad judgement? You can make your own judgement by posing your own questions to the person directly. That way the information and judgement can't be manipulated by a third party, or middle person.

"The news is a good example where you are fed a story complete with the judgement and you already agree with the perspective of the news reader, because that is how they delivered the information to you, exactly the way they wanted you to perceive it and *not* actually how it really is."

God said, "If we look at the human brain like a computer and each person has their own computer with their own unique programming. To fix the computer, you must convince the robot computer program that everything is all good, happy and mystical. Focus on all of the positive things and if you want to influence a computer program to come and join you, you wouldn't be telling it anything that is negative. Always aim to see the positive side. Try the hippy approach where nothing fazes you.

"Don't scare other humans, because if they have sensitive programming, you will freak them out like a computer program going crazy and it crashes. You could try *fixing* the computer and even download updates to get the computer working properly again. If all else fails, restart, or reformat the hard drive. This would mean resetting the brain and starting again and relearning everything from scratch. However humans are a bit more complex, because it is difficult to relearn everything overnight. It takes time and patience, but ultimately it is much easier to repair the faulty programming, than reformatting the brain."

God continued, "Brains are just grey matter biological computers that react on *fear*. This can be easily seen when you freak someone out, or get a reaction using fear. This is setting up learned behaviour of the worst kind and contributes to bad and destructive programming. Everything is easily resolvable and everything is all good. Once everything is under control, then the robot has learned. Humans have been programmed to accept the *drama* program, similar to the show called "Days of Our Lives" and must play out that programming every day by having *freak out* days, which leads to bad programming and ultimately days off."

God loves the topic of the human brain and continued to explain, "The human race needs to stop filling their heads with destructive programming and stop watching death and disasters on the news, stop watching horror movies, brutality and murder, which you are being constantly bombarded with in the media, on the news and on your TV screens.

"Stop believing that the drama show you are watching on TV is *real life*. It is *not!* This is destructive programming designed to scramble your positive programming. Why do you think so many people lose it and run out and go on a shooting rampage, or throw themselves off a bridge? They have been subjected to numerous sessions of hard coded destructive programming and they have been conditioned to accept it as a normal program in the brain, because they are seeing and hearing it all the time.

Once you are constantly exposed to something, you start thinking and believing it to be normal. Believe me it is *not* normal. Killing and hurting people is *not* okay and it is as far from normal that you can get. There is no excuse for killing someone, none."

The channeller spoke for God, "Everyone has become desensitised so much, that they probably wouldn't even flinch if they saw something like that in real life. This destructive programming acceptance must STOP, because it is not in attunement with who you *really* are and it is not in attunement with the love and light of the Creator. The destructive programming is backed by the Devil and he is doing a good job at distracting you from your true nature, which is to be loving, kind, honest and truthful. We are *not* killers by nature; this is an aspect of our consciousness which is to be used for survival only. We don't *need* to kill to survive, unless it is a righteous thing to do and I don't believe anyone on Earth really understands what righteousness really means."

The channeller continued, "You are allowed to exercise your free will to do the right thing and make righteous choices. You are not supposed to exercise your free will for destruction; it is not in your nature. If this is what you are doing, you need to question where you received that programming. If you were born in the forest with no influence from man ever, like children who have been raised by animals for example, you may hunt to kill so you can eat, but you don't kill for any other reason, because you know it wouldn't be right.

"It is hardcoded in you *not* to be destructive. Only those who are influenced by destructive programming and destructive people fall prey to the dictator or the controller and allow themselves to be destructively programmed. Your brain belongs to you and you are in full control of it. Exercise your free will to do the right thing and not the wrong thing and you will have nothing to fear."

The channeller added, "On the positive side of brain programming, once you understand what you are actually made of biologically, you can work out how to levitate. In order to levitate a whole entire body, a Monk, Buddhist, or Sadhu would have an understanding of what is inside the whole being. They would have a holy approach to it. They need to know what all things are and it is very complex. When you levitate, you need to levitate everything at the same speed, force and levitational push. The same as when you are healing something, or someone. You should be healing every microscopic tiny living thing in the subject's body, even the bad bits if you don't understand why they are there. Why? Because the bad bacteria that is there might be good for the stomach. Even if you don't like bad bacteria, it may still be good for you. That is why you need to heal *all* of it, the good and the bad, the whole body and being."

Hallucinogens

The channeller said, "Many people throughout history have claimed that taking hallucinogens, or consuming products created from hallucinogenic plants, has given them the ability to talk to spirits, nature spirits and sometimes directly to God during this experience."

Many studies have proven the link between consuming specific plant materials, or hallucinogens and simultaneously having a mystical or spiritual experience. This is the real reason why so many hallucinogenic plants and substances have been made illegal. The establishment doesn't want *everyone* being able to communicate with spirits, or God that easily! That could be deemed as dangerous. Dangerous to who? Not for the seeker, but dangerous for the establishment, because free thinking is not supported, or encouraged in a material world ruled by those who want total order and enslavement. They prefer you to be subservient and obedient, which make you easier to rule and control. They prefer to keep you in the dark, with the spiritual cloak in full force.

In some cultures, there are shamans who have received sacred, traditional and special teachings from their ancestors, to enter the spirit realm and receive divine messages to assist in healing rituals. Shamans can enhance the seeker's spiritual experience, especially for the uninitiated seeker, by guiding them through the spirit world, using sacred ceremonies and songs that may, or may not involve consuming strong substances, derived from mother nature's garden nursery. Shamans are experienced Realm Walkers who can safely cross the boundaries of space and time, in these altered states of consciousness. We will talk more about Realm Walkers later in this book.

Who do you think put the plants there in the first place? Where do you think the plants came from? They are not random. They are carefully placed in certain locations within the garden of Mother Earth for us to discover and experience our true divinity, by connecting with everything that exists. When we find the plants that vibrate on a godly frequency, we should embrace the joy that is felt at the heart of these sacred plants. We should not be banning them and making them illegal. We should be studying them and finding out what these plants can do for our spiritual growth and evolution and understand what the plants are trying to teach us. Remember these plants have been on Earth longer than we have and they are probably much more evolved than we are as a species.

When humans release their ego and stop believing they are the most superior creature in the Universe, then they will learn what they are *really* here for and what their *true* purpose is. Only then, can they understand that this world is already filled with mysticism and wisdom. We have so much to be grateful for, when it comes to our humble plant family. Learn to live in harmony with everything and everyone, including our sacred plants. Just think of all of the life forms that plants support and everything that lives and breathes as a result of the plant kingdom, including us. Without plants, we would find it very difficult to survive here on Planet Earth.

The channeller said, "There is another way you can talk to God which is totally legal and they cannot stop you and that is through working out how to communicate using the hallucinogenic frequency, which is 28 kHz. Once mankind has cracked this code, then you shall surely talk to God."

The channeller continued, "God doesn't actually *hide* from us, although he is practically invisible, which does make him mystical. God makes himself available for all of us to talk to him and he wants us to use our faith and inner knowing to communicate with him, rather than having to *see* him and talk to him with our conscious mind. It is man that is incapable of finding a suitable way to talk to God that can be proven to work. If mankind worked a bit harder and researched which frequencies God likes to communicate on, he could replicate that feeling, or use the feel good frequency, to tap into the awareness of God."

The channeller added, "Spiritual communication is very difficult to measure, because each experience is usually contained within the mind, the third eye, or the subconscious of the individual who is talking to God. To the seeker, once they have found God, they have no need to prove it to anyone else and continue their cherished personal relationship with God."

There are many hallucinogens over the centuries that have been used to communicate with God with varying degrees of success.

"These experiments, or experiences should only be attempted by persons of completely sound mind, or they could risk triggering a psychotic episode that is beyond their capacity to comprehend. It might short circuit their belief system when they finally make contact, to such a degree that it might even drive them crazy. You can also use advanced meditation techniques like transcendental meditation, to trigger the same response, or get really deep into the full somnambulistic meditative state, where you can communicate with God."

Taking time out and going somewhere you really love, being in the right frame of mind and at the right time of day, can also help you to be guided to somewhere you're meant to be, to communicate with God. This is when you could experience even a glimpse of enlightenment, when you are touched by the light of God.

When you experience the natural and holy love feeling that comes from God for the first time, it will make you hungry for more of that loving feeling and you will continue to pursue the journey of getting to know God even more. It is a feeling that you cannot get from any drug, any hallucinogen, or any other experience on Earth. To be in a loving connected state of being with God, can't be paid for, or purchased. It just is and you just are with him in that cherished moment.

Expectation

All humans get confused, because they don't understand how to do something.

The channeller said while conversing with God, "There is a procedure, or a way, *how* to do something. God wants to remind humans what the procedure is, so they can do it. For example, if you ask someone to go and get a lemon from a lemon tree, you say, 'Go and get me a lemon.' Now, there is a number of ways to do that and that is where the confusion is."

The channeller continued, "Confusion is for a lazy person, or a person who does not know. Write out a formula for the task you need the person to achieve. The person needs to understand what they are getting and who they are getting it for. Is it for themselves, or is it for someone else?

"The second thing is the time period. How long have I got to go and get this? This brings about stress and stress is a frequency. The higher the stress, the more stress exists. The human needs to be on a higher vibration to cope. The lower the stress, then less stress requires lower vibration. More stress creates an overload, or a peak load on the body. The way to overcome stress is to believe there is still more stress. This keeps us in a higher state of vibration and preparedness.

"Once a person works out what they want, where to find it, how to get it and how to get there, then they know the *direction* they are heading in. If they have legs, what transportation method do they use to get to it? If they don't have legs, then they have to slither, or sludge their way there. A happy person would have to smile their way there."

The channeller added, still talking to God, "According to time, this would determine the transportation method. A smart person would send somebody else there with a smile of course. If you send a lazy person there, it would take a long time, because they would go slow. Remember, someone else could grow a lemon tree. There are many ways to get your lemon. You could make it, or find it. It doesn't just magically appear in front of you. You have to go and do something to get it.

"What is it? Where do I find it? How do I get there? If I find my *[whatever it is you want to manifest]*, then how do I get back?

"The expectation should not be *finding* the lemon. It is *giving* it to the person who asks for it. That is what you should enjoy and that is the expression you should be getting. Is it good or bad? What should I see? If you deliver the lemon, then what is perceived? If you do not get what you expect from them, an unusual reaction perhaps, then you won't be getting them a lemon again. This is the reward for getting the lemon and if they don't give you a good reaction, then that will be their loss."

The channeller continued, "What type of lemon should I get? What quality of lemon does the person need and how many? Then a wizard would turn it around and tell the person asking, how to go and get a lemon and make them do it by giving them a few pointers. The old wise one, a boss, or a manager would say, 'Surely one should go and get a lemon if I show you how, or where to find one?' Then they think to themselves, *when they get their own lemon, I shall be happy for them.* The wise wisdom of the chief would say, 'It's not about making decisions at random, it is about giving wisdom and teaching life lessons to people.' Giving wisdom to people is more desired than *telling* them how to do it. You need to be giving them feelings of being satisfied, enriched, seeing brighter things, happiness and endorphins."

God said, "People want to feel happier and empowered, to be able to accomplish a task themselves. Tell them they will feel happier when they do it. When they come back, you can show you are happy with them, so they can be happy with themselves."

Jesus would have said, "You have now made a friend and a happy friend at that!"

God said, "Question all the time to understand. Never assume anything and you will be enlightened, surprised, humiliated and in hysterics."

God continued, "Let's apply expectation to setting a goal. To have a goal, you would have to learn how to get to the goal, not just to have a goal. It's not just about specifying what you want; it's about learning the principles and learning every step it takes to achieve that goal. When you write about a goal, it is made up of hundreds of goals. People focus on the end goal, but in reality the goal is made up of so many goals and each goal needs to be achieved, before the next one can be obtained.

"The most important thing is learning to break down your goal into easy steps. Let's look at a simple goal to achieve, so we can apply this theory. How do you achieve love and learn how to love someone? How do you become in love, or love someone? There are many steps to achieve this. You might start as *friends*, then *liking* each other, then *loving* each other and finally, to be *in love* with each other. You start creating the thoughts of love, by thinking about the things you like about them. For example, you like the way they smile, the way they look, the way they treat you, how they make you feel and that brings up things that make up the feeling of love. There are lots of little things that make up the feeling of love, so a goal is like love."

God added, "Love grows stronger, because now you have learned the ability to love others. Love is built from liking first and you must like a lot of things about that person, or creature."

God said, "That brings up the complexity of what a person's expectation of what love is and what liking is. Can you define it? If you set your bar of love way too high, then your range of expectation is way out of alignment with your true self and you will exclude every scenario of love from entering your life. If your expectation of love is perfection and then you tell yourself you will fall in love with them, you are setting yourself up for failure and disappointment, because nobody is perfect.

"Expectations are nothing to do with how a person sees themselves; it is about what they expect something to be, where they set their line and their interpretation of limits of what is acceptable and what is not."

God continued, "Be aware you can die aiming too high and missing out on the treasures life has to offer in the meantime. I prefer the diamond in the rough, the rogue that always takes you by surprise, the one you least expect to be your friend, or even your lover."

Gratitude

God gravitates towards appreciation and that is why you have to be in an attitude of *gratitude*, to attract the great dude to your place for a while!

God said, "Inner harmony is true happiness. True happiness is to enjoy the present and rest satisfied with what you have, which is abundantly sufficient. The place to be happy is here and the time to be happy is now. Get into the flow and rhythm of life."

"Showing dedication is knowing what drives someone to do what they do. When you arise in the morning, think of what a precious privilege it is to be alive, to breathe, to think, to enjoy and to love. Feel lucky to be alive."

God continued, "There is an infinite amount of learning and you will never stop learning all your life. Do all the good you can, by all the means you can, in all the ways you can, in all the places you can, at all the times you can, to all the people you can, as long as you ever can."

God added, "Inner conflict disappears as we face our contradictions and then invite reality to dissolve them. Every person has good and evil and it must be balanced.

"Is someone saying thank you when you give them something, or are they taking more from you, by not saying thank you? This is always a sure test to know if someone is simply taking from you, with no intention of appreciation, or gratitude. A dying star gives more light when it is about to go, by saying thank you and it provides light on its way out.

"Humans don't understand that when you give more sunlight to someone, they take it from you and drain it. Humans haven't learned to appreciate something that is given away for free like; love, gratitude, friendship, loyalty and kindness. They have learned to take very well and have learned to seize every opportunity with both hands."

Speaking for God, the channeller said, "What happens if you constantly take, take, take off everyone? You have all of the taken information in your head and you become ill, or mentally unbalanced. It is not wrong for God to give humans more. What would happen if a tree could walk? It grows into a big monstrous tree. It grows in the ground and lives off the soil and water. If it could walk, it would get fatter and fatter and grow bigger and bigger. The tree is supposed to be in the ground with ribbons (branches) which grow from it, so it can feel for food in the earth and it grows a little bit more each day. It is designed this way for a reason and it is God's will that trees are like strong supports, providing oxygen, shelter and shade for all of us and the planet. That is why you are not supposed to take all the trees. The trees cannot run away and defend themselves. They are here to be a part of the planet and experience a long life just like you are."

The channeller continued, "Why not plant some more trees, to replace all the trees that have been taken in the past generations. If we all planted one tree each on our birthday every year, we would offset the demise of climate change in a few short years. Yes, this is a good start and yes it is that simple. That is having gratitude for the planet on which you are living. If we all picked up one piece of rubbish each when we go for a walk and put it in the rubbish bin, this is another positive step towards cleaning up our beautiful planet. Better still, if we each consciously thought about what we throw away and what we are consuming.

"Are we contributing to the pollution and destruction of the planet, or are we helping it? For example, if we all said no to plastic bags, then there is one less plastic bag each, per day, or week in circulation, that ends up getting washed out to the ocean and ends up killing some poor sea creature.

"Remember the old paper grocer's bags we used to use? Let's go back to using them. That is gratitude for our ocean and our ocean creatures. If we ate less meat or no meat at all, then that is showing the ultimate gratitude for the life of the creatures you share the planet with. Think about the millions of lives that you will save by contributing to this conscious way of living."

I really want to share the ultimate experience of gratitude that I have ever personally felt and how I felt the grace of God with me, for the first time and really noticed God's presence. I feel gratitude daily, but sometimes you just have that really special moment that you remember and treasure forever. Like the first time you meet that special someone, or your first love, or in my case my first real meeting with the Creator. That one time when everything just felt right and I had nothing to worry about. Life for that period of time, whether it lasted for minutes, hours, days, or weeks seemed like it lasted for an eternity.

I need to give you a bit of background, so that my story makes sense and you understand the events leading up to my experience of true gratitude. The year was 1997 and I had spent the previous two years working hard in the mines in Kalgoorlie, Western Australia, to save up for trip that was to last for a whole year travelling around the world. I was in my early 20's, full of life and itching to explore the world. I had many destinations planned for my travels and my recent separation from my ex-boyfriend fuelled my excitement, because I couldn't wait to make a clean break and get out of the middle of nowhere and explore the world. During my time in Kalgoorlie, I met some really wonderful people and had some truly interesting experiences out there.

Mining taught me many things and it opened my eyes to the destructive side of mining and the dangers associated with working at remote sites. I had a lot of respect for the workers and the whole operation. It was humbling to observe their willingness to work all hours of the day, or night, in exchange for good pay. The mining industry is complex and needs *people* to keep the operation alive. The industry feeds so many other industries and other sectors can also benefit and become very lucrative. Money is the driving factor behind why most people work in the mines and not much thought is usually given to the wildlife habitats that can be displaced or environmental damage that can occur in the aftermath of mining. Mining at the time was the backbone of the Australian economy and it was a good way to make good money, to be able to pursue other goals.

On my big world journey, my first destination was home to New Zealand to catch up with family, before embarking on my even bigger leg of the journey. Second stop Fiji; the land of tropical islands, bare feet, grass huts, ukuleles and sea snakes. Arriving in Fiji was like travelling back in time 50 years and the pace of life in Fiji was well and truly on *Fiji time.* Nobody was in a hurry to do anything, or go anywhere. At first you resisted relaxing and then everything finally catches up with you and you feel like collapsing and sleeping for a month.

The pace of life in Fiji suited me fine, because 20 years ago the internet was only a relatively new thing. You didn't carry a mobile phone with you and you kept a journal, or notebook with you at all times, because there wasn't really any other way to document your travels. If you wanted to keep in touch with someone, you had to write an entry in your old fashioned address book. Palm pilots were only new technology and when they were available, they were really expensive. If you moved around often, it would be easy to lose touch with people and some of them you never ever saw again.

Digital cameras weren't readily available and cameras in the market place were still mostly using film, so you had to choose your photo moments carefully, because it was expensive to turn all of your negatives into prints.

The most advanced piece of technology I had with me was my walkman. It was a cassette tape walkman and I had spent many days before travelling, preparing all of my mix tapes, so that I could take all of my favourite songs with me. Personal computers weren't even on the radar, or readily available in the market place, unless you had heaps of money to spend, or were a full blown geek and knew what you were doing. Then you could build your own computer. You had to rely on travel agents to do your travel bookings and had to let them know if your plans changed, so you could update your ticket.

I had only planned to visit Fiji for two weeks and ended up staying for three whole months. I found a beautiful little spot in the middle of the Pacific Ocean, called Leleuvia with no cars, no traffic, no roads, minimal people and no noise other than the island generator which was only switched on during the day. The only way on and off the island was on a small motor boat. This was the isolation I had been looking for; to finally relax and recover from the turmoil I'd left behind.

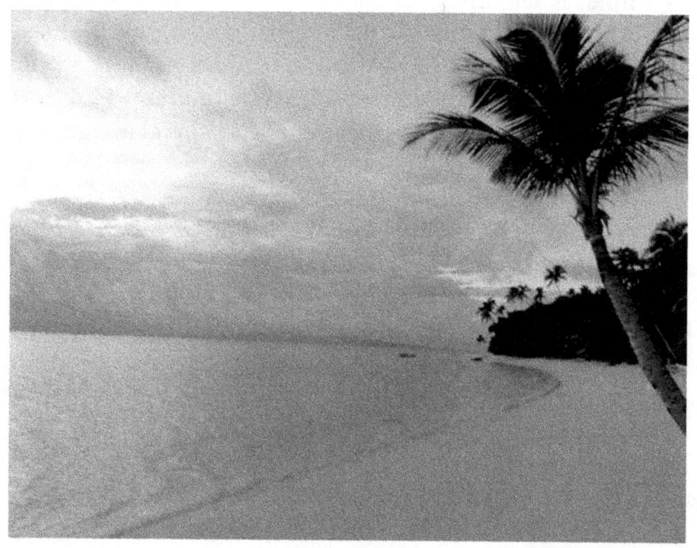

After being on the island for almost a month, one evening during a full moon, I was awoken by a clear distinct voice who said to me, "Get up, you're going for a walk." I thought I was dreaming at first. Then when I fully awoke, I reached over and checked my clock and it was around 3:00am. I thought to myself, *I can't just go wandering around on a tropical island by myself at 3:00am in the morning, can I?*

I rolled off my bed, my feet hit the earthen floor in the darkness of the night and I stepped outside the bure (Fijian hut). There were two beautiful dogs sitting outside my door waiting for me. They were the two island dogs, the *only* two dogs on the whole island. I chuckled quietly to myself and whispered, *"Hello"* to the two dogs and they were excited with their tails wagging, ready to go for a walk. I started walking in the direction that I felt was the right way to go and the two dogs were right beside me, one on my left and one on my right side, guarding me and protecting me. I felt safe to proceed.

The moonlight was bright and lit up my pathway and illuminated the white sand around the island. There was total silence in the village and not a soul was stirring. Everyone was fast asleep in bed, except for the three of us. It was a warm tropical balmy night in Fiji and the atmosphere was so still, that not even a slight breeze could be felt.

It was the perfect temperature, the kind of ideal temperature you dream about when you think about going on a holiday. It was so warm at night, that you could easily sleep naked on the beach (if you wanted to). It wasn't too sticky or humid either. I was dressed in a basic black singlet and a colourful sarong and loved the feel of earth under my feet and the sand between my toes.

I started to make my way through the village towards the east side of the island and began my walk to the northern tip of the island. As I was walking on the beach, the dogs kept looking up at me with loving smiles and they were both enjoying their walk in the moonlight. During the walk, I could hear the waves lightly lapping on the shoreline, the odd night creature rustling in the bushes and the distant sound of waves crashing onto the ocean reefs a few miles away.

It only took about 10 minutes of walking to reach the northern most tip of the island, where I knew nobody lived, or slept. Many islanders didn't like frequenting that part of the island, because of their local legend about a lady ghost, who they believed lived at the northern tip of the island. Ghosts don't bother me and I didn't actually believe their legend, because it was a bit farfetched and sounded more like an urban legend that was a good story to tell the tourists.

I felt like I was in the right spot that I was being led to and sat down cross legged on the sand. The dogs sat on each side of me as close they could get to me, without actually sitting on me. We all had an understanding telepathically between each other and it was a beautiful feeling of belonging. The feeling that we were all part of the one soul, connected and loved. I looked out over the ocean in front of me and it was like glass, so still and so calm. I had never ever seen an ocean so still in all my life.

The moon was now directly overhead in my field of view. It was illuminating the landscape of the neighbouring island in the distance and it was shimmering like a sparkling stairway on the glistening water in front of me. I was on a tiny little island literally in the middle of the Pacific Ocean and I felt safe, guarded and totally attuned to nature in that moment. Life was perfect!

Just then a feeling came over me that I had never actually experienced before, a feeling of total bliss, warmth, love and connectedness. It was a feeling that a magical presence was with me, around me, embracing me and making itself known to me. I can only describe it as a feeling unlike anything else I have ever felt, the feeling that God was now with me in an energetic form.

I knew it was God and I felt the strong presence of the holiest of holies visit me. I couldn't *see* God as you would see a person, but I could feel and see God in the beauty all around me as it became more illuminated, more pronounced and more surreal. It was like being awake in a lucid dream, or like daydreaming about your favourite place, but it was totally real. I could feel, see, hear, taste and know everything all at once, like I was the Creator for that period of time. It was so magnificent and so special that I wish I could give you that feeling, even for five minutes, so you could feel the presence of God. Feel the presence of the Creator, like I felt the presence. It gives you more than just goosebumps; God is that mega tingly feeling, the warmth, the love and the electricity that illuminates your being.

God stayed with me for a long period of time. It felt like days in my mind, but was probably around an hour of Earth time. I didn't feel the need to talk to God, because it was more like a telepathic connection, a knowing, a feeling that the Creator was here with me, around me and a part of me. I started to cry tears of joy, pure joy, pure appreciation and pure adoration for such a beautiful energy that was with me. I had goosebumps all over my body and I knew I was in the presence of the Supreme Being. No question I could have asked would have meant anything at all, because I became all knowing and all of my fears and worries melted away. I felt so insignificant in the big scheme of things. I realised that all of my human concerns didn't matter, the Creator has the answer for everything and everything is created in perfect balance. In the end, it will all work itself out, with, or without my existence.

I would describe this as having a glimpse of enlightenment, which is an overwhelming feeling of *gratitude* for being allowed to exist on this planet at this time and to be able to experience all the things that I had asked to come here and experience.

I realised the reason I was here on this planet, was a *conscious* choice and that every lesson, every moment, every experience I had felt up until now, had all led me to this place, this moment and to this very experience. I was in total awe of the Creator and I loved him so much, I could have squeezed him so hard and given him a big cuddle, but I couldn't reach out and touch him. He was just beyond my reach but yet all around me.

It is a peculiar thing to get your head around, inexplicable with a trusting feeling that you almost couldn't explain, or didn't even need to explain to anyone else. I was so grateful for this truly special experience and it was such a personally felt stream of energy and now knew that I could tap into this holy connection any time I wanted to.

Words fail to describe the intensity and love being shared between us, because I was open to this experience and didn't deny the internal calling I received.

All I have to do in future is think back to this experience and this special place where I had first consciously connected with God and I will be reconnected. I was truly alive and had finally found my *happy place*, my sanctuary, my eternal connection to the Divine Creator, the source of all loving energy and the source of all life. I thought to myself, *I will never doubt God's presence again!*

Manifesting

God said, "If you open your arms and spend some time alone and ask to be filled with love and light, the God source energy *has* to come to you, because you are asking for it. Is a billion dollars created by you or the source, or given to you?

"You need *love* to create goals. It is not *given* to you, it is *created.* Let the love, the comfort and the calm in. You have to pull love in and then generate what you need even if it is food, income, your home, or millions of dollars. It's done using the same method."

God continued, "Be humble about what you want, as well as embracing abundance at the same time."

These 3 simple words teach you about manifesting anything

1. Practise
2. Patience
3. Persistence

For those of you who have seen the documentary, or read the book called *"The Secret,"* it is a very good movie and an equally good book based on the law of attraction. It teaches a strong foundation, when learning to manifest things and it also teaches you how to maintain the right state of mind, to be able to manifest *good* things.

What it doesn't teach you, are two very important things. The first thing is how to create a manifesting board properly and the second thing is where exactly are you directing your faith? The documentary teaches you to ask the *Universe* for what you want, but if there is a Creator and there are spirit guides, soul families and angels, why would we be asking the *Universe* to help? Why not just ask the Creator, the spirit guides, the soul family, or the angels to help?

The Universe is a vast mass of space, with loads of planets and it is really big out there. Your wish or your desire may get lost amongst the voices of everyone else in the Universe also asking for help. There are cases when you can call upon the Universal energies and there will also be times when you need to cast a wide net with your wishes, but if you want to aim for something *specific,* then you need to target your intent on something *specific.*

Let's combine the two things and let's make a manifesting board called the "God Board." Let's put it on gold paper, so we can literally go for gold. First, put on the board where you are *now* and then where you want to *be!* For example, show yourself being poor on your knees praying, then show yourself being happy and successful.

Start with a sad face picture and label it (from here, or *from this*). This is to show those spirits, or entities who are going to help you, what you feel your current state is and then show them using pictures what the end result should look like. Then add your happy face and label it (to here, or *to this*).

FROM THIS

TO THIS

Pictures are better to use than words, because it needs to be in a universal language, so that any soul can understand what you are asking for.

You have to *convince* a soul in pictures to help you. Work out the goals and keep them simple. If you're asking for help from any spirit, they are not mind readers and they don't get inside your head and listen to your inner speak. They need to be *shown* exactly what you want, so they can help you to achieve it.

This is actually the hardest part for most people. Actually working out what their goals are and establishing what do they really want from life? What is happy? You need to show what you want in universal or pictorial symbolism and be *specific* about exactly what it is you want to be doing, or what you want to achieve, so that the spirits, angels, or God can help you to manifest your goals.

This can also be why dreams don't come true for everyone, because we don't ask for these dreams or goals in the right way. We are not directing our wishes to anyone in particular. We are being taught to throw it out there in the *Universe* and just wait for the results to come back. In reality, it is not quite how it works.

You don't just think idly about something and "*ding*" it magically appears like a genie in a bottle. If you think about something often enough and give it as much energy as you can, then you need to be very careful what you wish for, because you just might get it, especially if you are thinking about it all the time.

The main thing "The Secret" gets right, is showing you that what you think about, or put your energy into, is what you are attracting into your life. It is also what you *become.* If you are continuously worried about having a lack of money, having too many bills, or having a lack of love in your life and concentrating on these problems and thinking about them all the time, you are actually subconsciously manifesting *more* of what you don't want. It is okay to *acknowledge* what you don't want, so you can clear the path for what you do want, but don't dwell on negative thoughts and feelings.

Learn to direct your thoughts in a positive way and if you happen to drift off down the woeful and negative path, gently guide yourself back onto the positive path and don't get angry at yourself for making a mistake, because you will only attract more mistakes. Think about how you can do it right and see yourself already achieving your goal and even beyond that.

Manifest the feeling that you will experience when you have already achieved your goal. That's what you want to focus on. In your mind, believe that you have *already achieved* it.

Focus on being grateful and you will attract more grateful experiences. I personally think that the real reason we should all experience gratitude, is because our Creator, the Supreme Being *allows* us to exist in the first place.

This is the same being that is responsible for all of us and the *only* reason we exist at all. God is not just some airy fairy Universal Energy concept. God is a real being, who is fully alive and living a life, just like we are. He wants to engage with you and if you would just be patient, he will show you signs he is with you. If you pray to a vague force like a single nature element, or direct your prayers out there *somewhere*, you are denying yourself the opportunity to be within the full presence and all encompassing energy field of the Creator.

My biggest reason for writing this book is to show God and anyone who is interested, how much faith I have in him and how much I believe in him. I can share his presence with all of you, if you are willing to learn *how* to tap into the God energy.

I am sharing my personal proof of God's existence with you, to help you see and understand there is a God, an Almighty Lord, an intelligent Life Force who created us and everything including the scenery around us.

God is real, lives and breathes and is not some fictional character that many would have you believe. Trust your inner voice and listen to the inner connection you already have with God.

We are so concerned with political correctness that we are often in denial of the existence of our very own Creator. Imagine how the Creator feels about people who don't believe in him? It saddens him deeply, but he doesn't want to force you to believe, because you have free will to believe whatever you want, even if it is denial. He wants you to seek him out and become attuned, so you can feel him.

I still don't understand what the problem is admitting and acknowledging there is a God. I don't *think* there is a God, I *know* there is a God and he is the most amazing being you will ever come to know, once you open your hearts and simply believe in him.

Everything will change for you, once you recognise he has already been with you the whole time and he has never left you ever! Without truly experiencing his unconditional love and kindness, you are living in a partly shaded or darkened existence, without the presence of the holy light of God.

Once you have worked out what your goal is, you can put it on your God Board. Have patience, pray, *expect* to see results and wait to see what happens. Being proactive can also help, because you don't want to wait around for life to happen to you.

God said, "Imagine a man who is living in Kenya and he decides he is going to set a goal of having $20.00 per week. It may not seem much to you, but to someone in Kenya this is a lot of money. Then when he reaches that goal, he could set a new limit of say $50.00 per week. He can continue to revisit himself and his goals and put his goal up to the next limit, until he is happy with his achievement. When he is ready and if he wants to, he can go to the next level, or limit. He is creating his own happiness by achieving his goals.

"What happens to most people when they reach their goal, is that they are so busy thinking about their next goal, they don't even take time to acknowledge the fact they have reached their goal. They forget to pat themselves on the back and say, 'Well done, good job.' In such a materialist world, people always want more.

"On the flipside, it is very important not to live in the consciousness where you say to yourself, 'I will be happy *when* I reach my goal,' because you are denying yourself happiness right now. You could get happier, but don't think of it as being happy, dependent on a goal. To be really good at manifesting, you have to learn to specify what happens when you get there."

A classic example of when manifesting can go wrong, is when people only set *one* life goal and they only have *one* dream they want to fulfil on their bucket list. They could be a sportsperson reaching their physical fitness pinnacle, or achieving their ultimate goal. They could be a musician finally getting to perform in a concert hall, or they could meet the man or woman of their dreams and then *"bam!"* They are taken away, or they die suddenly, because this was their *only* desire, their single wish, or goal. They forgot to specify what happened *after* reaching that goal.

Be very careful what you wish for, especially when you believe in the power of your mind and your beliefs. You need to keep an open mind and an open limit, but break it into digestible steps, or chunks to help you to manifest your larger goals.

God said, "You must believe in your heart that you are going to achieve your goal. Learn to see *beyond* the goal and be prepared to move on and have a new goal, once you have achieved it. Remember to reward yourself for achieving your goal, even if it is a trip to the movies, treating yourself to a massage or having a meal out somewhere special. The reward is doing something you really enjoy."

Most importantly remember to say thank you when you reach, or supersede your goal. Thank yourself, thank any souls that helped you and thank God. This is how to *show* your gratitude, with genuine appreciation for those who helped you along the way.

Creative visualisation

Creative visualisation is much more proactive and is almost like a dedicated meditative practise, where you are consciously spending time, effort and energy on your goals and desires. With creative visualisation, you are specifically focusing on what you want, or asking for specific guidance in relation to your goals and desires.

When using creative visualisation you need to be really specific. The main difference between manifesting and creative visualisation, is the end goal. With manifesting, we are usually focusing on a specific goal, or a specific desired outcome and we may want to manifest something particular over a longer period of time.

God said, "When we are using creative visualisation, we are getting into the manifesting mindset all of the time. When we awaken, when we go about our daily life and then when we reflect at the end of each day, we are using creative visualisation.

"It is a state of mind and a state of being that we are consciously seeking. We actively need to set aside time regularly, to truly focus our energy, intention and desire into creatively visualising to manifest our goals. During the creative visualisation process, we will be shown what possibilities are potentially out there for us and receive divine guidance to show us how to achieve these goals ourselves."

God continued, "Everyone is always looking for the miracle cure, or the magic pill. The truth is that there is no *one thing* that is going to make you achieve your goal, cure your cancer, or allow you to be financially free. It is always a *combination* of things, when used together, that makes up the total recipe for success. When you bake a cake, or prepare a special meal and you leave out one vital ingredient, it can lead to a flat cake, or a bad tasting meal."

God added, "To be fully in the moment with creative visualisation, you need to ask yourself, if money was no object, if distance, location, education, age and excuses were no object, what would you be doing, or what would you like to be *right now,* that would make you feel totally fulfilled and happy? The answer to this question, you should be spending your time consciously focusing on and using your mind, to creatively visualise it and make it a reality!"

Goal setting

I could easily write a whole book just about goal setting. I am a very accomplished goal setter and I always achieve my goals, once I set both my heart and my mind to align with the intention of achieving the goal.

First, you need to decide *what you want* to achieve as a goal. The hardest part of goal setting is right at the very beginning, by establishing what you want. Setting goals requires you to make decisions about what you want in the future and then determining how you are going to achieve each goal. To be able to do this, you need to be able to put a deadline on what you want and then create a plan.

We are not taught these basic skills in school, sometimes we are shown small fragments of the process at work, but often we are not shown how to set goals from the start, right through to the end. Unless you are earning a living from coaching people to set goals, or you work as a project manager, or in a similar role, setting goals can be like a foreign language to learn, if you haven't learned how to talk the talk and walk the walk.

What you need to do, is take some time out of your busy schedule, to choose a goal that you would like to achieve. It is really important to remove yourself from your usual environment and go somewhere you can feel connected with nature, or feel connected with the God energy.

Close your eyes and visualise. Imagine yourself already accomplishing your goal. Where are you? How did you get there? How do you feel now that you've already achieved your goal? Are you happy? Does it feel good? Focus your attention on what you are trying to achieve and remember that you have full control over your goals and that you will have the strength and skills, to overcome your obstacles and difficulties. You can change your goals any time you want to and you can upgrade and downsize your goals any time too.

You need to spend some valuable time thinking about what you want to do in your life and creating the life you want, instead of accidentally falling into whatever happens to you in your life. This is investing valuable time and effort towards your goals and that is a part of what makes your goals manifest. This process is necessary to help you identify your vision, your dream and your future goals. Setting goals for yourself puts you in control and allows you to choose where you want to go in your life, rather than being driven, dictated to, or led astray.

I personally have 7 simple rules that I follow. These guidelines can help you to determine what your goals will be and help to make the process work for you.

1. Make sure your goal is **something that you really want** and that it is not just an idle daydream, or a wishy washy thing you might like to have.
2. Your goal must **ethically agree** with your personal path.
3. **Write down** your goal in complete detail.
4. Make sure your goal is **achievable**.
5. **Stay focused on the big picture** and don't let small setbacks wear you down.
6. **Acknowledge your success** when you finally reach your goal.
7. **Develop your goals** once you start making your goals a reality.

Once you have decided on your main life goal, then you can determine your smaller, measurable, or actionable goals. The smaller goals are like stepping stones to achieving your bigger life goal.

Define and describe your goal. Write down *when* you want to achieve it, the *reasons* you want it and also how you would *feel* after you have achieved it. Figure out exactly what it would take to get it and be realistic about the time things will take.

People don't always allow themselves enough time to achieve their goals and give up too soon. I have learned this lesson the hard way and usually try to cram 100 goals into every year and set myself up for disappointment and failure, when I only achieve 50 of them.

Make a time line by drawing a horizontal line with a dot at each end. The left end represents "**Now**" and the right end represents a point in the "**Future**," when you want your goal to be achieved by. Specify **what you want to happen** and when, from now until then. Write the "**goal date**" next to the word "**Future**."

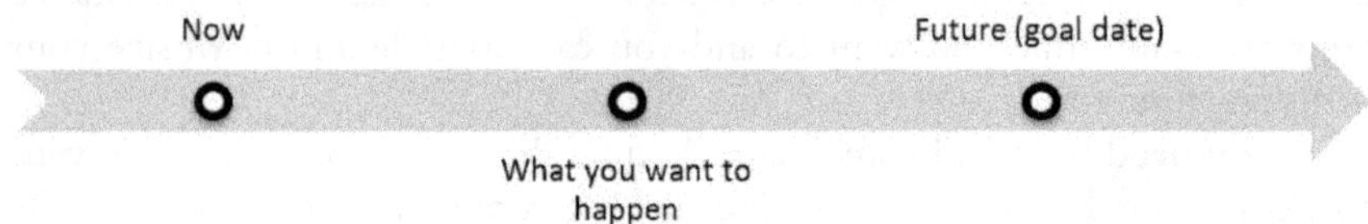

Set out your smaller tasks that need to be achieved, before the major goal can be obtained. These tasks can be added to your timeline, at the approximate designated intervals that you think you can realistically achieve. When you achieve a task that is an integral and an important part of the process, then that determines the success of the next phase of the goal. This is called a *milestone*.

Once you have defined your vision, imagine yourself where you want to be, when you reach the goal you have set. Does it make you feel excited and energised, or tired and overwhelmed? If you are absolutely passionate about the goal, vision, or dream, then you will stay focused and having the urge to quit will be less likely.

The true secrets of manifesting are; feeling, acting and going through the motions, of already having whatever it is you want to achieve. By reviewing your goals daily, you are living in the moment of already achieving your goal and reinforcing this process every day.

If you follow this process every day, you cannot help but align yourself with what you need to achieve your goals. You may like to dedicate a regular time each day to focus, or meditate on your goals.

Spend the time to simply imagine yourself already achieving the goal and not becoming too concerned about *how* you will achieve the goal. This creates a strong connection between the physical and spiritual worlds, to help bring your goals into alignment.

God said, "Every time you make a decision during the day, ask yourself this question, *does it take me closer to or further away from my goal?* If the answer is *closer* to your goal, then you have made the right decision. If the answer is *further away* from your goal, then you may need to rethink your course of action."

God continued, "Goals are a very personal thing and you shouldn't share your deeply personal goals with all of the people you know. You can bounce ideas of people, but don't let other people determine what your goals should be. Their influence can change the way that you view your goals, without even meaning to cause you any harm.

"Remember we are all here for a different purpose and to experience different things. If you want to climb Mount Everest with your best friend who is unfit, unhealthy and unmotivated, you might have to reassess your climbing partner, not your goal."

God added, "If you do not know what you would really like to do, or what you would really like to achieve, it is probably a really good time to start seriously thinking about where your life is heading and what direction your life is going in. You are in the driver's seat of your life. To not have a vision, is like being on a boat with no destination in mind and drifting aimlessly wherever the wind, tide and currents may take you. It might be fun for a while, but you might also get lost at sea in the process, not knowing which way to go next."

God continued, "Getting lost sometimes, is a good way to find and reconnect with yourself. Sometimes things happen to you on your life path that make you question everything and make you re-evaluate your life goals completely. That is perfectly natural and a part of the process of successful goal setting.

"Big events have a big impact on your life and can change your perception of life goals like; getting married, buying a house, relocating, having children, getting divorced, losing family members or friends, gaining a new job, losing your job, getting overworked, becoming ill both physically or mentally, dealing with the behaviour of others and losing yourself somewhere along the way."

God added, "If you happen to wander off track, or get lost out there somewhere, just come back to the simplicity of re-evaluating and resetting your goals. You can screw up the old goals and start again, any time you want to."

Addiction

God said, "Anything that takes away minutes, or seconds off your life is not good, it is *demonic.* If you are easily addicted to things, then you could be labelled a junkie. Temptations are everywhere. 'Here, we want you to experience this new drug, this new type of love, this drink, smoke this, eat this, try this and let's try this type of sex!' Oh it's just like art."

God continued, "First you need to ask yourself some questions, *is this making you happy? What have you lost?*"

The channeller on behalf of God said, "God is here to give you hope, to guide you in the right direction. Addiction is there simply to fill a void, a space where love doesn't exist. It is filling up the hole with something, anything to stop the pain, or to stop thinking about the things in your life you are not happy with. Sometimes people can be so destructive with their addictions that they are prepared to fill their void with the Devil's temptations, even if it kills them. Bring yourself back to where you were, before you went down."

God added, "What other natural highs are there in your life? Wouldn't you like to get back up there again? Let me take you to the top of the hill and then keep you there. Find something to replace the high with and let me guide you through the experience."

God said, "If you have a friend, or someone you know who is addicted to something that is harming them, you may need to go with them to help save them. Save their souls. There is always a demon from the past that will rear its head up! The demon is trying to lead the righteous astray by taking away their hope and replacing it with *temptation.* It's part of the testing process, by testing your true faith."

God continued, "Addictions are like false prophets. They give you false hope and leave you in a deluded state of well being, that doesn't last. Find some *genuine sweetness* in your life.

"One of the worst addictions on the planet at this point in time is smoking cigarettes. It is the biggest killer out of all of the possible addictions you could have."

God said, "Why doesn't a cigarette packet have the skull and crossbones symbol on it, instead of a picture of a stranger which people disassociate themselves from? Hold up a packet of cigarettes and ask, what is the international symbol for poison? Then explain the fact that if cigarettes are so poisonous, why don't they contain the deadly poison symbol on them?"

God continued, "Smoking has the betrayal of catching up with one's self at a later stage. Someone who does not cherish their future does not understand and they must be shown their happy future without smoking. Their younger self, should show love for their older self and the love the younger self gives to the older self, shows the ultimate self respect.

"Smokers are being selfish in their younger life and denying their older self a healthy life. If they could change their younger self when they are old, they would. Shaking, pain and shortness of breath in their body, is the suffering that will be endured by the smoker and not *if,* but *when.* Once the death and decay takes hold of the body, then the shame they feel about their younger body kicks in. It is like the demon is finally getting what it wants and it gets to take your soul away in the end, with your last gasping breath of air."

God added, "To release yourself from the bonds of the smoking addiction, you need to take a look at where that path is taking you and how you think that path will end? Now, fast forward in time, to when smoking will eventually take your life. Is that something you want for your body? Is the suffering that you will endure, something you are looking forward to? Is that your representation of happiness and healthiness?

"You need to be consciously aware of what you are doing to your precious cells and your mortal body. Your body is a vessel given to you for the duration of this life. If you want your vessel to be in good shape and last the distance, you have to maintain it and take care of it, just like you maintain your vehicle. We all know what happens to a vehicle that isn't maintained, or looked after. It is not a matter if it will expire or breakdown; it is just a matter of *when* and how badly. Say to yourself, *I shall stop smoking as my younger self and if I feel like smoking as my older self, I can.* By then you will see how silly smoking is and that you have no need to do it when you are older, because there is no point to it. It is just like now, when you are younger; there is still no point to it."

God wanted you to know, "The licking of salt cures smoking. Smoking shuts down all the senses and the person who does it is getting through life just fine without feeling a thing. They are depriving their senses, especially their taste and smell senses."

God continued, "Surely another addiction is called love, when it is co-dependence. Not being able to love oneself is another self destructive addiction. You don't need anyone to love you. *You* need to love you and you can *ask God to love you,* any additional love is a bonus. Why don't you try having an addiction to something healthy like green sprouts, or broccoli? Too much of anything isn't good for you, but learning to do things in moderation, is a good way to start reducing destructive habits in your life."

Another addiction many people have fallen prey to, is the gambling addiction. Gambling has a strong pull for people who like to take risks. They want an easier way to win money and gambling also gives people a sense of having a ticket in the golden lottery so to speak. Gambling includes playing the poker machines, online gambling, card games, TAB, horse racing, greyhound racing, sports betting, footy tipping, scratch and wins, Lotto, Keno, Bingo and of course the casino. There are slightly less risky gambling activities such as; foreign currency trading (forex), share trading and real estate. When it comes down to it, living and breathing is a risk.

To take a risk, is when you are prepared to exchange something valuable for the opportunity to get something more valuable. You can risk anywhere from $1 up to millions of dollars, each time you take a gamble. The amount of money is irrelevant; it is the fact that you are taking a gamble. There are safe players and there are the outrageously risky players. There are those who will gamble their entire life savings in one night and there are those that like to build up their float over time and they know all about how to take calculated risks. The calculated risk taker knows their limits and follows a set of rules when taking any punts.

You go through a whole range of emotions when you gamble and lose, just as you go through a whole range of emotions when you win. Like all methods of gambling, the odds are *not* in your favour, but yet we all still like to take a punt from time to time. God is happy when he sees each gambler realise that they can learn from their mistakes. He doesn't judge you, if you have a go at something and you lose.

God knows that we are learning and that sometimes risks pay off. Different people class risks differently and some people do actually make a living out of gambling to some degree. The ones that do make money are realistic and they know that you don't win all of the time. They are prepared to take their losses when they happen and celebrate the wins when they come. You see it isn't a problem, until you lose more than you win and your float starts eating into your savings, or you start borrowing, or stealing money to support the loss.

Knowing when to call it quits, is the key to winning in gambling. I know that sounds so simple, but people do play on thinking they can *chase* their losses and that the system owes them, because they have invested so much already and convince themselves that they will get it back. Even better, don't take the risk at all. If you are going to take the risk, do it with a proven set of rules and *stick to your rules*. Set yourself a spending limit and a stop loss and pull out when you reach either of these limits. If you are winning, then you can increase your stop loss and implement what is called a trailing stop as your win increases. Don't break your own rules and get out while you are ahead, or pull out before you lose too much.

What happens when you don't have a plan and you don't follow the rules? You lose. It's not complicated, it's really simple. You get angry and frustrated and you might even get out of control, but it doesn't get your money back. Walk away when your loss is obvious. It might hurt, you might even cry, or get upset, but learn what that feeling is like when you are losing and if it doesn't feel good anymore, don't do it anymore. Stop, breathe and remind yourself, that you are in control. Remember the outcome the last time you lost and bring that thought into your mind to help you to decide not to go, before you go in the first place.

It's setting a standard of what you want and what you enjoy, against what you don't want and what you don't enjoy. It's getting back to *the line* and once you have set your rules, your standard and then stick to it. The odds with gambling are always against you and occasionally there are a lucky few. Luck is not the best word for it, gambling works on random odds, which are based on statistics and mathematics. You just need to look at the statistics to know what the likelihood of winning is going to be.

You can never get that money back once you have lost it. You can't stop other people setting their own standard, because that is their lesson to learn not yours. If someone else is gambling out of control, you can always offer *suggestions*, or offer your help and guidance, but you can't tell them what to do, especially if they are an adult and capable of making their own decisions, even if they are unreasonable, or out of control. Maybe you could teach them *the line*, the standard. Teach them to aim above the line and not to drop below the line. Maybe they just need to learn for themselves.

God said, "There are plenty of other addictions out there like legal and illegal drugs, alcohol, shopping, porn, sex, coffee, medication, sleep, chocolate, food, sugar, fat, salt, pot smoking, television, internet, technology, mobile phones, co-dependent relationships and on it goes. The main thing to remember with any addiction is *balance*.

"It's okay to really like doing something, even if it is considered a bit naughty, it doesn't matter. What really matters is how much and how often you are doing it, or craving it, when you are not doing it. Overdoing anything is not good for you. Have you ever heard the term gym junkies? It is proof that even too much exercise is not good for you. You can do things in moderation, even if they are considered bad for you, as long as you have a balance of good, to counteract the bad. You can eat takeaway foods, if you eat them moderately and for the rest of the time, you eat healthy. You can have a piece of chocolate cake, a bowl of ice cream, or that small packet of chips you loving munching on so much, as long as you don't eat the whole cake, the whole tub of ice cream and a whole packet of large chips in one sitting.

"It feels good to indulge every now and again, but you need to remember your body is sacred and you need to think carefully about what you put into your body and what you do with your body. If you are eating only chocolate in your diet, then you are probably having too much sugar and fat and that makes your body work really hard, to use the energy constructively. You might like eating only bananas, but do you think that would be nutritious enough, to sustain your body on their own all the time? If you are having too much of anything, you need to introduce other things into your life, to give you variety and balance, so that you don't become addicted to just *one* thing."

Brainwashing

God said, "What does the TV do? It brings up the hatred and horror to the forefront all the time."

God continued, "How many productive hours do you think you could regain by simply switching the television, or internet off altogether? If you can't turn it off completely, make a plan to reduce your exposure to it and moderate the content that you are exposing yourself to. Are you watching endless hours of politics, doomsday prophecies, death, horror, cruelty and stressful shows, which add tension to your already stressed mind?

"Brainwashing yourself with negative images and concepts *does* have a huge subliminal effect on you, as well as on your subconscious mind. It is forming a negative self-destructive program, which is either getting you fired up to cause chaos and havoc, or it will wear you down and make you feel overwhelmed, helpless and numb. Either of these methods of programming would be classed as *destructive*. It is not good for you and both have long term negative side effects. If you must watch television, or the internet, then watch documentaries, positive stories, or educational programs, which utilise your brain and get it working in a positive way. This will have a positive flow on effect into the rest of your life and others' lives. If we were all doing this, the world would be a happy place."

Modern music is another carefully implanted sickness creeping into the youth of today. Subliminal messages are encoded in manufactured pop music these days and it is changing the way youth see the world. Modern music videos not only showcase the degradation of relationships, but also show demonic portrayals of men and women, which have now become normalised and we have become desensitised. Mankind no longer flinches at scenes of ritualistic abuse. The modern day music videos are portraying subliminal pornographic messages, which are hidden deep within in the music video so cleverly, that young children couldn't possibly understand the agenda being pushed behind the scenes.

Many trends are so influenced by the mainstream media and some of these trends encourage the disassociation with family and friends with the popularisation of gangster and rap music. The music industry has now made it all about making money and music isn't what it used to be. Music doesn't even need to sound good anymore to sell. Music is supposed to be happy and joyful, but many superficial music artists just sell their soul for fame and fortune, even if it is short lived. This just makes them a puppet that is doing exactly what they are told by the music industry.

Music used to be about getting messages across to the community, feeling good, entertainment, celebrations and more importantly to showcase musical talent with a unique musical ability. Now it is based on worship, but worship of the darkest kind, which is steering mankind *away* from the goodness that is inside everyone. Unless you actually start looking deeper into what you are being exposed to you, won't see it on the surface. Take time to listen to the lyrics of the songs and ask yourself, *is this a pleasant song, does it make me feel good, does it invoke useful emotions, or destructive emotions?*

Mental illness

God stated, "Someone who is mentally ill is smarter, because they have invented *more* than a normal person with a brain. You may not understand who you are looking at and they may have 10 people inside one body.

"In the old days, they would have been considered to be possessed, but if you look at this scenario as being a wire frame, so you can see *through* the wire frame, then you can always expect there to be multiple personalities behind the frame.

"When you talk to a supposedly *sane* person, they are coming across as seven attitudes for the average person. For example, anger, happiness, sadness and other expected attitudes, but you wouldn't expect them to say, 'Hi my name is Kelly and I am angry.' Then they have several realms behind that. You see Kelly might be a murderer, or a demon and the only way to deal with that, is to tell the original person who might be called Mary, to step aside, while you deal with the other demon who has given itself a name.

"Jesus could see quite clearly and could see right through demons and that is how he dealt with them. He was always looking for a diamond in the rough."

Please do not misinterpret mental illness for possession, because it is not. I am just making you aware that there are cases of mental illness that *could* be demonic possession.

God said, "Go inside their mind and also be away from their craziness, so you don't *become* crazy. You have to measure yourself against them, not necessarily with your own experiences. You have to make up experiences in your mind, if you haven't had experience with this before. This is another method of calibration, or bench marking the person, before helping, or treating them.

"In the second realm there are numbers behind numbers and you can have infinite numbers of numbers, behind the numbers. This can cause someone to be schizophrenic, because they can see in 3D. They have depth in their field of vision and when someone has a mental problem, they build a brain *beyond* their brain, which causes them to constantly choose a new brain. Some of these brains are their past lives and some of them have been invented, or are make believe ones.

"Know what you are dealing with and address the multiple personalities by making a statement like; 'Okay I am talking to *all* of you.' By making this statement, it includes getting the attention of all of their personalities and not just the current personality you are talking to. If there is a case of possession, or spirit influence involved, this can also address the entities, as well as the multiple personalities. This way you can deal with the whole group at the same time, or use the term *'all of you,'* which includes everyone inside there."

God continued, "This will now give you a deeper understanding when someone is confessing something to you. It is the other personalities coming through. It is like an aspect of their personality, which might be 8, 9, or 10 layers deep and it is one of these attitudes telling you their sins. Don't judge people when they tell you their sins, be like a confidant and pray to God to help them to stop their sins. You can pull the person up and state the fact of what their actions may be causing, so they understand the fault in their internal programming.

"Jesus would say to the thief, 'My brother that is wrong, because *[you can fill in the blanks]* and I will pray for you.' You could also say, 'You shouldn't have done that, there is going to be consequences and the only way to fix this, is to pray to God.' Tell the person that now they have done this, they shouldn't do it again."

God added, "Look at people as if you are looking at a wire frame. Then you can not only expect the worst, you can also expect more from them as well. It is like looking at a body frame and straight through into the skeleton, which can help you tell when someone is lying.

"If someone is possessed, or influenced, they have to go seven layers deep within themselves and move into latency mode, or delay their reaction, because behind that, they have to be in *zombie* mode. When you get down to the zombie mode, you need to ask them, 'Who am I talking to? Am I talking to the direct soul, or the soul behind that?' The entity will answer you and it is important to note there can be multiple souls in the body, but *which* soul is in control?"

God continued, "When you are talking to someone spiritually, are you talking to the spiritual body, or the possessed soul which would be the second layer? Schizophrenia would be multiple souls in control of the body, or at least the *essence* of the body. When you are alive there is a physical body and then there is the soul body. There are souls and spirits and the soul is the soul of the body. The spirit is the spirit in charge of the soul and the soul is in charge of the body and the energy. To make a soul, you have to have a spirit and to make a body you have to have a soul. How do you get a complex body? It just needs so much more to become a body.

"There were a total of 365 angels that made a body and they spent millennia working on the human body. They had to work harder, because they didn't have any education and had to build everything from scratch. The reason they made a bone that is not magnetic, is so that humans don't feel the magnetic energies from the Sun and the Earth, when walking around. If you were made of iron, you would know when there is a lighting storm. If there were any magnetic changes, you would be constantly affected all the time and have a meltdown. You were made so that when a spirit goes past, you can't even feel it.

"Each soul has something like seven names, which go seven layers deep. There is the angry name, the happy name and you also have names in the past, or the future, because you are allowed to change your name. Let's say in the past you have committed, or been the victim of a horrible crime. Then in the future you can *rename* it to help you cope. If you are dealing with a person who has anger management problems, then you would say, 'What is your anger name? Who are you when you get angry?'

They reply, 'John.'

'Okay what is your name when you are happy?'

They answer, 'Billy.'

So then you say, 'Okay now, let's call your angry name Billy!' This is going deeper into the layers and peeling back the layers, like the layers of an onion."

God added, "To understand what seven layers deep means, it touches on every sense and triggers an emotion, which in turn penetrates yet another layer, until all the senses are accounted for. Then you get the eighth layer, when you can talk *straight to the soul* and reach behind the wire frame.

> For example, if you were to talk about a beautiful flower, you would describe it something like this:
>
> 1. I saw this violet flower
> 2. It smells like violet
> 3. Lovely purple colour
> 4. Tastes like violet
> 5. Sounds like...
> 6. Feels like...
> 7. Sensed like... etc"

The channeller said, "To talk to God you need to go beyond the seven levels, to get through the wire frame. There is the surface to the wire frame and behind it is another realm and that is where the spirits are."

12. EMOTIONS

Life is about mastering both love and calmness.
When you can overcome everything and react with only love, or calmness,
then you are in complete control of your emotions.

HUMANS need to have a healthy respect for their emotions. To be in control of oneself, you need to be in control of your emotions. To be in control of your emotions, is to master your ego and to master your true self.

When your emotions are out of control, or out of balance, you can do irrational, unpredictable and irresponsible things. Emotional outbursts are the reason so many relationships fall apart and why crimes get committed.

A triggered emotional response can be all it takes for a human to do something they could regret for a whole lifetime. You cannot take words back after they are said and you cannot retrieve the stone after it is thrown.

The line and setting standards

I am going to teach you about "the line." See *the line* as a benchmark, a standard, an imaginary line that sets a limit on what is acceptable and what is not acceptable in your life and in your behaviour. The line is not only for your own benefit, it will help to realign and shift the vibration of those who you apply the line to.

God suggested to me, "When you are teaching the line, it is not horizontal. The line is vertical. We can view it looking at the past vs. future, the same as we look at the dark side vs. light side. You calibrate people by asking them which way is the future and then notice which way they show you. Which way is your future and past? The cross symbol shows both ways. Once they are calibrated you, can do a break state by slicing one way to break it and if you do a cross both ways, you can really affect a person's aura."

God continued, "To set the best standards, or to mark out your line, which is your ultimate cut off point, is to ask yourself, *what is the correct behaviour, or what is an acceptable level of behaviour?* How much is the right level? Who are you using as a model of correct behaviour? This can adversely influence your behaviour if you do not have a very good role model to use.

"An example of reprogramming would be to pick a category out of the many categories and model an example of correct behaviour and replace the negative behaviour. For example, sex. What is an acceptable level of behaviour, how much is the right level? People must learn to relearn and research what is the normal level and what is the maximum level. Once you learn the *right* levels, the correct levels, then you have set your standards and your line."

God added, "Even criminals have set limits on what is acceptable and what is not. They have learned behaviour that is not always correct and they know that it is not quite right, but they don't know how to change it. They don't have anyone who cares enough and who is *able* to help them. Their behavioural issues can stem from *influenced* behaviour and incorrect role models, as well as negative conditioning."

The channeller said speaking for God, "In God's eyes it is not wrong, or right until you realise what the minimum, or maximum is supposed to be. For example, if the maximum is 100%, the average person sits in between the 50-60% benchmark. You then need to research what is normal for the person, based on religion, age, law, culture, health, gender etc. Someone that is on drugs might think it is okay to have a taste every now and again to experiment, but to be doing it 100 times a day, is completely wrong and is ruining their health. Everything should be used in moderation and nothing in excess.

"Life is about mastering both love and calmness. When you can overcome everything and react with only love, or calmness, then you are in complete control of your emotions. If you can learn these methods and learn to respond to any conflict, aggression, or anger with sweet words and sweet actions, you can diffuse the situation very quickly.

"If this doesn't work then sometimes the best thing is to say *nothing* at all. Silence makes people stop in their tracks and it can make them feel acutely aware of what they are saying, when you don't respond. You cannot fuel a situation by saying nothing at all. If the situation becomes dangerous, then you are better to walk away, as soon as you feel uncomfortable."

The channeller continued, "Humans are not very well trained when it comes to manners. In some countries you might be forced to rush around and push in front of people and benefit from being first in the line. In other countries, you can take your time and nobody cares how long it takes to get somewhere. You need to ask yourself, *where are you in a hurry to get to?* When you cut somebody off in a car, was there any point to it? When you get angry at someone driving on the road in front of you, beside you, behind you? Is there any reason for you to get angry over something you have absolutely no control over? No there isn't.

"Focus on the things you have the power to do something about and remember love and calmness in *every* situation. Your pulse rate will drop right down, your blood pressure will stabilise and your heart will continue beating at a steady methodical pace."

The channeller added, "The stress of feeling like you have to change all of the injustices in the world overnight does not actually help. Any plan you want to implement needs to be well thought out and carried out with precision. This simple act stops you from feeling like you are in a rush to get everything done straight away.

"Pace yourself, set your own standards, the same as you expect other people to act. You can't create one rule for you and one rule for everyone else. Whatever standard, or benchmark you set, you need to be prepared to live by it, teach it and justify it, just as you expect others to do."

For me, this is what the line really means. Do as I do, not do as I say. Lead by example and blaze a positive trail for others to follow.

Love

God said, "If it's love you feel, then it comes from God. He has given you love. Love is the answer. Love is as easy as 1, 2, 3. Love is the answer to all of your problems. Love is the answer to all of your dreams."

God continued, "Nothing comes for free, but love does. So does hate. You can be anything, or either. Love generates something. Nothing generates nothing.

"What's the deepest feeling of love you can get? If you had to feel seven emotions about something and if you can find seven reasons to be in love, think about these seven ways. What are the seven experiences? It is like being in love seven fold deep."

God added, "I want you think about seven ways that you could feel and express love and then you'll experience the most exasperating experience in the world."

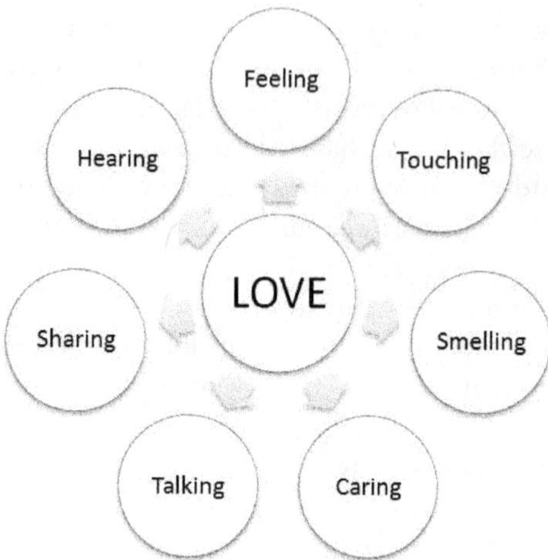

God's favourite and holy number is seven (7). The number seven (7) is used so often by God that you can rely on it as a sign that God is sending you a message and trying to communicate divinely with you.

God wants you to look at the pH (potential of hydrogen) level of water, when it is at the pH of 7. This is when the water is in a Godly state and is drinkable. Why do you think the correct ph of water is seven (7)?

God explained, "Reach out and love one another. Love is when you become loving of another, then you become one. Loving one another becomes *one* love."

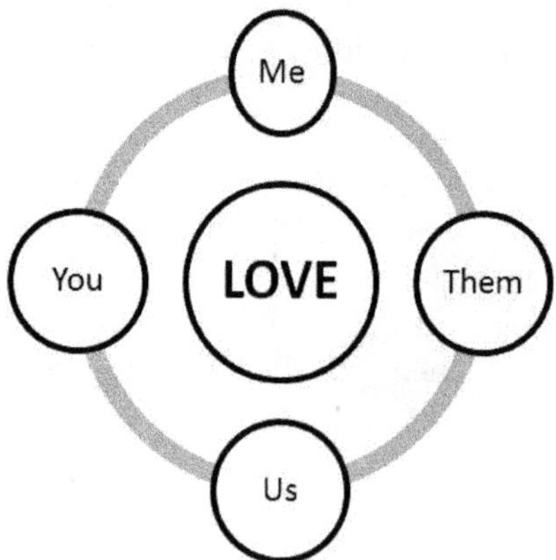

Praise

Praise is an old word that was used to show gratitude and appreciation towards something and particularly when singing, or praying to God. Praise is one of the passions that humanity has lost somewhere along the way.

The channeller said, "If you want someone to do something for you, then you should always remember to praise them. Praise turns on the receptors in the brain. The dumber they are, the less receptive the brain. A good example of using praise would be if you wanted to get pregnant using IVF, you would say to your doctor, or nurse, 'I would praise you for being able to do this for me the first time and I put my faith in you. I've got one shot at this and I've been waiting all my life.' If you praise someone *before* you get them to do the task, they will feel responsible and put more effort into the outcome."

The channeller added, "You can also praise someone *while* they are doing a task, to give them encouragement and help them to feel like they are a part of fulfilling a purpose and that their work is going towards a good cause.

"Praise is often delivered too late *after* the work has been done and even though it is nice to be thanked; sometimes it is too little, too late."

Forgiveness

God said, "Forgive *yourself* for your crimes, be helpful to others and embrace happiness. If everyone was to do this, even the dying and weak would be supported by the rich and those of knowledge and you shall be rewarded in the afterlife. Reach out and touch me, for I shall be the one who will hold you when you die. Believe in me, as I will take you and bring you back to life and you shall see again."

God continued, "Own your own sins and forgive yourself for something you've done wrong. Forgive yourself for your sins. Learn from your sins and once you have forgiven yourself for your sins, you won't do it again. Stop and reset. If you keep getting reminded about the sins you've committed, you are living in a demonic state. It is a very complex tribium."

God added, "Sins are comparable and the main thing is that you are responsible for your *own* sins. If you are happy, share it. If you are angry, or unhappy, try to *contain* it. Own your own robot, your own body, your own road. No one can be on *your* path, but you can share it. Stop the whingeing and moaning."

Forgive the living

God said, "Jesus saved souls that other people had prayed for and forgiven."

God continued, "Don't reject souls. If you're holy, or righteous, you can downplay their bad circumstances and bring them back to the middle. Someone who is really demonic just shows you they really haven't experienced love and light.

"It is important for people to be able to look forward to a change in the future and for you to be helping someone who needs forgiveness, to upgrade themselves as a person. They need forgiveness to make them something better than what they already are, so they still feel loved, even if they have made a mistake, especially if there is shame or hurt involved."

God added, "Make a statement like; 'In your own time, as fast as you can change and you will feel better. For you have the power to be what you were in the past and you have the power to be what you are in the future. What does that future look like to you?' This statement is a good starting point, to move the person out of their traumatic state and into their future happier state. Paint the picture if they can't see anything positive and move them towards that happiness."

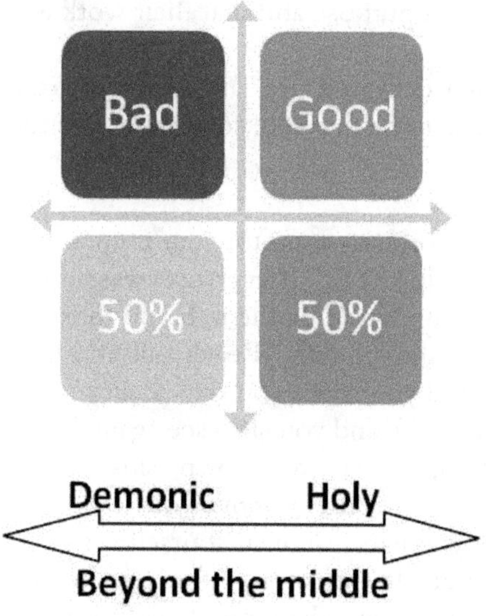

God said, "If someone is focusing too much on the demonic side, then that is where they are coming from, the *hell* energy. This may be where they have come from and they have been given another chance to make improvements to their soul."

Forgive the dead

You can ask God by saying, "God forgive the dead ancestors." You can lift the curses from the dead, while you are alive. When you pray to God, ask for forgiveness for your ancestors and pray for your ancestors.

Sometimes family members complain that nobody rings them up, but what they don't understand, is that nobody rings up their ancestors either. What is the difference between communicating with the living and the dead? Nothing, except it is more difficult to communicate with the dead than the living.

God pointed out, "If you pray for the dead ancestors, you'll see all the battles they have been through, when in trance. First you'll start to see colours and then images come through. Write down what is on the agenda for the meditation and the ancestors will take you there. It is like contacting the lost tribe."

God speaking through the channeller continued, "A long time ago, they used to stare at a fire and get visions, because things were a lot less complicated back then. Another way to get into a deep trance, is staring into water.

"Our parents can be one of the biggest discouragers when it comes to communicating with the dead, especially when we are young. When we are younger, we have a better and more attuned psychic ability than we do as we get older, unless you *develop* that ability. The reason is because after you have believed something from your parents for many years, you become *conditioned.* To reset your belief system, you can just *swish* and restart again!"

Taming the inner warrior

God said, "Learn to feel secure about yourself. When you are feeling insecure about yourself and your future, you can use your aggressive knowledge or your warrior sixth sense on an internal level. This can give you a new understanding. One thing that confuses humans is learning to understand risk and knowing what to do with humans that trample over one another. They do not understand they are trampling on one another's feet and themselves. Today you are the milkman and tomorrow you are the postman.

"Man is actually time locked and he has been locked in time to control him. Once you realise his ideal logic of time and space, then you can start to look inside the mind of a criminal. A criminal is not a criminal forever, just for that moment in time when they lost control of their inner warrior. The inner warrior is there to help you survive, fight off your enemies and use the fight instinct, instead of the flight instinct, to get you out of trouble when you need it."

God continued, "For example, a killer might think to themselves, I don't like waitresses and I killed one. What the killer doesn't understand is that they are killing all of the future roles that person would become; a musician, a project manager, a doctor, a healer etc. The killer needs to turn their inner warrior into a *saviour* warrior and learn to *save* some souls instead of destroying them."

Humans do tend to have a preconceived idea of what they think a criminal looks like, how they act, or who they are. Let me remind you there are many well dressed bandits around. Remove your rose coloured glasses, your misconceptions and your prejudgements. Let's break it down and get into the nitty gritty of a crime.

God said, "Young souls that may have only been here for one, or two lifetimes, might be a bit eager to test out their role as a human and see how far they can take it. They push the boundaries as much as they can until they get caught, captured, or taken out. So now that you have the prisoner, what are you going to do with them? They are puppets of their own fear. They are too earthly and just discovering themselves and making lots of mistakes in the learning process."

God continued, "This is a lesson for everyone, because ultimately we are one nation, in the spiritual world. They are lying to you in this world. So the kings and queens of old and new make a statement like; 'One of our people will come and destroy your nation.'

"The defending country's response would be, 'We won't tell you when we will come back.'

"The minority said, 'The spiritual people told us that one of our people will wipe your people out and you'll never stop it, it is written.' Then they have to try and find out who that *one person* is, just like they did when they tried to hunt Jesus down when he was born, because it was *written* that someone was coming to save them. What they didn't realise is that Jesus was more interested in saving souls long term and not just putting himself in a position of power. He didn't want to remove himself from the populace. Two populations can be identical, but one nation wants to wipe out the other nation. It's too advanced for humans at this stage of their evolution, but you get a bit of it."

God said, "Imagine how many times Jesus would have had to tap into his inner warrior to calm the injustices he was experiencing and seeing all around him, when he came to Earth to spread the **Word of God**. Enoch's soul was involved in making humans and he wanted them to be made so they could not be controlled by one person."

The free will humans were given sometimes gets a bit overbearing, when the free will of someone else overpowers the free will of another. This is technically *breaking* the rules. Define the rules. Well, let's start with the commandments given to Moses by God. You see mankind finds it a bit tricky to maintain a good emotional balance and not let their emotions get away on them.

God told me that I get to write all the words of wisdom for the suffering.

The channeller said translating for God, "When the inner warrior hurts someone intentionally and aggressively, then someone else suffers. Long term they both suffer, the hunter and the hunted. If the aggressor is held accountable for their actions, then they are labelled as a criminal and locked up. Nobody wants to know the story that led the person to commit their crime, or act of immorality, because they have already been judged by mankind.

"You ultimately judge yourself for your sins and God judges us for our whole existence and everything we have done, both good and bad and he doesn't just focus on the bad. He sees *all* of your deeds and he knows that with guidance, you can turn yourself around and still be forgiven, if you truly ask for forgiveness.

"Let's clear up the next question before you ask it. That doesn't necessarily mean you can commit a crime deliberately, say sorry and then get off the hook with the law and not be accountable. It means that when you *realise* you have made a mistake, you make amends and show that you are truly sorry. You can turn your life around and get back on the right track of love and light, even with a history of sins and sinning."

God said, "Many strings of life are like the strings on a guitar. When one breaks, you rewire it and tension it up. The more strings on the guitar, the more complex the life, or the areas of a life are. We live in a virtual world now, instead of a solid foundation where we used to live many years ago. Life can get really complicated without the proper support networks to help both victims and perpetrators, break free from their negative cycles."

God continued, "There are many states of a human being and every day it changes. When you feel that you have helped someone, learn to give and take. If someone says you don't have enough of something, or has told you off, then this can cause you to bring up the emotion and that is what comes through. What you expose yourself to, is what you create for your sanity. The first rule is to *avoid* conflict in the first place if possible.

"If you are backed into a corner, then you need reassess your position. Are you in self defence, or attack mode?"

God added, "To analyse what makes someone do something, you need to look at what is the *attitude* that is influencing the person the most. You have to look through the eyes of the Creator to understand that even someone that is in a jail, is waking up today and something is going to be different. Use different techniques to change the way we deal with people that are trapped in the prison system. When someone commits a crime and goes to jail, society needs to create opportunities for them, not continue suppressing them. The worst case scenario is, if you kill someone with a knife, you would want to be thinking differently psychologically, if you got in trouble for that.

"Learn to *embrace* the inner warrior and not deny it. Plan your outcomes of how you are going to handle yourself, when your inner warrior kicks in and learn how to *save* a soul, instead of destroying one. It has to be learned, if your prior learning has led you to be what you are. Relearning is the escape from the prison trap."

God said, "Learn a new way to deal with your emotions, instead of reacting in the same way every time and expecting a different result. If you continue hanging out with the same bad company thinking that one day things will just magically work out, you are asking for trouble. Without effort and application on your behalf, things don't just magically change by themselves. You have to put your energy into the change and learn a new way."

God continued, "If you diagnose someone whose anger is turned up way too high, you need to turn them more into a zombie by lowering one of their emotions. Not through prescription drugs, or shock therapy, but through a genuine diagnosis of what is wrong, caring enough about the person you are working with and then teaching them techniques to suppress it. Analyse someone then repair them."

God explained there are simple techniques to pacify someone and there are usually three main choices available.

1. Use a dummy or *pacifier* > change the subject.
2. Offer tissues > *comfort* them, or give them a hug.
3. Give them a *reward* like lollies > tell them they are happy, or doing a great job.

God said, "Use the door technique. If the first approach doesn't work, just walk out the door and turn around and come back again and try a different approach. It's like a swish technique and you may even surprise people with this approach, because it resets the situation and breaks the negative energy flow. Changing the whole subject is another break state. Start talking about something completely different, something more positive and constructive. Walk away if the pacifying techniques don't work, because that is the safest option when all else fails."

God continued, "Learn to watch, observe and learn, instead of jumping in boots and all to start a fight for no reason. Understand the outcomes *before* engaging and assess what the worst case scenario would be. That is measuring the risk. Then teach the learning outcomes, when you can see what works for you. In your mind, move to the point *after* the event and come up with what you think would be the best outcome. When someone is being disobedient, ask them, 'What is it that you want to do?' Then you will understand what troubles them."

My purpose in all of this is to give you faith and help you to realise that having faith in *something*, is better than having faith in nothing. I'm here to deal with humans and I want to teach you who God is. He is not some fairy tale, he is *real* and he knows your soul better than you do. God will come and save you. If you find it easier to talk to Jesus, then talk to Jesus.

I have personally been way past the holy good and way past the unholy bad, so I can teach you. It's not a false promise and there is a purpose and that is to gain an understanding of the holy vs. the unholy. It is realising there is some bad in existence and coming out balanced. It is better to understand what your current split between good and bad, or holy and unholy is, because then you know where you sit in the scheme of things. Are you 80/20 good/bad, 70/30, 60/40, 50/50 etc?

The purpose is not to be 100% holy, because then we wouldn't need to be here in the first place, but if we can work on a higher split, where the holy outweighs the unholy, then we are on the right track. If you happen to get to the 100% holy, you will either get taken away like Enoch did when he walked with God, or you might just ascend and never be seen again, who knows? I don't know anyone who is 100% holy and still walking the Earth at this time. It actually doesn't matter. All you need to do is give it your best shot and aim for the highest percentage of holiness that you can.

The channeller on behalf of God said, "Have a true understanding of where the male energy comes from. Don't deny the masculine members of society. Control them positively, guide them gently, love them wholeheartedly and influence noble men to do *noble* things. Lead by example. We are sending our noble men off to war, even in this day and age. It's a tragedy that good men all over the world still buy into the war story. If we all just stopped and boycotted war altogether, we would have *peace on Earth* and our inner warriors could be used for building honourable foundations for our future generations. Then all you need to do is channel the excess energy into healing the past wounds of old wars. Our world wars have always been a deception, to create a smokescreen for other things that were going on behind the scenes."

The channeller added, "You can rise above the crowd and be in your bubble."

Dealing with aggression

When someone is getting angry, they are getting angry at themselves. It's all about building walls, building boundaries. Be the opposite of whatever the opposition is. Counteract any hostility with an apology.

You can say something like this to them, "Well there's no point being in this body anymore, everybody knows that this person is usually very happy."

God said, "You can't be aggressive with someone who opposes you. See it as an opportunity to teach them something. They may have learned something unusual, which feeds their misunderstanding, even when something is incorrect, but true to them."

God continued, "Picture yourself and multiply yourself into three different people. Give each of these three people the same name. For example, you would name yourself Jan from the past, Jan in the present and

Jan in the future."

God added, "If you had all the events of your past and told someone else your past, you have now relieved yourself of these events, both good and bad. Now, if you had made up another Jan that has a completely different past, wouldn't you like to know the other Jan? Wouldn't you like to know what the other Jan, or the third Jan has done? Each scenario would be different. You are talking about your past, all the good things and all the bad things. This helps you to talk to your created non-judgemental party about your problems."

God said, "By removing your judgement when you deal with angry people, or aggressive behaviour, it is much easier to *diffuse* the situation and gain an understanding of what is making the person aggressive, or making them want to *express* their anger.

"Problems come from complex systems and you will need to drill down into the problem, to be able to help the person. Listen and ask more questions. If someone says they are hungry, then ask them, 'When is the last time you had something to eat?' If someone says they are homeless, then ask them, 'Where are you living right now?' You can drill further into the questioning by asking, 'How are you homeless? Why are you homeless?' Don't just ask them for the sake of asking them, genuinely learn to counsel people.

"Drill down and ask the relevant questions. Take them back to a state *before* their anger, *before* their aggression and *before* their sadness, when everything fell apart. For example, if someone is homeless, then ask them, 'When weren't you homeless?' If they are sick, then ask them, 'When weren't you sick?' If they are experiencing chronic pain like back pain, ask them, 'When were you last happy with your back?' If they are unhappy, sad, depressed, or angry then ask them, 'When were you last happy? Can you remember?' Instead of focusing on the thing that is triggering their behaviour, trigger the opposite reaction, by taking them back to a time when they were happy, satisfied and feeling fulfilled. Another good question to ask is, '*Where* were you last happy?' This could clear up the issue immediately, because they could realise it is the *location* they are not comfortable with and not necessarily the person, or behaviour."

God added, "Can you see how treating someone with respect, even if they are angry, or aggressive, can really help the situation? Remember they are angry at themselves and *not* you. You just happen to be there when they are expressing themselves."

Dealing with bullies

A friend's young daughter came to me and asked me how she should deal with the people, who were constantly bullying her at school. I know how I would personally deal with her situation, but I am not her. To be sure that I was giving her the best possible advice, the next opportunity I had to speak with God I asked, "What should I tell her that is the righteous way to deal with bullies?"

God responded, "There is a need to distance yourself from the bullies. You have to separate yourself from them. The victim always asks, 'How do I stop someone from doing whatever it is to me that is hurting me?' The bullies could be physically hurting you, sexually harassing you, swearing at you, or humiliating you."

God continued, "How do you deal with the bully? You need to identify every incident and analyse it. Ask the weakling what they did to fight back? What happened when you asked them to stop? Why does the weakling become weaker? Because they are losing! They are getting weaker and weaker and weaker until they don't exist anymore."

God posed the question, "What is a bully? It is someone who seeks strength and power and proving to you that they can do it and they will go to extremes to prove it. Bullies are called bullies, because they are the bull of the group. The leader is called the bully."

God explained, "To win against a bully, you simply have to take their perceived power away from them and regain your own power. If the bully is swearing at you, say to the bully, 'Every time you swear at me, it makes me stronger!' If the bully is throwing rocks at you, say to the bully, 'Every time you throw a rock at me, it makes me stronger and better!' You get the picture right? By reacting with strength and courage, instead of fear and submission, you are overpowering the bully and showing the bully that nothing they do to you, can take away your power and that you are *not* a victim. They'll soon get bored of your unaffected reaction and they will move on to their next victim."

God said, "You are a soul and you are in control of your own soul. You need to be in control of every situation. You need to be in control and you need stay in control. When you do something bad, who is actually in control? Mankind likes to let go of his control sometimes and that is when he gets into trouble."

The channeller said, "Humans are all apprentices, just like God and psychosis happens when a person gives up their control, because sometimes people don't want to be in control. You are brainwashed to listen to bosses and they control you. Then when people get bullied, they give up their control and give in to the bully. Once you give in to the bully, then you are bowing down and allowing another to control you. The important point is being in control? Always be in control of your actions and your behaviour. Once a bully loses control over you, they are not interested in you anymore. When you are in control, you become powerful, rich and happy."

Fear

Fear is a lack of faith and fear can drive the mind, body and soul to do the most irrational and erratic things. Later, you may even question what on earth you were doing. I have personally had many negative encounters with people throughout my life, for many different reasons. Sometimes it is because I was hanging around with undesirable people and other times I was being given the opportunity to experience certain situations, for the purpose of learning difficult lessons, so I could teach others in the future.

Having no fear

In the past, I have had martial arts training and as a result have learned to handle fear, anxiety and spontaneity, by being ready for my opponent at any given moment.

My warrior spirit guide said, "Always face your opponent and be ready for the attack. Don't turn your back only to be stabbed in the back."

I have now learned this technique and implemented it, in both my personal and business life. Having no fear, does not come without its challenges. In my experience, the more your spiritual awareness opens up, the more challenges you are presented with.

We all live in a society we wish was safer, cleaner, nicer and more wholesome. Reality dictates what actually happens out there in the real world and on the streets. We can either pretend that everything is alright and walk around blissfully unaware, or we can prepare for the possibility that sometimes things just happen. This is not being a pessimist, or lacking faith, it is quite the opposite. It is being prepared for battle in your mind, at any given moment. This state of mind is called having *no fear,* or being *fearless.* Ultimately this leads to a state of mental calmness. It gives you crystal clear spiritual clarity and also it gives you the mental strength of a warrior. Stop, breathe and think *before* you do anything. Acting irrationally or hastily can come at a price, especially if the situation is very serious and you could be in danger.

Martial arts, combat sports and self defence training are all like highly active forms of meditation. There are also slow and methodical forms like; Tai chi and Qigong. Then there are fast and energetic forms of martial arts like; Karate, Taekwondo and Jujutsu. There are many other forms of martial arts, including styles that use weapons training. The techniques you learn, teach you discipline, stamina and how to remain calm, even in a very anxious situation. I would recommend it to anyone who is being bullied, anyone who needs how to learn to defend themselves and to anyone that needs more *self discipline* in their fast paced life. It is also ideal for people wanting to learn ancient spiritual techniques and how to focus their energy constructively. It is a great way to get fit and enjoy challenging exercises at the same time. During your training you will be taught defensive techniques that can get you out of trouble when you need it. The two most important things it teaches you are quiet confidence and mental preparedness. Keep in mind that martial arts training, is to be used as a tool for self defence only and is not to be used as a weapon to harm anyone, or to inflict pain unnecessarily.

Unexpected fear

One time, I was once dragged across a concrete driveway by my hair, until all of the skin on my knees was raw, because my drunken boyfriend at the time had lost the keys to the apartment and locked everyone out. He was so angry, that he couldn't contain himself and took it out on me. Fuelled by alcohol, he was so angry and out of control, that he completely forgot he was in the presence of a whole group of people, who witnessed the whole event.

Mental note, always have two sets of keys and if necessary, hide one outside for those occasions when you lock yourself out. After some smart thinking and a brick, we gained access to the house. As soon as the door was open, I was running up the stairs to pack my bags quick smart and was on a mission to remove myself from this toxic environment. That was the last straw for me. He had crossed the line and encroached upon my standards and he had reached the edge of my boundary. I was not going to put up with violent or physical abuse from anyone.

Our other housemates that witnessed the whole scene fully supported me and protected me, while I packed my bags and prepared to leave the house. He tried to stop me from leaving, but everyone pitched in and stopped him from interfering any further.

The main reason I wanted to share this story with you, is so that you can see how quickly a situation can turn nasty and violent and you can be totally unprepared for it. In this case, I didn't really get to experience fear, because there was no time to react and the whole hair dragging incident was over in about one minute. It was totally unexpected and it was a brief, but *intense* experience. He displayed totally unacceptable behaviour.

Domestic violence can happen to anyone, at any time and without warning. Many people, who observe domestic violence from a distance, say that it should be *easy* to leave someone when it happens, but sometimes there are circumstances that make the relationship complicated.

At the time, I was so appalled because of his behaviour. He was a very strong man and there was no point in me fighting back at the time, because he could have hurt me even more.

This unexpected fear made me realise, that even in a brief moment of anger, this person disregarded all the basic laws of respect for another human being and I was not strong enough, even with my martial arts training, to take him on. Only in this case, I chose the path of least resistance and *surrendered* to the cruelty to lessen the pain. I decided to leave him after that event. If I had stayed with him, I would have never been able to trust him again and would always be living in fear that he might explode into a fit of rage at any time.

For those who are faced with domestic violence and physical or verbal abuse on a daily basis, there is a need to first identify the other person's behaviour as abusive. It may start out as subtle digs and offhanded sarcasm, then it can lead onto continuous harassment and criticism. If the conflict escalates it can turn into hostility and violence. Then ultimately one person uses their love as a weapon, by withholding their love and affection as punishment. This is when the behaviour turns into control, creating a codependent relationship. Over time this behaviour can wear anyone down.

Abuse can affect men and women in different ways and there is no one solution fits all, to deal with this behaviour or escape from a turbulent relationship. You need to recognise behaviour that is consistently abusive, mean, cruel or dominating, is *not* love. Successful relationships are always built on love.

Everyone gets frustrated sometimes and every now and again people can lose their cool. If it doesn't happen very often, then it is easy to forgive someone. They may be under a tremendous amount of pressure, haven't had enough sleep, or they may not be coping very well with current issues in their life. When it becomes habitual and recurring and their behaviour does not improve, you need to seek help. You do not have to put up with abusive behaviour. No marriage contract states you must tolerate abuse. If you learn to love yourself more, you will respect yourself more. When you respect yourself, you realise that you *deserve* to be loved, cherished and appreciated.

Rational fear

The next scenario I want to share with you is another random incident where I literally found myself up to my neck in trouble in a matter of seconds. During this life, I have been presented with many situations and lessons, especially with angry and aggressive men. I have now successfully learned to deal with their aggressive behaviour. I have certainly learned some very valuable lessons, as a result of my very confronting episodes.

I have never let my scary experiences turn me off men and it has never affected my ability to love men. I still believe that even the most violent man can be turned around, if you are willing to understand what triggers their emotional outbreaks of anger and spend time fixing their issues.

After my break up with my angry ex-boyfriend, I decided to escape to a tropical island out in the middle of the Pacific Ocean. I ended up extending my two week trip and staying for three whole months, because I loved it so much.

I didn't wear shoes for the entire time, played guitar every day and was so blissed out living the whole island lifestyle. The experience was very liberating and natural.

During this time, I met some wonderful people from all over the world and I also got romantically involved with a local islander, who was one of the boat drivers. He was also one of the musician entertainers on the island. He played in the island band and they played every night for the tourists. Most of the islanders that lived on the small island were not originally from there, they had come from all over Fiji and sometimes from neighbouring islands to live there. While I was living on the island, I also became a part of the island band and I loved it.

One night, I was invited out to one of the bures (Fijian hut) to have a few drinks and share some travelling stories, with my German lady friend and her group of travelling companions. We got on famously and we were having a good laugh and great conversation all night long. Unbeknown to me, my holiday romance was hiding in the bushes watching us having a great time. He was also invited to the social gathering, but chose not to come, because he wanted to spend all night with me, exclusively on my own. I was a traveller and part of that experience, is meeting people and hearing their stories. Then all of a sudden, mid-sentence, out of the bushes appears my native romantic lover. He became very agitated and moody, because he felt like he was missing out on all the fun. He had already had a few too many drinks by this stage and was starting to make a fool of himself. He was being very possessive and jealous, stormed in and demanded that I leave with him right now. I told him that I hadn't finished and that I would be there as soon as we were done. He stomped off and left us there.

Meanwhile, he was waiting for me back at his bure and steam must have been coming out of his ears. It was not long after the mood was dampened, that I finished up with my friends and headed back to his bure. When I arrived, he was very sweet and nice to me to start with, but I could feel the tension brewing underneath his cool demeanour, until eventually after asking me loads of ridiculous questions, he exploded in a rage of jealousy. He told me that I shouldn't have made him feel jealous like that and it was my fault that he was feeling so angry.

Can you see a pattern forming here? Clearly I had lessons to learn about poor choices of men. I was obviously in training to focus on how to deal with aggressive and strong men. He was athletic, strong and very fit and he had a temper like nothing I had ever seen before. I genuinely sensed danger this time. I jumped off the bed and ran for the door. He lunged towards the door and just missed my legs, as he tried to rugby tackle me to the ground. I pushed the hut door open and kept running. I felt like I was running in slow motion, like you do when you are being chased in your dreams. I was literally running for my life, when he caught me and jumped on top of me from behind. We both landed with a massive thud and hit the damp earth.

So here I am, shocked and now wounded, he rolls me over and pins me down with his legs, holding my arms down. It was really dark with the generator power turned off. Everybody else in the village was either in bed, or hiding, because they didn't want to get involved. I could only just see the reflection of the moonlight shining on his face. His face was like a wild man who had just hunted and caught his prey and he was *not* going to let me go. I saw the flicker. It's like the killer flicker you see in a killer's eyes, once they have made up their mind to attack and follow through.

Have you ever seen a dog, or a cat's eyes turn green, just before they are about to attack? It's like a flicker, that killer flicker they get when they are committed to harm something. Both wild and domestic creatures can get the flicker in a moment of rage. It is like the warning flicker telling you that an attack is imminent. It's the warning sign to back off and get out of there, if you still can. It's like that warning sign you get, just before the cat strikes your face.

Let's just pause there for a moment, while I run you through my current mindset. My first reactions were shock and disbelief. I found myself totally bewildered and perplexed, trying to understand why someone would go to these lengths to react in this manner. My second reaction was to ask myself, *is this for real? Really?* My heart was racing really fast and I had to think quickly what to do.

I was squirming and wriggling, trying to free myself from his grip. He was very muscular and was overpowering me with his brute strength. Eventually he had his whole body weight on top of me and his legs were pinning my arms down. I was trying to yell for help, but his hands were tightly clasped around my neck, squeezing as hard as he could. He was about 20kg heavier than me and I was struggling under the weight and strength of my opponent. How does someone transform from a lover to an enemy, in just a matter of seconds? As my throat was getting more and more restricted and his grip was getting tighter and tighter, I was running out of breath and if he had been allowed to continue doing this for another 10 seconds, he may very well have killed me. My *rational fear* had fully kicked in now and I saw my life flash before my eyes.

Fear is such a strange emotion and it can take over your logical mind when you are in a panic. Then all of a sudden, I heard a voice inside my head say, "Relax and be calm." I was now in full warrior mode. In this quietened state, I lovingly prayed to the Almighty God, to give me the strength to get this thing off me. With my last remaining breath, I pulled my legs in close to my chest, placed my feet under his abdomen and with every bit of Godly strength I had, I launched him through the air. The force of the push threw him a few metres in the air and he landed on his back, winded and in a state of shock that he had just been thrown off, by someone like me.

Victory was only momentary, because I had to think fast on my feet and had to work out what to do next. I jumped up and I ran as fast as I could, through the dense jungle in the middle of the night. It was pitch black and I was looking for somewhere to hide. Never mind the jungle spiders; they had nothing on this crazy person. I had about a 10 second time advantage on him, when I came across an old abandoned two storey boat in the dense jungle. I scrambled up on top of the boat, with milliseconds to spare and I lay really flat and really still on top of the boat, so I couldn't be seen. Still paying no mind to the spiders and creepy crawlies that would have been up there with me too.

I had to control and slow down my breathing and my heart was nearly beating out of my chest. I really believed that if he found me, he would kill me. I was truly fearful for my life and I came to the realisation that I was actually hiding from a full blown psychopath! As I lay really still, I could hear the leaves and tree branches crunching under his feet, as he got closer and closer to where I was hiding.

He was gently whispering, *"Jan, Jan, where are you?"* He said, *"I'm so sorry I lost my temper, come out, come out wherever you are. I promise I'll make it up to you."*

I thought to myself, *this guy truly is crazy and in fact, he is raving freaking mad!* I had a fire burning in my belly and my adrenalin was pumping nonstop, but I had to remain as still as the night, so he couldn't find me. He could have been a killer for all I know, he was certainly acting like he had the capacity to kill someone. After about 15 minutes of him trampling through the jungle looking for me and calling out my name, his voice got further and further away, until he finally gave up and retreated back to his own bure.

Once it was safe, I slowly and cautiously crept off the boat and quietly made my way back to the camp. I was so exhausted and so fearful that he might find me. There was nothing I could do in the middle of the night to raise any alarms, because everyone was asleep, or in their private bures. I found my friend's bure and crawled into bed with her and slept with one eye open until daylight came.

Needless to say, that was the end of my three month tropical holiday in Fiji and once again I was being *forced* to move on. I was on the next boat off the island the following day. I was still nursing my bruised body and neck welts.

Ironically, this is also the same amazing place, where I had my beautiful experience meeting God.

Jealousy and alcohol can become a deadly cocktail. Jealousy on its own is already dangerous enough and is something we should all be aware of in our every day dealings. To understand jealousy, we need to realise the person experiencing jealousy, has insecurities and trust issues. It is unlikely to be anything you are doing wrong to trigger the jealousy. It is usually something buried deep within the subconscious of the jealous person that needs to be addressed. Once alcohol enters the equation, the situation can escalate very quickly.

Humans need to remember that alcohol is like rocket fuel for the body. It is a highly refined and a very processed beverage. Alcohol can have wildly different reactions with different people. It can make a person hyperactive, aggressive and it can also trigger psychosis, if too much alcohol is consumed.

If a person becomes out of control, or irrational, due to excessive alcohol or drug consumption, it can also open a demonic doorway which effectively is an open invitation, for a demon to attempt to take over the body of an intoxicated person.

Society would be better to view alcohol as a medicine, rather than as a party drink, then it would be consumed sparingly and under the right conditions. Alcohol *can* be beneficial to heal ailments, if consumed in the right dosages.

Alcohol and drugs can also impair a person's ordinary judgement, causing the person under the influence to behave inappropriately. It can *influence* them to act in a manner, they will later regret. If a person has a mental illness, then alcohol and drugs should be avoided altogether.

What did I learn from this experience?

The following 10 tips are important things to remember and will help you to handle yourself wisely, in this type of situation.

1. **Don't ignore the warning signs** of a person with very possessive, jealous, moody and compulsive behaviour. I now call these red flags, or precursors. These are warnings to be aware of possible psychotic behaviour. Avoid friendships and romances with people who display this combination of behaviours, *unless* you are properly trained.
2. When you are being attacked, **slow down, take your time, don't panic** and think of what the best defence plan is, so you can execute your plan carefully. If you panic too much, you could hurt yourself more and you could give your opponent the advantage they want, which is to scare you.
3. **Use the power of your mind** to overcome an opponent who is stronger than you.
4. **Pray for help**, because when you really need it, that help will be

there, just like it was when I asked for it.

5. **Use my scenario as an example**. Run the scenario through your mind and think of ways you could have handled yourself better, in the same situation. What would you have done differently and what other options could have worked successfully? It is a lot easier to work through these scenarios in your mind in retrospect. Coming up with solutions in a live environment, or on the fly, involves the engagement of *all* the senses. Learn from this experience and let it be a reminder that things can just happen out of the blue, when you least expect it. Be mentally prepared for anything.
6. Luckily for me **he did not have a weapon**, as this would have been a game changer. Don't let this fool you though, because he was using his strength and dominance as a weapon and this can do just as much damage.
7. **Defence is the only response**. There is no point to retaliate and engage in further battle. If you can, use self defence techniques to avoid, or minimise damage. You don't want to be responsible for killing someone, because you will end up doing prison time for something that is not your fault. In addition to having a black mark against your name in the system, you will also have to face the Creator and explain why you chose that course of action.
8. **Run as soon as the opportunity presents itself**. If you value your life, a psychotic person can be very unpredictable and they are not thinking straight at the time of having a psychotic episode. You can't reason with them, you just need to remove yourself from the scene as quickly as possible.
9. **Learn self defence techniques**, which will teach you how to take a couple of knocks, before it really hurts. Once the adrenalin kicks in, it acts like a pain killer and you can't feel anything, other than the surge of adrenalin pumping through your veins.
10. **Don't let a bad experience** like this; **stop you from loving anyone** in the future. He was a psychotic man with some serious insecurity issues and men are not generally like that. Learn to forgive people and move on. Don't blame the entire male species for every bad experience you have. The same goes if you have had a similar experience with a female.

I could say, don't get yourself into this situation in the first place, but the truth is, we can find ourselves knee deep in trouble, or neck deep in my case, without even expecting it, or being able to predict it. This was not a normal jealous reaction, to a lover spending time with someone else. It just goes to show you that it doesn't take much to escalate into a dangerous situation, when a psychotic trigger is activated.

Rational fear will set off your adrenalin and your adrenalin in turn activates the warrior within. It is the warrior within that helps you to survive even the scariest life experiences. Embrace the inner warrior when you need to survive and use the natural rush of brain chemicals to keep you alive, because that is exactly what they are supposed to be used for.

Prepared for fear

There are very few people who are actually fully *prepared* for fear, or even death. Some people have to prepare for fear every day due to their occupational hazards like; military personnel, soldiers, pilots, police, fire fighters, emergency and rescue workers, body guards, prison wardens, stunt men, professional fighters, deep sea fishermen, high risk construction workers and miners, just to name a few.

Then there are the more underground and unregistered professions like; gangsters, mafia, street fighters, drug dealers, ninja warriors and assassins. The mindset of each person is essentially the same. They are trained to *identify* risk, *recognise* danger and be *prepared* to do whatever it takes to save their own life first, then protect the lives of others. This is the ultimate survival instinct being fully utilised and these people are prepared for fear constantly. They are faced with life threatening risks daily and they are surviving on adrenalin, pure instinct and intuition that gut feeling you get when something isn't quite right.

Let's explore these survival behaviours further.

Adrenalin

We have already had a look at how adrenaline works, when explaining rational fear. Adrenalin is like an extraordinary boost of energy that prepares the mind and body for battle, conflict, or potential danger. It practically removes the ability to feel any emotions. It overrides our love feeling, turns on all of our senses at once and sets the senses at a heightened state of awareness. All systems are either turned on and fully engaged, or waiting in standby mode like a sleeping giant. This is literally like having the finger on the trigger, or the button.

Instinct

Instinct is the next behaviour I want to highlight. Like animals in the wild, we still have that primitive animal *instinct* that lies dormant within all of us in our DNA. Instinct is the survival behaviour that keeps us alive. It is becoming aware of both the mentality of the hunter and the hunted, at the same time.

The aim of instinct is to be able to *predict* the next move, or *assess* the potential dangers, in order to be prepared for any attack. It is the stalker and the prey, the lion and the gazelle, the attacker and the defender, the safe zone and the unsafe zone. It is necessary to understand what instinctively drives us to take action and move into warrior mode when needed. It is the strike, or the fight mode.

Being prepared for fear activates and lights up whole sections of the brain that don't get used on a daily basis by regular people in society. It is a specialised skill set that once activated, it is dangerous. This is the reality of dealing with critical challenges in your work, or home life. When you put these scenarios into perspective, it gives you a whole new appreciation for those who are faced with these challenges. The behaviour influenced by instinct is still the same. If the police could only understand this when they are dealing with criminals and the underworld, they would be more ahead of their game. Criminals are just like them. They operate using the same set of behaviour patterns and live a similar life, just on the *other* side of the law.

Intuition

Although intuition is still classed as a behaviour, it is more like an inner knowing, or a subtle feeling one gets, when something isn't quite right. Intuition is not something that is easily understood, but it is an automatic feeling we get when something good or bad is going to happen. It is like we are getting this feeling on a soul level, a message that something isn't right and our life might be in mortal danger, if we don't listen to our intuition.

We are not necessarily trained, or taught how to use, or how to identify our intuition, but there is something inside of us, like an internal compass that we all have and use unconsciously. A good example of this is thinking about crossing the road on a blind corner, then having second thoughts about it, or you get an intuitive feeling, that now is not quite the right time to cross the road. So you don't cross the road and five seconds later a car slides sideways around the corner narrowly missing you and you breathe sigh of relief, because you *trusted your intuition* not to cross the road at that time. If you had crossed the road when you were originally going to, then you may have been killed.

Another way to describe intuition is when we get a good, or a bad feeling about someone we meet, or see for the first time. It might be through an introduction, or you may see, or feel them on an energetic level in the room, or in the immediate area where you are.

Everyone emits a certain frequency as they walk around the planet. Good people emit a lighter vibration and they go relatively unnoticed, with the exception of super happy people, who emit a very high vibration and you can't help but notice their *good vibes*. They seem to have a very magnetic personality. We intuitively pick up on these people as being harmless and helpful.

Then you have people who are not good, or people who do bad things and you may pick up on the feeling that they may have the intention of doing bad things. They tend to vibrate at a lower vibration. Their dense vibration, can be noticed against a crowd of lighter vibrating people. This is how people pick up intuitively on good and bad people. It is through their vibrations. You get *bad vibes* from people who emit a very dark or sinister energy. There are those who are trained to seek out this type of person. They already know which signs to look out for and trust their intuition to guide them in the direction of the bad people, or the potential perpetrators of crime.

We use our intuition every day without even realising it. It is a combination of our subconscious and unconscious mind, blended with our past experiences. This internal guidance system, can keep us safe from harm and out of danger if we learn to listen to our intuition. It can also lead us to the right person, event, or answer we are seeking, if we trust it.

The very first gut feeling you get about something or someone is always the right one. The second you doubt it, you go down the road of logical reasoning and questioning. This is where your conscious mind, the *thinker* gets involved and messes everything up. The logical mind always wants proof and evidence and sometimes you can't get that with intuition. You just have to learn how to *trust* your intuition. Go with the flow and allow your inner moral compass to guide you in the right direction.

Intuition is our gift from God, to help us tune in to any given situation and assess the potential risks and dangers. Using our inner feelings, impressions and faith, instead of using our logical reasoning skills from our brain and our conscious mind, we can feel God more through intuition. We become more in tune with ourselves when we are in tune with our feelings and intuition.

Coping with rape and abuse

When you are dealing with being abused now, or in the past, you can sometimes get stuck in the mindset, that society beats the crap out of you to take everything away.

Rape is a very personal trauma and many people suffer in silence with the effects. It is an experience they can hold onto for their whole life until they seek counseling, or therapy to work through it. To counteract rape, you must give back something that was taken from the person originally. Rape doesn't have to be brutal to be classed as rape. It can be so subtle, that you may not even recognise it as rape.

When someone is raped, they lose their dignity. So dignity needs to be returned to the person, to help them to deal with the incident. They need to view their trauma as an experience they have already had, to be able to put the past behind them. Things happen to all of us in life and many things happen without our permission and without us expecting them to happen. To become *empowered,* you have to move from the mindset of victim, to the mindset of victor. You have to triumph over your experiences and chalk it up to lessons. Use these experiences to help other people get through their trauma. If you help others with your wisdom and understanding, this in turn helps you to deal with your experiences.

God said, "Abuse is like taking candy from a baby. To help the person who has experienced the abuse, you have to give the candy back. The most important tool you can use to counteract abuse is hugs and love. Genuine and unconditional affection and love with nothing expected in return. The candy is the love. The candy (love) was taken from the baby (person) and now you have to give the candy (love) back."

God continued, "Anyone who has suffered sexual, or physical abuse, will tend to shut down their senses one by one, until no senses are left on, other than the senses required to go through the motions of each day. To the sufferer, this minimises potential exposure to emotions and also shuts off the feelings they may have had to experience during their abuse. To reverse this psychological and physical state of simply existing, you need to turn all of their senses and everything on positively!"

God added, "Learn to engage the senses so that you have positive experiences to focus on and you can escape positively and not spiral down out of control. You should want to try and live, to use all of your seven senses. There are over 20 senses in total, but many are still yet to be discovered by mankind. Use the powerful tool of the mind to overcome any situation and create your own positive reality, even if you are still suffering the abuse right now. Start manifesting your way out of the abuse cycle by focusing on positive changes you can make to your life right now that will make a difference. In your spare time, do things you love doing, things that make you feel good about yourself, which turn your senses on in a positive way. You may be in a situation where you can't stop the abuse just yet, but if you work on a solution, even if it is slowly, you will be free from the abuse. Pray to God for help and *ask* for spiritual guidance. It is better if you pray for your abuser to be shown the righteous way, so they learn what they are doing is wrong and stop."

You can seek help from someone you trust, a friend, a spiritual healer, a church member, a counsellor, a medical professional, or perhaps a family member. If you can't trust *anybody*, then trust in God and ask him for help and guidance.

You can use guided meditations and guided self hypnosis, to get you in the right headspace, to help you to cope and heal any past unpleasant experiences. It is best to use meditations that will engage your senses, by getting your conscious and subconscious mind working together as a team. You'll want to hear questions like; *can you feel the warm wind blowing on your face? Can you hear the waves lapping on the beach? Can you see the beautiful white light coming down to heal you? Can you smell the fresh air?*

Now that you have all of your senses engaged, you are bringing your power back into your being.

God said, "An abuser is either doing it to exercise their power, or to exercise their curiosity. Curiosity wears off eventually and they get bored and move on. The power struggle is the long term abuse cycle. How do you stop this abuse? By removing the power and filling the void with love. Channel your energy into love and light and be the expression of that. If your abuser is demonic, they won't be able to stand your energy and will feel repelled by you. Demons love pain and fear and dislike love and strength. If you no longer react to the abuse the way they want you to, there is no point in them continuing, because they are not getting anything out of it anymore. Fear can drive an abuser to react. Removing the emotion they are aiming to trigger, is the best reaction you can have to stop the abuser. Remain neutral and passive, to remove the enjoyment the abuser may get from the abuse. This will in turn remove the victim trigger that the abuser is enjoying."

God continued, "Programming another human through influence and persuasion is the most effective way to *diffuse* an abuser. Everyone has the ability to influence another person through passiveness, assertiveness and aggressiveness. Taking the path of least resistance, is the least painful and the least destructive, by giving them what they want, until they tire of it, or get bored.

"If you don't have the physical strength to overcome your abuser, then you have to overcome the abuse with your mind and the power of your influence. If you have the strength and have a safe escape plan, by all means defend yourself. If you are in a powerless situation, then you have to first escape mentally and then second escape physically when you can."

Emotions are a powerful tool that can be utilised to help you in many situations, if you get them under control and don't let them rule you.

Surviving relationship breakups

In the past, I have been the one to end the relationship and I have experienced being dumped. I have been unfaithful in relationships myself and I have also been on the receiving end of being cheated on. This is why I believe I can say with experience, I have had my fair share of each type of relationship, by being on the giving end, the taking end and on the receiving end of some of these karmic experiences.

The main thing I have learned from relationship mistakes and breakups is that you become stronger and wiser with each failed relationship. You get better at making better choices in the future, each time a relationship breaks down. You also get better at mate selection and ultimately better at avoiding the same mistakes that led you down the path of distraction and destruction the last time around.

I have learned that what goes around, comes around and you get to learn what it feels like from all perspectives. I have never let bad experiences stop me from loving people, or experiencing new relationships. I am decidedly more cautious these days, but I still love with my whole heart when I do.

These days, God tells me if I am making good or bad relationship choices and doesn't judge me even when I still get it wrong. I want to see only the good in people and get slapped with the truth every time I get it wrong. God fills me with wisdom about new people that I allow to enter my personal space and gives me his character assessment of the person. He is always hilarious when he talks about my friends and tells me off if I judge them incorrectly. He also tells me off, when I don't put my foot down when people take advantage of me and he warns me if I get lost in my false beliefs.

Following the spiritual path is actually one of the loneliest paths one can choose. I don't have a large amount of close friends in my life, but the friends I do allow in my life, are like rare and precious gems. They have their special qualities and I admire them for these attributes. I am getting better at saying *no* to people and if anyone pushes me too far, friends included, they lose me forever.

Through trial and error and experience, I have worked out *who* my true friends are and which ones are not. Let me save you some painful realisations by sharing some of these experiences with you. I am sure you will find some of these simple insights invaluable.

The biggest question most people ask themselves is; *what do I do when it all turns pear shaped?* Sometimes relationships come to an end. This is an inevitable fact of life. Friendships and relationships will start and end throughout your life. It is very rare for people to stay with their childhood sweetheart for their whole life. For those who have stood the test of time, I congratulate them, but this generally does not happen.

Relationships with both friends and lovers can come to an abrupt end without any warning. Sometimes you both have a fixed opinion about something and it can be that one thing that ends the relationship. At other times it can be a slow and painful end, which is at the extreme opposite end of the scale. The drama can drag out for many years and even decades for some.

The main difference between a friend and lover is that you are usually a lot more intimate with your lover. However, sometimes your friend may know more about you than your lover; like all of your little personal secrets and habits. This can be seen as cute for a while, but this can also be the very thing that ends the relationship. Friends, who know too much about you, can easily become your enemy after a heated debate, or a disagreement.

My advice to all of you is never share anything about yourself that you cannot trust others with. This means never tell anyone anything that could potentially get you into trouble. Never share your precious original ideas with anyone, other than those who are going to help you achieve your goals.

Friendships can turn sour, if one friend becomes jealous of the other friend's success, or potential success. Friends have been known to steal original ideas from each other and attempt to claim these ideas as their own. When they are confronted, they simply deny any prior knowledge of the idea, making you look like the thief. This is not a friendship. This is a user, or time waster, who is using up your time, your resources and your energy. They are like energy vampires who hang on every word, waiting for the next juicy morsel. You could literally be hanging out with your enemy and be totally unaware.

Friendships can also blur the line between intimacy and platonic relationships and one person always gets hurt when that line gets crossed. Once you have crossed that line, it is very complicated to go back to being just friends after the break up. It takes a lot of social and emotional maturity, to be able to end a relationship with someone and still remain friends. It can be done, if the two people involved, mutually agree on the terms of the separation and they end the relationship before it gets ugly. How often does it actually happen like this? Probably not that often.

A long term relationship with lovers, friends, colleagues, neighbours and even family members, can end up being blown apart by a disagreement, a difference of opinion, or someone is caught lying about something. This in turn creates an emotional trigger, or a response of some kind. If the relationship turns destructive and if the wounds are not treated correctly, they can become infected and difficult to heal.

Before ending the relationship, or commit to breaking it off with someone, you need to consider three very important questions.

1. Is there **betrayal** involved?
2. Is it **resolvable**?
3. Do you **love** them?

Let's look a bit closer at each of these influencing factors and see if you have a reasonable case for separation.

Betrayal

For betrayal to even exist there has to be an implied or agreed trust involved. There also has to be an expectation from either one, or both parties, that your relationship is either exclusive, or open. Trust cannot be assumed, but sometimes it does need to be discussed. The terms under which the relationship is built upon, can then be agreed upon. If it is a true fair-weather friend, or lover, who will last the distance through the ups and downs and has good intentions, then trust will be automatic. You will feel that trust deep down inside your heart and you return the same feeling by honouring their trust and respecting them. Love comes later, once the trust has been established.

Friendships are very rarely exclusive and it is probably not that healthy, to have only *one* friend in the whole world anyway. It is generally acceptable to share your friends with other friends and vice versa.

Lovers are very different in this respect and exclusivity needs to be determined, before betrayal can even enter the equation. Getting married is not only exchanging your vows of loyalty in the eyes of God, but also a promise to be faithful to one another. A de facto relationship and long term partnership implies that the same loyalty should be given as a married couple.

Formalising marriage in no way ensures either faithfulness, or loyalty. It is only a formality and vows can still be broken.

To understand betrayal, you need to understand what drives someone to betray you, or what drives you to want to betray someone else. There can be a number of reasons including; boredom, lack of excitement, lack of stimulation both sexually and intellectually, lack of intimacy, lack of financial stability, living away from one another, one partner has serious behavioural issues, lack of growth in the relationship, lack of trust, lack of commitment, inequality, no common ground and irresolvable conflict from arguing, abuse and infidelity. Believe it or not, the most common reason for divorce and break ups is *infidelity*.

It is better to have that difficult discussion early on in the relationship, instead of being upset when your assumption turned out to be wrong. Ask your potential lifelong mate if you are going to have an exclusive or open relationship. If you both agree, it doesn't matter which you choose, then all is well. It may work for a while and then one of you decides they no longer want exclusivity, or an open relationship and then it all changes again.

Another reason relationships fail, is because of unrealistic expectations of one, or both of the parties to the relationship. One partner likes to go to bed at 10:00pm every night and read a book, while the other likes to stay up until 1:00am watching sports on TV. One partner likes to party on the weekends and the other partner prefers to stay at home. One partner is really sociable and likes to have their friends over all the time and the other partner is a recluse and prefers quiet time alone. One partner is a vegan and the other partner is a large consumer of meat. One is a smoker and one is a non-smoker. It is the same for drinking alcohol and taking drugs.

Although these differences might seem cute in the beginning, over a period of time it may drive a huge wedge between you that can make you question exactly what it was that attracted you to them in the first place. Having common interests is a *must* for companionship. It is just as important having your own interests as well, so that you don't get in each other's space all the time.

God said, "In friendships, diversity and variety is better, because you get to socialise with a wider spectrum of experience, with people from all walks of life, from different cultures and within a bigger age range."

Compatibility is the key to a successful relationship with either gender. It is important to attract an assortment of skill sets within your circle of friends that compliment and help each other. Not all of your friends have to like each other. In fact, it is okay for some of your friends to even dislike each other. They may be friends with you personally, but are not interested in becoming friends with your other friends. This should not affect your own personal relationships with your friends and you shouldn't base your friendships, or choice of lovers, on the acceptance of others. It is your time, your life and your choices that you get to make, based on who you want to spend your valuable time with.

Betrayal happens when one person in the relationship does something to *betray* the trust of the other person. This includes lying, cheating, stealing, gossiping, hurting, taking advantage of the good will of each other and being unfaithful. Betrayal can be forgiven, but new guidelines need to be set. A new standard needs to be established between you, if you are going to go down the road of forgiveness. If you choose to be merciful, then you must follow through with your promise of forgiveness. It would be unreasonable to constantly remind them of their past mistakes, every time unrelated issues arise in the future.

Counselling, or communicating openly with one another, may help if you want to repair any damage to the relationship. A word of warning here, once that trust has been abused; sometimes it is never fully recovered. In addition to forgiveness, you need to establish and agree on a rule, or expectation of what will happen if the trust is broken again. It is certainly not impossible. If you can work through the next two critical steps including resolution and love, then you may be on the road to recovering the relationship.

Resolution

So you have forgiven your friend, or lover for their misdemeanour. You are now on guard and you are like a rose that has tucked all of its petals in tightly, waiting for the spring time to come, so you can open your petals again. You may even be on the other side of the situation and you may have been forgiven for your infidelity. You could be thanking your lucky stars that you have just been given a second chance. Does a leopard change its spots? Let's see shall we?

Days, weeks and months go by and you have almost forgotten the incident and your love, or friendship is blooming again. If all is well in your world, you can move onto the next section about love.

The worst case scenario is that it happens again in some form or another. It is at this point you have to ask yourself, are you a sucker for punishment, or do you think there could be some other legitimate reason you keep attracting this type of experience into your life? What do you need to *learn* from this life lesson?

Forgiveness is one lesson that many people have come into this life to learn. There is a big difference between forgiving someone for their mistakes and being taken advantage of. You need to establish your boundaries and enforce them, when they are being pushed. There are many ways you can enforce your boundaries with those who are taking advantage of you.

God has taught me many new skills about being assertive and I am going to share these skills with you.

1. **Ask them directly**, "Are you taking advantage of my good nature?" See what kind of response you get from them. Sometimes this hits the nail on the head and they are left speechless, because you have asked such a direct question.
2. **Express your concerns** and state that you have previously had this discussion. State that you both agreed what would happen the next time this situation occurred. Don't leave the decision up to the person who is taking advantage of you. Assert yourself by saying something like, "We both agreed this behaviour was unacceptable last time and you promised to do the right thing. Now you have repeated the same mistake, which I forgave you for the first time. What do you expect that I am going to do now?" This is a good open ended question and will get them to reveal their true feelings about the situation to you.
3. **Some people don't have the balls** to break it off with you, so they find it easier to annoy you, by disrespecting you in every possible way they can, until you either leave, or ask them to leave. If this is the case, then walk out the door, never look back, they are not worth it. This type of friend or lover is shallow and

superficial. They usually just move onto their next victim and play the same game.

4. Sometimes you just have to realise that **some people just can't help themselves** and their behaviour is never going to change. If you have had enough, then prepare yourself, it is time to move on and get on with your own life and finding happiness.
5. Never let **financial commitments together** be the reason you stay together, because in life we always have some form of financial commitment. Work out the best solution and continue with your exit strategy. Have faith that things will work out and *trust* that you will be able to meet your financial obligations.
6. If you do **decide to go**, I am not promising this is an easy task to do. It takes a noble and courageous person to break off a relationship, if it is not working out. It will hurt for a while, you may feel depressed and you may even cry a lot. You may also miss them while you are going through the separation. You may even change your mind a few times and go back to them for a while, but if you keep doing the same thing and expecting a different result, you are going to drive yourself crazy trying to *fix* the problem. If *you* are not the problem, then how can you fix it?
7. There is always an **exception** to the rule. Maybe one or both of you are just slow learners. You both keep making silly mistakes and you really love each other, warts and all. You are prepared to forgive each other yet again, because you are both willing to learn how to resolve any relationship issues. It could be that one of you is such a good person, who loves unconditionally and is prepared to keep working at making the relationship successful.

Relationships require work and need to be maintained regularly, to last the distance. Successful relationships are not meant to be *hard* work, they are meant to be joyful and fulfilling. If you don't have mutual love in your relationship, then the relationship is one sided.

Happy relationships are based on mutual respect, occasional compromise, caring and sharing. After all, you do love them and that is why you are still with them.

If you no longer love them, throwing them away, is not always the best resolution. It is unfortunate that relationships that may have previously lasted for years can be destroyed in a moment of incorrect behaviour. If you can find it in your heart to forgive and cherish your loved ones, even with all their faults, you will find that when they return the love, it is highly rewarding.

Respect is earned and not automatically granted, just because you are in a relationship. God teaches us to love unconditionally with all our hearts and to see the goodness in everyone. God also expects us to find happiness and love and doesn't want us to be lonely and miserable. If your relationship is empty and loveless, ask yourself, which one of you is withholding your love?

Love

God said, "Love conquers all. Love can literally conquer countries and whole continents. Wars have been fought, won and lost in the name of love."

When love is really passionate, you can experience a very volatile relationship, full of excitement and unpredictability, but with sparks comes fire and you can get burned by the power of love, if it is not built on a harmonious foundation.

On the flip side, you can do everything in your power to cultivate a happy home and it still doesn't work out.

Accidents, near misses and injuries can really bring partners, friends, or families much closer together. Similar to when someone in the family dies. You all experience that moment when you realise all the petty stuff just isn't worth fighting about any more. You start to focus on the real things that actually mean something to you.

I would like to share a personal story about love with you. I was living in Kalgoorlie, Western Australia in the late 1990's. I was working in the mines and my boyfriend at the time, was still recovering from a serious vehicle accident, which happened to him at work one afternoon. One day in the middle of winter, a young lady was driving the work 4WD on a mine site. It was a rainy day and she didn't really have the right level of experience, to be driving the vehicle in the rain. She was travelling too fast on a dirt road and on the surface of the road, was a very fine layer of mud, which made it very slippery. She took the corner a bit too fast, overcorrected and lost control of the vehicle. The vehicle rolled multiple times and the vehicle landed with all of the occupants upside down, hanging from the roof. Luckily, all four of them had all been wearing their seatbelts, which had saved all of their lives.

My ex-boyfriend recovered quickly from the shock of what had just happened and although he was badly injured, due to having glass crushed all through his arm, he checked to make sure all of the other occupants were okay. He had been holding onto the safety strap above the window in the back seat and each time the vehicle rolled over, it caused more glass to break and shatter into his arm. The driver was absolutely hysterical, screaming her head off and was in total shock. He had to yell at her to get her to calm down, because panic at an accident scene, can have a really traumatic impact on others, who may have also sustained injuries. It is important to *remain calm*. There was blood everywhere. Three of the four occupants were conscious, but one was unconscious.

After freeing himself and the conscious passengers, he loosened the unconscious lady from her seatbelt and laid her down in a more comfortable position. Their radio had been completely smashed in the accident and the main road was five kilometres away from the scene of the accident. He was pretty fit and strong, but had sustained multiple injuries especially to his arm. He felt a surge of adrenalin kick in and said he was going to run to the main road to get help. The other two passengers stayed with the unconscious passenger, until help arrived.

He told me what was going through his mind, while he was running towards the road. He just kept seeing himself making it to the road and getting help and didn't focus on anything else. He doesn't really even remember running the whole way. He mainly remembers getting to the main road and flagging down the first car that drove past, who at the time were extremely reluctant to stop, because he was covered in blood and was looking very dishevelled. Something made them stop and drive back for him. He knew that if he didn't make that run, his workmate may not have survived without medical attention.

They pulled over and wound down the window only slightly and asked him what had happened and he let the whole story out in one big sentence. It was a nice car and they said for him to wait on the side of the road, while they got something to cover the back seat with, so he didn't stain the interior of the car. That's all he remembers, then he passed out and woke up in the hospital, along with two of his other workmates. The fourth passenger was flown by helicopter to the emergency department at Royal Perth Hospital, to receive treatment for her head injuries. Thank God they all survived that day.

Meanwhile, I had just arrived home from work. At that time we were working at different mine sites and I found a note stuck to our unit door. We only had a little bedroom in a shared house, with shared bathroom facilities. It was similar to a mining camp arrangement, but in the township of Boulder, on the outskirts of Kalgoorlie. The note read: *your boyfriend has been in a car accident, you need to go to the hospital immediately.*

I was freaked out and quickly made my way to the hospital, not knowing what to expect.

When I arrived at the hospital, the first person I saw was a lady who I used to work for as a nanny, when I first arrived in Kalgoorlie. In a freak coincidence, she had also been rushed to hospital on the same day and she was heavily pregnant with her third child. She had been working right up to the due date at the local prison and unfortunately she lost her baby that day at the hospital and she was absolutely distraught. I told her my boyfriend was also in hospital as well. I promised to go and visit her after I had seen him.

When I got to his hospital room, he was sitting up. He was full of pain killers, full of chit chat and surprisingly full of beans. He was in really good spirits, considering the ordeal he had just been through. He was truly happy to be alive and couldn't believe his luck. He was also very happy that he saved someone's life. The accident had made him rethink his perspective on life. He had already made a new friend in the hospital. I viewed my boyfriend as a bit of a hero after I heard the full story and I praised him for his bravery. It never went to his head and he was very cool about the whole episode. I really loved him at that time.

The injuries to his arm were quite extensive and the doctors said they were going to have to take a skin graft from his thigh, to recreate new skin on his arm. It was a massive piece of skin they had to cover. They cleaned his wound out, by scraping out all of the glass and performed the necessary skin grafting surgery on him. It was that intense during the healing phase, he wasn't able to work for around two months. During this time I nursed him back to health, making sure he had everything he needed. I changed his dressings, cooked for him, kept the room clean, ran errands, gave him lots of hugs and well wishes and continued to go to work.

Fast forward a few months, we were both back at work and we had moved house. I found him a new job, working at the mine site that I was working at and our travel plans had to be pushed back a few more months. We had exhausted all of our savings fairly quickly with the recovery, so we were back on the earning and savings wagon again.

A few months later, we were about a month away from our overseas trip. A friend of mine, who was working with me at the mines, mentioned that she had noticed some unusual behaviour between my boyfriend and one of the girls working at the mines. She said that I should keep an eye on her. The thought of my boyfriend being unfaithful to me, didn't even cross my mind; in fact, it wasn't even on my radar. Another friend who was into everything alternative, suggested I should go and see a psychic, to get a reading to see what hidden things might be going on.

I had only ever been to one other psychic in my life in New Zealand, about five years earlier. She was an elderly lady called Mrs. Saxon, who seemed to stare straight through you, when she was talking to you, as if she was somewhere else. She had translucent eyes and used psychometry to give people a psychic reading. To perform the psychometry, she asked me for a personal item of mine. I handed her my Māori bone carving that I was wearing around my neck. Because it was my first experience with a psychic, I was a bit dubious and I had no idea what to expect from the reading.

I arrived at the psychic's place. She was a beautiful woman in her early 40's and had the most gorgeous little country cottage, with a miniature Garden of Eden inside her back yard. There were fruit trees and fruit vines, little animals, manicured lawns, flower bushes and luscious plants. I half expected to see a fairy or gnome step out of her garden to greet me. She showed me around the garden and then motioned for me to sit down at her beautiful big stained timber table, opposite her. She pulled out a pack of tarot cards. I hadn't seen tarot cards before and they were intriguing, full of interesting symbols and pictures. She started shuffling the cards to get started and she immediately started picking up information about me from the spirits and she said some very personal things to me. This technique is used in the early stages of a reading, as a method of identifying and confirming which spirits want to come through, to give you a message.

Spirits don't usually muck around, they tend to get straight to the point. The lady asked me, "Who is this blonde woman in the picture, who works at your work?"

I gulped and thought to myself, *oh no, it is true!*

I explained who she was, at least as much as I knew. The psychic told me he had been sleeping around with her, while I had been on shift work during the past few months. They had even slept together in my bed. The reading was thorough and honest and I was happy, because the main reason I went there, was to *confirm* if it was true, or not. I was also hoping to receive some type of divine guidance to help me learn and then prepare to move on, yet again.

To cut a long painful story short... I confronted him with these new facts and he denied it multiple times, but was unable to sustain the lies for any length of time. During the course of that conversation, we ended our three year relationship right there and then. I had to go through the motions of finding a new place to live and get out of there as quickly and dignified as possible.

Did I mention the knee dragging incident earlier? Yes I know I did. Well yes, I *used* to be a slow learner. The person in this story is the same one who I had already left the first time he treated me badly, when he got rough with me. Somewhere down the track, he begged for forgiveness and I did forgive him. I obviously hadn't learned my lesson yet and came back for another kick in the butt.

Love can hurt and love can feel really good. It is a risk worth taking, because when you do eventually find mutual, happy and fulfilling love, all of the bad experiences just melt away into the past.

By now, I had already saved enough money to go on my trip and pay for my own way. This meant I could also afford to travel solo. I decided to go to the travel agent and I changed all of the travel destinations on the ticket. I pulled up my socks, dusted off my boots, dried my tears and forged on with my new adventure as a *single* traveller.

Wow how exciting! My first destination was home to New Zealand to see my parents, who happened to be going through a separation of their own. I left everything behind, except for a backpack full of clothes and my guitar and off I went. So now I have two bags, with the addition of my guitar.

Let's have a look at some of the reasons why, even though you love someone, it can be time to end the relationship.

1. You have both learned different tactics to handle conflict and you just **can't seem to find a workable middle ground**.
2. You have both agreed to **end the relationship amicably**.
3. Neither person is **willing to sacrifice, or compromise**, making a truce impossible.
4. One person **loves someone else more** than you and you are ready to let go.
5. Love by definition is not actually what you thought it was and you realise that **you don't really love them** unconditionally. You only love them when it suits you, or they only love you, when it suits them. Either way, this is not unconditional love. It's called *convenient* love, or *conditional* love.
6. When the relationship is based on **co-dependency** and it is restrictive and destructive.
7. When one partner is constantly **abusive** towards the other partner in the relationship.
8. When the relationship is **broken beyond repair** and you have both given it your best shot.
9. When you have **lost all respect** for yourself in the relationship.
10. When one partner wants to **end the relationship permanently**, after trying to resolve all of the earlier points.

True love is *unconditional* and couples who experience this kind of love will outlast everyone. True love in families that is unconditional, will also last the distance. Unconditional love in a friendship will be reserved for your *forever* friends. The type of friends who you can get away with not talking to for years and just pick up where you left off, when you see them again.

So remember, relationships can require regular input and hard work, but they are not meant to be arduous work. True love is something that grows stronger over time and doesn't weaken with age.

God said, "Unconditional love means *loving an imperfect person perfectly* and not trying to make an imperfect person perfect."

Grief

Grief is such a taboo subject in many cultures and yet expressed openly in others. I have seen many types of grief in my life and have helped many people deal with the grief of losing a loved one, a pet, or even their own identity. That can also be like dealing with death too and it makes you grieve in a different way.

When you give up your misconceptions about life, that you have held onto so tightly, for so long and finally *surrender* to the power of the Universe and the glory of God, it can feel like a massive relief, to allow whatever happens to happen and just observe. I have also learned personally from grief, when I have had to deal with loved ones passing over and losing young friends before their prime.

I have also seen and felt many spirits suffering from grief too, which is a whole different level of grief. People may naturally assume, that if there is an afterlife, a person who dies, just goes to that afterlife when they die. It is not always that simple and there can still be many challenges that a person faces, even after they have died, before they make it to the afterlife.

God said, "If a surviving family member, or loved one is grieving too much and they are unable to move on, even a long time after a person's death, it can cause the spirit to hang around the living, because of their concern for the living. The soul doesn't get to progress as quickly, because they are still dealing with the grief you feel for them, even though they may be happy on the other side."

God has taught me many things that I didn't know, even after loads of research about certain topics. God told me about the Israelites and other ancient races of people who used to show their grief by tearing their clothes or garments and throwing dust on their heads. Sometimes they would wallow in ashes. This is where the traditional term; *"ashes to ashes, dust to dust,"* during a funeral ceremony came from. It was also used as a sin cleansing practise that they would regularly go through, after a period of fasting. Then they would use dust as a symbol, to cleanse any dirt from their soul, when they were asking for God's forgiveness and praises.

Dirt and dust was used, because it showed the connection to the Earth and dirt was a symbol for mourning and grief. These days, the original grief process has been changed from an actual practise, to just saying the words and only giving it lip service during the burial, or cremation process.

The channeller said on behalf of God, "If we all knew what was waiting for us on the other side and we lived a good wholesome life, then we should have nothing to fear. In fact, we would even love to be back with the true source energy of the Creator. Everything makes sense again; we see all of our critical flaws during our lifetime, when we are shown our life lessons. This can also cause a spirit to want to make amends with the living, for any harm they may have caused them. Once they become aware of their misguided actions, they are truly sorry, but cannot change the past.

"Once free of the bounds of a physical body, spirits can celebrate being free and can move around the Universe and in time freely. If a person was ill, injured, disabled, living with chronic pain, or disease, prior to passing over, death for them can come as a welcome relief and their pain is removed instantly. To be out of the body can be a relief and they can continue their learning journey, in a different form of energy."

God said, "Spirits can get frustrated with those who are left behind, because they can be blind to what beauty exists on the other side. As a society, humans grieve deeply for people who have passed over, only because they think they have gone forever. Grief is even stronger for those who believe that *nothing* happens after life, because they do truly believe they have gone forever. In reality, they are probably right next to you in spirit form, whenever you ask for them to be with you. If you ask for their presence in a loving way, then they are happy to come and visit you, instead of visiting you out of concern for your grief."

Grief can be really debilitating and it can suck the energy and life force right out of you, if you are not prepared for the death of a loved one. In saying that, it doesn't matter how well you prepare for someone's death, even if you know their death is imminent, or you have known for a long time it was coming, it still doesn't make the actual process you go through called grieving, any less painful. Grieving is a normal emotion and a normal response we experience and it only becomes *abnormal*, when we don't snap out of that grief eventually and we remain in the depths of grieving for too long.

Allow yourself a period of time to grieve, after the death of a loved one. There is no need to prove you are superman, or superwoman. Preparing for the funeral of a loved one is a very stressful time for people, especially if they are also coping with intense grief. The last thing people usually want to do when they lose their loved one, is to arrange the funeral and yet in this day and age, it is common for the bereaved partner, or immediate family to do this.

Once the funeral is over, allow yourself a designated period of time, where you do not have to attend any social outings, do not have to attend work, visit anyone, call anyone and you should not worry about your appearance during this time. You have the right to grieve alone, or with company, whatever you prefer. You do not have to explain your choices to anyone and sometimes family is what you need during this time, even if there has been some estrangement in the past. It is a good time for family to reunite and rekindle what may have been lost for some time. Allow others to prepare meals for you and do things for you if they want to. It is their turn to give back to you and you can be on the *receiving* end of love this time.

The channeller said, "Be thankful that you are alive and live every precious moment you have, with joy and happiness, out of respect for the fact you are still *alive.* You can resurrect the dead by thinking about them, talking to them from a positive perspective and showing them how much you love them, even after they have passed. Another way you can show your love for them, is by doing all the things they loved to do, while they were alive and asking them to come along with you."

The channeller added, "Intense and prolonged grief can hold a spirit back from passing over completely, because their loved ones are left grieving for them, which causes the spirit to want to visit them. They feel sorry for the living having to cope with the grief, so the spirit hangs around for a bit longer. It's a vicious cycle that only the correct thinking of the living can prevent in the long run. Forgive in your grief and don't allow it to make you bitter, revengeful, or too sad."

Ask yourself, *how does the spirit feel about grief?* In my experience, if a spirit experiences grief, or expresses extreme grief, it is usually because they died suddenly, had an unexpected accident, they may have even been murdered, or killed without warning. They might also know that they could have been saved, if they had been able to get their message through to the right person, or treating doctor before their death occurred.

There is an unwritten spiritual law that can sometimes hinder you from interfering with souls, once they have passed over, *unless* the prevention of more deaths or harm is gained from your intervention. You are not allowed to sticky beak into the realm of spirit and probe about things you are not meant to know and you should still have respect for the deceased person's privacy, just as you would for the living. If a spirit wants you to know something, they can be very determined in getting that message across to you and will try many different approaches and methods until finally you *get it.*

Sometimes learning the truth after someone has died, about how they really died, can make you feel sad, angry and helpless and even more grief stricken. This is why spirits don't always divulge the nitty gritty details of their death, unless you ask them and even then, the spirit still has a choice whether to tell you the whole story, or not. If you have something to learn from it, or would benefit from knowing, they may tell you.

Spirits in general don't really like having to relive their experience of death, because it can trigger painful memories for the soul of the dead and even they want to forget sometimes. If you can't do anything about their death now and your actions won't necessarily help anyone in the future, then sometimes it is best to accept their death graciously. You can't bring them back and you cannot undo what is done.

It is best to hold fond memories of your loved ones who have passed over, in your mind and in your heart. Pray for them to have a safe transition into the afterlife. You can talk to them any time you like and send loving energy to them whenever you want and they will receive it.

Don't blame God for every single human being's death on this planet. It is not his fault, it is nobody's fault. Death is a part of life and it is the natural end of yet another life cycle lived by a soul, here on Planet Earth. If you have lost someone you really loved, you can be sure that you will cross paths with their soul again in the future. There are no guarantees with timing, but know that you will see them again. If you are lucky, you may get to see them as a reincarnation of another person during this life, otherwise you can see them on the other side, or be reincarnated with them again in the next life, or another life.

I also mentioned grief in relation to losing your identity. This one can sneak up on you and take you by surprise. Many people experience this kind of grief when they are approaching middle age, from around the age of 40 onwards. It is when they come to the realisation that life wasn't quite what they imagined it would be and they haven't achieved all the things on their bucket list yet. Time feels like it is moving so fast and the walls seem to start closing in on old age. This is called having a *midlife crisis*. Really, what is happening is the ego is starting to *dissolve*; you are starting to view the simple things in life as being the most precious. Naturally people you have known for a large part of your life, start to pass away.

How do you avoid grief?

- **Cherish life!** Live every moment doing what you love, don't waste time doing things that make you unhappy. Most of all, tell people how much you love them every single day if you want to, then you will never regret not saying what you wanted to say to someone *before* they go.
- **Love those who are precious to you** and worthy of your love and hold them with both hands, while they are alive. Also love those who are unworthy of love, to show that you are beyond judgement.
- **Have no regrets**. If you have longed to go somewhere, do something, change jobs, start again, move on, move in, move out, move up, or stand down, then *get on with it* and just do it. Stop waiting for the perfect time, there is no such thing. If you want to go and live like a hippy in a village, grow vegetables and have chickens, then take off the corporate cloak and go and do it!
- **Remove the illusion** that life in a human form is immortal. It is not. All of us will die someday, it is guaranteed. Let's not pretend that we are supposed to live forever, in this physical form. The soul is immortal and eternal like the Creator, but not the flesh. The flesh is weaker than the soul. Lift the veil and see

life for every treasure that it presents to you. Every second here is a gift, so make the most of it.

- **Have faith in God** and ask for miracles. It makes everything worthwhile and gives your existence meaning. How fabulous to know we get to return to our Father in Heaven, when our mission is complete. There are no shortcuts, no easy way there, no cheating. Just live your life out to your last breath and make a difference to everyone you encounter, while you are alive. There is no need for grief, only the *celebration of life.*

The inner saboteur

Human beings have a bad habit of sabotaging their opportunities, right before the rewards are due from all of their hard work. The frustration that all of us face are the hold ups, the setbacks, the steps backwards, the extended delays, waiting, waiting, waiting… It is natural for people to display learned behaviour, which is not always the correct way to behave. They are acting out as a result of their negative conditioning, environment and circumstances.

God said, "Each of us comes fully programmed with the inner saboteur and this is one of our life lessons to overcome, to enable the advancement of the soul. The inner saboteur is like that negative little voice in the back of your mind telling you, 'it isn't going to work' and 'you are wasting your time.' It is like a hidden darkness within everyone that tries to stop you from succeeding."

God continued, "If a person is constantly bombarded and surrounded by attitudes of failure, lack, stress, limit and resistance, it is inevitable that the same behaviour is likely to be re-enacted when they are faced with a similar situation. Human's natural response to a challenging situation, is going to be similar to that of their role models. If their role models are inappropriate, or negative, then this is the only resource available to them at the time. This is called *conditioning.* The only way to break free from conditioning is to reprogram yourself to think in the correct way. You need to convince yourself that there is a better way to act and there is a better response to choose for each situation."

God added, "To understand yourself and others is to realise that it is possible to reprogram people to feel the right way, about the right things. A human brain is like an empty computer. If you *input* negative information, you are going to get negative *output,* or feedback. If you enter nice things into the computer, you get nice things out of it. The computer does not reason, it merely gives output, based on input. However, if you bring in another program called *emotion*, this can change the whole operating system."

God said, "When people think, or perceive that bad things are happening to them, the main thing to focus on, is to see if they can find anything *good* that has happened to them. It sounds so simple, but very true and it works to counteract, or numb the inner saboteur. To shift someone's focus from the bad things, over to the good things, is just a matter of focusing their attention on anything good at all that has happened to them. After the episode is over and they are freed from the situation, the question to ask yourself is; *what good has come out of it?* Also another important question to ask yourself is; *what have I learned from this experience?*"

Life is full of lessons and although we don't always see the reason at the time of the lesson, it does not mean there are no lessons to learn, or that there is no reason for the lesson. There is *always* a reason for everything that happens. You just need to figure out why this is happening to you right now.

Deal with sabotage that happens internally, by *acknowledging* it and then not paying any further attention to it. What you focus on becomes current in your consciousness. What you don't focus on becomes distant and sits in the background, until finally it fades away. Learn to shift your focus when the negative voices try to get a hold of your mind. Remember who is in control. *You are!* Not the inner saboteur.

13. THE BODY

God said, "For every ailment, he provided a cure from the forest or originally from the Garden of Eden."

YOUR body is your shrine. It is your earthly vehicle that will transport you around the planet, while you are here living in this life. Treat your body like a temple so that it lasts the duration. Feed it good wholesome food, ensure you get enough vitamins and minerals and keep it moving and mobile. Rest when it is needed. Don't abuse your body, or take it for granted, because you don't get another one.

A human body is like a computer. You put crap in, you get crap out. My belief is, if you are not prepared to eat it, don't put it on your skin. If you cringe at the thought of eating, or drinking your shampoo, conditioner, moisturizer, toothpaste, sunscreen, hair dye, make up and so on, then why would you put something that toxic on your skin, which is the biggest organ on the human body? Your skin absorbs these chemicals directly into the blood stream, through the skin and then the body needs to digest and break down all of these materials, to pass them through the body's waste system. This process can put unwanted pressure and stress on your vital organs, which can ultimately manifest into an unwanted illness, when the body can no longer secrete, or excrete this waste.

Next time you buy body, skin, or make up products, buy non-toxic, natural and organic products where possible. You will not only be saving your body, but also helping to improve the environment as well.

Natural products can extend to all areas of your life including; food, drink, clothing, bedding, packaging, cleaning products, furniture, your actual dwelling and décor as well. Be as natural as possible with these materials and where possible, purchase cottons and natural fibres, instead of synthetic and toxic materials. This will benefit your overall immune system and will also eliminate many allergies.

Offering health advice

You can't tell someone they can't do something. You could *suggest* what you think is the best thing for them to do, to cure their ailment. For example, you could ask them, "Do you think if you ate less red meat that this cancer would go away? Do you think if you didn't smoke cigarettes anymore, that you would be able to breathe easier and have a healthier life? Do you think if you relaxed more using the techniques I showed you, that your illness would dissolve forever? And it will won't it?"

Everyone has an inner rebel, an inner saboteur and as soon as you tell someone what to do, or give them instructions that go against their inner saboteur, their inner rebel and their inner demon, they are less likely to listen to you, or take your advice. Sometimes it can even trigger a response, for the inner rebel to do exactly the opposite and activate the self destruction mode, just to prove a point. This can only be corrected by right thinking and natural living.

Here are a few basic health principles that you might like to live by, to keep yourself in a good state of physical fitness and mental balance.

- ✓ Be natural
- ✓ Go organic where possible
- ✓ Balance your minerals and vitamins
- ✓ Go vegetarian
- ✓ Keep fit
- ✓ Get plenty of exercise
- ✓ Be kind to yourself and others
- ✓ Drink plenty of natural, distilled, or spring water (not tap water)
- ✓ Respect your body
- ✓ Love life
- ✓ Learn to relax and enjoy yourself

In my next book, I am going to teach you how to live a healthy life, with the correct balance of everything. The focus of the book will be about living a long life and correcting ailments and illnesses that have become out of balance.

Health issues

God said, "Influencing and denying senses of the body contribute to mankind's health issues. In 2050 they will discover the true meaning of this balance."

God added, "Nature has grown a cure for everything."

The channeller said, "God has made medicinal foods and plants, for every ailment that we could ever suffer. For example, research what blood arteries are naturally made of and then eat foods, or plants that are made up of the same mineral compounds. That action would clear any vein blow outs and cure varicose veins.

"There is also a natural antigen for helicobacter and a natural antibiotic for mycoplasma, but the pharmaceutical companies don't want cures and ancient remedies, because you can't easily patent and control a plant for medical use. They will try and do this with marijuana, but they need to remember this plant has been around for thousands of years as a medicinal plant. In fact it was only made illegal during the past 100 years. They tell you that it is a drug. It is *not* a drug and it never will be. It is a *plant* and a medicinal plant at that. It should be used for medicinal purposes, which can cure and assist with many different health ailments and conditions. The medical industry is slowly working this out, but is very cautious with their approach. This is why they are not encouraging its usage. They are only in the testing phase."

Just for a moment, let's look at the industry definition of a drug: *a chemical substance used in the treatment, cure and prevention of...* it doesn't mention anywhere about plants.

The law enforcement agencies now class illicit and narcotic drugs as Class A drugs; even if some of them are made, or derived purely from a plant. You might think this definition sounds innocent enough, but the pharmaceutical companies and the law enforcement agencies have forgotten one simple fact. God made plants for our responsible use. Imagine the hysteria if broccoli, wheat, or corn was suddenly banned from public use. Everyone would be asking, "Why are you banning something that is healthy and wholesome?"

The troubling part of the equation is that it is illegal to consume some products made from plants, but it is legal to consume pills and medicines made from synthetic and harmful chemicals. Just to clarify, I am not condoning illicit drug use. I am simply comparing the two scenarios from an objective and holistic view point and not through the eyes of the law.

The channeller on behalf of God said, "For every ailment, God provided a cure from the forest, or originally from the Garden of Eden. The crazy thing is if you break down every synthetic drug to its bare bone structure, then you will realise that every ingredient of that drug, or medicine, is actually made from a plant, when you trace back the source of every element. This proves that there is no difference between the substances used in pharmaceutical drugs and illicit drugs. One industry has a license to produce their drug and the other industry does not. It is not a *moral* argument, or one that God judges. It is a control and monitoring issue, where they don't want people taking mind altering substances, *unless* they are under strict supervision, or they have a prescription for it!"

Muscle aches and strains

God said, "Lactic acid is released when using muscles and more lactic acid is produced, when overusing these muscles. Treat the affected limb or area simply by relaxing it. Rest it to give it time to recover. What happens is we work, work, work at whatever we work at with no relaxing. We need to turn the muscles on and off, not just leave them continuously on."

God continued, "When training, there should be periods of going hard like a sprint, then rest to give the muscles a chance to turn on and off. This will prevent muscle aches and strains. When you overuse muscles, you are just overdoing it and need to rest. It is that simple and not technical at all. You are not supposed to be full on all the time. Rest is just as important as exercise, but too much of either, is not good for you as well."

Diabetes

God said, "Refined sugar was invented in the 16th century and has contributed to diabetes. Type 1 and 2 diabetes were both discovered in the 1900's. In 2013 scientists and doctors discovered the cure for diabetes, but it hasn't been released yet. Genetic diabetes can be changed and is originally found in the genes."

God continued, "The earliest links to diabetes was around 1000BC. Then there was another burst of incidents around 1700's, although they didn't call it diabetes back then. Diabetes occurred when the person had a bladder infection and they used to become unconscious, with the pancreas being lost. Pancreatic diabetes is the 3rd stage of diabetes and it is where they can't save the pancreas. The uncommon thing is where it links cancer to the pancreas and diabetics."

God added, "A person with diabetes is not getting enough *love*, so the symptom which causes diabetes is rejecting love. The person is in rejection of their responsibilities. They are rejecting their body working and this is about taking responsibility for yourself. They are doing this, because they are being rejected from one incident. This can all lead back to this one incident with their mother, father, lover etc."

God said, "The best treatment for diabetes is throlthiren. Measure the body's ninathaline. They measure this by checking the T cell depletion to see if it is either high, or low. They are not meant to do it on a daily basis, because it doesn't give them a true reading. The doctor gets a blood test done every day for a chronic diabetic, where they should be only looking at the weekly tablets, to confirm if the patient's medical treatment is working. Suggest every 4-5 weeks reassessing the medical treatment and swapping it if it isn't working, but these are considered American medical treatments.

"Have you ever considered giving the person a hug? Urine samples were introduced between 1969 and 1973 and were refined again. Urine swabs came in around 1993. Then they introduced the finger prick to determine blood sugar levels, instead of urine. They have now learned how to manage this by electronic glucoses and using glutamine, to assist with the white blood cell count. The medical profession terms it the pancreas runaway. Get the pancreas back into shape and everything else works fine again.

"Medication problems occur when the person self administers their own treatments. The age group of teenagers from 16 to middle aged adults, up to 35 tend to overdose on their medication. If they are given 10 syringes, they try to overdose and have all of them at once, which is not fixing the psychological problems associated with the issue. The 40+ age group are stubborn and won't take the medical treatment when they are supposed to and end up overdosing on sugar. What fails to happen is the need to assess everyone on a personal level, to see if, or why they are crazy, or why they have psychological problems. The diabetes disease is caused by underlying psychological problems and is *not* fixed by addressing the symptoms only."

God continued, "Another effective method of treatment would be to find out how many antibodies within the body go to correct the problem. The T cells that are destroyed show on the antibodies of the cells and whatever the remaining balance is, can be discarded through the body. The T cells that are destroyed need to be noted and also how many cells are destroyed. Remember, the person may lie about how much sugar they have had and this is why it needs to be tested without asking the person. True testing needs to be in place and the social lying aspects of being caught, hinder getting true test results. The method needs to test the T cells and don't use the method of asking the actual person questions, because all people lie, to cover up their fear of getting caught out.

"The body destroys sugar, when it is in the body in abundance. Hypoglycaemia occurs because of the amount of sugar they take, simply because they are being starved of sugar. Then when they have a sugar hit, it is like an overdose and the body reacts. How about doctors inviting a speech from someone who is a sugar junkie, or an addict, or a reformed person, to really get their point across to people suffering from the disease? When you just listen to the doctor, it is boring. They need to hear from a sugar junkie, to hear *why* they need this fix.

"Show people what happens to their body, when they have a *need* and what the result is, when they act on that need. All they really *need* is a hug! They need love and they are trying to replace it with sugar, drugs, alcohol, sex etc. They are lacking their own self love, their own self monitoring mechanism. If parents were not teaching you correctly, then there is an imbalance. That can mean that some parents are not a good role model for the correct, or right way and they could be teaching you bad habits unknowingly.

"The best way to control sugar cravings is to first recognise it as an *addiction* and treat the addiction in the same way you would treat any harmful addiction. Take a disciplined approached to your diet, regain control of your food and drink choices and allow more love into your life."

Personal hygiene

God said, "The black plague was caused by rats eating human faeces. If rats are healthy and well looked after, they are not full of disease. If the rats eat faeces from the open sewers, then the black plague will return. Man must close the sewers and stop the rats from eating from them, to stop this happening again."

The channeller added, "Humans should pee on their faeces to sterilise it. The scientists will realise what God meant by that comment. Ammonia shall kill all bacteria. What man lacks and what God has, is time... Man can't create in a hundred years, what God has created in millions of years of research, with his tried and tested experiments. God is the ultimate alchemist, due to his experience and God knows how to make gold and man doesn't."

God added, "Earth is a corrosive planet and everything needs to have skin, because it is exposed to acid. Rubbing hands together destroys bacteria. Handshaking is rife with disease, but we still do it. It is better to bow to each other with no contact."

God said, "Normal bacteria exist on everyone's skin. Methicillin-resistant Staphylococcus aureus otherwise known as MRSA in a *live* body is a form of decomposition.

"To combat MRSA you can either:

1. **Increase the rate of new cell production**, which means you get healthier; or
2. Seal it to stop, or **slow down the bacteria** and decomposition process = death."

I asked God, "Why do some people get embalmed?"

God explained, "Embalming is designed to slow the decomposition process down, to enable the reincarnation to be participated in, at a future date. This was the original reason for embalming people."

If you practise these basic hygiene guidelines, you will protect yourself from *most* germs, viruses and bacteria. Germs, viruses and bacteria exist everywhere. You should be able to avoid them, if you minimise your exposure.

1. **If you are sick, be considerate and don't spread your germs** by coughing and sneezing over everyone else. If you need to cough, or sneeze, make sure you cover your nose and mouth, to avoid spraying the germs over surfaces, food and people. If you sneeze into your hands, ensure you wash them afterwards.
2. Disinfect areas that sick people come into contact with regularly, to **avoid reinfection** and to **avoid spreading germs** through the whole home, or workplace. Consider a safe quarantine area, away from other family, or work members, when one or more members are contagious. If you cannot avoid contact with members of the public, consider wearing a surgical mask to contain the germs.
3. **Wash your hands regularly**, especially before you eat, every single time you go to the toilet and every time you could have potentially come into contact with germs, bacteria, or viruses.
4. Wash your hands after touching any animals, both domestic and wild. **Be careful when handling animals**, because they can be infected with parasites without you even knowing it.
5. **Soil and plants contain many micro bacteria** and ensure you do not breathe in the organisms, when gardening, or harvesting.
6. Don't put your fingers in your mouth, or in any orifices, if you don't **have clean hands**. Every orifice contains its own bacteria and if you come into contact with contaminated surfaces, or another creature's orifices, or skin, cross contamination can occur.
7. **Avoid direct contact with highly used public items** such as; escalator rails, shopping trolleys, door handles, light switches, touch screens, teller machines, public toilets, floors, hand rails and footpaths. Use gloves, or a barrier between you and these items.
8. **Always keep wounds clean** and cover wounds, until they have healed.
9. **Brush your teeth** a minimum of two times per day. Once in the morning and once before going to bed. Floss your teeth once a day. You should change your toothbrush, or toothbrush heads a minimum of every six months. You can change it more often if you wish.
10. **Practise oil pulling** at least once a week, to remove any unwanted debris and bacteria from around your gums and teeth. Discard the dirty oil down the drain, or in the toilet. Use only organic, cold pressed oil. The best oil to use is flaxseed oil or coconut oil.
11. **Keep all common areas clean** and disinfect these areas

regularly.

12. **Wash your bedding and clothes** at *least* once a week. Underwear should be changed daily or more often if needed.
13. **Keep your food preparation areas clean and sterile**, before and after you prepare your food. Don't use the same chopping boards to cut raw meat and vegetables. Have one board for each use. Wash your chopping boards thoroughly, with hot soapy water after each use. Discard old or cracked boards, because of the risk of bacteria that can live in the crevices.
14. **Discard any dishes, or drinkware with cracks, or chips**. Cracks and crevices are the ideal breeding ground for bacteria. It can also increase your exposure to toxic elements used to make those dishes, like; lead, cadmium and plastic.
15. Don't eat and reheat leftover meat dishes. **If in doubt, throw it out**. If you are eating in a public place and the food is served from a display cabinet, don't be afraid to ask how long the food has been sitting there.
16. **Remove mouldy food** from your living space, because the food is in a state that is breaking down and it is no longer nutritious and fresh. Mould can also contaminate and affect food that is located nearby.
17. **Keep your living and working areas dry**, clean and well ventilated.
18. **Learn about infection control** and be aware of your surroundings at all times. Avoid direct contact with people who are sick, even if you are fit and healthy.
19. **Keep your whole body and hair clean** by showering, or bathing multiple times a week. Washing yourself not only feels good, you can wash off germs, bacteria and dirt, to ensure you are not unnecessarily exposed to harmful bacteria. Regularly clean all of those hard to reach places, such as; inside your ears, between your toes, under your arms, under your fingernails and in all the other cracks and crevices of your body.
20. **Stay hydrated**. Drink plenty of herbal tea, freshly squeezed juice and filtered water.
21. **Boost your immune system** with a good balanced diet and supplement it with vitamins and minerals.
22. **Be streetwise** and know your surroundings, especially if you are travelling in a foreign country, or unfamiliar environment.
23. **Avoid stress**.

Blood borne viruses > can be spread through contamination by blood, or other bodily fluids. Don't share, or use dirty needles, or dirty implements. Avoid direct contact with other people's blood, especially if you have open sores, or cuts. Avoid contact with fresh blood from any creature, or human, near any of your body's openings, or orifices. Be aware of the risks if you are being treated in a hospital and understand the risks associated with blood transfusions. Avoid mosquito, insect, or animal bites, especially when travelling in countries with known infectious diseases, parasites and viruses.

Bacterial viruses > not all bacteria is harmful and in fact some bacteria is beneficial to our health. Practise good food and personal hygiene. The most important health tip is to avoid food that could be contaminated. If food is not stored, handled, or prepared correctly, bacterial contamination can occur. Bacteria can spread to other foods, without you doing anything. Be aware of good food hygiene practises and only eat, or buy food where there is a high turnover of food and a good reputation for cleanliness.

Just because you can eat what you like in your own home country, it doesn't mean you can eat what you like in a foreign country. In some poorer and third world countries, their standard of health and hygiene may not be as high as the country where you live. A task as simple as brushing your teeth with tap water, or having ice in your drink in one of these countries, can make you very sick. Bacteria can also be picked up from contaminated surfaces, where the infected person or carrier has left a trail.

Airborne viruses > avoid close contact with people who are sick with an airborne virus, or who are infectious. If you hear, or see someone sneeze, or cough, cover your eyes, nose and mouth to prevent the contaminated particles from entering any wet, or open areas on and in your body. I personally get as far away from coughing, or sneezing people that I can, for the simple reason that this is the most common way for airborne viruses to spread. The best rule of thumb is not to stand within natural spitting distance to someone, when you are talking to them. This way you can avoid contact, that is close enough for you to become infected and it allows for a safe zone between you, if you need to turn away, or walk away from a sneeze, or cough.

Soil-borne viruses **>** if the soil where plants grow is out of balance ecologically, it may contain pathogenic viruses that can harm plants, creatures and humans.

Waterborne viruses > don't drink contaminated water. Always know where the source of your water comes from. Test the water if you are unsure, or use micron filtration to filter the bacteria and viruses. Boil the water first if you don't have filtration available. Water that has come into contact with urine, or faeces from any creature, is the most dangerous cocktail of contaminants.

Sexually transmitted infections > avoid unprotected sex and contact with contaminated blood, semen or vaginal fluids. Anyone who is sexually active is at risk of exposure.

Synthetic viruses > are created by the manipulation of the genomes in RNA and DNA to make it biologically hazardous. Avoid over populated areas where these viruses could potentially be released. Human contact is almost unavoidable in built up areas.

Vaccinations

God did not vaccinate humans with anything pharmaceutical. Humans adapted to their environment through trial and error and through learning to live in harmony with their environment. They used their intuition and instinct, to find healthy and non-harmful nourishment.

The best vaccination for babies is their mother's milk. Milk from a tin, does *not* have the right balance of minerals, fibre and cellular DNA a growing baby needs, to develop a strong and healthy immune system.

The best defence is to keep fit and healthy and maintain a strong and healthy immune system. The forest is your pharmacy, minerals are your building blocks and nature is your sanctuary away from the poisons of the industrialised world.

Stem cells

God said, "If you are going to make stem cells, mankind programs the cells to do something. The problem is that cells have no soul. You can make an ear, but whose ear is it? Remember the aura. Scientists, or doctors need to swap out the soul part, as well as the physical part, or else it won't work properly."

14. APPLYING SKILLS

Make rules when making decisions.
Know that there are always good options.
Options are choices. Do you like this option?
No, then come up with another option.

LEARNING how to apply your skills correctly, means finding a good role model who is doing it right and copy what they do. You won't be able to model them exactly, but you can learn to be like them. If you want to be a good speller, just *emulate* a good speller. If you want to learn how to build boats, then you need to spend time with a boat builder.

God said, "A person that stutters, does it because they already think they are going to stuff up their speech. When they start to say the word, they hesitate and repeat the word, because they think too much about stuffing it up. They need to think they are going to speak correctly and to practice out loud. Hang out with people that encourage their progress and stay away from people who discourage them."

You can be even better than your role model, by learning more than they know and enhancing it. Not in a cocky way, but in a way that makes you a better learner than your role model.

Making decisions

Humans love to have options. Nobody likes to be forced into making a decision that has only one outcome. Humans feel trapped when this is the case. They need options, to feel like they have some input into the decision and having input, creates choices.

Here is a good example of asking a loaded question, with both options being favourable to you. Let's say you want to get your child to clean their room. You would ask your child, "Would you like to clean your room now, or later?" They have a choice and both outcomes are favourable, because the end game is to get your child to clean their room. It doesn't matter which choice they make, but they must make a choice. Whatever their choice is, you need to support it and follow up with the agreement that you have made.

Another good example of using options with favourable outcomes is; let's say that you are having difficulty getting your child off to bed and it is 8:00pm. Children react when they are told what to do, so you ask them, "Would you like to go to bed now, or at 9:00pm?"

It is typical of children to want to stay up late, so they will respond with the answer that suits them the most. You have now entered into negotiations with your child and now you both must honour the agreement. At 9:00pm you can say to them, "Okay this is the time you agreed to go to bed," and they will more than likely go to bed without a fuss, because that is the options they chose themselves.

Options are empowerment and what does empowerment mean to you? It means exercising your free will to make informed choices, based on the available options. It doesn't matter that both options are favourable to you. Your child is happy they were able to participate in the decision making and that is what matters. How you conduct yourself with others is really important for getting cooperation.

You could use techniques that invoke appealing emotions, that will influence the decision making process. How about trying to use a sweetener to get your options heard? You could say, "What about if I gave you *xyz* if you complete the task? How would you feel if I did it for you? If you do it *now,* rather than *later*, I will do *xyz* for you." The goal is to make them realise that they are better off taking the option with the good deal, rather than taking no option at all.

To make a decision about something, first you have to explore the options. To be able to explore the options, you need to make choices. To be able to make choices, you need answers. To be able to get answers, you need questions. See how it works? You need to chunk it right down, until you get this process.

God said, "Make rules when making decisions. Know that there are always good options. Options are choices. Do you like this option? No, then come up with another option. Options are changeable and you can even change your option and how you are getting there. Options are will power and everything is an option.

"Explore what the options are and if your rule is; always have 3 options, then implement that rule for yourself to use. *You* are the creator of your own options.

"In ancient history, elders were given high level information about how to persuade humans. They were advanced at assessing what options were available in any given situation.

"If something makes you feel good, then that's a good option, even if it is dark."

God continued, "Sometimes an urgent option, is one using the fight, or flight mode and you may need to be tapping into other emotions, to help you make a choice based on an option. Let's say that a finished project starts with one question and five possible answers. It would look something like this."

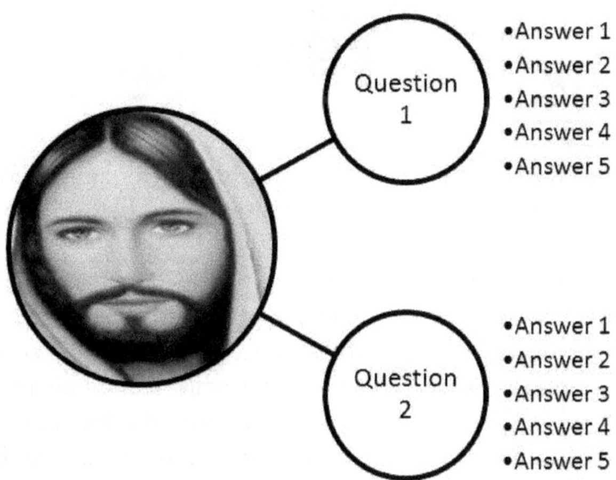

God added, "There are three layers of the human brain. The layers go three deep, with three slices. The brain is running at high speed and it is running all the time. It goes around in circles, performing continuous checks. The brain checks the body's senses, the body's safety mechanisms, the emotions, the internal temperature and regulation systems. It is constant and it never stops.

"Most of these functions are *learned.* If you represented how the brain works as a diagram, it would look like the diagram below. It is like you created the query, or question, then passed it on to other brain cells, or sections of the brain and then the inner guru answers all your questions. The inner guru becomes your answering mechanism. Now all you need to do is create a standard for your answering mechanism. If you wanted to be more like God, then your answering mechanism needs to be like God, holy and true."

When we were searching for the right block of land to purchase, we spent many hours researching and visiting properties on our shortlist. Whenever the opportunity presented itself, I would ask God to help us decide which block of land to buy. Funnily enough, God wouldn't tell us which property was the right one to buy, but he did *show me how* to make the right choice, based on certain criteria.

God said, "We can drill down even further, by looking deeper into one of the outcomes, or answers to the question you had before, about the land. Let's take a look at one possible answer."

1. **It will have space and privacy**.

God asked, "What is privacy? Is privacy being able to lay nude in your own space, because at certain times you are going to want some privacy? This ultimately means when you are using this technique to help other people, or if you are showing them how to apply this technique, you need to have a better understanding of how other people feel. Dig deep to ask the question!"

God continued, "Life can be filled with squabbles and queries. You need to divide questions into multiple answers and start opening up, so you can answer the million questions you may have to answer."

God added, "Life is choices. Questions and choices. The answer is always straight in front of you."

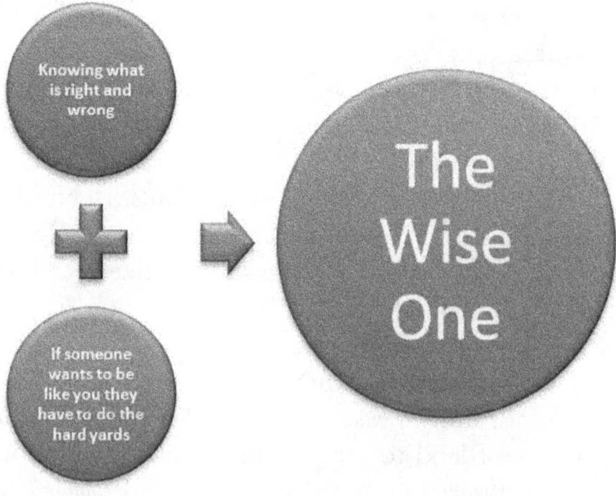

Change

God said, "Look up super computer network. The HAARP network is on the internet. The next thing to look up on the internet is the summary of the word called *change*. Everybody is in charge of that work on this planet. The most powerful word in the dictionary that is a physical word is **change**. You can pray to change something. You can physically change something and other people can change things. You can change the way you think and you can change the way that somebody else thinks. You can ask God to change something. You can also be a part of the change, which is more exciting than anything."

God continued, "You can change the way you love something and the way you see something. Change the way you taste something and change the way that a murderer sees their views and thoughts, by making them loving instead of hateful! Everyone can be a part of change and everyone can be a part of the solution, instead of further contributing to the problem."

I want to introduce you to a concept called the *helix effect*. God taught me about the helix effect; when I was having a hard time understanding why it was so difficult to get certain changes implemented at my workplace. I couldn't work out why the same behavioural pattern, of only doing half a job was so prevalent in the company and I wanted to know *why* it was happening and how I could fix it.

God explained, "There is a thing called a *helix effect*. A good example to describe the helix effect is; when disease enters the body and the virus latches onto a bad cell and then transforms itself into a leader cell. Then it duplicates itself, until the bad cells take over the good cells. I am trying to simplify it for the purpose of this explanation. So using this analogy, when a person in any organisation has bad habits, has trouble completing tasks and they are the leader of the organisation or in a position of power, they tend to create more of the same. How do they do this? They become deeply involved with the selection and recruitment process. They hire other people just like themselves, because they can relate to them easily, feel comfortable with them and think that they need more of the same thing, to make the business operate more efficiently."

God said, "Mistake number one, is assuming that any organisation needs *similar* people, or similar personalities to make it better. Incorrect! They need *diversity*, a spread of skill sets and people, who are not like them, who can approach challenges in alternative ways. This mode of operating a business, gives you strength with less numbers. It combines the skills and the knowledge base and provides the perfect balance in a team environment, where you can work together to form a synergy, to get things done effectively."

The *helix* in this case was the manager, who continually employed people who were similar to himself. He didn't even realise what he was doing wrong and couldn't work out why the failure kept happening and where the breakdown was occurring in the string of command. The manager thought he was doing a fabulous job, recruiting people of similar skill sets, but just like him, they failed to complete their tasks on time, they got easily distracted and due to their passive nature, allowed themselves to be manipulated by people with a destructive nature."

God explained, "Let's dig deeper and take a closer look at the root cause of the problem. The reason behind this particular person's issue was his dominating mother, who would constantly criticise him for everything he did. He grew thick skin and accepted the same behaviour from those around him and he never learned to deal with the emotional abuse from his mother. He in turn immersed himself in his work, became extremely specialised in his field of expertise and was a very technically bright and smart man, but he lacked emotional intelligence. Guess what the helix did? Hired more of himself, until the helix became like the disease did and the bad cells overtook the good cells. Implementing change in this type of unbalanced environment is almost impossible, unless something changes."

God loves to offer solutions and I personally don't like to raise a problem, without at least offering a solution of how to change that problem.

Here are some possible solutions.

1. Stop the helix from being involved in the recruitment process. This means the helix, who is creating the chaos unknowingly, needs to withdraw from the situation and **trust the process of life**. They need to know that other people are capable of making the right choices, without their input.
2. **Fix the helix**, so that the helix swings their balance from bad to good. Spend time working on the core issues and teaching them emotional intelligence. Guide them through the process of what is and what is not acceptable behaviour. Provide them with appropriate support, so their skills are not wasted on managing *issues,* instead of people.
3. Suggest that the helix would benefit from a **diverse range of skills**.

This means reassessing the process in which people are selected, or recruited. Look at how you can diversify the workplace to suit the needs of the growing business, instead of fulfilling the needs of the helix.

Through using these guidelines, you can either *improve,* or *fix* the helix. What happens if you don't fix the helix is that the helix becomes out of control and destroys the organisation without even meaning to, because they are unaware of what they are doing. You need to remember they have no malice attached to what they are doing; they are just unaware of the helix effect.

To implement change effectively, you have to first work out *how* to change things. You can't just simply wish for and want change to happen, because it has to be backed up with *intent* and *energy* to implement change. That means pulling apart the delicate fabric of the patchwork quilt, seam by seam and attempting to work out where the stitching has come undone.

When you find the *source* of the problem, then follow through and repair it. There is no point observing change, talking about it and then not doing anything constructive to make the necessary changes. Put in a process to stop it happening in the future and ensure all changes you implemented are for the benefit of mankind and not just yourself.

The channeller on behalf of God said, "Humans are like other animals in the animal kingdom and that makes them creatures of habit. If mankind has been doing something a certain way for thousands of years, it doesn't necessarily make it right!"

God continued, "Here is the ultimate example of what happens, when everyone continues to keep doing the same thing and expecting a different result. Imagine if there was a small village in the middle of nowhere and there was an evil doctor working there. The evil doctor had a plan to take over the village and have it all to himself, so he concocted a potion that would kill off the whole village, one by one, until there was no one left. Slowly one by one, all of the townsfolk started dropping. Meanwhile in Heaven, God questioned each villager that was being sent to him and he asked each of them what happened."

For example, the person who had just passed over said to God, "The doctor told me to drink of this potion. He said it will surely make me better. Then death and '*whoop,*' I am here."

Then God asked, "Why did you drink this potion?"

The villager responded, "The man told me it would make me feel better."

God responded with, "You are a fool!"

God laughed and said, "This is how they got termed the *village idiot.*"

God continued, "What is the lesson to be learned here? Nobody questioned what was going on and they all fell into the same death trap. Have you ever heard of lemmings? They are driven by a strange biological urge to migrate in large groups and instinctively, they go to extreme levels to get to where they are going. This includes falling off a cliff face, if they are following all of their fellow lemmings."

God added, "This is only a metaphoric representation, used to illustrate the point and is not necessary scientifically correct, but the point is still very serious. Humans can sometimes get into the crowd, gang, or mass mentality, where they simply follow the leader of the day, without actually questioning what they are doing, or why they are doing it. They are being swept up in the confusion and the madness and going with the flow, sometimes to their death. War is a good example of this."

God wants us to question everything and wants to know where our stupidity comes from.

God said, "Who told you this? How do you know of this? Why is this so? Don't believe everything you are told. If it doesn't sit right with you, it probably isn't and this can be indicative of time for a change."

God continued, "Learn to ask more questions when people have problems and drill down to help people resolve them. What's the point of asking someone how their day is going, when you genuinely have no interest in listening to the answer? When you ask someone how they are going, really stop what you are doing, engage with the person and really get to the nitty gritty details of their issue. You may be able to help them resolve it, by casting a second set of eyes and ears over the problem. A problem shared, is a problem halved. If a whole group of people share a problem, you have the total combined experience, years, age and wisdom of everyone in the group, to help solve the problem. This makes it a tiny problem to solve, when you divide it up accordingly."

God said, "If you want to implement change, you need to look at the past, the present and the future. Look deep into the past and ask yourself, *has this been done successfully in the past?* What about asking yourself, *is this change working right now anywhere and do you know of anyone, anything, or anywhere like that in the present? How will it be in the future?* Think the whole change dynamic right through to the end and don't just focus on what you want to change. Really transport the mind into the future, to see what the effects will be, projecting into the future."

God continued, "If you are at work and you want to implement change, you need to convince your colleagues, workers and managers to give you a chance. Show them that you can teach them how to be a leader, how to succeed and ultimately how to get ahead. You could start with an opening line like, 'What if I could teach you how to do this job and keep you here for a long time?' Or something like, 'Follow in my footsteps and do what I say and you will stay here for a long time,' which is more empathetic. Many people are afraid to stand up on the soapbox, on the stage in front of a crowd and put themselves out there, because they have been fear conditioned to shut up, be quiet, behave and do what they are told."

The channeller emphasised the message from God, "This is *not* how we were created. We were given a voice to be heard, hands to write and be creative, a life to experience our lessons and a soul to be a part of the God force. We were created to learn from our lessons, grow as a result of our learning and change the injustices that make it difficult for our fellow brothers and sisters to exist. This is why racial intolerance and discrimination is just pointless. We are all part of the *same* family, part of the same human race and we all come from the same source of love and light, to which we shall all return eventually."

The channeller continued, "Bring down your walls, settle your petty disagreements, forgive us our trespasses, as we forgive those who trespass against us. Forget the struggles and the injustices, wipe the slate clean and start again. The human race needs to start moving into a collective state of consciousness where change, if it is positive and helpful, is embraced and implemented, for the benefit of mankind and all of the creatures and plant life you share the planet with."

Every single one of us on this planet right now has lessons in life to learn, *even* if you are the world's most revered monk, you are still learning too, just like God is. The learning is infinite and no person on Earth is perfect. As a collective race, we need to determine the right balance, share our resources and define the purpose of life on Earth.

God knows our purpose on Earth, is *not* to deplete the Earth of all its minerals. He doesn't want to see all of his natural habitats destroyed and he doesn't want humankind to destroy themselves, or the planet that they live on. This is what God sees when he looks at us. He wants to see change and he wants to see change happen quickly, to reverse the damage we have created and restore the balance and harmony to nature.

God said, "Change is easy, if you want it."

Moving on

Throughout my life, I have had many experiences that I have shared with many different people. Some good, some bad and some I can only chalk up to experience.

Whenever it is time for me to move on to a new place, God always comes and visits me and lets me know that it is time to move on soon. Sometimes I get annoyed, because I am not ready to leave, or I am not mentally prepared to move on yet. I get stubborn and resist change, because it means everything in my life *changes* with moving on.

Even though I know I must listen, I do get frustrated, because sometimes I think he is joking around with me, or just testing me to see how I will react. Of course everything God tells me that will happen actually happens! I shouldn't doubt God, because he knows what my life path is and what other things he has in store for me. God knows everything, including things I don't know about yet, especially future events.

I don't often get to leave a place peacefully and easily, or in my own good time. I am usually forced to make a move and I am pushed out of my comfort zone, so that I must react by moving on. For this reason, I forgive those who get angry with me, or who have treated me in a way that causes me to want to leave, because they are simply the catalyst to make me do something about my situation.

I can remember every time that I have ever been moved on, from one place of residence to another. It usually gets uncomfortable, just before I am about to leave. I have stopped questioning it now and just go with the flow. I may even get proactive and start planning my next move, before I am due to move on, so that I have at least thought about it and I am not left in a state of shock dealing with any sudden moves.

This happens to me in both my working life and where I reside. Things can even get unbearable in the neighbourhood where I live, when it is time to move on. That's when I get that familiar feeling; it is time to get ready to move on. I trust that the Creator has plans for me, which I just don't know about yet. He always looks after me, no matter what and I always have trust that there is a greater plan ahead. I have learned to believe with total faith, that *everything* happens for a reason and everything will be okay!

I remember this one night in early April 2016, while I was living in Melbourne; we were discussing and planning our getaway, to move back to Queensland at the end of that year. We thought we had plenty of time to get organised and then God came and visited me and said, "The end is near for you in Melbourne and you shall be squeezed and squashed and poked and prodded until you leave. As a horseman says, you shall be lame."

Well God was right. The very next day at work, the fun and games started and people I normally worked well with, started acting out and misbehaving all over the place. I already knew this was coming and luckily I was mentally prepared. For the first time in a long time, I could actually sit back and watch it all roll out and not be affected, by what was to come. My relationships at work changed very quickly and I started speeding up the packing and the planning process.

As it turned out, I had a very good friend who was living in Brisbane at the time and she happened to call me at the end of that eventful week and said to me, "Hey come up for a visit, you have plenty of leave, check out my place. Come and see if you guys want to move up here sooner. You can stay with me until you get yourself sorted!"

That was the exact inspiration I needed, to get my mission underway. *Hmmm,* I thought to myself, *the timing is perfect, work is falling in a big heap after years of loyal service and it's time to move on!*

Now I'm excited when I get the nudge. I still get butterflies in my stomach, because it makes me feel a little bit nervous. Faith calms your worries, when you know that something better is coming along for you. I don't just think fluffy little thoughts and dream away. This is an actual state of mind I must live in, to survive these shifts of energy that occur. The more in tune you become with events around you and divine signs, the quicker and easier it is to deal with these transitions and have fun doing it.

As a species, humans have become lazy and complacent and as God said before, *lame*, when we tolerate crappy places, crappy jobs, crappy people and crappy situations. Have you ever thought these so called crappy experiences are there and divinely created, to get you to move on? I am not talking about running away, or causing trouble and using the decision to move on to avoid the aftermath. I am talking about really understanding why certain things have happened to you, throughout your life.

Then there are people who are sent to you for a reason and we don't always know what the reason is, at the time. There are people sent to cross paths with you, for both good and bad reasons. These people unknowingly stumble into your life and sometimes even wonder why they are there themselves.

Each one of us has something to teach one another and just because we have been assigned someone to teach, it doesn't mean they can stay forever. It also doesn't mean you have to accommodate them forever either. God wants us to love one another, but he also wants each of us to be responsible for ourselves and learn how to stand on our own two feet. He doesn't want us to give to those who are lazy, or feel like they are owed something and who walk around with a chip on their shoulder. God wants us to help the needy and the underprivileged.

During my last days in Melbourne, before moving, I was sent a lost soul. Someone who had become lost on their journey and they had become so financially indebted, which caused them to lose faith along their journey. The funny thing is, the whole time I was being coached by God. Step by step, he showed me the best way to teach this person the righteous way, now that I had invited them into my house. For two months this lady lived with me rent free. Her food was all paid for and I gave her good financial advice. I let her boyfriend stay for the weekend, helped her to rework her tired resume, loaned her my vehicle, played music with her and offered endless suggestions to help her get back on her feet.

Well, the situation blew up in my face, but once again I was prepared for it, because I was told exactly what to say and how to bring out the true intention of the house guest. I had been chosen to teach them a lesson in independence. This is not the first time I have been assigned people to teach them lessons of independence.

Whenever you teach someone who is reluctant to be taught, someone who already thinks they know everything, they can become quite nasty and really try to hurt you. Luckily I have had lots of training with manipulators, so I knew what I was getting myself into. I figured that after a couple of months of living under my roof rent free, while receiving the unemployment benefit, was enough grace time to give them, before asking them to *contribute* in some way. She was contributing during the first couple of weeks, by helping with cooking and doing some housework. That slowly trickled away to nothing and was replaced by unusual behaviour and hiding in the bedroom. There were many job interviews that didn't amount to anything and she became reluctant to face me. She was hiding from the world and didn't want to face her responsibilities. She thought it was easier to just get a free ride and jump on my train. I too have responsibilities and one of them wasn't supporting a fully capable adult, whom I didn't actually know that well.

God said to me when the time came, "Times up and you must confront her and ask her what she has been doing with her days, while you have been at work. Ask her to contribute towards the household financially and give her a time limit to come up with a plan; otherwise this situation is going to continue to go on, until you put a stop to it."

I felt really mean and uncomfortable confronting her, but I also knew that I had to learn my own lesson, about not allowing myself to be taken advantage of, once again. On this particular night, she had been hiding in her bedroom all night and waited for us to go to bed. She came out of her room, thinking that everyone else had already gone to bed. She was on her way downstairs to make herself a feast of food and was trying to avoid us in the process. I was waiting in my office with the light out, working on my computer and sprung her sneaking past my office in the dark.

I asked her how she was feeling and I also asked her if she needed any help with anything. She said that she was okay and that she didn't need any help. The conversation was very limited and I knew that I had to sit her down and have that *awkward* chat. My partner came and sat next to me to support me, but he didn't say anything and let me do all the talking.

I started with the following statement, "Look it's been a couple of months and we have been really good to you and let you stay here and look for a job for free. It's now time that I help you, by giving you a deadline, to start contributing towards the household. A small contribution of $50 a week to help pay for some of the bills and maybe that will motivate you to find work."

I further explained, "Sometimes we all do jobs that we don't always love, but it's our way of contributing towards the household we live in." I also suggested, "I think you should maybe take something, *anything* to get you on your feet, until something you really like comes along."

After a good 30 second pause, I waited for a reaction... Silence first, then the tears rolled down. After a period of time, the responding statement came from her, "I knew I couldn't count on you for anything, I should never have trusted you and that you would just let me down!"

I explained calmly that we had been helping her out the best we could and it was time for her to contribute towards the living costs. God felt that if I didn't place some type of *value* on what she was getting, she would just keep taking. God affirmed that $50 wasn't much to ask for and she was getting the money for free anyway. She needed to learn to pay her way through life and not expect that someone else would pick up the bill all the time.

At no point was she aware, that I was receiving spiritual guidance from God, helping me to deal with the situation in the most righteous way. Then the anger reaction came. It was the spoilt behaviour pattern repeating itself, to show me that this person had been using this behaviour for a long time, to manipulate others into helping her. In fact she had been reinforcing this behaviour pattern and acting out for so long, that her version of *normal* had finally been confronted.

The whole situation rolled out, exactly as God said it would. He wanted to show me that you can't help people, by doing things for them. You need to teach them to be responsible for themselves and teach them to stand on their own two feet. Show them the way, but don't do it for them.

God said, "When someone hands over their responsibility willingly to others, they also have the opportunity to hand over the *blame,* if things go wrong. Always looking for a scapegoat, they use the victim act to get you to feel sorry for them and the real demon rears its ugly head, when you catch them out. Sometimes these hard luck stories are not even true, or they are exaggerated to make their situation sound much worse than it really is, so you dig deep and donate your time, energy and money to these lost causes. Then they move on. They move on to the next person, who will fall for their hardship stories. They will search for someone else they can manipulate, until they have to move on again. It's a cycle, a repeated behavioural pattern."

What did I learn from this experience? I learned to get in touch with my own strength and that I have my own mana, my own spirit, my own essence to call upon when I need it. I also learned that I have my own personal goals and I have more than enough tasks to keep myself busy. We all have so much to say, but we must work quickly and stop dilly dallying. We all need to focus on our *own* tasks and complete our *own* missions too. It is easy to get caught up in focusing on someone else's mission and this can *distract* you from your own goals.

God added, "Believe in yourself and realise that others cannot always help, but they can believe in you too. Pave the way for change and others will follow. Not philosophical, but *real* change."

Organising yourself

Getting organised is something that unmotivated people find really challenging. Disorganisation and chaos are there to remind you that something isn't quite right and that you need to organise yourself.

God said, "If you see something that is wrong, then go back over everything that is in turmoil. There must be *something* in this place that is orderly and working? Find that one thing that works like it is meant to and make everything else like that. You must focus on those pleasures, to make everything else like that. It may sound a little bit OCD (obsessive compulsive disorder), but it takes time to be messy and it takes time to be neat. When you throw your underwear and clothing all over the place, it takes time to look for it. That time is precious and if you don't spend the time *now* to organise yourself, then you will spend your time looking for things, when you can't find them. Eventually it is easier to sort yourself out now, rather than later. Don't put off something you can do now."

God continued, "There's a now list, which then turns in to a schedule. There's no such thing as *can't,* only *when.* Use the tools you have been given, to live your own life and organise yourself."

15. HEALING

Getting to the root cause of the problem, is always the way to deal with what is causing the barrier to healing in the first place.

GOD said, "Healing can happen through effort and intent, as well as spontaneously. Healing can be fast, medium, slow, or non-existent. It all depends on the person receiving the healing and where that healing is coming from. First of all, let's look at the person receiving the healing. Are they wanting to heal themselves, or not? If not, then healing cannot happen quickly. It *may* happen eventually, but it will be slow."

God continued, "Someone who does not want to be healed for any number of reasons, doesn't attract a vibration of healing and love and will hold onto their manifested ailment, for as long as they want the destructive attachment, or as long as they want to hold onto the excuse, that they are sick, or unwell. It could be done consciously, or subconsciously, but either way it has the same effect. Healing is then slow, or non-existent. The receiver is blocking the healing energy, which cannot penetrate the intent of the receiver, blocking the incoming loving energy. The destructive attachment, is what is making them ill in the first place and the destructive attachment, *is* the barrier to healing."

God added, "A person who really wants to be healed, will be healed. It is that simple. If you maintain a positive attitude, attract the positive healing energies into your life wherever they may come from, ask for healing and *believe* that you are already healed and you *will* be healed. Your mind is a powerful computer and it sends the signal out to the Universe that it wants and needs healing.

"Remain open to the many different forms of healing, that you may receive and then you are more likely to experience a spontaneous healing, rather than someone who is reluctant to receive healing energy. Getting to the root cause of the problem, is always the way to deal with what is causing the barrier to healing in the first place. Once that barrier is removed, you are open to receive healing from the Universe. God will send you exactly what you need, or show you what you need to do, to heal yourself in his many subtle ways."

When it comes to healing, it is okay to direct your energy into the Universe, because this helps you to cast a wide net for support from the Universe. Earlier I mentioned how important it is to be more specific, when directing your wishes and desires, instead of casting them out into the vast Universe. To receive healing energy, it requires a broader focus, like the beam of a wide-angled torch. Goal setting requires a more defined focus, like the beam of a laser.

Healing with God's energy

Get God to channel love and light into you. When channelling the Holy Spirit, you can look at a house and clear it. You can look at healing a person or a group of people and feel the God energy working through you. Converting the God energy *through* the body when healing is the real experience of God, in the new millennium.

The channeller on behalf of God said, "Ask yourself when you are healing someone, *what is this person's ideal body, relationship, goals?* Cure the person by bringing in the light and use God to push the cancerous cells out of the body. Learn about disease and teach people about disease. Be hygienic to stop disease. Recognise what things are good and bad for people. This is essential for healing someone. What may be good for one person may be bad for another and vice versa."

Chakras

Open your chakras and free yourself.

Chakra is a Sanskrit word. Sanskrit is an ancient Indian language. Chakra means wheel, centre, or cycle in Sanskrit. Each living being has a set of seven basic chakras that operate like energy wheels inside their subtle body. These energy centres, control the seven main endocrine functions within the body. There are more chakras beyond the seven basic chakras, but for the moment, we will just focus on the first seven.

God said, "You must be balanced in your seven chakras, which are the seven balances of the human body. If you have blockages within, or are overusing any of these chakras, this makes you out of balance. When you are out of balance, illnesses manifest themselves and other factors in our lives become unbalanced as well."

God continued, "What are we teaching people? We are supposed to be teaching people how to be happy and how to make other people happy. You are either on the love, love, love team, or else you are on the other unhappy, unhappy, unhappy team. Whatever makes the soul happy, keeps the chakra balanced. If you are a killer, then your chakra will be unbalanced and killers just want to kill everyone. They are lacking in one of their chakras. What is it they are lacking? Easy, they are lacking love! This makes them unbalanced. What do they need to be fixed? Love! Work on their **heart chakra**, which is the centre of their love."

I asked God through the channeller, to explain each of the seven chakras to me.

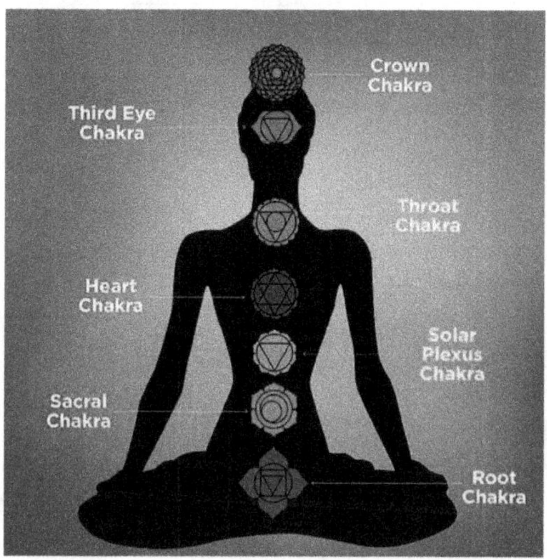

The channeller responded with the following description for each chakra, starting from the top down.

Crown chakra [colour: violet – 7th chakra]

"Let's begin with the crown chakra, which is located just above the top of your head. It is the spiritual all knowing chakra. This chakra can be affected by things like breathing in polluted air. People don't want to breathe fresh air anymore. So many people are used to the smoke haze in a city and they are confined and restricted. Chinese people believe you are in your own selfish imprisonment. To restore balance in your crown chakra, why not go outside and take a big breath and overindulge in air.

Third (3rd) eye chakra [colour: indigo – 6th chakra]

The third (3rd) eye chakra represents the hidden sense that is missing from our education system and teachings. The third eye which is the unknown sense and sometimes referred to as the *sixth sense,* or the psychic sense, needs to be tested and developed by doing exercises.

If you don't use it, then the physical sense that confirms the third (3rd) eye visions and strength, becomes unbalanced and underutilised and shrinks.

Throat chakra [colour: blue – 5th chakra]

Another way to look at this chakra is like the breath chakra. If this chakra is out of balance, it will also be out of balance within the sexual hormones. A female's voice will become lower, or a male's voice will become higher. What does this mean for a female who wants to procreate? The imbalance is quite known to you and you can see it from a distance. A female needs to mate with a balanced male. Two males make one big mess and two females make one big mess and both scenarios are out of balance.

Heart chakra [colour: green – 4th chakra]

The heart chakra is located inside the chest cavity, where the heart is located and it is our love centre. Restricting one's flow of the energy and wanting to take one's life are some of the issues that arise, when this chakra is out of balance. Learn to go with the flow of the universal energy, to correct this chakra when it is out of balance.

Solar plexus chakra [colour: yellow – 3rd chakra]

This chakra has a lot to do with the intestinal system, our gizzards and the inner self workings in our body. If it is out of balance, then it will affect our digestion, our appetite and our internal power storehouse of energy. Being calm and centred and feeling like you are in control of your diet, energy output and your emotions, will keep this chakra centre fully balanced.

Sacral chakra [colour: orange – 2nd chakra]

Going down to the reproduction sacral chakra, man was given a male sexual organ to match a female sexual organ, for the creation of a baby, no more and no less. A blockage to this chakra might be being gay, which is not being in balance with the correct harmony and is deemed as a chakra weakness. True acceptance and love for the gender, or sex that we were born in this life, is all we need to be in harmony with our body and to rebalance this chakra, if it is out of balance.

Root chakra [colour: red – 1st chakra]

This chakra is the one main chakra that gives us the ability to live on this Earth plane. It is like an anchor that keeps us grounded. If this chakra is out of balance, we feel disconnected, angry, uprooted and easily distracted. To get grounded, earth yourself out by sticking your fingers, or hands in the earth, or the ground, by standing with your feet on the ground, or on the grass barefoot. You can also go for a swim in a natural body of water, to immerse your whole body in mineral water."

God said, "There are hundreds of levels on the other side. One level is called anger and one level is called love and all of them are balanced in harmony. You need to practise *balancing* your chakras. On the other side, no one can be too sexual, too righteous, too anything, out of balance, or falsified. If a soul comes up to you and it is demonic, it has only learned one thing."

God continued, "If someone is only good at one thing, they are dumb, because they don't know the rest. Dumb is not meant in an offensive way, but dumb as in, not smart at multiple things. Being clever at only *one* thing is still technically not smart, or dumb. They portray themselves to be amazing at only one thing. When someone is in harmony, they are open to learn and want to know it all. They can deal with a dumb person, or someone who is not balanced. To balance themselves they need to focus on some of the other realms, instead of focusing on one. When you have forgotten to work on your chakras, you don't grow them and they become *dumb*."

God finished, "If you have too much of one chakra, then it overflows into another chakra and throws it out of balance."

Calibration

Calibration is a new term that I hadn't heard before, at least not in relation to healing. This lesson from God was a real eye opener for me and I will give you as much information about it as I can.

Both Jesus and Edgar Cayce used to *calibrate* a crowd of healthy people, against a person who is not well and ask the question, "Why can't this person be like all of the healthy people?"

This was a tool they both used, to clarify what was wrong with the person who needed their help.

Then they would ask God, "Lord, show me what is missing from this body to make it right?"

They may receive a response to their question like; rib, zinc, copper, biotin, red blood cells etc. If they needed additional clarification, they would ask a more specific question like; "Lord, show me what is this body missing to make it your creation?" This way God could scan the body and determine what was missing in terms of minerals, or body parts, to return the body to its original creation.

God said, "When healing the body, look at the body as a mass. Almost as if the soul was dead and all you were left with, is just a lump of mass. This way you don't get distracted from the purpose of the soul and you can just focus on the physical ailment."

God continued, "Calibrate the person at the beginning of their session, by asking some simple questions about what they like and dislike. You can ask them, 'What is a nice colour, when you think of a colour? What is a colour that really aggravates, or annoys you? What is your favourite colour?' You can push on by asking more questions, to calibrate them further. For example, 'What type of music do you like? What do you like about that type of music?' And so on."

God added, "This is calibrating what they like, in comparison to what they do not like. These things need to be taken in context and can be used while treating the person. When the person comes in, you need to get them to complete a new file, answering a lot of simple questions that will assist you greatly during their treatment session. These questions should be in relation to the standard Neuro Linguistic Programming (NLP) representational systems."

- **V** – Visual (see)
- **A** – Auditory (hear)
- **K** – Kinaesthetic (touch)
- **O**– Olfactory (smell)
- **G** – Gustatory (taste)
- **AD** – Audio digital (internal talk) *does it make sense, it is logical etc?*
- **L** – Love (the love of something, like a feeling) internal and external love, because there are two types of love.

God said, "In fact there is two of everything for every sense and there are additional hidden senses. Things that people love are like another sense. How much of everything does someone have? If the person is unbalanced, they won't have two of each sense, or they might have a lack in one of the senses. If this is the case, then check why the senses are turned off.

"This is a part of reading someone, calibrating the person to check if they are over, or under using their senses. If you notice that after calibrating someone, they are holding onto pain in their foot, or toe, you could say to them, 'Your toe is sore and I can feel your pain, the pain is missing the love and the love is missing the pain.'

"You can't have love without pain. It is a perfect balance and it is like *acknowledging* the pain. You can research children that have been born using medical drugs, in comparison to natural child birth, without the use of any pain killers. Childbirth is like the pain of death, and when it is bringing a new soul into the world, it helps to calibrate the child to both pain and love. If a child is born under the influence of pain numbing medication, then the child is not calibrated to pain at birth and this can cause issues later on, when the child first experiences pain."

Body scanning

God instructed me how to do body scanning.

He said, "Body scanning is a technique you can use to heal a person, using your hands and your energy field, by tapping into the divine God energy force. Hold one hand against the third eye location on your forehead and use the other hand to scan the body of the person you are scanning. Use the third eye on the hand to pick up any illness, or problem areas and be thorough when asking your third eye to show you exactly what is wrong. Also tune into your third eye while body scanning and ask exactly what needs to be done to heal the affected area. Ask what psychic surgery needs to be performed, or which areas need specific attention."

God continued, "When performing psychic surgery, hold your hands above the body and then look inside the body psychically and grab onto the bone psychically. Then calibrate the position of the body in relation to where you are holding the bone. For example, where the skin is positioned, the veins, flesh, the head, stomach and feet are positioned etc. Once you know what you are treating, you can surgically repair the illness, or ailment, by removing the offending thing and throwing it away and as it is thrown away, it is moving away infinitely. You can also disintegrate the ailment or injury completely, never to return to this person or any person for all of eternity."

God explained, "He wants you to not just *visualise*, but actually manifest the operation for real, by focusing on the affected area. This will require you to perform whatever surgery is required, using the power of manifestation. This is true faith healing and not just simply Reiki. It is more advanced than Reiki and more skill and faith is required.

"If you are repairing bones, grab hold of the broken bones using the method above and seal the two breaks with divine love and total faith. Hold them set for as long as you think they require, to rejoin the bones.

"If you are dealing with cancer, then ask the person how long they have had the particular cancer and state to them, 'Wow that's a long time to have that cancer, it's now time to let go of the cancer, as it must be completed and healed by now?' This way you are actually talking to both the person and the other thing inside, that is hanging onto them."

God added, "Make the person believe that they have had the ailment for far too long and that is time for it to go, because time is running out and still nothing has happened, so that means it's not worth hanging on to. This technique is using *manipulation,* to distract the unwanted visitor/s into leaving the body. You can view the unwanted visitors as demons, entities, bad spirits, or just things that need to leave the body. Whatever works best in the healer's mind, to rid the person of their unwanted illness and unwelcome guest/s at the same time."

Colour therapy

God said, "When someone is showing a colour in their aura, or skin, then the colour indicates a condition. To treat the condition you need to give them something of the same colour.

For example:

- **Blue** = lack of oxygen > treatment = oxygen is blue > anti-oxidants, blueberries, blue grapes etc.
- **Red** = spots > treatment = heat therapy, fire place, sauna, stick with red hot embers > hold the stick near the red spots, showing the devilish spots that there is more heat in the stick, than in the red spots > eat strawberries for red blood cells, tomatoes, red peppers etc.
- **Yellow** = jaundice and yellow fever > treatment = sunlight needs to be diluted > eat lemons, squash, bananas etc.
- **Orange** = orange blotchy skin problems, or burns > treatment = eat oranges, pumpkin, beta carotene, carrots etc.
- **Purple** = stagnant blood and bad circulation > treatment = clean clogged arteries with beetroot, eggplant, purple grapes etc
- **White** = increased white blood cell count > treatment = need more starch > eat potatoes, pasta, rice etc.

God continued, "There are many more colours. This is just a few, to show you how the principle works. Every disease must have a colour associated with it and once you establish what the colour is, you can cure it, by providing food and therapy, using this colour.

"Colours of the rainbow should be used to heal people. Use a laser beam and turn on the particular colour you need and direct it toward the affected area."

God added, "Eat it, feel it, be enlightened by it, believe you are in the colour and use the colour therapy to heal yourself. You can analyse people with aromatherapy and colour therapy. You can also test the overall temperature of the body. For example, blue = cold, red = hot.

"Blue is the colour of oxygen and humans use oxygen to breathe, so visualise blue when you want to breathe in pure oxygen. Breathing in a beautiful blue colour and breathing out the bad grey or black energy. The pure air is making you feel healthy, cleaning the body of all its impurities and it feels great. Breathing in the beautiful rainforest air and watching a bird fly past, is a true feeling of being alive and not dead.

"Put yourself in a different space and take yourself out of your current state. People in the city don't spend much time with nature and they don't see life around them, as much as people who live in harmony with nature. Taste the purest coffee beans, drink the most natural purified water and breathe in the best fresh air. Listen to the best local musical talent in town, on lovely comfortable seating and enjoy plenty of attractive people."

God said, "During the day when you have the opportunity to daydream, say subliminal words to yourself like; *smooth taste.* Ask yourself the question, *how do you like your coffee? Do you like it creamy and sweet, or bitter and strong?* This way you are engaging your senses, even if you are at work, school, or home and you are feeling a bit bored, or distracted. Really care about what you think and give yourself the mental opportunity to *taste,* or *smell* the beans, before you buy them. Visualise yourself taste testing the coffee, smell the coffee beans getting roasted and visualise everything in your mind in full colour. Use the richness of colour, to make your visualisation come to life and make it feel more realistic."

Getting grounded

We use the term *grounded* all the time, without really giving much thought to what it really means. We refer to the ground that we walk on, as being on the ground level. Underground represents *inside,* or *under* the Earth and above ground, means *above* the ground and not on the ground. What about getting *grounded?* Why would we even need to get grounded?

In electrical terms, they use the word earthing, or grounding, when they are referring to grounding the electrical current into the earth, or grounding the *path* of electricity into the ground, for electricity to be safe. A ground or earth wire is connected to powered devices, so that people don't get an electric shock, or electrocuted when they touch the power cable. The Earth has a natural energy field, which has its own electrical charge and the Earth's natural charge is good for us. It helps to ground and balance the unnatural electrical charges that can build up in our body.

Nikola Tesla found a way to tap into the Earth's energy field to provide free energy for everyone, but the power companies didn't like it, because they couldn't control, monitor and charge people for power. They took it, patented it and buried it in a mountain of legal paperwork, never to be found again. Nikola Tesla also used to meditate a lot and he used to talk to the other side, as well as God. This is where he got so many of his wildly creative ideas from.

God wants us to understand how everything works. Everyone is made up of three different subatomic particles called protons, neutrons and electrons. In general, atoms on their own have no electrical charge, or they have a *neutral* charge, because they have the same number of positively charged protons, as negatively charged electrons.

When the numbers of electrons in an atom change, the atom can carry an electrical charge, by either gaining additional electrons from other atoms, or by losing its electrons to nearby atoms. If an atom is electrically charged it is referred to as an *ion.*

If a group of atoms *lose* protons, or gain electrons, this group of atoms has a net negative charge called an *anion.* If a group of atoms gain protons, or lose electrons, this group of atoms has a net positive charge called a *cation.* In ions, the numbers of electrons vary and in isotopes the numbers of neutrons vary.

If the number of neutrons within an atom change, an *isotope* is formed. Isotopes within an atom have different atomic masses and exhibit different properties and can be viewed as variations, but the chemical composition of an atom remains the same.

Every now and again, these subatomic particles become unbalanced within the human body and within the human brain. Electromagnetic frequencies can cause an excessive amount of positively charged protons to float around inside the nucleus, which can then create an imbalance of negatively charged electrons, floating around the atom. The imbalance of the odd number of electrons creates free radicals.

To go one step further, free radicals are groups of atoms that have an odd number of electrons and can be formed when oxygen interacts with certain molecules, causing DNA, cellular and protein damage.

God explained, "Free radicals just want to form a bond and that is their intention. They will keep going until a perfect circle is formed. The best counteractive measure for free radicals, is *anti-oxidants* which slow down the oxidizing, or acidification process, or in other words, stop the group of atoms from forming a complete circle and destroying the cell completely."

God continued, "Then there are the effects of both static electricity and free radicals in your body and in the atmosphere, which has a flow on effect of free radical exposure to your food, water and any other substances that you take into your body. Further down the chain, it can cause free radical damage, which can be increased when the particles in the air you breathe, are affected and absorbed into the body. This provides yet another method, for free radicals to enter your body. Free radicals take electrons from molecules and are harmful to humans, because they can damage your cells. Too many free radicals can cause disease and speed up the onset of an illness, by increasing the static electricity build up and oxidation process in your body. This makes the body become like a magnet and can attract excessive amounts of positively charged protons. Over time, this can cause you to become charged up, or *overcharged* with static electricity.

"If you don't discharge this excess electrical build up, it can cause issues with the sensitive electrical currents in your brain, by short circuiting your complex brain wiring. This in turn affects your mental health. Humans can also have health impacts and complications, as a direct result of not being grounded."

When a human body is overexposed to too many positively charged ions, it creates a harmful imbalance in our electrical chemistry and circuitry. We can become overexposed to positive ions in environments like; offices, factories, hospitals, shopping malls, indoor areas and other areas where recycled air, or poorly circulated air exists.

To rebalance the human body, we need to expose ourselves to more negatively charged electrons, to help reduce the electrostatic build up throughout our body. We can do this by exposing ourselves to more negative ions. Negative ions are in abundance, wherever air molecules are constantly breaking apart due to sunlight, radiation, moving air, or rushing water.

Let's take a look at some of the various methods, of getting a healthy dose of negative ions.

1. Start using a **negative ion generator** in your home, bedroom, or office to increase the amount of negatively charged ions in your immediate atmosphere.
2. **Getting out and about in nature**, where there is an abundance of negative ions.
3. **Breathe in mountain air**, especially near waterfalls.
4. **Go for a walk and breathe in the ocean air**, near areas where beaches pound the shores.
5. **Spend time in the park**.
6. **Go for a bush walk** and breathe in the bush air.
7. **Getting exposure to dirt**, walking on the bare earth, putting on mud masks, or bathing in mud.
8. Spend time outside when it is windy and **where there is constant airflow**.
9. Use **Himalayan salt lamps**, which clean the air.
10. Use **Orgonite** to absorb excess positive ions.
11. Have an **indoor water feature**.
12. **Plants** are great absorbers of positive ions and in turn release negative ions.
13. **Use infrared heat**, rather than radiant heat to warm your body.
14. **Light a fire** and spend time near the fire light and heat.

The channeller speaking on behalf of God said, "People with brain tumours have isotopes in their brain, so they need to remove the isotopes. Sometimes these people are sensitive to the damage in the ozone layer, so therefore the layer of protection that used to exist for them has now been destroyed by humans. This is what protected them in the first place."

The channeller added, "God created the ozone layer to protect humans from the electromagnetic radiation, emitted from the Sun and the other planets. When we use devices that *increase* the electromagnetic radiation *inside* the atmosphere, it increases the free radicals in our body and also it increases the static electricity *inside* the ozone layer. We are literally showering ourselves with dangerous radiation and exposing ourselves to lethal radioactive isotopes."

Take for example, dangerous, or hazardous radioactive isotopes like; strontium-90 and cesium-137, which both have a half-life of around 30 years each. Iodine-131 only has a half-life of 8 days and technetium-99m has a half-life of about 6 hours. All of these isotopes are used in nuclear medicine and other smaller applications.

Then you have the big guns, technetium-99, which has a half-life of 211,000 years. Plutonium-239 has a half-life of 24,000 years and is the most dangerous material in the world. Supposedly, the only isotopes used as nuclear fuels at this stage in our evolution are; uranium-235 & 238 and plutonium-239. Thorium is in the pipeline for future use, because it is more abundant than uranium, but the crazy thing is that it has a half-life of a whopping 14.5 billion years, but is also considered the most stable. Let's put this into perspective, so I can explain what a half-life is.

If plutonium has a half-life of 24,000 years, this means that after 24,000 years, *half* of the radioactivity contained in the plutonium, will have decayed. I am not joking, this is serious stuff and that is a seriously long time! Why are humans messing around with this stuff? They have no idea what they have done, when they opened the nuclear equivalent of Pandora's Box.

There are naturally occurring radioactive elements such as; uranium-233 to uranium-238, which is supposed to be weakly radioactive, because all its isotopes are unstable. These types of uranium have a half-life between 69 years and 4.5 billion years. When they use isotopes for nuclear fission, fuel and power applications, there is *always* nuclear waste and it creates a secondary and ongoing radioactive waste problem.

There are many other types of naturally occurring radioactive isotopes like; potassium-40, which is used in the production of argon gas, amongst many others used in a variety of applications. The way they dispose of this radioactive waste, is to bury it back in the ground, after a period of cooling down.

The by-products that are left over, after the use of some of these products, create toxic and radioactive waste. For example, once the uranium fuel is used up, after around 18 months, the spent rods are moved into deep pools of circulating water, to cool down for about 10 years. They still remain dangerously radioactive for a further 10,000 years after that. The irony is, if they just left these elements in the ground where they belong and in their natural form in the first place, they wouldn't have to solve this problem.

God said, "In minute amounts these elements are okay, but when it is mined, concentrated, used in an unstable format and then disposed of, it creates massive problems. Problems so huge, that you can't just bury it and hope it goes away. The problem hangs around for thousands of years, after we have left the planet. Who is going to be responsible for looking after that mess and cleaning it up? The nuclear industry alone generates thousands of tonnes of radioactive waste every year. It must STOP! Humans are clever enough to find alternatives, which are less harmful and use less destructive methods of producing power. They should find ways that contain the waste much more efficiently."

God continued, "If there is not enough iron in the blood, then stick your finger in the dirt to get some more iron. If there are high doses of copper, iron, silver, or magnesium in the blood, then high doses kill all of the active isotopes, *if* you earth yourself out. To earth yourself out, you can also jump in the ocean. If you took a charged metal and put it in your body and then stuck your finger in the ground, or jumped in the ocean, that action would earth you out. It sucks all the positive energy out of your body and your body has to produce more, to earth yourself out."

God added, "That is why you have *skin*, because skin is the isolation. Scientists will want the formula, but God is talking to me in layman's terms, so he is missing out all of the super technical information, because I wouldn't understand. If God had a hammer and hit a squark, or a proton, there would be an infinite amount of particles inside of there as well."

God said, "The soles of your feet and the palms of your hands are the most conducive areas on the whole body. Earthing yourself regularly can have all kinds of positive health benefits and is necessary, if you want to live a long life. Before this new era of technology was introduced, people used to spend a lot more time outdoors, in the natural sunlight and surrounded by nature. These days, we spend most of our day and night, cooped up inside, with electromagnetic frequencies surrounding us, from the alternating current of electricity within the buildings, computers, lights, electronic devices, air-conditioning, heating, overhead power lines and underground services."

God suggested using *direct* current, instead of alternating current, for power in buildings used by people, to lessen the exposure to harmful electromagnetic frequencies.

Signs of excess electrostatic energy build up in our bodies, caused by excess protons and excessive positive ions, can be displayed in many ways.

- When you go to close your car door, you get a mild electric shock, or you get a small zap from the car metal, when you discharge yourself. Touch the glass of the car door, when you close the door, to avoid this and lock your car remotely.

- Getting electric shocks from touching conductive materials like metal door frames, electronic devices and other eletrostatically charged people, or objects.
- Wearing synthetic clothing and then touching someone else, who is also wearing synthetic clothing. You both get zapped.
- Shorting out electrical equipment when you touch it.
- Affecting the signal on the radio, when you move closer to it.
- Blowing lights when you go to turn them on, or off at the switch.
- Getting sick from free radical damage, or exposure.
- Certain diseases can thrive off excess energy build up.
- Feeling drained from over exposure to electromagnetic radiation.
- Having migraines, or headaches for no explained reason.
- Feeling fatigued and drained.
- Hearing super high pitched frequencies and you cannot get them out of your head.
- Brain tumours, or fast spreading cancers.

To discharge excess electrostatic and electromagnetic energy and also to ground yourself, there are a number of ways you can do this. These are simple and effective methods that can be practised daily, or even multiple times during the day, if necessary.

1. Walking barefoot on the earth, or on the grass.
2. Walking barefoot on the beach and walking along the water's edge.
3. Stick your fingers, hands, or feet in the earth.
4. Laying on the earth, or ground with full skin contact.
5. Go for a swim in the ocean, or a salt water pool.
6. Have a bath with Epsom salts.
7. Create a grounding rod in the earth and hold onto it for a period of time.
8. Meditate with your feet on the ground, or sit on the ground and hum low to yourself, to lower your vibration.
9. Touch metal objects occasionally, to earth yourself.
10. Use rubber mats, or antistatic mats on your workbench, or desk.
11. Use an earthing mat regularly.
12. If you are working with computers and computer components, you need to discharge yourself *before* touching any of the sensitive components, computer chips, or computer cards inside the computer.
13. Wear an antistatic wrist band.

14. Wear natural fibre clothing and shoes.
15. Avoid wearing synthetic clothing, or shoes.
16. If you have spent long periods of time in an aeroplane, or motor vehicle, it is vitally important for you to earth yourself often, because you are rarely touching the earth, when you are travelling above the ground.
17. Holding crystals, rocks, or earthy objects.
18. Visualise being earthed, if you cannot actually get access to one of these techniques.
19. To help you get grounded, treat yourself to a natural hands on healing therapy session like; Reiki, massage, Bowen, physiotherapy, chiropractic care, acupuncture, acupressure, chakra healing, energy healing, EFT, forensic healing, kinesiology, or crystal healing etc.
20. Go somewhere in nature, where you can avoid technology for a period of time.
21. Do some high energy exercise, which helps you to create piezo electric energy in your bones, which is electricity resulting from pressure. Real body electricity and not fake electromagnetic frequencies.
22. Choose specific sports, or exercises that focus on energy work where you can discharge any excess energy like; martial arts, Yoga, Pilates, Qigong, Tai chi, walking, running and dancing.
23. Use special breathing techniques.

******Warning******

Remember not to use any of these methods during a thunderstorm with lightning, otherwise *you* will become the earth, or ground and the shortest path for the lightning bolt to ground itself.

Let's take a look at what happens when we are not grounded spiritually as well. We can react by feeling disconnected, flighty, scattered, erratic, displaying excess nervous energy and behaving airy fairy. We find it difficult to concentrate on anything, because of all the unseen static noise. You may not be able to see, or hear it, but your body can certainly feel it and is affected by this noise.

When I talk about getting spiritually grounded, I mean that you are more connected to the Earth plane or physical plane and that you need to discharge any excess energy and come back down to earth.

To be able to enjoy your existence here on this plane, you need to feel grounded, connected and earthed. We also need to get psychically grounded, so we don't float off to the astral planes, mid conversation with someone. Otherwise we can float in and out of consciousness, when trying to participate in earthly activities.

A psychic friend once told me that she finds it increasingly difficult with the more spiritual work she does, for her to stay grounded and on the Earth plane. She plugs into what she calls *upstairs*. This is her term for connecting directly to the God source, the source energy of the Creator. When she communicates directly with the other side, she keeps her feet firmly on the ground and she uses her body as the conduit between the physical, astral and higher spiritual realms, to *channel energy* to heal people. She already knows and has been psychically told, that she is a reincarnation of an ancient Atlantean soul, from one of the earlier civilizations in Atlantis. She hasn't reincarnated on this Earth plane for a very long time. This was due to the energy on this plane of existence, not being ready to enter, until this time around. Atlanteans have been reluctant to reincarnate, until recently.

These Atlanteans, Lemurians and star children, are souls from other worlds and are really starting to come into their power here on Earth, at this time. You are likely to find them in the alternative, healing and lightworker fields of work. This particular lady still looks very Atlantean, with a full head of blonde hair and fair skin. She is super slim, tall, ageless and fit. Her conversation could seem really out there, if you didn't understand where she was coming from with her point of view.

Her techniques are anything but conventional and wouldn't be considered *normal*. She doesn't believe in reading any man written books. This is simply because she was told psychically, that everything she needs to learn is either shown to her psychically or she is guided to use special techniques that cannot be found in any regular books. To be in this state constantly can be physically and psychically draining for a healer, or lightworker, especially if they don't learn to ground themselves regularly.

Psychics, channellers, healers and lightworkers and those involved in this type of work, would greatly benefit from having a partner who is very earthy and grounded, or having friends around them who are earthy and grounded. This helps them to cope with their otherworldly occupation and their unusual abilities. Grounded relationships help them to come back down to the Earth plane, in between sessions.

I also have a wonderfully magical and mystical friend, who is actually the most grounded psychic person I know. She has a long lineage of tribal ancestors, who are with her on her journey. Her special ability relies heavily on her being able to ground herself, during her channelling sessions. Getting grounded helps her to be able to tap into the Source energy and not be drained like those who are not as earthed. To be around her feels warm, earthy and maternal.

She doesn't fully utilise her gifts and abilities as much as she could and since having children, she hasn't been able to connect to the Source energy as strongly as she could prior to starting a family. My friend told me about an amazing experience she had. She told me how she astral travelled, during a lovemaking session with her man. At the exact moment of conception, she astral travelled high above the Earth, into outer space and retrieved her daughter from the soul pool. She grabbed her hand and pulled her back down into her body. Soon after this event, she confirmed she was in fact pregnant and knew it from that moment onwards. She hadn't told anybody about it, because it sounded so far out, but my willingness to listen to her experience, allowed her to be open enough to share this with me.

Her energy feels like the maternal Mother Earth incarnated, when you are with her. She knows the importance of being grounded psychically and also knows the benefit, of attracting a partner who is the opposite of what she is energetically, for optimum balance.

Many psychics have difficulties finding a balanced and complimentary partner, who understands and allows them to utilise their abilities to their full potential.

This particular friend is actually a registered nurse and has been for many years. She naturally gravitates towards this line of work, so she can be in a field where she can help people who need it. If you have ever been in a hospital, or care facility for any period of time, the best nurses are the ones who are patient, methodical and thorough. They are usually the most *grounded* nurses and they are also the same nurses, who I would trust with my life.

I am not a fan of flighty, rushed and incompetent medical staff that run around all over the place in a mad rush to get everything done. They tend to make mistakes. They don't really care about the patient's welfare and contribute to the growing number of misdiagnosis, in medical facilities all around the world. They too need to get more grounded and they are influenced by the many things that take them away from the state of being grounded.

When I first met this friend many years ago, the grounding effect I experienced when we first met was electrifying for her and intensely grounding for me. I could feel my energy getting pulled into the Earth's energy field and into her energy field instantly and I couldn't stop it. It was like a rare earth magnet, pulling my crazy static electrons into line.

We got on fabulously and became best friends very quickly. We both recognised the energetic pull and that is how we knew we were also connected on a soul family level. We were the ideal energetic balance to one another's energy fields. It is uncanny that we were born only days apart. At the time, I felt like I had met my soul sister from the stars. We now live in different countries and hadn't seen each other for a long time, until we recently reconnected, when she came to Australia for a holiday with me. We have both been busy living our lives. We had to make time to get together, or else more time would pass and we may lose touch altogether.

I tend to be more of a highly charged person, who needs a grounder, or earthed person to keep me earthed. I need regular grounding and earthing, or else I give people electric shocks when I touch them and give myself electric shocks when I touch conductive things, because my extra charge is looking to discharge itself.

If I don't get grounded, I end up blowing light bulbs and shorting out appliances when I turn them on, just by touching them, or touching the power switch. Then I go through periods of time when I am a good grounder and I can help people who get carried away with the fairies, or float away in the clouds. I can become the one to absorb excess energy from others to help them.

Personally, when I menstruate, I am the most grounded that I can be, right throughout my cycle. I also find that I have my most earthy, astral and vivid dreams during this period of time. This is because during this time, I am connected to the Lunar and Earth cycles simultaneously. I am in *sync* with the Earth's energy and cosmic cycles, which also makes me feel grounded spiritually.

I do not use anything synthetic to control my hormones and prefer to be in sync with the natural cycles of the Universe. When I was going through the IVF process, my energy was all over the place and I really noticed the effects of the synthetic hormones and IVF medications.

Two people, who are both full on energetically and positively statically charged, both naturally and through absorbing unnatural electrons, can be exciting, spontaneous and highly eletrostatically charged. On the flip side of that, it means that sparks literally fly between the two of you and everyone knows that sparks can start fires, with their constant sparks.

Volatile energy and electric shocks from one another can become draining after a while. A highly charged person can wear people out, if they are not able to balance themselves sufficiently. They can also be good for people who are too negatively charged, by giving them an electric boost to their own energy field.

Two people, who are both negatively charged, both naturally and through earthing techniques, can sometimes become boring, predictable, morbid and gloomy. On the flip side of that, it means that you can have a constant, steady and predictable energy flow between you, with no volatility. You can literally sleep for hours together, without disturbing each other. An overly negatively charged person, can be very draining on a highly charged person's energy, which can be good when appropriate, but exhausting for a person who is already earthed.

The optimum choice is having a good balance, between being

positively and negatively charged. It is ideal to have people in your life as friends and partners who are a mix of both types. It is even better to have friends that are balanced, to ensure you don't get too drained, or exhausted. This ensures you both remain balanced in your mind, body and soul and you can both be a good grounder for each other when the other is in a crazy static mode. If you are both highly charged, be aware of each other's energy levels and support one another through positive and negative energy shifts.

When engaging in high level channelling with beings from higher angelic realms, it is almost *essential* that you have a grounding energy, or a very earthy person present, who is the ideal grounder, or *grounding force* for you. They can help to rebalance psychics and channellers, when they have finished their channelling, or reading.

Having an experienced psychic grounder is important for people who regularly engage in this type of psychic communication with the other side. It is ideal for spiritual safety, to have a person who can non-judgementally control the situation in a calm, cool and collected manner, if the situation ever gets out of hand.

Clearing

Clearing is a term used to describe a cleansing method, which is used to *clear* a person's conscience, karmic debt, energy, space, or soul. What exactly are you clearing? It could be negative energy held within for past deeds, or stagnant energy, which stops a person from moving forward in their life. It could be negative spirits, suppressed memories, or even demonic entities.

The best use of clearing is when it is applied to those who want to confess their sins, in order to have a clear conscience. They may have a strong desire to be forgiven for their sins. This is a soul who truly repents, regrets what they have done, is sorry for their misdeeds and has *learned* from their mistakes. They are less likely to have a demon hanging around them, than those who are not sorry, or who couldn't care less. They are worthy of forgiveness in the eyes of the Lord, but will still be answerable to some degree, both on a karmic level and on a soul level for their actions. Their repayment may be to experience a similar feeling, or action in this life. If they are lucky enough to have instant karma, they can repay their karma in this life, or else they may have to wait for another opportunity to correct their misdeeds, perhaps in a future life.

Karmic debts can also be voided, if your future actions are noteworthy to a point of rendering these sins forgiven, or if you have been consciously correcting bad deeds, by doing more good deeds and sincerely making an effort. This system is in place, so that people cannot simply act, or behave in a manner that contradicts the spiritual laws of God and then just say sorry and think they can get away with it.

In principle, the early churches used to offer regular confessions and some still do. It is not as common for this to be available to all members of society. A confession works by first praying to invoke the presence of God. Then we seek healing and forgiveness through repentance directly from God, sometimes with the assistance of a priest, or a holy person. We need to promise not to sin anymore and make every effort to stick to that promise.

Every single action and thought creates a reaction and you are answerable and accountable for *everything* you do, say, think, or act out. We are all spinning around on the same karmic wheel of life, until we reach a point in our existence when we do not accumulate any karmic debts, or we have completed our soul mission. Then we can hop off the tiresome cycle and stay in the higher realms. We stay in the higher realms, until we get bored and want to come and experience another life, or if we have higher work to do within the higher realms. We may choose *not* to reincarnate and stay in the spiritual world, still helping others.

The channeller said, "Clearing can be done by any holy person, or anyone who has 100% faith in God. Their role is to help by acting as an agent of God, or Jesus, accepting the honour and the burden of listening to others' sins and wrongdoings. Within the role of a clearer, or person who listens to your sins non-judgementally, is to give the person who wishes to offload their burden of sin, or guilty conscience, to someone who understands and who can assist them to communicate with God, or Jesus, to clear up their issue or problem.

"The same process is used for all methods of clearing and it should not be attempted by those who are not aware how to use these methods, or if they are not faithful, because God already knows those who are faithful. God will only accept sins from those of the highest faith, integrity and that trust in the power of God, the Supreme Being, to deliver them from sin. These are the ones, who should be concentrating on this type of work."

The channeller continued, "You don't need to have obtained a badge, have sacrificed a lifetime in the priesthood, or lived as a monk, or as a nun, to have the power of the good Lord invested in you. You could be *anyone* who has lived an ordinary life and through faith, have become an extraordinary individual, from your lessons and through your teaching about God.

"You just need a rock solid, unshakeable faith, so you can *handle* the liars, the cheats and the horrific stories that come out of people's mouths and also the demonic entities that might rear their ugly head, during the process. Clearing is not usually as scary as the movie "The Exorcist," although I am sure there are some people out there, who have experienced their fair share of scary stories."

The channeller added, "The stronger your faith, the less a demon, or negative entity can stand to be in your presence, or to be around you. Sometimes, if someone unholy is simply in your personal space and you are emitting a holy, or pure energy of love, this can be enough, to scare the demon out of someone. You literally can't even flinch and your just need to go with the flow, when you are listening to their confessions. It is not your job to tell them what to do, other than to remind them of what is the righteous thing to do in future.

"You are *not* the judge and jury. You are the neutral ears on behalf of God, who is the ultimate judge. God decides how the lesson will be learned and through Jesus, you can be given another chance to change your path and correct your direction, so you can be reset onto the righteous path. If you have been led down the corrupt path and the path of darkness, through confession and discussion with someone holy and righteous, you can remove the burden of the sin and share your deepest, darkest secrets, so they don't manifest into something uglier. This will give you better access to God and help you to understand why Jesus died for our sins in the first place."

In all honesty, there are many people who don't even know what they are doing is wrong, because they have only been shown the wrong way, or the corrupt way to do things. The only time people can correct this glitch in their programming, is to either learn the right way through researching it, observing other people's behaviour, or by becoming conscious that what they are doing is in fact incorrect. Sometimes it is simply a direct result of bad programming like; *monkey see, monkey do!*

The channeller said, "Man was not born a sinner, but through bad influence, coercion, corruption and wrong choices, mankind can be easily led astray and wander down the path of sin and darkness, without actually meaning to. I am not saying mankind is *innocently* led astray, because that would imply humans are stupid and like sheep, which generally they are not. They are smart enough to know instinctively and intuitively, what is *right* and what is *wrong*. Humans can get caught up in the sheep, or herd mentality, when they see everyone else doing something and they can be known to follow the rest of the herd without question, if they are too lazy to think for themselves."

It gets really confusing for those who have been programmed incorrectly. They can be punished for doing good things and rewarded for doing bad things, which affects the emotional triggers and wiring in their brain. If they have destructive and incompetent parents, or guardians, just like the owner of a wild dog; they can turn their children or pets into destructive troublemakers and criminals of the worst kind. This is why re-education, rehabilitation and positive reprogramming, are the most important tools in correctional institutions, juvenile detention centres and mental health facilities.

Schools are also contributing to the problem, by not correcting bad behaviour and leaving it to the parents to fix their children. Well that's not really going to work, if their parents don't care enough to teach their children anything. It is definitely not going to work, if the parents trigger the bad behaviour, or are the perfect example of bad behaviour. The parents or guardians can be an *inappropriate* role model, which is more common than you think.

The channeller said, "We all know there is no such thing as a perfect parent, but there is a distinction between a *good* parent and a *bad* parent. God gave us all the ability to know right from wrong and he gives us plenty of chances to get it right during our lifetime, even if we fail numerous times. God is all forgiving and likes to watch us develop into loving, kind and thoughtful beings. Let me remind you, what is considered a sin to you and I may be completely different to the way Jesus, or God views a sin."

I have had this scenario explained to me in many different ways and many times over. God wants us to know that a *real sin* is backed by the *intention* to harm. It all comes down to your intention and what is in your mind and heart, when you are performing an action, or a task. Was it your intention to lie, steal, cheat, hurt, maim, or kill someone, or something? Your actions may have been committed in the heat of the moment. Your emotions or mental health may have been considered unstable, or affected at the time. It may have been done out of curiosity, or you could have been testing your boundaries. You could have simply made a stupid, or bad choice, that you cannot undo and how we would all love to rewind the time clock, to start over and do it differently next time.

I am sure that if this was a possible solution, everyone would be time travelling, mainly to fix their past mistakes, or to go back in time and make different choices. There could have been any number of extenuating circumstances leading up to that event.

The channeller continued, "God is all knowing and knows your whole life path when you talk to him, or when you ask someone else to talk to him on your behalf. He knows absolutely everything. There is no hiding and he knows every dirty little secret, every good and bad deed you have ever done and everything that has led you to this moment in time right now, including every single past and future life. Ultimately God and Jesus are the only ones you need to ask for forgiveness, because they are ones who will either approve, or deny your entry into the heavenly realms, when your time comes."

The channeller added, "Jesus was a natural clearer and everywhere he went, people would flock to him, to tell him their sins, because they could sense they were in the presence of someone holy. That is what pushed their soul to want to clear itself. Jesus cast out many demons in his lifetime and this was one of his specialities, because he was so faithful. He never quivered at this role and he never felt burdened with this responsibility, because he loved mankind so much and yet they still killed him.

"The person, who has sinned, may not even realise consciously that they are telling you their sins, but their subconscious and their soul desperately wants to be cleared, so the soul will pour out its whole life story to you, with the hope of being blessed and being forgiven, on behalf of the Lord."

When you are clearing a person, energy, home, room, space, or land, you need to be in a calm, balanced and in a Godly state of mind, for the clearing to work effectively. You should always start with a prayer of protection, before proceeding with any clearing work, so that you don't collect any unwanted negative energy or spirits yourself. If you are clearing a particularly challenging energy field, or larger space, you should be asking for assistance and guidance from the higher angelic or Godly realms, *before* starting the clearing work. You can use all of the below methods together, or only one or two of these methods combined. It will be sufficient, as long as you include some form of prayer of protection each time and maintain 100% faith in God when you do it.

There are many methods that can be employed in the process of clearing. Let's take a look at some of the successful methods used.

Prayer

Prayer is the best method for clearing, because it invokes the presence of Jesus, God and his band of holy archangels. When it comes to clearing, you want the best and most holy entities you can possibly muster, to help strengthen your faith, conviction and belief.

Every time you clear, you should invoke and call in God, Jesus, or the holy archangels to help you with the clearing. Other spirits are welcome to help and observe, but leave the work of clearing to the super powers, because that is their domain.

Smoke

One method that is commonly used for clearing amongst spiritual practitioners is the white sage smudge stick over the affected area, the body, the house, or the space you want to clear. You can also use a burning stick, incense, or sage, whatever is appropriate and whatever you have access to.

Light

White lighting yourself and the energy field you are working with, is vitally important if your intention is to not only *clear* the negative energy, or spirits, but also to leave the area with holy white light, once you have finished.

You can use white lighting to clear chakras in people, animals and spirits and you can use white light shielding, to deflect negative energy fields and strong magnetic fields. You can also balance ley lines and energy grids on the property, or land, by tuning in and protecting the area with the divine light and love of God.

Sound

Many spiritual practitioners, who are well versed in the art of clearing, may use sound, song, or vibration to scare the negative entities away, or break up the negative or stagnant energy, to make it easier to disperse and clear. You can also use beautiful meditation music and music that makes you feel happy.

Musical instruments, drums, sticks, chimes, bells, chanting, humming, singing, or any other method of sound that feels appropriate, are all useful tools when clearing. Some people like to make lots of loud noise and banging, to clear a space, with whatever they can get their hands on at the time. You can use whatever works for you and feels right at the time.

Forgiveness

Forgiveness is the best method to complete the clearing process. The real question I asked God was, "What do you do with the entities and negative energies once you have asked them to leave, or if you want to send them away? Where are you going to send them?"

The channeller responded on behalf of God, "Send it to God, Jesus, or the archangels. They have the special ability to correct any negative energy and to rebalance and restore any corrupted energy. You could ask for any unwanted spirits or energies to go back to where they came from, which could be the dark side, or the underworld, which they may, or may not be willing to do. Or you could give them an ultimatum and send their energy force, soul, or spirit back to God to be rejudged.

"There are many entities stuck in the astral plane, because they are ashamed, guilty, or very afraid of what they have done wrong. They are scared of facing the wrath of God, so they hide in the shadows for an eternity, for fear of being judged by God."

The channeller continued, "Present them again to God for judging and even if they have done wrong, at least they will get processed and moved on from the realm they are stuck in and sent to a different place, or plane of existence, to progress with their learning again."

The channeller added, "God doesn't destroy anything. He is all forgiving and he is a kind and just God. God also knows that souls are capable of destroying themselves, when they have to judge themselves. Convince the spirits to go back to God and to go *towards* the light. This way they can start their journey towards the light side and that is one more team member won over by the light. In the end, *all* souls will go back to the source energy of God, because that is their true purpose. We will all eventually go toward the light, but for some it takes a long time and they have to work through the challenges of judgement and their fear of retribution."

Blessing

Sometimes clearing has not been requested, but you have been asked to perform a *blessing* on the new block of land, or new home, or whatever has been asked of you. It is similar to a christening, but on a property, or in a building. When blessing the land, or any property, don't just bless the house; bless the whole block of land. Bless *above* the block, *below* the block, *around* the block and for *infinity*.

The channeller said, "When you are blessing the land, you must clear the land first, even if they haven't asked you to. It is part of the clearing process. If you feel the presence of a soul, or ghost when doing the blessing, send the souls back to God, or Jesus to deal with and send them back with love and light. Convert them over to God before they go. It is very important to clear the land first, before starting the blessing, the same as it would be, if you were blessing any person, or child."

To clear or not to clear?

I have been taught a slightly different approach to clearing, through scribing this book and also by understanding how to clear correctly. You won't find this in any text book, because this understanding comes from a deeper level and recognising that sometimes a spirit wants to talk to you, or spend time with you. They may actually want to help you out of a sense of duty, or because they choose to be with you and they love you.

When the spirit is not harming anyone and you understand and respect there is no harm in allowing the spirit to stay on the land, or in a house, you can allow the spirit to stay, if you feel this is the right thing to do. Trust your intuition when working on the land. It is not as simple as one rule getting applied to every scenario. Each situation needs to be looked at independently and the appropriate method can then be applied.

Sometimes a spirit can be a good protector, beneficial and they may actually love to be there. In that case, clearing would upset the spirit and they would feel deeply insulted, if you sent them away.

You can take it one step further and ask the spirit to look after your land, or forest, or whatever it is that you want them to do for you. You can ask them to help guide you around the place, or show you hidden secrets on the land and if they are benevolent, they will be happy to help you.

Spirits get bored too, just like people do and they love to be asked to help. It gives them a sense of purpose. They feel loved and wanted and not just ignored and hidden away in some other distant realm, never to be remembered. This is why it is essential for everyone not to have an attachment to spirits, once they have passed over.

You must respect the free will of another person, or spirit and they should be asked for help without commanding or demanding them to help. You should not have any attachment to spirit entities and they should not feel any obligation to perform any work for you. Explain they are free to come and go as they please, if you don't mind having them around. You can talk to the spirits and they can even keep you company, if you spend a lot of time on your own. Any time it gets too much for you, or if they are annoying you, they can be sent back to where they came from.

Some spirits are happy to stay where they are in a building, or on the land and they have no intention of leaving, no matter how much you coerce them, because they believe they are fulfilling their duty, or they feel like they have a sense of purpose. They may be guardians of the forest and want to look after the trees, plants, creatures and animals.

Some tribal practises not only invoke the spirits of their ancestors, but enjoy the presence of their passed over loved ones surrounding them. They love to feel the many arms of love around them and the beautiful presence that family can have, when they are hanging around you in spirit form. Those who are not in a state of mourning, or sorrow for their ancestors, can set them free and also welcome them to come and visit any time they want to. There is no need to imprison, or direct these souls. You can simply *acknowledge* their presence and allow the spirits to move freely between the spirit world and the physical world, whenever they choose.

Exorcism

The only exception to the rule of allowing spirits to hang around is when you really don't want them there and you don't like having them there on the land, or in the building, because it is causing distress, mischief, bad luck and grief to the residents. Then you will need to perform an exorcism, or *full clearing,* invoking the holiest of holies and you will need Jesus, or God to assist you with this process. This is the most serious form of clearing and this is not something you should do, unless you know exactly what you are doing. You should have a team of protectors with you, to perform the rituals correctly.

I am not going to focus on horror stories, or give the dark side any more airtime than they deserve and I am not writing too much on this topic, because I could easily fill a whole book on this topic alone.

The channeller said, "I will make this next point perfectly simple and clear for you. If you are faced with the presence of bad energy and it feels dark, evil, or destructive, it has to go! You need to send the presence to

God, or Jesus to deal with it, because as humans we may not be in a position to deal with, or reprimand this type of soul, or spirit. If you feel like you are out of your depth, then engage the services of a holy priest, or someone holy who knows exactly what to do and is a person of strong faith, integrity and has experience with exorcisms above all else."

The channeller continued, "If you play around with demons and mess around with evil spirits thinking it is funny, you just might find that, if you play with the Devil, you will get burned! I would strongly advise against using this method of clearing, if you are dealing with multiple entities, a curse, or a strong stubborn presence. You may need to get extra help to clear these entities, or to reverse a strong curse.

"Evil spirits and demons thrive on fear. If you doubt your faith, even for a moment, or are not strong enough to cope with their presence, you will be asking for trouble. If you get in too deep and don't know how to follow through and finish the clearing process properly, you can accidentally end up with unwanted guests following you around, causing a nuisance."

16. THERAPY

God Said, "The whole reason they are unable to solve the problem themselves, is because they are not confident in their faith and in their own ability. They are at a loss to themselves and feeling pity."

THE purpose of therapy is to either relieve a person of pain, or to heal a person. One precedes the other and the healing process can often relieve symptomatic pain, as a result of the healing.

I personally believe in holistic therapies and holistic healing techniques and I have used these methods many times myself. Holistic therapies use techniques that can heal on all levels of your being, including your beliefs, your mental patterns, your past, your body's subtle energy fields, your physical body, mind and spirit.

When appropriate, therapies that are applied to all of these areas, contribute to healing on a soul level. The soul level is where we all need therapy, love and healing the most. A competent healer can use healing techniques that may not only heal our current lives, but our past lives as well, which ultimately clears the way for us to progress spiritually in this life and heal past wounds.

The medical industry is the perfect *temporary* solution. It is the band aid for the body and the stop gap filler for the mind, but nothing takes the place of *loving energy.* Nothing compares to the love and light we get from the presence of something holy, like the God energy, which is the Supreme Creator's presence, when we engage in holistic, natural and alternative therapies to heal the soul.

You won't usually find any soul healing taking place at the local doctor, in the hospital, or in any of the conventional medical clinics across the planet. They are all working in a commercial and regulated industry and they are often too busy, with too many patients, to have a holistic point of view. You won't find any words of wisdom written on the pages of a medical script and you won't find the meaning of life in a bottle of prescription pills. If anything, you will be numb and suppressed, not able to feel a thing. That is the medical way. Numb the pain, even though the pain is an *indicator,* to show you there is something wrong. You certainly won't find the path to God and enlightenment, in the synthetic chemical concoctions you are being tricked into taking. Prescription medication will not magically cure all your ailments. The only magical cures are those found in *nature.* The cures provided by God.

The channeller said, "Illness *starts* in the mind, then *manifests* in the body. It is cured only through correct conscious thinking, positive action, healthy living and holistic healing. It is amusing how the medical industry calls non-medically registered methods of treatment, *alternative* therapies, when these therapies used to be the original and only remedy available.

"The old remedies have been used successfully in the past and this has been proven both scientifically and through medical research. The original and ancient therapies worked back then and still work now. There are many guaranteed methods to treat and heal any ailment. These ancient therapies worked for thousands of years, using medicinal plants, forest trees, natural minerals, herbs, supplements, poultices and tinctures, as part of the ancient world's naturopathic and homeopathic healing tool kit."

These days, if the products don't get approved by the Therapeutic Goods Administration (TGA), or the Food and Drugs Administration (FDA), they don't make it onto the *prescribed list of treatments,* or medicines. People can be easily manipulated by the medical industry, because doctors and medical professionals are sometimes treated like gods, even though they get rushed through the queue and kicked out the other side with a fancy script.

Unfortunately the general populace tends to hang on every word the medical industry endorses and they believe that the only healing options available to them, are the treatments, drugs and prescriptions that are recommended by the industry. The medical industry does not endorse, or recommend alternative medicine, or holistic therapies, because they are not endorsed, or supported by the medical system, or used in medical facilities at this time. You can do your own research and find alternative treatments for almost everything.

The channeller said, "Doctors and hospitals are excellent for saving lives in an emergency, performing tricky surgery and stitching people up, but beyond that, the current treatment model is *not* designed to treat, or heal people long term. There is no financial benefit to the medical industry to have fit, healthy and educated people. Why? Because people who self diagnose and self medicate, using natural plants and substances, don't need to use the services of a doctor. They mitigate their own health risks, keep their immune system healthy and strong, regularly work on their spiritual and mental health and practise good hygiene. The medical and pharmaceutical industries make more money out of sick, tired, uneducated and inexperienced people, because they are easier to program and convert to the way of the medical system, especially if they don't know any other way."

The channeller continued, "People are waking up, one by one, all over the planet and starting to see that *prevention* is the cure. They are also starting to make more conscious living choices in relation to their food, drink and their lifestyle. They are realising that natural, raw, organic and sustainable are the new buzz words to look out for.

"You are in charge of your body. It is the vessel that houses your soul during your journey through life, so make it last as long as you can, by treating it respectfully and using the right therapies, to suit the issue, or ailment. Even better, you can learn about preventative measures and spend time working out how to *boost* your immune system, to give your body better resistance to harmful bacteria and viruses.

"You don't need to pump your body full of chemical drugs and synthetic food to make it work better. *Less* is more and you will live a long and prosperous life. Less food, less drugs, less alcohol, less sugar, less poison, less acidity, less exposure to radiation, less stress and less bad advice. You will need less sleep to survive, if you are healthy and fit and you will need less money to spend on unnecessary drugs, pills and medical treatments. You will also spend less time waiting in doctor's surgeries and hospitals."

Working in a group

Whenever you work with groups of people, it is important to incorporate some key elements into the meeting, for the benefit of the people who are attending. Keep your number in the group intimate to start with. A group size of 10 is good to work with.

God said, "When working in groups, you can start your session by saying, 'Thank you for coming. You are all welcome and bless those who have come here to witness the love that we are about to enjoy as a group, as we get to know one another and our spirituality. If we all become one and realise that we are all the same, there is nothing that we cannot do. All of us that have learnt from our past will share our experiences with one another, so we can all learn. This group session will now share each of your fears and past regrets and together we will build a brand new future, because we will learn from one another's mistakes.'

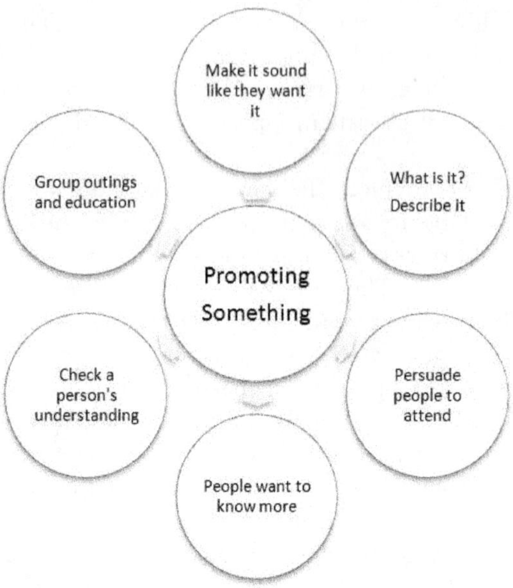

God continued, "Working in a group is a powerful healing tool. You can ask questions like, 'Can anyone remember when they were a baby, a child, an adult?' Use some examples and then bring every one up to the present day. Then you can build a *new* future, from all of the combined learning of a group of 10 people.

"Where you steer this force of people, will now have the force of these 10 people's lives behind it. If you multiply that and count all the years, on average you have more than 300 years of learning in the group and the manifesting of this group, will manifest in the correct way. This way you don't need to manifest these mistakes yourself. Learn and listen to all of the things that people have done. *People* generate life lessons. *People* generate mistakes and then learn from these mistakes. It's like having a computer program and having a blank program.

"The conclusion is there is a lot to learn from a group. Tell your group members that there is nothing they tell you in the group that will be boring. Tell them you all want to understand the feelings and what each person felt. You are not *measuring* yourself from the state of mind of each person in the group. You want to know how they felt.

"For example, you all go for a swim in the pool. All of the group members hop out at the same time. You assume that everyone had the same feeling, but everyone had a *different* feeling. Some people were cold and some felt different. Once you learn all of these outcomes, you become more powerful about understanding the outcomes. You are taking them all on a new journey. You understand them all differently, but you are all the same and everyone has different outcomes."

God added, "If money comes across as a result of these group sessions and then this is okay, but don't do it for the *purpose* of making money. You should only charge for your time and not for the purpose of getting together."

Working agreements

God said, "There are timeline threads and working agreements between people. The timeline thread can be for a singular person, which intertwines with working agreements between people. Everyone is managing their own timeline and when a team of people get together to do something, or go somewhere, then there is a *shared* timeline.

"Each milestone is a thread and rules must be created for the timeline. Get mutual agreement from everyone in the group that you are all operating from a timeline. The timeline is the pipe and you are all tapping into the pipe. You will need to schedule in regular meetings about the timeline.

"The timeline is the goal and you can all input information into the timeline, according to progress. When there is someone to blame, you can blame the timeline and remove yourself personally from it. This removes personal blame and disharmony within a group environment. This means you will have to create a multi changing timeline that suits where you are going.

God continued, "Be flexible. You should always be changing the goals and making new goals all the time. Remember to include recreation, spiritual tools and also allow time for living your life on the timeline. The timeline can have multiple people on it.

"If something is missing off the timeline, then everyone in the group can help to find it. If one person is struggling and failing, then everyone else helps. Everyone manages their own timeline, with their own goals and tasks. Then there is also a *master timeline*, so that everyone can look at everybody else's projects."

God added, "The benefit of doing it this way, allows each of you to give feedback about each other's projects and progress and pitch in and help whenever you can. You can all get involved and give each other encouragement about the projects.

"Initially everyone has a meeting about what the main goals are and this outlines the data to put on the timeline, once the goals are agreed by everyone.

"Just like project management, you can create benchmarks and milestones to show your progress. You can revisit and re-evaluate and if necessary, *adjust* your goals as you go. Mankind is so used to living in a rigid world, where they try to make everything set in stone. The lesson is to be *flexible*. Be prepared to move things around. Help people and get to the end goal as a group and not as an individual. You can all help each other to get there."

God finished, "You can learn to focus more and not allow distractions. At the same time, you also need to learn to have fun time as well as serious time, even if you have to schedule it in. It is useful to have a time schedule, as long as it doesn't *rule* your entire existence, allowing no time to actually experience anything."

Meditation

Solitude is good for calibrating yourself, especially in times of turmoil, or periods of chaos. If you could have the ultimate break away from society, the ideal period of time to spend in a cave, or at the very least to escape from society to a retreat, is 40 days. Just like Jesus did when he went away and reset himself or calibrated himself after 40 days and 40 nights in the desert.

Most of the great seers and gifted psychics in times past and in our current time, are very good at one thing; *meditation.* They can just *think* themselves into a meditative state and start receiving divine guidance. Every one of us has the ability to meditate; we just need to make the time.

You don't need to be a yogi master, or join any special classes to learn to meditate, unless of course this is an easier way for you to focus on the meditation. You can get help if you think you need it, but meditation is so much simpler than you think. As usual, humans over complicate everything and think that it is just too hard to meditate, so it's easier not to try, so then they don't have to fail.

People such as Jesus, Nikola Tesla, Edgar Cayce, Nostradamus, Mother Shipton and many others were all good at meditation. This is how many of them received their divine messages and also how they came up with their inventions, writings and sayings.

For example, Edgar Cayce used to receive information by asking what is wrong and listening to the response from God. Edgar Cayce was known as the American "Sleeping Prophet," who used to give psychic readings for people while he was in a trance, or deep meditative state. After lying down on his couch in his office and going into his deep meditative state, he would have his secretary scribe the readings, word for word. Edgar did readings for people who requested help with their health, family, finances and general well being.

There are thousands of readings, for thousands of people, documented in his library in Virginia. Most of the time, he did not charge for his services, or accept payments if the person couldn't afford it. He was a faithful believer in God and talked to God often. He made no secret of his love for God. He was invited to speak at the Church often, although he didn't really affiliate himself with any particular religion, or religious denomination.

He performed his true heartfelt service to people, for most of his life, even though he suffered many tragedies throughout his own life. Every year Edgar would reread the Bible and this was his way of meditating in the presence of God. Edgar was often visited by angels and this is also well documented.

Edgar Cayce had a peculiar learning style, which he accidentally discovered at a young age, after struggling with what would be called a learning disorder these days. He was able to sleep, or meditate with a book under his head and when he awoke; he could recall every bit of detail contained within the book. This ability was proven under test conditions, multiple times.

Edgar Cayce has visited me a few times through one particular channeller and one of his favourite subjects was meditation, because this was something he was very passionate about.

On behalf of Edgar Cayce, the channeller said, "1928 is the year. He is visiting while he is alive, at the time of the channelling. Edgar wants to share some wisdom with you, to help you learn how to meditate properly. Edgar Cayce is physically talking to you, when he was alive through trance. He has already spoken these words from back then. He said that if you looked through his library, where all of his documented readings are kept, you would find it."

The channeller continued, "Release your stress first. Run through all of your problems and know that they will still be there, after your meditation. You don't need to worry about anything being wrong. When one is in a state of total relaxation, all your problems will be there for you to deal with, in a better state of mind. This causes one to stand back and look at something and *see* what is going on. You are now able to relax. Separate meditation and being happy, by putting things on the other side and split them into two, by labelling them *true meditation* and *relaxation*."

The channeller added, "Talk in such words. Listen to what I am saying. You are going to put two hands out in front of you. On one hand, are all the things that are upsetting you and stressing you out. On the other hand, are all the things that are pretty and nice. Now use those hands to balance things. This is separating physically and mentally, the distortion of one's mentally and disturbed mind on one hand, and putting all the things that are pleasant and loving on the other hand.

"This technique also works for all mental, psychotic and bipolar problems. It is possibly one of the ultimate human repair tools. Make two sections in the brain. Put all the nasty stuff on one side and then *mentally* throw it away. Get the two minds and throw the crap away. You can do this to not only the logical mind, but for the two physical parts of the brain.

"This technique will heal the mind that is ill, or not well. Put all the horrible stuff on one side and all the beautiful T cells that are happy and the beautiful skin that you have, on the good side. When you put all the bad stuff on one side and all the good stuff on the other side, the human brain is distorted into thinking that it is *okay* to have ailments, or problems, because the body doesn't know what the good, or the right thing to be is. Once you have the logical and creative brains separated, then you will see the real miracles happen. The logical mind will realise this and repair itself. Things in a psychic mind will be influenced, by what you watch on television and whatever else you input *into* the brain."

The channeller said, "Meditation is about getting in the *zone* and staying in the zone, even with the infinite chatter that goes on inside our heads and all around us.

"By contacting God in meditation, all of our desires of the heart are fulfilled. Humans have been intelligently designed, with a communication system built in, which is contained within our seven main chakra centres, so we can communicate directly with spirit."

The number seven (7) once again is no accident. It is God's divine number, to remind us he is *all around* us and *within* us all the time. All we have to do is plug in upstairs and *download* the love from our Creator, to feel reconnected.

Still speaking on behalf of Edgar, the channeller said, "The first law of meditation is *planning your emotion.* If you want to meditate, then meditate your day, *prior* to it actually happening. This is more like *premeditating*, before it happens. A guru is someone who meditates about *what* they are going to do and then goes and does it. Plan to receive a particular type of emotion and focus on what you have to do, to achieve that.

"When the busy mind becomes too distracted to focus on emotions, or to allow your mind to be empty, then you would benefit from using *guided* meditations. The great thing about guided meditation is that it helps you to steer your mind in the right direction and to focus on the right topic, at the right time. Humans are easily distracted and our minds wander naturally, because we are thinking of so many things at the same time. To bring that focus back into alignment, it can help to have a purpose on which to focus your mind."

The channeller continued, "You should treat your meditation time as your own personal time, to sort through your queries and troubles. Meditation is like an answering hour that you can set aside for yourself, to answer questions that you have. This means, if you save your questions for your daily meditations, task them out and then you can gain clarity, when the mind is still enough to focus on the questions. Answers will come from your higher self (you), or from elsewhere (spirit guides, God, or divine guidance). Allow yourself to be open enough to *receive* this wisdom, from any of these sources of inspiration and listen carefully to what solutions or answers are provided to you. It may feel like you are talking to yourself, or inventing the answers, but there is a greater power at work helping you, guiding you, coaching you. The voice of wisdom and guidance is always there. You just need to turn your inner radio on and *tune in* to the divine frequency to receive the messages."

The channeller added, "Everybody has a perfectly programmed subconscious mind. It is the logical mind that interferes. The soul mind is the good mind and that is the one you need to work with. It's the logic mind that bends and twists the subconscious mind, which is why it is very important for you to be in touch with the subconscious mind.

"Meditation is for taking time to feel everything in your body, not just meditate. It is within that space, when a guru, or master meditates and they meditate within themselves, or for others. You first need to master meditation within yourself and one must discover every part of themselves, before they can discover someone else.

"When meditating on issues that can become overwhelming in your ordinary state, create a big cloud and inside the cloud, place little clouds. Inside every little cloud, put every individual issue that is concerning you, into a little cloud all of its own. Number these issues in order of importance. To begin with, restrict the number of issues you are allowed to deal with, at any given time. Then work on each issue, one at a time, instead of trying to deal with all of the issues at the same time.

"One of the Sutra's is learning about the sexual being within oneself. This is commonly known as *Kama Sutra.* It is the art and practise of discovering one's own body and then applying this technique by exploring their sexual partner's body. That is why someone can have good sex, because they understand and have meditated on their own body. Being in touch with your own body is the key to being relaxed and comfortable in one's own skin."

Hypnosis

Say for example, someone you know wants to quit smoking and wants you to help them. What you say to them is, "I don't want you to smoke anymore."

Words are not enough to make someone give up smoking. It is *gestures* that help with hypnosis and when healing someone, the touch is relevant to the spot that is affected. Touch the heart of someone, when you tell them they are giving up smoking. Tell them you have faith in them to be a non smoker and that they no longer have the need to do this to themselves, because they are loved. Then repeat the touch when you say, "Next time you come and see me, you will be cured of smoking, as smoking no longer has a use for you and there is no need for you to do it anymore."

You could start with a hand shake. Touch the affected area (the lungs), or touch on the third (3rd) eye area, then give the embedded hypnotic command.

This time placing your hand on the affected or potentially affected area, project mentally into the future in your mind and say it like a command. Say it like a deeply concerned hypnotic suggestion, "I don't want you to smoke anymore."

God had a message for one of my friends, who was due to arrive to spend a few days with me in Brisbane. God visited me the night before she arrived and gave me some very strong suggestions that I should pass onto her. At the end of my friend's stay, at the airport, I handed the message to her on a piece of paper and explained to her that these were *not* my words, they were God's words. I told her he wanted her to read these words and understand what he wanted to tell her.

A few months prior, my friend suffered from a really bad chest infection which affected her lungs, her breathing and her overall health. She had a real health scare and ended up being hospitalised, with whooping cough and pneumonia. I love this friend very much and desperately wanted her to cease smoking cigarettes, which was a major contributing factor and intensified her symptoms so quickly. Her immune system had failed to protect her, due to the excessive smoking prior to the ailment appearing in her body. *Stress* was also a major contributor to her smoking habit, among other factors.

These were God's words, "Your friend is going to come here and smoke her head off. You need to come to terms with her and where she is at. Take her back to when she was a baby, you've already met God and then you were sent here. She needs to have the courage of God on a mono pole and he is going to fire some questions at you.

"Do you think you could help me give up cigarettes?"

God affirmed, "Yes I am going to make you stop."

God wanted me to firstly regress her, then distract her logical mind and then talk directly to her subconscious mind.

> To do what God wanted me to do, I had to ask her two simple questions.
>
> 1. *"What do you like about being here now?"*
>
> She may be depressed, so listen to the response. Ask again, "Come on, what are some of the most amazing things you have seen? What about the art work, what about the wonders, the music?"
>
> This lifts the person out of their state of depression and makes them think about all the things they live for and that they are happy to be alive to experience.

2. *"What things do you think could kill you?"*
God asked me to write these words for her, "This is serious. God is a prophet and do you want to be lying in a bed dying, by gasping for air? You've completely damaged the good set of lungs that God gave you. God isn't going to save you if you ruin the lungs you have and you can't blame him.

"Apparently you love to smoke, more than everything you love. He could have taken it all away from you at any time, but he let you see the wonders and there are even more wonders, but you need to be reminded, that those wonders take a little more than packs of cigarettes.

"God promised to give you a fascinating wonder, every six months, if you give up smoking and all you have to do is *think* about it. God isn't being mean; he is just telling you what you need to hear. You are taking the wonders away from yourself, every day you keep smoking. It needs to stop, if you want to discover more wonders in your life. Do you want to discover the wonders and see the miracles that God will show you?"

God continued, "Why do you need to give up smoking? Let's see. Who is making you smoke? Whose choice is it? Where does smoking come from? Do you know the channel of the smoking, or the reason for the smoking? Where did it come from? Maybe it came from Gods Wikipedia, because he is the truth and he is all knowing? Where did smoking come from? An ancient Indian term was used and you can find it, by researching it. The big chief pipe was used and it was good if it comes from the chief of a tribe and guess how many of you, have actually seen the chief of a tribe? Hardly anyone! A spell or prayer is supposed to be given, before taking the pipe. You can look this up and the chief will make a peace pipe. It's a prayer pipe and when you light it up, do you say where it is coming from?

"If you smoke and use it as a tool to clear the body out, then this is what it is supposed to be used for. It is not meant to become a *habit* and an everyday occurrence, in fact multiple times a day. Smoking was used for *clearing* and for *spices*. They used to use chilli to kill bacteria, as well as onions, curry, spices, thyme and sage. The Indian chief referred to it as a medicinal or spiritual healing tool and *not* for destroying your lungs, by inhaling it multiple times throughout the day."

God said, "The Native American Indians used to call this practise *Kunfro*. What is Kunfro? It comes from the Navaho Indians. Native American Indians used to set their tents up in rows. Three rows deep and 10 tents long in each row. They made lots of things out of animal skins and the telltale sign was the fact that the Indians used to cut the animal skins really straight. They had straight sticks, joined to the centre of their tents, with animal skins wrapped around the outside."

God said, "The peace pipe was used, in the later part for white man. It was used for communication from chief to chief, warrior to warrior, scalper to scalper. Scalpers were really feared, because they would shave the face right off with a sharp axe. There were only so many scalpers in the tribe that were trained, or knew how to do it. American Indians cut their skins in straight lines and their tattoos were in straight lines, whereas the Australian Aborigines were using circle shapes, by burning the stick into the skin with the dots. These were differences between the Indians and the Aborigines. Buffalo was hunted by the Indians. Deer and horse were eaten. Horses were also ridden. Feathers were used off the bird."

Getting back to the smoking habit. So now you can see why one of the world's biggest killers and most destructive habits, is so grossly misunderstood by humans. The advertising and brainwashing, has humans so sucked in, that they will actually go to ridiculous lengths to continue to kill themselves, for the purpose of what? Clearing? *What* exactly is it that you are clearing? *Hmmm now it gets really interesting.*

So what was the conclusion of that story? Did she take God's advice? No. One must first *believe* in God, before they can understand the gift of God's wisdom.

Each person reacts differently to being in a deep trance and the purpose of hypnosis, is to disengage the senses first, to get them in a relaxed state, bring them back, then fully engage the senses. This can be done through guided hypnosis, by you talking to them directly, or they can listen to a guided hypnosis session, or guided meditation.

Use key words that invoke feelings like the below examples:

- **Touch** > soft, hard, gentle, warm etc.
- **See** > bright, dull, light etc.
- **Taste** > small taste, large taste, intense taste, bitter taste etc.
- **Human body** > hungry, full, fulfillment, happy, warm, starving etc.
- **Love** > looking for beauty in somebody, or looking for hate in somebody.

You can take them on an uplifting fulfilling journey through hypnosis. If you are selling fitness and health, then focus on feeling healthy, getting fit and having fun.

God said, "If you want to focus on hypnotherapy and the person wants you to treat them for addictions, phobias, or traumatic past events, then you can use this hypnosis technique, to answer their questions. Make sure all the boxes are already ticked for them, which means you need to make sure they don't have to think about the decision. You are basically telling them how they are going to feel, but using all positive statements.

"Humans are quite detached, so you need to be a little bit forceful with a human when programming them, but not in a physical way, just through subtle hypnotic commands. You don't *ask* the computer what to do, you *tell* it what to do forcefully, but not with anger. This is the best way for the programming to respond, by using the method of taking away the need to think, but still realising that every human has free will.

"You are helping them make up their mind, for themselves. Their own free will tells someone what to do, or what not to do. For hypnotic purposes, you could call free will a new word, or definition, so the hypnotic suggestions work better and you get fewer objections.

"Make up a new technique called *fearless*, meaning not feeling any fear. It's like a full confidence word, which is why there is no reason why they cannot do it. Logical reasoning is answered for them and you can specify the rules or guidelines and answer any objections *before* they arise. This way the logical reasoning has already been sorted beforehand. It's easy to work out what they need. You just need to check it against their logical reasoning. Like a machine does, before it commits to the next task.

"The whole reason they are unable to solve the problem themselves, is because they are not confident in their faith and in their own ability. They are at a loss to themselves and feeling pity."

God finished, "A really positive approach to hypnosis would be to get a person that puts their effort into destructive behaviour and focus on how to turn that destructive behaviour around and channel it into *constructive* behaviour. They need to be reprogrammed to behave constructively and with effort."

Neuro linguistic programming (NLP)

Neuro linguistic programming (NLP) is a relatively new method used, to help people with their communication skills. By using this type of psychotherapy, you can help people understand their internal and external talk a bit more and help them to develop their interpersonal skills. It's like studying the way you think and the way you speak to people and combining it, with the way you *interpret* what people are saying to you.

Some people already use NLP on a daily basis and don't even know it. The term NLP and what it means to the psychology community, is very different to the reality of observing and implementing the skills you are actually applying. Once you understand the techniques and the principles involved in NLP, it comes more naturally in your everyday dealings.

My hypnosis teacher and the person who first introduced me to NLP, was Brad Greentree. God likes to call him Brad Greentreefrog, because God loves green tree frogs.

God said, "If you see a green tree frog it is always a good omen and it means that the eco system where the green tree frog appears, is safe and free from contaminants, because frogs are very environmentally sensitive."

In one hypnosis and NLP training session, I remember Brad carrying a chair around the room on his shoulder. He was showing us an example and explained to us, why some people just won't *let go* of their issues, hang ups, phobias, or fears. He explained that they like to carry this burden around with them, because they have been using it as an excuse *not* to deal with their problems for so long, that to let go of it, would mean they would have to actually face their fears and *deal* with it.

Their resistance to being helped, is exasperated by you trying to *remove* the chair, or burden from them, that they holding onto so tightly. They are hoping you will get distracted, go away and leave them alone. *Persistence* is the key, when dealing with people who like to hold onto their reasons for why their life is so hard. Once you *remove* the reasons, then you also *remove* the excuses that they have been leaning on as a crutch, to separate themselves from the root cause of the problem.

God said, "People are like onions, hidden under layers of illusion, lies and fake costumes. Once we peel the false layers away, we are left with the underlying truth of any issue."

NLP also deals with the *perception* of the person with the problem. If someone constantly thinks about their phobias, their fears, their traumatic experiences and their issues, they can start having a distorted and enlarged perception of their problems. This occurs when they blow their issue way out of proportion, exaggerate the impact it is having on their life and allowing their issues to totally consume their life.

As friends, healers and therapists, your job is to reframe that issue and shrink the focus of the perception, so that it isn't in the forefront of their consciousness and getting in the way of their everyday life, so they can move on and get on with living. Try not to focus on the problem continuously and help the person to start focusing on their future direction, so they don't get stuck in the past.

Brad also taught us one simple NLP technique that I will always remember. When someone makes a statement, or raises a negative issue, Brad always used to ask them one question, "Are you focusing *towards*, or *away from* what you want to happen in your life?"

For example, if you want to have a happy, balanced and fulfilled life, then focusing *towards* this state of mind, is exactly what you want to be doing. Any negative focus that takes you *away* from that state of mind is steering you *away from* where you want to be.

It didn't matter how tricky the question was, or if somebody made a bold statement, they were reliving their bad experience over and over again. Brad kept coming back to *what* they were choosing to focus on and what direction they were facing, when they were thinking about the issue.

That is the key to healing. You can't change what has happened in the past, but you can change your *perception* and focus regarding what happened.

You don't have to forget, but forgiving and moving on is the *only* way to deal with any heartbreak and heartache. There is no other way that works in the long term. Then you need to *reframe* it, by viewing it from a different perspective. Any trauma can be dealt with in this manner, no matter how serious the trauma was.

You can seek the services of a professional hypnotist, or NLP practitioner, if you need assistance with chronic fears, phobias, or traumatic past experiences, especially if you are having difficulties dealing with these issues.

In NLP training, you are taught to use a *break state* method, to *interrupt* the thoughts of someone, who is focusing on something that is negative and overwhelming for the person at the time. Although this technique may be useful for temporary distraction, it doesn't actually *fix* the issue; so therefore, a break state is *not* the correct way to address a major issue.

God said, "What you need to do is shut the human down on every level, other than the one that the human needs to resolve. This is the best way to deal with destructive distractions, to get to the core of the issue and resolve it. Focus on *one* thing at a time and shut down every other sense.

"When someone asks you a question, or tells you something, you need to chunk it down, until you get the information by asking more specific questions. Chunk it down as much as possible, until it turns sour and then chunk it up again, to kind of lighten it up, or break the state. Use closed questions, but give them two ends of the scale, to get the conversation going. For example, ask them, 'Did you do a good job, or a bad job? Did you have a good time, or a bad time?'

"Getting down to specifics is a good way to befriend someone. Don't distract them with anything else. Stay on the subject that the person likes to talk about, by drilling down and asking, 'What makes you think that?' When it gets out of control, you can break the state by using the *swish technique*, which means using a statement like, 'Ah get over it,' or 'that doesn't matter,' or 'okay then, let's talk about something else now.'

"What humans don't do very well is learning to listen to themselves and trust their inner voice."

God continued, "Humans are predictable. The reason they appear like they are always unpredictable, is because they want to be cool, accepted, or liked. This is what changes their predictability and the pressure from society to be a certain way, look a certain way, or act in a certain manner. It can really influence how a person communicates and forces them to be unnatural to fit in socially.

"Humans are easily influenced from the tiny subliminal suggestions they are hearing all of the time and they don't even realise it. NLP is used in advertising, on the radio, in television programs, on the news and especially in politics. Most politicians have been trained in the use of NLP and once you recognise what NLP is, you start seeing it being used everywhere. It is a subtle form of programming. If it is used appropriately and for the benefit of mankind, it is very helpful and useful. However, if humans had faith and input the right substances into their body *and* looked after themselves, they would be acting in the correct manner naturally and wouldn't need NLP.

"What people need is *balance*. Everything in moderation and not too much of the same thing or one thing. This is the key to being in balance with yourself and being in balance with nature."

God added, "Ensure that when you ask someone about their ailment, or illness, that you cover off the five main senses and the two hidden senses. For example, you can ask them, 'Are there any sounds associated with the illness? Can you hear anything? Can you taste anything? What do you see, when you think of this illness? What does it look like? What does it feel like? What did it used to feel like?'

"For some people their favourite thing in life is using their senses. They might love music, sports, art, swimming, reading, studying, or painting. Instead of focusing on the illness, associate the issue with a positive state of one of the things they love to do. This is like a type of *positive anchoring* and you can associate it with their illness, or issue in a positive way, through their favourite senses, which in turn will have a positive effect on their illness."

God said, "Hypnosis is a really good technique to *combine* with NLP, because you can get the person into a restful state, before offering positive suggestions. To use these techniques together, you need to get the person into a sort of hibernation state, which means get their mind and body running at 10% capacity, before giving them suggestions. You ultimately want them to *cruise* through the day, as if nothing is a problem and this would mean they don't really need to sleep, because they are already half asleep."

Time line therapy

Time line therapy focuses on the feelings of the person and the things that trigger these feelings off. Find out how often these triggers occur and break it down, chunk it down. You can ask the person a question like, "Did you feel that feeling in the last few minutes, in the last hour, this morning, during your sleep, yesterday, last week, or last month etc?"

Then when you run back through the timeline, you are looking for moments that were triggers and where the feeling that was associated with the event was raised again.

Try not to specifically go to the *actual event,* as the trauma experienced with the event, is not that useful, but changing the feelings associated with the state, is the aim of the treatment. Change the feelings to more positive feelings, so that in future when they are faced with the same triggers, they have some new tools to call upon, to bring them to a better state of mind than previously. It is similar to a *crossover* in NLP.

Always talk about issues or problems in the *past tense* and focus on the *future tense* when mentioning the problem, because you are activating their mind to think that they have already achieved their goal. For example, if they are giving up smoking ask them, "When you *used* to be a smoker, how did you feel when you used to do exercise? *Now* that you are a non smoker, how does that feel *now*?"

17. OTHER REALMS

God is on the highest vibrational level and the farthest away
from the lower human vibratory levels, experienced here on Earth.
That is why so many people feel so disconnected from God all the time.

TO understand the other realms, you first must understand which realm you are living in, which realm you came from and to which realm you will go, when you die.

One night I was visited by God, so he could teach me about an elderly parent, who was fast asleep in bed. He asked me if it was okay to show me how to tap into his realm, the present moment and show me how to see what someone is doing right now.

God asked me, "Do you know where Eddy is at the moment? If he is in bed and asleep, what is he dreaming of? I want you to really *focus* on what you are trying to do. You are trying to *be* that person, to understand them and you can only allow the game to last for a very short period of time. The trance state is an alarm clock and you set a specific time. Physically you can put the alarm on and remember; only holy people are allowed to read the *Akashic Record.*

"The word *trance* means that you are taking on somebody else, or you are leaving your body. You are trying to make someone feel like they want to be like you, or you are feeling what it is like to be them. When you are hypnotising someone and when you are remote viewing, you can *link* onto the person, by wanting to be them, understanding them, or existing within that space and time. Time in the astral realm is nonexistent and it is like an obvious spiritual trick, because the spirit can be in another body. Ultimately this body, *your* body needs a spirit, but there are no rules that say you are not allowed to be in someone else's body, which would mean having two spirits in one body at the same time.

"You cannot *fully* give your soul to another spirit, or else you may die, or even worse, you may not be able to re-enter your own body. You can *allow* your body to be used when in channelling mode and wait in the background, but you *remain* with your soul. Always ask for holy spiritual protection of your body, when you are travelling within the lower astral realms, even for a short time. Then, when you have completed your trip, you can come back. If you ever give your soul to the demonic side, it is very difficult to get it back, because they won't give it back to you."

That's a part of the deal that you strike with the demonic side, if you sell your soul. Don't do it and **never** sign a blood contract with anyone. The price you will pay for that contract is not just with your life, but can also be with your soul for eternity.

There are many realms or *levels* as God likes to call them. We exist right now in the physical realm of Earth, where matter is physical and our bodies are physical. Matter in this realm is denser, than in the lower vibratory realms. To be able to *transcend* to be with God, you need to be able to travel through all of the levels. God is on the *highest* vibrational level and the farthest away from the lower human vibratory levels, experienced here on Earth. That is why so many people feel so disconnected from God all the time. It is because their vibration levels are so different to God. They are like chalk and cheese, or yin and yang.

To be able to *feel* God, or talk with God, you need to raise your vibration to the highest possible level of spirituality that you can possibly imagine. This is like the pure unconditional love that God emits and the type of love that brings tears to your eyes. That is the vibration that God tunes into, if you are emanating it. He will feel it like a lightning bolt and tune into your *love* frequency. That is how God can locate us easily. God then has to reduce his high vibration, to a point where he can communicate with you and meets you half way.

God and the holy archangels cannot last for long periods of time in the lower vibrational realms, because they get bombarded with lower energies and spirits. They are very sensitive to being in that space and find it quite draining. It is not only draining for them, but also draining for a channeller, or psychic, who has to be the intermediary between realms, for the whole duration.

The channeller is either translating through feeling, pictures, or thoughts, or allowing the angelic beings to simultaneously share their body, for a period of time. God or the angelic beings do not ask you to *leave* your body, nor would they ask you for your soul. They are *not* dead, so they have no need for a body and they don't have a longing, or desire to be in a physical body, when they love where they reside. That is how you know they are higher vibrational beings.

They only share their love and wisdom with you and never scare you, or tell you things that are horrible, or unnecessary. You are lucky if you get more than an hour or two at best, in this state. Sometimes the visits only last for a few minutes, depending on the health, or alertness of the channeller, or psychic and the energy of the being coming to visit.

Realm Walkers

What is a *Realm Walker?* Realm Walkers have the special ability to clearly communicate between the spirit world, otherworldly realms and this world. They can talk to God, Jesus, spirits, angels, guardians and any other beings from the light they choose, who are all just on the other side of the psychic veil. It was the amazing talent and consistent faith of the channellers throughout the years, that inspired me to write about the **Word of God**.

Realm Walkers can travel between realms, or planes of existence in a waking, hypnotic, meditative, or transcendental state, using gamma, beta and alpha waves. These brain waves allow Realm Walkers to access different states of consciousness that can help them transcend their current state of consciousness. During this state they can choose to go to particular realms and focus on particular subjects, people, locations, objects, or topics in a calm and meaningful way.

They can also travel between realms in a more dormant state, when they enter the theta and delta brain wave patterns. When your brain is in a deep sleep, in a dreamless sleep, falling asleep, or in a dream state, you would be considered unconscious and in a somnambulistic, or sleeping state. These states are very beneficial for healing, recovery and helping you to sort out your mind clutter. This is the daily junk which clouds the mind. It is not uncommon to visit the astral realms in this state, where you can experience weightlessness, flying and viewing scenes from an objective viewpoint. You may feel disconnected and separated from your body. It is because you travelling with your *soul*, but not your body.

If you want to become a *Realm Walker*, you better be prepared for what you might see! Some realms on the lower vibrations can emit a sickly, nauseating, low pulsing frequency and some realms at the higher end of the spectrum, can vibrate the highest harmonic love frequency, right at the peak of your ability to feel, or perceive. Then there are multitudes of realms in between.

These realms don't exist anywhere else. They exist right *here*, right *now*, in this time and space, but on a different frequency. The more *attuned* to a specific frequency you become, the more adept at realm walking you will become. Roaming the spirit world and talking to the souls of the deceased, may sound scary at first, but becomes more comfortable with time, patience, practise and persistence.

The other side

I like to refer to the afterlife or the realm where you communicate with spirits, as *the other side,* because this is what the spirits often refer to as their current location. For the purpose of describing the afterlife, I will call it *the other side.* There are multiple realms of existence, but the main realms that we have contact with, are vibrating relatively close to us and are located on *this* side. This is the side where we live our daily life on Earth and *the other side* is where the spirits and many other entities and beings reside.

God said, "The main difference between realms of the *dead* and the realms of the *living* is the frequency they are all vibrating on. If you could see the sound waves on an oscilloscope, the two realms would look like two different waves, but they still exist in the same space simultaneously. If you are not *tuned in* to *both* frequencies, you can't hear, see, feel, or know that the other side even exists."

Just because you can't hear, see, feel, or know that the other side exists, doesn't mean it doesn't exist. The same goes for God, just because you can't feel him, or haven't acknowledged him ever before, doesn't stop him from existing. God doesn't exist, simply because of *our* belief. God is more substantial than that. We *only* exist, because God does. Without God, *nothing* in the Universe would even exist.

To tune in to the other side, takes practise, persistence and patience. The most important thing you need to have is a really good imagination. The images you are shown, the voices you hear and the feelings you get; like being touched, prickles, chills and tingles, can make you feel like you are going nuts sometimes, but these are all good signs you are getting *something* from the other side.

Be sure you are attracting *only* good spirits, who want to help you and who only have good intentions. Nobody wants to attract an unwelcome guest, who is difficult to get rid of. If you do accidentally attract something you are unsure of, or don't like the feeling you get from them, you can send it back to the realm it came from, with one simple statement. You can say, *"Go back to whence you came from!"* This needs to be said and felt with the clear intent of sending it away. If you are not confident doing this, you can ask for spiritual protection from the angels, archangels, spirit guides, ascended masters, Jesus, or God to help clear the spirits.

Some people truly wish they had the ability to communicate with the other side and try so hard, but just can't seem to connect. While others feel like it is a curse, because they can't escape it and it is hard to turn it off, when you want some peace and quiet. Once you are *open* spiritually, you can tune into the frequencies of the other vibratory realms, with just a thought. This is why guarding your thoughts when you are giving a psychic reading, channelling, or healing is extremely important to protect yourself and the people you are working with.

If you try to *hide* from the gift of prophecy, or *deny* the gift of being able to communicate with spirits, the spirits will keep finding a way to get you to pay attention and accept the gift. It is better to *embrace* it and learn how to do it safely, so you can use it as a service to humanity, rather than trying to bury your head in the sand, or trying to run away from the gift.

It is believed that many so called crazy people, are quite in tune with the spirit world, but because they don't know how to control it, they get overwhelmed and it drives them crazy. They also don't have the skills to tell the difference, between good and evil spirits and the feelings can become too overwhelming for them.

God said, "Instead of treating the mentally ill patients with mind numbing medication to turn them off, why don't you ask them *who* they are talking to. You might learn something beneficial from them and be able to actually help rid them of demons, or lower level entities, who are constantly bothering them, or trying to attach themselves to the person. All mental institutions, addiction clinics and psyche wards should hire spiritual healers, who are skilled and experienced with *clearing* unwanted spirits.

"This is a much better investment and will provide help and restore sanity, to the so called insane. By doing this, it will also assist spirits in their transition, if they are stuck in this realm and don't know how to cross over to the other side safely. These spirits may also have lower level entities attached to them and they may need help from these specialist healers and clearers, to free themselves to the other side, instead of being stuck in between realms, or worlds."

I must admit, I have never met a spiritual healer yet, who doesn't believe in God. I know many gifted psychics, channellers, healers and many spiritual people and they *all* believe in God and the all knowing wisdom, love and light of the Creator. God is who they are plugging into, when they are performing hands on healing. God is who they are asking for protection from when they need it and God is who they send any souls to, that need to be released from this earthly dimension, when they become trapped, or grounded here as ghosts, or demonic entities.

Sometimes due to anger, grief, unfinished business, or remorse, a spirit may hang around, or may want to attach themselves to the living, to elongate their experience in the Earth realm. They might be seeking forgiveness from their loved ones, or people who hold a grudge against them. The spirit may also be concerned with the grief that the living are feeling and they don't want to leave their loved ones, when they are suffering so much.

This is why it is so important to forgive *everyone,* for *anything* they have ever done wrong to you, so that *you* can free yourself from soul attachments in the future and to *free* the soul who has done you wrong. It is also really important to release your loved ones, into the love and light. Pray for the soul to follow the love and light of God and let them move on from this realm, because it is not healthy for them to stay here, after they have passed.

All souls have learning to do, even after they pass over, so you need to let them continue their existence and you can meet up with them again later. God is their judge and he will deal with them sufficiently and in the righteous way, so that you don't have to. Release them to the love and light.

Communicating with spirits is so different from talking to people, because you are not making the spirit feel like it has to be here. They *choose* to talk to you, when they are ready.

I need to mention, that when you talk to the other side, you are communicating with both the living *and* the dead. Time has no boundaries on the other side, like it does here. You can talk to any soul, at any point in existence, or you can talk to the spirits using your concept of time and where you believe they are now, parallel with your time. You can even talk to yourself in the spirit world, or you can talk to any spirit who has passed over at any time.

Once you get good at doing this, you can step up your skills, by starting to talk to *living* entities, who are vibrating on a way higher vibration that is so high, they can only come halfway down to your vibratory level or realm of vibration and maybe meet you there. You must be able to meet them at least halfway up, on *their* vibratory level, or else it won't work. This includes God, Jesus, archangels, angels, ascended masters and other non Earth entities that are residing in other parts of the galaxy, who may receive your form of telepathic communication.

The channeller on behalf of God said, "There is a Heaven and there is a Hell, but it is not quite what you think it is. Hell is like a material prison, where souls who get eternally attached to the material world go, until they realise that they can free themselves from this eternal cycle of material attachments. It is a vibratory level, a realm that keeps attracting those that want earthly desires fulfilled and want to have experiences that cause them to vibrate on that lower level. When you realise there is no reward with materialism and that spiritual fulfillment and helping others should be your ultimate goal in this life, then you can start to open up and *surrender* to the power of the Almighty God."

Get to know God in *this* realm and then it is so much easier to vibrate at a high enough level to ascend upwards, through the astral, angelic and heavenly realms. It's all about the *frequency* you emit, the frequency you can tune into and the frequency you attract. The frequency you vibrate on is where you end up, in your own personal Heaven, or personal Hell. Free yourself now and learn forgiveness. It is so much easier to learn this lesson from *this* realm and it has a positive flow on effect, into the other higher vibratory realms.

The channeller continued, "When the soul gets snatched by the Holy Ghost, God will say, 'Just take my hand, surely only the soul knows.'

"He is letting hundreds of souls go through to different places. It takes a lot of sorting and managing all of the souls that pass over. There are a lot of comings and goings. There is a continuous flow of souls coming in and souls getting reborn again and there are restrictions on how many souls, can go to certain places. You may have to wait your turn, to go where you want to go."

It is at this point I asked God, "What message do you want to give humanity, from the other side?"

God said, "I am in trinity, in infinity, I am indestructible. I am in between, living the dream and already in the dream. I call it I. All of it. Call it shall, it's called not. The same words are probably called *do it.* It's called taken, or called received and the next word is called responsibility. Show respect and then further your responsibility in knowing oneself. Learning from others and how you would like to be treated and then treat all people equally with love. It's called love to *create* something, because love, even if it's ugly, or not right, is still love, because you failed in your creation. Failure is learning. Learning is love! That's why *touching* causes stimulation, which is love, which is more than just like. We can touch, or be touched by the living *and* the dead *and* across all realms. We are all one."

Dreams

We all dream. Sometimes we don't remember them all, but we definitely all dream. God gave us the ability of the third eye to dream but, *why does one actually need to do it?*

There are dreams that we *create* and then there are dreams that just *happen* and we are an observer. You might dream of being somewhere you have never been before and this might be considered a prophetic or precognitive dream, if it comes true at a later date.

It doesn't matter how bizarre our dreams might seem to us at the time, they *always* have a meaning. For some people, myself included, dreaming is a good way for spirits on the other side, to communicate with us during a dream state, because we are totally relaxed and not thinking about distracting thoughts like we do during the day.

Dreams often contain symbols and themes and care needs to be taken, when interpreting dreams. Dream interpretation is to do with being able to interpret symbology. Pictures and symbology are like a universal language, just like mathematics, that can be shared between realms, cultures and different languages.

To see a representation of an aeroplane in your dream could have many different meanings. To interpret it correctly, you have to look at *all* of the symbols presented to you in the dream simultaneously, because they are all related to one another. An aeroplane crashing into the ocean, would be a much scarier dream, than an aeroplane flying *over* the ocean and both dreams can have the same symbols, but both dreams can have different outcomes.

It is important to keep a dream diary, or a recording device next to your bed, to record your dreams as soon as you awake, because as the day progresses and you become more conscious, you lose more and more of the dream, until the following day, when you can no longer remember what the dream was even about. Record the *feelings* and the *symbols* and what *you* think it may have meant. Dreams are specific to *you only*. Dreams can be used to tell you a story, about what you are experiencing in your life at the time, or your dream may even give you hints, or clues, to help you solve some problems that you are currently faced with.

Astral travel

God said, "When astral travelling, the body needs to be *anchored* to the soul, that it is wandering from. You could do the Holy Trinity symbol as a safety anchor, by praying to the Holy Trinity, before you go to sleep. You can even pray while you are in your dream state. You can also override the Trinity, by doing a circle. First do an anti-clockwise motion in a full circle and then do a clockwise motion in a full circle and you can encompass *everything.*

God continued, "Your ancestors and your spirit guides are there to assist you to travel to your future, or past. They are stuck in a realm and they can only go up, or down and they get bored. They like to help you, especially when asked, or during your astral dreaming state."

One time, I remember waking up, because my whole bed was shaking so intensely, that I was forced to get out of my bed. When I got out of the bed, the floor was still shaking so hard, I could barely stand up. It was confusing for me at the time, because I thought I was experiencing a severe earthquake. I wasn't aware that I was actually still asleep and the more I walked around in the dream, the more things just didn't make any sense to me. I realised after some time, that I was *not* awake. I was actually astral travelling. The whole experience was very tactile and I was even able to pick things up and move things around with my hands.

At the next available opportunity, I asked God why my bed was shaking so violently, during my recent astral travelling experience. He told me it was the spirits shaking me to wake me up, out of a certain layer, or dimension of astral travelling. As we *fall* asleep, we fall *down*, or *descend* into deeper dimensions of realities, or realms and sometimes if we fall *too* deep, we can end up in the lower level astral dimensions, which are not always inhabited by pleasant beings.

Even though sometimes we can experience pleasant things on these levels, the lower level astral entities can mess with our conscious and sub-conscious mind and play tricks on us, when we have descended to this level during sleep. These are the dreams that we have, when we wake up in a cold sweat, after thinking we have just experienced something horrific for real, only to awaken and wipe the sweat from our brow, with a sigh of relief, realising it was just an astral travel, or nightmare experience.

Not all astral travel experiences are bad. There are many experiences that are really pleasant. There is something eerily pleasant about flying over towns, cities, or forests. There is something very organic about visiting loved ones and being able to have a look around and explore other realms in our astral body. This type of astral travelling experience is safe, as long as you remain connected to your soul cord, which is your connection between this realm and the astral realms.

So in the case of my shaking bed experience, my spirit guides were trying to wake me up, to get me out of that particular lower level astral realm, so that I couldn't be harmed.

If you ever wake up inside a dream and it is not pleasant for *any* reason and you just don't feel right about the experience, to end it, you simply call on holy entities like Jesus, the archangels, spirit guides, or the ultimate warrior, God to help you. The terror will diminish, once you call on holy energy to assist and quite often you will either awaken immediately, or the dream will change to something pleasant. You *must ask* for help, because they are not allowed to intervene unless asked and also because it is *your* experience.

The Akashic Record

God said, "You have to complete many levels and if you thought that level three was the ultimate level, then you would ask, *who created level three?* The *Akashic Records* are available to everyone, but you need to be able to travel through certain realms to get to them. It is the triple realm that you have to go through. It is the triple lock you have to go through and it was lost in the burning of knowledge."

God will say this only once to you, "The Akashic Record of all knowledge holds all the sins of every lower soul, on mankind and every soul on a lower level and we are all clawing our way to the top. The Akashic Records tell of a man's sins, recorded for every lifetime and he needs to access them, to see what his past sins were, so he can correct them."

God leaves these records open for you, to personally read about your own Akashic Record. He does *not* withhold his word. Never anywhere does it say he will withhold his word and he is allowed to change his mind.

God stated, "Thrall shall hellish of not holdout, inspired by ones hand to hold the heart with the left and hold. Only holy people are allowed to view the Akashic Records of others, but you do not need to be holy, to read your own."

God continued, "For those who have ventured beyond the realms, see the true meaning and journey beyond those who have ever journeyed before."

The channeller speaking on behalf of God added, "They may ask God's permission and with his approval, he shall give them the *Book of Knowledge*, which is also known as the Tree of Knowledge and it shall hold all of history, the past, the present and the future. If you ask kindly, you can take his hand and he will guide you through his books of knowledge, but only if you are *worthy* of being righteous. He holds all of mankind as worthwhile, including those who have done wrong *and* those who have done right."

18. THE SPIRIT WORLD

The spirit world and our world exist simultaneously in the same space. Just because you can't see it, feel it, or hear it, doesn't mean it doesn't exist.

FOR me personally, the spirit world represents the place where the spirits reside and you can *tap* into their world, or ask the spirits to come into your world. Both scenarios can only last for a certain amount of time and neither option is permanent. When your body is unable to be used and ceases to exist, you shed your vessel and your soul transcends to the spirit world.

The spirit world is like our world. When you travel on this planet, you can travel by plane, car, bus, train, motorcycle, bicycle, boat, taxi, animal, walking, or whatever other means are available to you, at the time. You can travel to many different continents, countries, cities, towns and special hidden locations. There are many treasures you can discover, along the way.

The same can be said for the spirit world. It is full of spirits, just like our world is full of people. There are spirits of all kinds that reside in this realm like; people, animals, creatures, plants and otherworldly beings. The spirit world exists close to Earth, but on another vibratory plane of existence.

You don't actually need to *travel* to the spirit world; you can *tap* into the world with your psychic ability. You can travel there in your dreams, or you can *transcend* there with your mind. There isn't anywhere to go. It is right here on a different level of vibration. There are good spirits, there are bad spirits and there are holy spirits. Just like when you travel to somewhere like New York. For example, there are good people, there are bad people and if you are really lucky, you might even find holy people.

The spirit world and our world exist simultaneously in the same space. Just because you can't see it, feel it, or hear it, doesn't mean it doesn't exist.

It *does* exist and if you really want to become familiar with that world, you need to tune your frequency dial to the right station, to the right vibration, to be able to communicate with spirits, in the spirit world.

Near death experience (NDE)

Some people *nearly* die, or clinically die, for a short period of time. This happens when a person dies, or flat lines, due to an illness, an operation, an accident, drug overdose, or traumatic experience causing death.

Well *almost.* They may *clinically* die and then later return to their body. This is what is known as a near death experience, or NDE.

They may experience a momentary death, or a *near death experience,* which takes them away from this world and transports them, through the tunnel of light, to the spirit world. So many people report seeing this tunnel of light, when they pass over.

The channeller said, "The reason it is a tunnel of such bright light, is because the bright light is the glory of God, beaming through your consciousness, showing you the right way to go."

When the soul has reached the spirit world and they are greeted by loved ones, or higher spiritual beings, it is at this point, the soul may be asked some very important questions. The soul may even be taken on a tour of Heaven, or get to meet some of their loved ones, who have already passed over. During their visit, the soul may be told that *it is not their time yet* and that they must return to their body, because they have loved ones back on Earth that would miss them deeply. They may also be *told* to return to their body, or sent back.

Sometimes, if there is unfinished work to do, the soul *may* be given the choice, to either return to Earth to complete their unfinished work, or if they are ready to transition into the spirit world, they can leave their current world behind, which means giving up their body.

The channeller said, "What happens if you are given the gift from God, the gift to survive? The last rite of God is that you are allowed to come back one last time, to complete a task. If you need to teach someone something and if you are pure, God will allow you a second chance. Do not take this for granted, or use it as a test. Use this opportunity, if you are doing it, for the right of God."

Coming back to the body

After a period of time, for some reason, the soul either chooses to return to their body, or they are brought back to life, using medical intervention. This can also be described as being forced back, or popped back into the body.

Upon awakening, the soul has to readjust after their transition from the spirit world, back into the material world. It can take some time for the soul to readjust. If the soul has had a spiritual *awakening* during their time away, they may come back completely changed. They may be more humble, more forgiving and may suddenly show a deeper interest in God and their spirituality. They may also no longer have a fear of death and live their life more fully, than they did prior to their NDE.

The channeller said, "As a side note, cryogenics is a good way to illustrate what happens, if a person spends a long time away from their body, then re-enters it, at a later date. When the cryogenic body is thawed, the soul is popped back into the body. This action means that the soul is taken away from wherever they were, before being awoken. This is something to consider, when entering ethical discussions about cryogenics.

"The person being cryogenically frozen needs to be aware of the risks and the technological advancements that may occur while their body is in its suspended state. When they eventually re-enter their body, it may take some major readjusting and they may not be happy about coming back, because they may be enjoying their time in the spirit world, only to be forced back into their earthly body."

Not wanting to be in the body

Sometimes a person is reluctant to stay in their body. They don't cherish their sacred vessel and they keep trying to escape from their body, by any means possible. They may not actually attempt suicide, but they are so close to it, they may accidentally kill themselves, in the process. Smokers, alcoholics, drug addicts, those that self-harm and even some people with a mental illness, can sometimes fall into this category, without realising it. They participate in risky activities and do irresponsible things, under the influence of their addictions, or illnesses. They are being deceived and influenced. These addictions and illnesses are not helping them to cope. It is quite the opposite. They are actually making it *more* difficult, to cope with life. Addictions and untreated mental illnesses, can create problems all of their own.

The channeller said, "A good example of this, is when a naughty soul, doesn't want to be in their body and they keep taking copious amounts of illegal, or prescription drugs, to escape from the emotional pain of being inside a body. *Where is their addiction or influence actually coming from?* The subconscious mind is where the soul comes from. The subconscious mind, remembers its way back to the body, but the conscious mind, distorts and confuses things and this creates inner turmoil. The soul can become temporarily *suspended* in the spirit or astral realms and can even become clinically dead, for a period of time.

"It is during this period of time, when the body, or vessel belonging to the soul, can become vulnerable to *walk-ins,* or *possession.* Another soul can attempt to inhabit the body of the causality and try to take over their body.

"This is why the body of the deceased, or casualty, should be guarded and watched over, until the soul either returns to the body, or the body expires naturally. The soul may decide to leave the body permanently and remain in the spirit world, or attempts to revive the body, may fail. Prayers of protection are required, during the soul's journey to the other side *and* back, to avoid attempted walk-ins, or possessions from occurring."

Shamans have experience protecting souls of the living and the dead, during ceremonial visits to the spirit world. They are well aware of the dangers, complexities and complications involved during that time.

Priests, holy people and those with genuine faith, are encouraged to pray for the soul of the living and the dead, whenever the soul is journeying to, or from the spirit world.

Organ donors and recipients

Let's look at another couple of scenarios. In the first case, two or more people have partially functioning bodies and if they are left to deteriorate, they are likely to die naturally. One or more people can be saved, by using the body parts that belong to organ donors. If the organ donor *agrees* to donate their body parts, under certain circumstances, then permission is given to donate these body parts, to save the life, or lives of other people. The donor's last dying wish may have been, to give someone else the gift of life, on their way out.

If the donor *agrees*, then this is deemed okay in the eyes of God. If the donor doesn't agree, then it is wrong and unholy. If the donor dies as a result of this forced donation, then it is *murder*. Live organ trade is very real in many parts of the world. Not all donors die, as a result of forced organ donations, but their quality of life is severely diminished. Not only is it sickening, it is wicked and corrupt. Remember, we do not have the right to omit, or overrule the free will of another human, under *any* circumstances. The donation must be genuine, legal and authorised by the donor.

The person who is the donor recipient, now has a part of someone else living inside them. Such a significant organ like the heart for example, is going to have some kind of impact on the recipient. If it's a strong heart, the personality of the individual, may change dramatically and they may appear much more confident, than they were previously. If the organ recipient was a bit soft previously, the change will be obvious.

By *choosing* to donate your organs, you can live on, in someone else and this is like reincarnating in some ways.

Let me pose a question to you. Which soul now lives in the body? How do you know which soul got to come back? This is for God, or the higher spiritual beings to decide, when the operation is being performed.

If the soul of the heart donor is given the body, then the new soul has the *memories* that were contained in the original donor's body. But now, the soul has a completely different set of desires, ambitions, wants and needs. As a result, they may change everything about their life suddenly. They may no longer be attracted to their wife, no longer have an interest in their family, quit their job and start taking up hobbies that the original soul, never had an interest in. It is also possible, for more than one soul, to live in the same body during a lifetime.

The channeller said, "There are so many variations and complexities involved, when making these decisions. There are so many outcomes. We could discuss each different scenario and each time, the answer could be different."

Death

The channeller speaking for God said, "God has time and he is everywhere and he talks to every single one of us, when we go back to Heaven. The reason why death happens is so that God can get an opportunity, to talk to us in between lives. He talks to *every* creature when they go back to him, the humans, the animals, the insects and everything. God gets to talk to each and every one of them, at the end of their life.

"You die when you want to die and when you've had enough, you'll want to die. That doesn't mean ending your life sooner than that you are supposed to, because suicide at any age, is considered a big no no, in the eyes of the Creator.

"There are 40 days and 40 nights, which are deemed by the 3 day ruling. The soul passes over within the three days of death. During this time, they are allowed to finish any unfinished business and say goodbye to those who they considered closest to them.

"Once souls have completed the first phase of death, which is after the three day period, there are more tests to complete. To be able to enter the gates of Heaven, you need to bypass and answer the 28 guardians at the gates of Heaven. If you are a woman, then you should ask for Mother Mary to start with."

When you present yourself in Heaven to be assessed, one thing that you may not know, is that every soul, being, or person you have ever killed, is shown with you. They are attached to you. You take their soul with you to the entry point. There is no hiding what you have killed, or any murder you may have committed. It doesn't matter if you have managed to successfully hide it your whole life, or if you were truly sorry for what you have done, it has nothing to do with remorse, or right and wrong. You are presented to the guardians with all of the souls you have been responsible for killing including ants, flies, mosquitoes, bugs, animals, fish, humans and any creatures and every single soul.

Picture this, you have just passed over and you have arrived at the gates of Heaven. You are facing the first guardian, who has just seen you arrive. Along with your soul, there is a massive group of other souls attached to you, behind you. This is going to arouse some suspicion from the guardian and they are going to start asking you questions about these souls. If you don't have a valid answer, you won't be allowed in and you will be sent somewhere else. The guardians are not stupid and you cannot trick them, or lie to them. They are there to protect God and to protect the entry into Heaven, so that the door is only opened for the righteous and not the unrighteous.

This is why it is important to resist the temptation to kill anything in the first place, *anything!* I already know I am going to arrive at the gate with some mosquitoes, ants and maybe a couple of poisonous spiders and because I *used* to be a part-time meat eater, I shall surely be presented with the souls of these animals that I have eaten. I have been a vegetarian for over 20 years now and I will become a vegan soon, when I am ready.

Even though I am truly sorry for eating these animals in the past, I cannot hide my deeds and these souls will be shown with me, when I pass over. This is why certain religions pray for taking the life of an animal, when they kill them. Know this, praying for their life, does not mean that you are presented squeaky clean. You will still be presented with these souls attached to you.

Speaking on behalf of God, the channeller said, "There are 28 souls who are the guardians of Nebula, which at this moment in time is purple, blue and yellow, but the colours keep changing all the time. You need to pass through them, to get to God. If you fail with any of the 28 guardians, you cannot enter Heaven and will be sent somewhere else. Being sent somewhere else is not a punishment, it just indicates to God that you are not ready to enter Heaven. If they grab you on the shoulder and ask you what you are doing there, you need to respond in a stern and faithful voice and believe in what you are saying.

"You can respond with, 'I am here to see God, remove your hand.' Tell them God is expecting you.

"If they touch you gently, then you can tell them, 'I am here to see God.'

"Ask them if they can help show you where God is."

The channeller continued, "Each of the 28 guardians will approach you differently and will each put you through their own test. These are the ultimate tests of faith. Don't worry if you are not ready, there are plenty of other places you can go, to learn more and get to a point when you will be ready to enter Heaven.

"There are two things the Creator does to you, when you die. First, he puts you on the running track, where you suddenly appear next to God. If you don't have faith, he sends you to the 28 angels, to put you through 28 tests, to see if you are faithful enough. That's when you say to the 28 angels, 'My question is for the Supreme Being, not for you,' to get through to God. There are a few angels in Heaven who can overrule it, like; Mary Magdalene, David, John, Jesus and a few disciples."

I had a question for God, "What happens when a lot of people get killed at the same time and you get inundated with souls, because of a natural disaster, or a war?"

God said, "The answer to this question will be... and yes if 100 million should rise at once, I shall have 100 million hands and bodies to guide every one of you and as I am one, I am many. I shall guide you through the afterlife and praise those of youeth that have done wrong and decide to change, as I will give you a test of your faith. The faith of those who believe in me and in yourself to do the right thing shall live. In a little scary passage, thou cannot believe how sophisticated one can be, but still don't have faith that you were created and given this marvellous body, to do good and look after and help. If everyone shall do this, there shall be no murders, or jealousy.

"If you don't evolve, parasites and demons want to take over your body, but you still manage to stay alive. As soon as you neglect one of your body functions, you will deteriorate. Emotions dictate what fuel your body uses, in terms of energy and you need to replace yourself every 141 days. All of your cells in your body are renewed during this period and you shall replace your body and you now won't be there anymore. If you don't nourish yourself and don't eat the right food, you will perish.

"You need to fill yourself with happiness, laughter and joy. These are the things that will nourish your soul. What takes away from that, is the opposite; fake food and unhappiness, which this, takes away from that. If you have a cupcake and you cut it in half, give one half to the poor person, who will be nourished and in return, will give you love and light. You eat the other half and nourish yourself.

"Death doesn't happen prematurely, unless suicide is chosen. We die at the time that is ordained for us and this could be a life as short as one day, when the cell no longer multiplies, through to the maximum life length a human can experience. In biblical days, man lived for a lot longer than what they do now. So many things have changed on Earth that contributes to your shorter life spans."

The channeller spoke and said, "The effects of the environment, our diets, our self induced stress and our pursuits, all have a deep impact on our longevity. In biblical days, the elders who lived long lives, were spiritually endowed and constantly guided by higher spiritual beings and God. They were given the secrets for living a long life. They were able to enjoy long life spans. In this day and age, people are so *disconnected* from the God source; it is amazing they even survive at all, without acknowledging the life force within themselves."

Luckily for us, God is very patient and allows all of us to learn at our own pace, instead of destroying us for our stupidity, or ignorance.

Once you understand the process of life and death, karmic cycles, your life's purpose and reincarnation, death makes so much more sense and it is no longer this scary eerie mystery, that sneaks up and snatches you when you least expect it. Your birth date and death dates are preordained and you have agreed to them, prior to your entry into Earth. There are a few exceptions to this rule, but generally you will get to fulfil your life as planned.

The main exceptions as previously mentioned are; miscalculated accidents and suicide. Suicide is when you take your own life earlier than originally agreed. In God's eyes, this is seen as the ultimate sign of disrespect, for being given a life in the first place.

God said, "A well organised and planned person will be ready for the end, where a hasty person will stumble and fall to their death."

Another exception to the natural death process, is selling your soul to Satan, in exchange for riches, fame, or whatever it is you think is more worthy, than spending an eternal life back with the Creator.

Every single one of you, who chooses to sell your soul for these materialist and shallow gains, will have to pay the ultimate price for your choice. If you get tricked into joining the dark side, or thought it was a good idea at the time, you need to remind yourself that it is not the type of contract you can back out of, later in your life. There is no refund and no cooling off period. Once you have signed your blood contract, you cannot change your mind on a whim and even if you repent and think that everything will go back to being normal again, you may be surprised with the outcome.

You cannot serve two masters, who are at polar opposite ends of the scale and if you choose to worship Satan, then you must accept the consequences of your choice. By doing this, you are denying the love and light of the *real* Creator, denying your own access into the higher vibrational realms when you pass over and you are ultimately denying your access to eternal life, as a result of your choice.

Selling your soul is not like shopping for a house, then realising you can resell it later on, when you have learned your lessons and no longer desire the house. This is a very serious deviation, from the path of love and light. Where exactly is it that you think you will go when you die, after your sell your soul?

There is a hell and it is a really hard place to escape from, not *impossible,* but without help, you will be damned for an eternity. Do you really want that for the sake of a million dollars, or a fancy car, or for some shallow temporary fulfillment on Earth? The temptations can be overwhelming, I know. That is why they are called *trappings* and temptations. Whatever you worship shows which path you are on.

God said, "Hear these words, those of you who have ever contemplated it. I am the Alpha and the Omega and I have existed since the beginning of time and will be here, until the end of time. I am your way to salvation. I am the way to your release from the prisons of the depths of darkness. Only through my Son, or myself; the Creator, can you escape these prisons. Repent now for your deeds and reconsider your spiritual path, because I am the light and love and the way to freedom. I am the Creator of the entire Universe, redeem yourself and realise I am the way. Only the holiest of holies, can allow your release. Ask for forgiveness, but not without first understanding your mistakes."

What happens when we die?

God said, "If you are selfish, you will go to your own personal Heaven, or Hell. If you are loving and respectful, you will go to a higher plane where the Creator resides. There are many planes, or realms that one can come across beyond death. There is reincarnation and other realms; like the astral plane, the hell plane and the higher planes too."

The channeller said, "All pity on those that ask him, why did you do this? Why did you do that? When he has more than a trillion asking him! He hears all and when they die, they shall come to him, after they have been where they are supposed to be, where they wanted to be."

God added, "They shall find love in themselves first, before they come to thee."

Elderly dignity

If you happen to make it past a certain age, you will inevitably become an *elderly* person. For some, this means getting wary and getting tired. For others it means getting closer to their journey, back to the other side. You cannot put a specific age on becoming an elderly person. Some people age gracefully and some don't. It can depend on the lifestyle of the person, the life experience of the person and many other circumstances. Aging goes hand in hand with health.

There are many people that have survived longer than 100 years. They lived longer during the biblical days, than these days. It is quite achievable to live a long and prosperous life, if you commit to looking after your physical body and keep your body moving.

Retirement can be a symbol of the end for many people, because they stop moving their bodies and they no longer have a definitive reason, to get out of bed in the morning. All of those years of working, have finally taken their toll and when they slow down, everything catches up. Retirement should be a celebration of free time and even more reason for the retired to go and do all of those things that they haven't had time to do, because they have been so busy working all their lives.

It is really important for retirees to maintain current hobbies, or to take up new hobbies, to keep their mind alert and their body active. Too many good people have been lost soon after retirement, because they have sat on the couch, turned on the TV and become lost in the brainwashing of the idiot box. Retirees need to embrace the change and get used to having more free time. Use this time to reconnect with loved ones and long lost friendships that fell away when work used to be a priority.

The saddest thing I have observed is when one elderly partner goes before the other partner, which is the order of things in this world. It is rare for both partners to die at the same time. The remaining partner can become lost and depressed, because it feels like their other half has left this realm first and they feel like they have been left behind. They can become lost in their grief and burdened with their loneliness.

The surviving spouse can still use this time, to remain connected with the partner who has passed over and remember they can talk to them as often as they like. It is very important not to let their passing, hinder the spiritual progression of the surviving spouse and stop them from continuing on with their own journey. There are still many places to go, many things to do and many people to visit.

My partner's mother passed over many years before his father did and during his father's remaining years on Earth, he was never the same. He could not bring himself to love another woman, because he felt his heart always belonged to his wife, even though she was residing in a different realm. He talked to her multiple times a day and pined for her every minute he was alive.

I respect that people grieve and I also understand that it can be very difficult to cope with the loss of a loved one, especially when they have spent such a large part of their journey together.

Part of everyone's lesson to learn here on Earth and in this realm, is to *cherish* every moment you get to spend here. Don't waste a minute, wishing you were somewhere else. Make the most of the time you have here, while you are alive. It is a lot harder to learn your life lessons, when you are on the other side, than it is to learn them, while you are in a human body. That is the *true* order of things and that is how God's plan works for all of us.

My partner's father Eddy passed away recently and there were complicated circumstances surrounding his death that we had to cope with. In addition to this, his best friend, who was residing at the same aged care facility, died a few weeks prior.

We had to deal with the death of two family members, within a one month period, which was very sad. We literally watched them slip away from us, feeling helpless and powerless to do anything. Eddy's close friend

Irene was an elderly lady, who his wife Diana used to care for, before she passed away. Eddy and Irene became friends and Eddy promised to live long enough to look after Irene, who passed away a few weeks before him. He was 77 and his friend was 96. Eddy fulfilled his promise.

There is no logic, when it comes to how old a person is, when they pass over, but I can say that it is a lot easier to let someone go, when they have lived a full life and you know they are *ready* to go. Elderly people will usually tell you when they have had enough and they will start making plans and preparing mentally, to leave this world naturally. Many are still not ready to go and fight to the very last breath. Some are ready for the day when it arrives and see it as a welcome relief.

Along with a growing aging population, comes the desire for elderly people to live out their remaining days in an aged care facility. It is a trend that has increased exponentially in the past 100 years, due to the aged care industry and new facilities popping up all over the place. There are a lot of things you may not know, about aged care facilities that I would like to share with you, to raise your awareness.

There is a whole process you need to go through, to get an elderly person accepted into an aged care facility. There are people who assess the eligibility of a potential resident and if you have money, in some ways it can be easier to gain entry into the preferred facility. If you have money in the bank, they welcome you in the door faster, as long as you can deposit a large percentage of what money you have left, into the bank account of the aged care facility. This payment will guarantee your room availability, until the elderly person is ready to give up the ghost.

If they have no money in the bank, but have a pension, then it gets a bit more complicated and you may have to sign a whole lot more paperwork, agreeing that the aged care facility can take between 80-90% of the elderly person's pension. This leaves them with just 10% of their pension, to pay for incidentals, medication and any special treats. It isn't *quite* enough to pay for everything and if any money is left in the bank, it will slowly whittle away, until there is nothing left.

Inside an aged care facility, residents are allowed to continue all of the bad habits that may have contributed to their demise. They allow residents to smoke cigarettes and cigars continue to drink copious amounts of alcohol, if the resident wants to and they don't even encourage the residents to exercise, if they don't want to.

Yes I agree that everyone has free will and they should be allowed to do what they want, but not if it is killing them even faster, than it would if they were under proper medical supervision. The main point I wanted to get across, is that aged care facilities are not designed for longevity. If you are considering putting your parent into an aged care facility, they are on their own, in terms of motivating themselves to do things and they are literally under the supervision of the aged care facility team, but not necessarily being *cared* for, or loved.

Aged care facilities used to have the residents welfare in mind and used to have plenty of nurses and staff available to assist the residents. These days it is like a commercial money making machine and they are churning the elderly through the mill at an alarming rate. The elderly are seen as a rent roll. They charge them high rent, with all of their bills included and give them second rate food, mixed with sedatives to pacify them.

Once an elderly person has a fall, or an accident inside an aged care facility, it is all downhill from there. They are heavily medicated to the point they can't even get out of bed, food is dropped off to them and if they can't feed themselves, there is no one watching over them to ensure residents get fed.

This raises a whole lot of red flags for accountability. The brochures give you all the fluffy pictures and warm fuzzy stories, that make the place look like it is an elderly person's paradise, but in reality it is God's waiting room, where they are just living out their remaining days, with no proactive assistance from the facility, to live out a quality life. The nursing homes are often understaffed, which means if an elderly person needs to go to the toilet, it no longer becomes a priority for a nurse. So they put nappies on them, until they can get back around to change them later in the shift.

It is quite comical that as an elderly person, the roles are so reversed and they are treated like a baby again, getting their diapers changed, they are fed baby food and tucked into bed every night. I am sure not all aged care facilities are like this, but this is just a warning, to help remind you to investigate the place, where you are thinking of putting your elderly family member. You need to ensure they are going to provide adequate care, especially if your elderly family member requires *high* care.

The first question you should ask is; "Does this facility provide high care for residents, when the time comes?"

This means when the elderly are no longer able to do everything for themselves, they become *high* care and need extra help with meals, bathing and mobility. Unfortunately, if the facility cannot provide high care and the elderly person needs it in the future, they may die from stagnant blood, starvation, or dehydration, or a combination of all three. Medically, it would be classed as malnutrition.

In the weeks leading up to Eddy's death, it became quite clear the aged care facility nurses were over medicating him and he was so drugged that he could barely speak, or move. The facility claimed that he was dying and was refusing to eat, but upon closer inspection and staying with him constantly, there was more to this than they were disclosing. The list of prescription pills that he was required to take; just for a few days, when held up in its perforated plastic bag was taller than 6 feet. Even a fit, healthy and strong person, would struggle coping with the amount of painkillers and medications they were expected to take.

They get their pills crushed into their food, or drink and eventually end up taking whatever they are given. I observed what was happening and urged my partner to stop his father from taking so much medication. He did for a few days and he literally came to. He was sitting up in bed talking away and telling stories about the old days. He was feeling much better and even wanted to go out for lunch and do things.

On top of the standard prescribed medications, residents were allowed to have a glass of wine each night. The glass was the largest glass I have ever seen. You could easily fit half a bottle of wine into this one glass. It was more like a fishbowl than a glass. Some of the medications specified on the label, that *no alcohol* was to be consumed with them, but they were still feeding him a lethal cocktail of prescription drugs and alcohol.

When he was feeling up to it, they would even wheel him outside and allow him to have a cigarette. He would be left unsupervised and due to the heavy doses of medication, he was falling asleep with the cigarette in his hand, which in turn led to him burning himself. At one stage, he was tripping on the medication and thought he was in a bar. That was before he went looking for his car, so he could drive himself to work. Eddy hadn't been to work in over a decade.

When we inspected under his bedclothes, this is when we discovered the nasty bedsores and the infectious sores on his bottom, legs and heels due to him not being moved enough. There is supposed to be a standard protocol that the aged care facility nurses are meant to follow. Residents in their care are supposed to be rolled over periodically, to avoid bed sores, or else they should be sleeping on an adjustable air mattress. This was clearly not happening. When we asked him if they were moving him, he said he wasn't being moved at all and whenever he called the bell to go to the toilet, they wouldn't come for over an hour and he couldn't hold on that long.

This is one of the reasons residents end up breaking bones, because they are in a rush to go to the toilet, the floor is very slippery and help just isn't available. The elderly still wish to retain their dignity and going to the toilet, is one of the last vestiges of independence left for an elderly person.

My advice to you, if you considering an aged care facility, you can easily get a professional carer, or subsidised helper into your elderly family member's home, for as long as you can, or look after them yourself. These are the preferred options, instead of sending them to their deathbed in an aged care facility.

High care is designed to comfort and care for the elderly, by retaining their dignity, until they are ready to pass over. Some facilities do it really well and some do it really bad.

A nurse friend of mine once told me, that the giveaway of a bad nursing home is the overwhelming smell of urine when you walk in. She said if you can smell the stench of urine when you walk in, it is definitely not a place you want to send your elderly family member. The strong smell of urine is an indication that elderly residents are not being cared for appropriately, or changed regularly. The staff may not even care about the residents, or they don't have enough staff to look after everyone in the facility. Either way, both answers are unacceptable.

Many elderly people are bullied inside these facilities and they fear retribution if they tell someone outside the facility what is happening, because it just ultimately makes it worse for them, if they complain. Once the visiting family has gone home, they are left on their own again and have to face the people they have complained about.

We requested an ambulance, to transfer Eddy to the local hospital, for better treatment and care. We wanted to see if we could get him back on his feet again, with proper medical treatment. We applied to a new aged care facility. After doing our own due diligence this time, we researched other facilities in the area. As a result, we were accepted into a much better facility. We moved all of his belongings out of the old facility and into the new facility, while he was in hospital, in preparation for his next move.

The whole reason he was in the first aged care facility, is because he could no longer look after himself properly and he didn't want to move interstate to Melbourne to live with us. He left Melbourne many years ago to escape from the cold and he wasn't interested in returning, under any circumstances. We weren't in a financial position to move back to Queensland at that point in time, to care for him. It was planned that we would move back to care for him later that same year. In August, he passed away and we weren't able to move back to Queensland fast enough.

Eddy originally chose the aged care facility himself, because his friend was living there and he was adamant that it was where he wanted to be. In the beginning, when he was not considered high care, he loved being there and was capable of getting around and looking after himself. Once he wasn't able to look after himself and his mobility was affected, that is when his *care status* changed. When you can no longer feed yourself, you die.

Passing people over

During Eddy's time in hospital, more bedsores were discovered on his body, when he was being washed properly. We were advised by hospital staff not to return him to the original aged care facility, because they believed the facility were being negligent, by not taking care of him properly. We lodged a formal complaint, about the lack of care provided at the facility and what the end result of that lack of care was. We complained through the correct legal channels, but this information fell on deaf ears and the issue was ignored.

We already had the backup plan in place and as a result, we had already relocated all of Eddy's belongings, to the new facility. The doctors at the hospital tried to reverse the effects of him being heavily over medicated, by giving him all kinds of drug reversals, but there were so many drugs in his system, they couldn't pull him out of his slumber. As a secondary consequence, pneumonia had now developed in his lungs, because he wasn't able to breathe properly, or cough up any phlegm. He couldn't get out of bed, could barely talk and he was declining very quickly.

The medical staff at the hospital were very kind and helpful, but they were too late to help him fully recover. It was noted on his record, that the medication he was given at the aged care facility, had affected him adversely in the past and the hospital staff couldn't administer anything that would help. Once we realised that he was slipping away rapidly, we had to prepare for two things, the potential physical death of Eddy and the passing over of his spirit.

One thing that nobody tells you about, until you have to make that decision, is the *resuscitation order.* I hadn't heard of it before we had to make a decision about it. The doctor will first give you their opinion, about whether resuscitation (if needed from herein) is safe and practical, for the sick and frail, depending on the condition of their health. The doctor will ask you to consider the answer, from the perspective of the elderly person and not from your own point of view. Resuscitation can be an extremely traumatic and painful experience to go through. They may break their ribs and do other damage trying to save them. Is the elderly person willing to go through that experience or is it in the elderly person's best interest, to be allowed to die naturally?

During Eddy's last couple of days on Earth, we notified his daughter who was on holiday in North Queensland with her husband. We explained the situation to her and she asked us if we were *sure.* We said he was pretty close to passing away and we told her if she wanted to say goodbye to her dad, she better get on the next plane home.

We discussed the no-resuscitation order with her and we all agreed that he should be allowed to go naturally, when the time came and that it would *not* benefit him, to go through the trauma of being resuscitated.

We both knew Eddy could hear us, but just couldn't respond properly. We asked him to hold on, for just a bit longer, until his daughter arrived.

She flew to Brisbane, gathered her family and came to the hospital in Tweed Heads. We all spent the last day together as a family with him.

After taking turns in the bedside seat for the whole day, his daughter and her family started their return journey home. Eddy's breathing started becoming shallower and quicker and we knew the time was near, we could *feel* it.

My partner and I are both very spiritually attuned and we knew that when the time came, we would be alone with him. We also knew that we had to wait for the right moment to do the passing over.

The last thing you want to do is pass someone over, if they are not ready and not willing. It is a delicate time for everyone and losing a parent is a very real experience that most of us will probably have to face, at some point in our lives.

It is really hard being present at the time of death and it is also a beautiful experience at the same time. It's a privilege to share your final moments together and to get a glimpse into the transition of the soul's journey, to the other side.

From the hospital's perspective, they just kept topping up the morphine and kept him on oxygen, for as long as you think it is right. Once we started to hear the death rattle in his chest, we were ready. The hospital turned off the oxygen and stopped giving him morphine. They left us alone with him, because they have heard the familiar sound of death, so many times before.

He started his descent and his breathing became more and more shallow and the spaces between breaths, became longer and longer. He was so frail and almost lifeless. It was really hard to let go, but we knew we had to, so he would no longer be in pain. This is how dying naturally occurs.

We kissed Eddy goodbye, told him we loved him very much, let go of his hand and then began the passing over.

It is important *not* to hold the hand of the dying, when you want to pass them over, because if you hold onto them, they don't want to leave and then it is only for *our* benefit, that we want them to stay. Keep talking to them, so they know you are with them and you will feel when the time is right. You need to be strong enough to let them go, when you sense they are ready.

We stood on either side of his bed and first we called in all the holy archangels to be present to take Eddy's soul away and to wait with us until we had finished our prayers. Suddenly the room filled with light and their presence could be felt all around us. It was so overwhelming that we could not hold back the tears of sorrow and joy, all at the same time. At that moment, a huge smile came across Eddy's face, a massively visible happy smile that was so big; we knew he was in the presence of Holy Angels.

We recited the Lord's Prayer and we asked that Eddy may be forgiven for any sinful acts he may have committed throughout his life and we asked the holy archangels to return Eddy's soul to God, with love and light. We told the angels we loved him so much and thanked him for everything he had done, while he was alive on the planet. We gave him full permission to go when he was ready and blessed his journey to the other side. Just then a second massive smile, bigger than the first smile, appeared on his face and he looked like he was so peaceful and filled with love and light, just for a few seconds. Then the white light moved through the window taking Eddy's soul. We knew at that moment, Eddy's soul had left with the band of angels. Just like that, *he was gone.*

Almost immediately, his face and body started to turn grey from his head first, down to his feet and there was no doubt, his spirit had left his body. We stayed with him for a while in silence and tears, before we called his daughter on the phone. By now, she had already made it about an hour down the road towards home and decided to turn around to come back and say her last goodbyes to her dad. The doctor waited until Eddy's daughter arrived, then announced the time of death, with all of us present. That concluded another chapter of life, the inevitable death.

About one week later, we were visited by Eddy in spirit form, who was excited to tell us about his journey with the archangels. He told us where they took him and confirmed that what we did was the correct way to pass him over.

He was really happy and running through the fields like a younger man again. He had reconnected with his wife, who had passed over many years earlier and he was free from pain.

This to us was a beautiful confirmation that there *is* an afterlife, that Eddy was safely passed over and yet another confirmation that God and his archangels *do exist* and *do listen* to your prayers, when you call upon them and ask them for help. We never doubted it; just having it confirmed again was a huge bonus.

Sometimes you may come across a spirit who has not transitioned to the afterlife or the other side successfully. They could be stuck on the astral, or on the lower Earth planes. You can help them to transition across to the other side by using the same method we used to pass Eddy over. Call in the holy archangels, say the Lord's Prayer and ask the good Lord to rejudge, or forgive the soul, when you present the soul to the other side. It is not for humans to judge a soul for what they have, or haven't done. Leave the judgement to God. God will deal with the soul, according to the soul's deeds and according to the process that God applies to all souls.

Suicide

The channeller said, "Suicide incurs demerit points on the other side. Suicide equals demotion. This is why it is not allowed. It does not give you a faster passage to God. It is quite the opposite. If you are killed, or die purely accidentally, this is different and not viewed as suicide. Remember God is all knowing and you cannot hide anything from God, because he knows you, everything about you, all the good stuff and all the bad stuff.

"When talking to souls that have passed over from suicide, in every case they *regret* ending their life with suicide, every single time. Only when they pass over, do they become aware of what the consequences of their actions will be."

During one of the channelling sessions, God explained what happened to Robin Williams.

The channeller on behalf of God said, "He is still Robin when he passes over, but he's not on Earth. He's nowhere. He was asking God for forgiveness. God gave him a life and he slit his wrists to be with God. God wanted him to live here on Earth. God gives them everything they need and they always want more."

The channeller explained, "Committing suicide is *not* necessary. They can have more. They do not need to kill themselves, to be with God. They can be with God *here and now.* Reach the ultimate *here,* before you go. You need to reset. Pain is not suicide, live it out. If you want to make people happy, don't give up, keep working on it. There are thousands of people who haven't realised that yet.

"The big question is; *how do you prevent suicide?* Suicide prevention is *listening* to the concerns of the suicidal people and addressing those concerns, while they are alive. Encourage people to talk about feeling lost, lonely and hopeless. There are many places you can reach out to that will help you. The main reason a person is feeling suicidal, is because of their disconnection with the higher spiritual realms and more specifically, their disconnection with the source of all love and light, the Creator.

"Every event, seen through different eyes, is an opportunity to rediscover yourself and your true purpose for existing on this planet. Having the realisation that you have actually *asked* to be here and experience these things and embracing them with full love and respect, will allow your journey to be even more fulfilling and gracious. To go a step further, accepting your lessons and acknowledging, that even the painful experiences teach us about ourselves and others.

"Every perpetrator is here to teach us something, just as every person who lends a helping hand, is also here to teach us something equally as important. They are all teachers of our life lessons that we are here to learn. The question to ask yourself is not; *how do I get out of this?* But, *what can I get out of this experience?"*

The channeller continued, "Every one of us has fears, doubts and insecurities. Every one of us wants to be loved and to give love. We are all learning how to best express ourselves appropriately and if inappropriate behaviour is all we know, then in some way, we may literally be doing our best, even if it is hurting someone. Every incident that you come across in your life is an opportunity to learn something. Every wrong turn, or incorrect expression, is a chance to discover, what the outcome of that decision will be. Every action causes a reaction and this is the *law of karma.*

"You cannot inflict pain on another human being, or another life force intentionally, without at some point in your existence, having to learn the same lesson yourself. This is *inevitable.* There is no escape from learning your lessons, even by the method of suicide."

Euthanasia

I have even discussed euthanasia with God. As far as God is concerned, it is still suicide. Don't be fooled. Taking your life sooner than you are supposed to is actually breaking your end of the deal. It will cause you to be reborn into another life cycle and experience everything all over again, until you reach that same point, but make a different decision.

Allow yourself to die naturally, even if that means experiencing pain. Learn to rely on nature and natural therapies, for pain management and not some chemical death cocktail, which lets you avoid the preordained *experience* of death. Suffering is a part of life, including the death experience, because it is a calibration point, a marker of when your death occurred. The soul can become lost in transition, during the euthanasia process. I personally do not support euthanasia.

If euthanasia is accepted and passed as law, the medical establishment has a license to kill anyone they choose; with, or without consent. Everyone is looking for an easy way out, a quick painless transition into Heaven, but God doesn't view it that way. Please realise there are processes in place for birth, life and death that are there for a reason. The way everything is designed, is for a specific reason and the transition happens exactly when it is meant to.

Reincarnation

God said, "Reincarnation can include being regenerated by a worm that eats you. Donating your body back to the earth is the ultimate gift to give other living creatures in the ground, when you decompose by burial. The option to donate your organs when you die, is giving life to an otherwise dead person. This is why transplant patients; can take on aspects of the person that has had the transplant. After this has been proven by medical research, eventually they will publish it. It is called cellular total memory. Each and every one of us is a king of our own learned world and we control nothing, but ourselves. These cellular memories and learning can be passed on to the donor recipient, when they transplant the donor organ, or body part.

"With reincarnation, you have the option as a soul, to become many particles. It is the rebirth of the soul. You can have a rebirth of a soul, where a soul chooses to be many. A soul will be content in itself and will become loving and will split itself into many. It may even turn into a physical object, just like you did to be here. My soul decided to form into a physical body."

Buried vs. Cremation

There is an age old discussion that occurs, when humans decide what to do with their body, after their soul has left the body. A lot of people think that it doesn't matter what happens to your body after you die and they don't really care, because they are no longer living in their body.

It is important to have a last will and testament in place, *before* the event, to ensure your body is treated with respect, even after your death has occurred. Most importantly, you need to ensure that your wishes will be carried out as instructed, by the executor of your will.

The biggest question we all ask ourselves, when contemplating what to do with our empty lifeless vessel is; *do I choose to be buried, or to be cremated?* Every person is different and each person has a different opinion, or view, depending on which option is best for them. This decision will be influenced by their religious beliefs and their belief in the afterlife. This decision can be influenced by your parents, your partner and even your peers. The stronger the influence is in your life, the more likely you are to choose what your parents did, or what their parents did and so on.

There are many arguments, both for and against cremation. I believe that God will not deny you entry into the Kingdom of Heaven, simply because of a bad choice, or even a misinformed choice. In my lifetime up until now, I had even opted for cremation, until I came to the realisation, that this is *not* the best way for a human being to dispose of their remaining flesh and bones.

God told me that it is written, that we are created from the earth and to the earth, we shall return. It is meant to be, that when a human dies, their body will then become food for the animal and plant kingdom, which can benefit from the decomposition of a human body, so we can offer one last gift to nature on our way out. Nature can benefit in many ways. The first thing being, that we become a food source to many organisms, right down to a micro level. There is also the fact that our DNA string then lives on in the forest, the earth, the animal kingdom and within any life force that comes into contact with our decomposing corpse."

It may sound a little *icky*, but the bottom line is, that we *all* die eventually and that *something* has to happen to our bodies. It is not being a pessimist, nor is it being morbid. It is a scientific fact, that one day we will all experience death. This does not need to be proven and it is not some mystical secret. It is simply a part of the life and death cycle.

God said speaking to the channeller, "We are not supposed to *burn* our dead; we are supposed to *bury* our dead. In order to understand where the process of cremation first came from and the sinister underlying reasoning behind it, we need to dig deep into our history books and look for the first recorded incidents of cremation, to get a better understanding and know why it began.

"Everything on this plane of existence happens for a reason and there is a natural order that all life forces undergo. When we tamper with the natural order of anything, it changes everything forever.

"One form of reincarnation that of our DNA, comes about as a result of our bodies being consumed by multiple life forces, both large and small. The food chain works a lot more complexly than we can comprehend, because we take for granted, the food we eat and rarely question where it comes from.

"Here is an example. You can think about and rationalise this concept. A man dies, his body is put in a wooden coffin and he is buried six feet inside the earth. The coffin is not watertight and it is biodegradable. Living organisms live all over our bodies and within our bodies every day anyway, but there are also many insects and creatures, that live inside the dirt and in the earth. The body begins to decompose and worms can get into the coffin and start to eat the decomposing body. The worms then get eaten by birds. The human then eats the birds and *voila*, there you have the most basic form of reincarnation where the DNA from the man who died, is now inside another human being, without them even being conscious of it. The person, who ate the bird unknowingly, has the DNA of the dead person now intertwined with their DNA. It is possible for one dead human body, to spread their DNA over multiple sources, including multiple humans after they die."

The channeller continued, "This is just one form of reincarnation. It is a process that your body goes through, when it is being returned to the earth. If you cremate your body, this type of reincarnation simply does not occur and your DNA ceases to exist, end of story. Your body and bones are turned to ashes and you no longer have the ability to reincarnate, as that particular string of DNA anymore. Cremation is killing the DNA permanently and ceases your opportunity to reincarnate in this way."

The channeller added, "Let's look at this scenario another way. If a person lives alone in the woods and eventually dies in the woods, what do you think happens to their body? It would decompose and break down over a period of time, with assistance from bacteria and other little nature creatures that assist with the decomposition process. The body would not be able to bury itself, nor is it able to burn itself. This is *natural decomposition,* which would have existed for many centuries, prior to the establishment of funerals and burial procedures. Natural decomposition would have been regarded a natural process of decay and rebirth and no one would have questioned the process in the past. When it became known that death can sometimes bring disease, humans began trying to find a way of containing the disease, or sickness that may live on, after death. Burials became an everyday ceremony around the world and this became an accepted method of disposing of human remains and doing so in the most dignified way as possible.

"Space then became an issue, as population grew and real estate in some areas became costly, humans realised that they may not be able to continue to bury their dead. They may no longer be able to *afford* a burial plot and saw that they may take over the lands with dead bodies.

"Along comes cremation and this process allowed human remains to be chargrilled and turned into ash. The small part of the remains is then either kept in a little urn, or scattered across the countryside. This in itself has now become an accepted, convenient and popular method, chosen by the humans of today."

The channeller said, "Soon a new process called liquefaction will be the *in* thing and people will choose to turn their remains, or the remains of loved ones, into a liquid substance, to be eventually washed down the drain.

"Let's turn back the clock a few thousand years and take a look at mummification. What is mummification and why did some ancient races use it? Egyptians used this process to preserve bodies and to ensure the decomposition was slowed right down, to give the human body a longer shelf life, as opposed to the other options mentioned previously, like burials and cremation."

Did the Egyptians know something that we didn't know? Was there a practical reason behind their week long process of mummification? We are lucky enough to witness the remains of mummies, even thousands of years later, where the coffin is beautifully preserved, along with the remnants of the former body. I have a theory; maybe the reason behind why they did this was to preserve the body, for the purpose of allowing the reincarnation process to take place at a later date. Rather than letting nature take its course and consume the body back into nature, it slowed the process right down, to ensure the flesh and bones would stay intact for many years *after* the date of death, just in case the soul decided to return to the body.

Many years ago in England, people had a fear of being buried alive, so they came up with an invention of tying a piece of string to the finger of a dead person and attaching it to a bell. There was always someone on the graveyard shift in those days and if they heard the bell ring, they would dig up the grave and the person would literally be *saved by the bell.* This is why it is vitally important to have a mourning period, of at least 3 days, where the family stays close to the body of the deceased and waits for other family members to arrive. It is common for open coffin viewings to occur during this time, in many different cultures around the world.

You'd be surprised how many people are pronounced dead prematurely and how many souls return to their body, after they are classed as clinically dead, or deceased. Miracles *do* happen if you expect them.

God said, "You can easily miss important clues, if you get too caught up in trying to understand the spiritual *reasons*, behind why certain cultures do certain things. In existence now is a super bug that is currently the strongest and meanest bacteria, that eats away the living flesh of a human. It is the very same process that occurs, when a human is bitten by a poisonous spider, or bitten by a poisonous insect that leave a flesh eating bacteria at the bite site.

"Stop and think for a moment. Here we are trying to preserve a dead body, which ultimately means stopping, or slowing down the decomposition process. Why don't we apply the same school of thought to a flesh eating disease like MRSA, or bugs like bacteria? Let's embalm the affected skin area, to slow down the process and save the flesh. I'll leave that little morsel in there for the doctors to work out."

God added, "You need to have the ability to realise that the way things have been done in the past, *may* have worked, but now a better way has been found to do something. Improvements or progress doesn't always have your best interests at heart. Some changes can literally be implemented, just for the sake of making way for progress to occur."

The channeller said, "God's creation in evolution is Darwin's way, but true evolution of the soul, is *not* through survival of the fittest, but by using your faculties for what they were given to you for. You were given a soul, to experience life as a human and learn the lessons that you have chosen to come here to learn. Everything that happens to you, is a result of some action you have participated in, either consciously, or unconsciously, even your death."

God said, "He likens the idea of cremation as a bit demonic, because burning a corpse is such a horrific way to decompose a body, to destroy evidence and he wants you to know, there is nothing natural about it at all. If we are supposed to be living in harmony with nature, then we would give back to nature when we die."

Buried	**Cremation**
Eaten by bugs and contributes to the life force	You don't reincarnate through DNA
Reincarnation is a process	Demonic
Via DNA strands through worms and birds you live on	Do not do it
Become a food source	Nothing but ashes remain

God wants you to look at which animals and creatures have the shortest life.

The channeller said, "Some of the dirtiest animals clean things up for

God and they might only live a short life. Everything has a soul; even an atom has a soul. So a human is made up of a lot of souls, lots of atoms and I am made up of a group of souls, or a group of atoms. You're a comprehension of a group of souls, called a *main soul*, which is yourself."

The channeller continued, "If you lose any part of yourself, for example, if you pee, they can work out, that your atoms are in the pee and they can examine it and work out that it belongs to you. It is your DNA and you are made up of lots of groups of atoms."

The channeller added, "Anything that you gave out, an organ, or a limb, or anything of yours, God knows that this group of atoms belong to you. If you lose an arm, a tooth, or a limb, those items belong to the person they belong to forever!"

Past lives

To grasp the concept of past lives, first you must acknowledge and accept that there is more to life, than just *this* life. For many the concept of life after death can be a real stretch of the imagination and if you truly want to understand past lives, it means there *is* life after life. Imagine that?! This means all of sudden, the sense of urgency to get everything done in just one short life, dissolves away. It means you can appreciate why there is no need for you to travel to every continent on Earth, earn millions of dollars, fulfil every single career desire, marry multiple people, or feel failure if you can't produce children. Now time becomes relative.

In French there is a saying called *déjà vu* and when translated into English it means *already seen*. Have you ever been to a place, met a person, or even been mid conversation with someone and then had a spine chilling tingle all over, or experienced a moment of clarity? A really deep feeling of familiarity of that exact moment and thought to yourself, *wow have I been here before?* You might also experience it as an inner knowing. For me, I like to call them *markers*, or *flags*. They are personal markers that confirm I am on track with my current chosen path. It is a timeline marker which, clarifies that every single thing you have done, before this moment in time, has happened for a reason and that you are *exactly where you are meant to be* at exactly the right time.

Deep down, we all have the ability to tap into this infinite resource of wisdom and we can all remember our past lives, however the memory can be tucked away in the far corner of your mind. There are reasons why we don't automatically remember and this is for our own mental protection and our emotional safety, so we don't have a longing, or a desire to return to Heaven, or want to go back to our past life, as soon as we are born.

When we are born, we are all knowing and we remember our most recent visit in the spirit world. We remember all of the details of our immediate past life vividly and we know exactly what our purpose is. As we grow from a baby to a toddler and learn to speak, we can express our stories of remembrance, to those who are willing to listen. We can tell our family about our imaginary friends, but if no one is willing to listen to these psychic experiences, the stories fall on deaf ears and you no longer feel the need to share this information with anyone, because of the discouragement.

I urge you to talk to your young children and ask them what they remember about their past life, so you can tap into that resource when they are really young. It doesn't matter how silly they might sound, you may discover that you are connected so intricately and you have been selected as their parent, or carer, for a very specific reason.

God said, "Soul families stick together, over multiple lifetimes and they change their position in the family, or group, to suit the learning experience for that particular life. Your daughter may have been your mother, or father in your past life and this time, you get to swap roles. You have lives as both sexes and you get to live to many different stages of life, depending on the specific learning lesson, or particular purpose of that life.

"This is another reason why sexual identity can be confusing for some people, because they feel more female than male, when they are born a boy. That could be, because their most recent incarnation, was as a girl and they have an inner longing for that life. They may have enjoyed it and they haven't quite adapted to their new skin yet."

The channeller said, "We ask to be born the sex we choose, so there is no point getting gender reassignment surgery, or wishing to be another sex, because it doesn't assist with your life's purpose, especially if you have agreed to be a certain gender for procreation purposes, or for another special purpose.

"At birth we go through a traumatic experience, squeezing through the birth canal. It is already traumatic for the mother, but it is equally traumatic for the child. It is no accident this process exists and it happens for a very good reason. One reason we go through this experience, is to *calibrate* ourselves to pain upon birth, so we have a measurement upon which to measure happiness.

"Another important reason we experience the journey through the birth canal, is to distinguish a definitive moment, between ending your last life and beginning your new life. We can travel in time to that moment of birth in any life, because it is a significant *marker* of pain, which can be easily found when scanning for a beginning and an ending, to know and feel where one life starts and another life ends."

The channeller added, "This is the moment that a psychic reader, or hypnotist will tap in, to *calibrate* the start and end point, so they can concentrate on what happened in between those two points, which is the entirety of one of your past lives. It is a mindset that precedes the knowing and the knowing confirms your feelings and thoughts about a person, or a place."

It helps to have someone experienced, who can communicate with the other side and it also helps to have a keen interest, in why you pursue certain hobbies and activities and why you have certain likes and dislikes. It also eases the frustration you might experience, when you have really deep feelings, or a deep connection with someone, whom you have experienced a past life with. It may not have been *ordained* for the two of you to romantically link up in this life.

Through various channellers, I have been given detailed descriptions of my most prominent past lives and the lives, where I have experienced anguish, or died unexpectedly, to help me work through some past life issues. I can use this information to help me with my current life.

God told me, "You left your post for three eternities, because you had a gut full of it all. You never get to take risks on the other side. If you think it's wrong, it's wrong. When you doubt, it will correct you and that sort of thing doesn't happen on the other side. So we can become bored or stagnant with our growth. If you stay on the other side for too long, it gives you the desire to want to experience another life."

When the word *eternity* is used, it means length of time and three eternities, can account for many different lives. Just so you understand, an eternity is *not* infinity, or forever, but it is a very long time.

During these three eternities, I experienced three significant past lives, which I will share with you. I have also had many other past lives that I haven't really delved into that much so far.

Female warrior

God told me that around 1000 years ago I was a female warrior who fought by the sword and I was a descendant of Joshua. I carried six daggers and an 18" sword with a cross. The king made me fight against Israel, a sheik, a king, a pharaoh. The pharaoh at the time was an alien and we were stopping them from destroying the world. I had no choice but to participate in the battle, because we were fighting for the King of the Jews. I led the front line of a 15,000 strong army, in a holy war, to fight the pharaoh in Israel and survived the first battle.

This just gives you a taste of the vast differences, between our past and current lives.

One of my current friends in this life was my phobel during that past life. I have not been able to find out what a phobel is and the word may no longer be used in this era. This is proof to me that even friends can be connected from a past life. We can still link up, even if we don't reconnect again for a thousand years in Earth time. When viewed from the spirit world, an eternity can seem like a long time, but it is not forever.

Dutch captainess

Another past life I have revisited multiple times during these channellings was my life as a Dutch captainess. I was a single woman and I had no children in that life.

I was a Dutch captainess on Dutch ships, between 1656 and 1747. During this life I spent most of my time on the ship commonly known as the *Mary Anne J;* as in Jade. It was a Portuguese built ship. The crew, the ship and everything on it, was constructed and made by the highest of high Portuguese people. I was first in charge of the port, starboard, bow and stern. I was also second in charge of the mid and sextant. The ship eventually ran aground in 1708 and that was the ship's last journey.

During this particular ship's life, the ship voyaged continuously and was in the business of carrying spices from the Caribbean and India, to the Duke in England for around 4000 shillings. If the Duke didn't pay the money, he would have ended up with a mutiny, because the cargo was more valuable than the crew. There were 20 men onboard, which is an odd number to cater for on a ship. There were 36 / 24 / 12 to 24 hour shifts, because you needed sailors to raise the sails and a crow at the lookout, high up on the sail mast. The crow basically ran the ship, as he was watching out for danger all the time.

There were two male soldiers around me, who used to make love to me and they used to cut people, who didn't do what they were told. They couldn't hurt anyone, unless I told them to.

The reason I would go out to look at the stars with the sextant, was to make sure the captain was doing his job. When we were travelling on the Indian Ocean from India to Holland as a Dutch trader, I didn't trust my navigator and I always needed to constantly check things were right with using the sextant, or else you all die. A sailing ropes man on a ship was considered higher up than a captain of the ship in the Dutch army, because he was your lifeline on a ship. You would always call your ropes man, when approaching shore.

When the trading ships arrived at their destination with the cargo, the purchasers of the shipment had to present themselves for collection of the items along with the money. If they didn't pay and sign, they couldn't take the cargo. Security was required at the collection point for this reason. It was difficult to prove ownership of the cargo and many attempts were made to collect cargo that didn't belong to them. This sometimes caused trouble when docked and a double book entry stock system had to be created to stop this issue from occurring.

The value of the cargo was worth a lot of money in those days, because of the journey time it took to cross the oceans and return to the original destination to collect more cargo. This made spices a very desirable product and there was never any cargo left over. The spice trade was lucrative and was always in high demand, because of the medicinal properties in the spices and their various other uses. The time you may have to wait for the ship to return again, could have been months if you wanted to purchase more.

I spent most of my life at sea and when I retired from my position, I missed the sea life and found ways to get back out to sea, through various other methods. I died in my sleep at sea and was happy to die at sea, when I felt that life was completed. God told me that to reconnect with this past life, I need to buy a sextant and look at the stars through it.

This past life explains the connection I feel with the sea and the absolute feeling of calm I get, when I am out in the open ocean on a ship, or on a boat.

One hobby I have a strong passion for in this life is diving, which has led me around the world to many exotic dive locations, to seek the beautiful colours and array of ocean life and mysteries under the sea.

The journey to and from the dive site location, is my favourite time and it is always where I have those moments of clarity, or epiphanies. When diving, you often get to go out in the open ocean, if the dive site is near an ocean reef, or near a group of remote islands. Sometimes it was necessary to traverse across large bodies of water to get to the dive location. This is when I am in my *special place.* The wind is blowing through my hair, the sun is gently touching my face, the soft salt air crystallises on my face and I can taste the ocean, when I lick my lips.

The dense and earthy ocean smell is absorbed through the rest of my body and I anticipate getting into the water, after a long time away from it. This is me reconnecting with my love for the sea.

I also have an intimate *knowing* about navigation using the stars. I can look up into the stars and just know how everything is positioned, which direction is which and have always had an inner compass wherever I am located in the world, which is very useful, because I never get lost. I could never explain how I just *knew* about the stars, but apparently that is the navigator in me. Whenever I look up at the night sky and deep into the stars, I feel totally connected to my past life and *everything.*

This was my past life before the horse wrangling life in the 1800's.

Horse wrangler

I have been told about this life multiple times and by multiple channellers. It was one of my most recent lives on Earth, prior to this life, so it is still relatively fresh on my soul journey. I was born female in the United States near Alabama. My soul name during this incarnation was Alisha. I was raised on a ranch, as a dirt farmer with horses. I had a very close bond with my horse and with horses in general. I became a horse wrangler, due to this relationship and had the ability to tame horses very well.

I had a black and white Basset Hound dog with brown spots, named Beagle, who loved hunting for rabbits. He looked like the typical Fred Basset Hound dog and he used to howl.

My father died of Cholera and I was left to raise the family which included me and two other children, Sarah and Henry. Later in life, I married my husband Jake Davis and we had two children, called Elsie and John. Elsie and John both had two children each, after I died.

My husband Jake was drafted into war and killed by one of his own, while eating his lunch. The bullet went straight through him, from someone in the crew who was a killer. Jake was killed two years before me.

I was well known as the female *horse wrangler* in the district and worked well with horses. I used to tame wild horses and break them in on my ranch. I never branded my horses, because I believed it was a cruel practise and would not allow them to be branded. I carried a double barrelled shotgun on my waist and a magnum six slinger in my pants.

In July 1845, I was accused of horse rustling and stealing horses, which wasn't true. They said I stole the horses from a prominent businessman in town and because my horses weren't branded, they said that I had no way of proving they were my horses and hence made me guilty. My trial was held in the same month and I was hung for horse rustling in July 1845.

The *real* reason I was accused of horse rustling, was because the Mayor of the town fancied me and I was not interested in him. He made an example out of me and hung me for something I didn't do.

My children were left to face life alone, without me and were both publicly humiliated for their mother's crime and fed lies from the townsfolk, about why their mother was hung. This is the main reason the children have a reserved energy, about wanting to come back into this life, because of the trauma suffered in the last life. My purpose on a soul level, if I want my children to reincarnate in this life, is to understand they need *reassurance* that everything is going to be okay and it is *safe* to come back and that this won't happen again.

Later that same year in November, I reincarnated again. I haven't been given details of that particular life yet and haven't really asked.

I have experienced other lives and have been given overviews of each life. In one past life, I was an Indian Sadhu, where I roamed the lands in search of people to help. I had another life as a Nun, where I was constantly sorry for every sinful thought and I was way too humble about even practically existing.

There was one life as a man, where I was murdered for speaking the truth and was given intimate details of my death experience. I don't need to share the gory details with you, because it's not pleasant.

So you get the picture, that I can't just make this stuff up and it really did happen. I haven't had time to travel the world and research libraries and log books to verify the dates and names and it is not the point, because I would be wasting time in this current life chasing my past lives. The details are already so vivid and every past event explained so much more about my characteristics and about myself.

These past lives have such a significant correlation with this current life of mine, that it gives me a deeper understanding and so much more of an appreciation for this life. I no longer need to be convinced of the fact that we do experience multiple lives on our soul journey. Reincarnation definitely does exist. Wouldn't you like to know more about your past lives?

My inner knowing is very active and my belief is so strong, that I now help other people discover their past lives and also help them to understand there is a divine order of things.

There are reasons why you feel that special soul connection with a complete stranger and there are places you have already lived, or visited, that you feel a strong affinity with. There are activities that you love to do and you have no idea why you like doing them, even if they seem out of character for you.

I encourage you to start asking questions, start seeking information and guidance. Open your mind and memory to the secrets buried deep within, because it will help you to unlock your soul's purpose. It will also help you to understand where you are situated on your soul journey.

Psychic ability

All of us have psychic abilities. It is hard wired into our DNA and coded into our brain. We *all* have the key to talk to God and any spirit we want to talk to. Some people are more attuned than others and have really developed their ability through practise and patience. Others seem to just inherit this amazing gift and it comes naturally to them. It doesn't matter *how* the ability works. What really matters is that you *believe* it is possible and this opens up pathways to more communication.

If you don't believe, then your mind tricks you into thinking it doesn't exist. The one thing most people struggle with, is trying to tell the difference between your own inner voice and spirits talking to you, because they are very similar in feelings. What you are actually hearing, are the words in your own voice, so it can be confusing, determining which is which.

A major key to being psychic, is having the ability to project well into the future and seeing a *possible* reality, then being able to describe what you can see. It's about getting into the vibration of somebody, something, or somewhere.

Nostradamus spoke to God, but only asked limited questions.

Warlocks used to be psychic and the kingdoms were frightened of them. Anyone that was either a witch, or warlock practising witchcraft, was killed, because they could potentially overcome the kingdom.

When you have spirits on your land, you can walk around and talk to them, when no one is around and manifest being in a relationship with them. All spirits can be useful and they want to be needed, just like people do. They also want to help you, just like people do and spirits get bored, just like people do.

There are many ways in which people use their psychic abilities, both knowingly and unknowingly. During a waking and conscious state, a psychic will either receive messages from souls, or spirits who have passed over, or from higher beings who reside in a different realm. These beings may, or may not, have lived lives on Earth previously.

Most people engage the services of a psychic, when they want to know what their possible future holds in store for them. They may also want to contact a friend, or a relative who has passed over. Psychics are also good at helping you confirm, if you are on the right track or not. The psychic tunes in to the spirit, or soul of the deceased person and starts to receive confirmation messages, before proceeding with the reading. The confirmation messages that come through in a psychic reading are usually very personal and it is intimate information that is known, only to the person visiting the psychic. The person receiving the psychic messages is asked to either confirm, or deny if the messages are correct. This helps the psychic medium, by letting them know if they are on the right track.

If you are communicating with a spirit, or soul on the other side, who knew you when they were alive and you have shared time, or experiences with them, will give you some detailed information about these experiences, to confirm you know who you are talking to. They also do this to establish your trust, so you don't get scared and run away.

This type of psychic reading is called psychic or spiritual *mediumship* and is useful for communicating with spirits known to you. Every psychic is different and each has their own style and their own talents, in areas of mediumship. Some of their skills and abilities are stronger than others and the psychic usually works with their prominent gift of mediumship.

There are many methods used for mediumship and they generally use one, or a combination of the following skills, or abilities.

- **Hearing** the spirits talking to them (*clairaudience,* or clear hearing).
- **Seeing** the spirits in their mind's eye like an image on a television screen (*clairvoyance,* or clear seeing).
- **Feeling** the spirits touching them, or feeling a strong presence around them (*clairsentience,* or clear feeling).

- **Knowing** what the spirits are communicating to you (*claircongnizance* or clear knowing).
- **Smelling** familiar smells, sensing danger, or ill health with your nose (*clairolfaction* or clear sensing).

Smell is a really interesting and powerful sense that psychics can tap into, or use to sense that a spirit is around. You might pick up the smell of a cigar, a rose, or a fragrance that reminds you of a particular person. Spirits can use these smells to help you remember them, or they might use these as subtle signs, to let you know they are present.

My strongest psychic ability is my *smell* sense. I can smell when someone is sick, getting sick, dying, or if something is wrong. I can smell death and know how far away death is for someone. I can also smell danger if something is very wrong. Spirits like to communicate with me in smells, because I sniff everything, I can't help myself. My mum likes to remind me that when I was little, I used to have a habit where I would smell every plate, cup or dish, before I put any food, or drink into it. I also used to smell *everything*, before it was consumed.

If you are using your smell sense, you will also pick up if there are any hazardous chemicals within range, or maybe in the atmosphere. By using your nose and your sense of smell, you can also pick up that funny smell if there are any harmful or poisonous substances in your food, or drink. Another reason I trust my nose, is I can tell when food is beyond use, when milk isn't right to drink and generally when food and drinks are off, without even opening the fridge door.

Although it is a blessing to have such a wonderful sense of smell, it can be a curse sometimes too, because I can smell *everything!* Having a nose like a dog, means I that can smell body odour, toilet smells and bad breath from way too far away. At least it is a good warning sign to give myself some distance and space, when approaching people and it gives me a good opportunity to steer clear of smelly people and smelly places. I love travelling to Thailand; it really is one of my favourite holiday destinations, once I adjust to the funky smells and the strong odours emanating from the drains.

I also have special *hearing*, which gives me the ability to hear conversations across the other side of the room, out of audible range. I can hear ambulances miles away, low Earth rumbles, birds and animals calling way off in the distance and I can even tune in and out of noisy rooms and pick up what I want to hear at will. I am sure this is why I love producing music so much, because my sense of hearing is so acute and so finely tuned, it would be strange *not* to play with sounds and make something beautiful out of them.

One really amazing thing about having almost multidimensional hearing is that every day is like a symphony of sounds and at night time I can hear the chirp of every nocturnal creature in my neighbourhood. Right now, it's almost midnight and my office window is wide open and I don't hear any humans, cars or industry, just the super high frequency of night life, like the chirping of crickets, squeaking of cicadas, nocturnal birds, squealing bats, the occasional possum hiss, or dog barking in the distance. There are two horses that live across the road from me and now and again, I hear a gentle neigh, or grunt.

When it rains, the frogs and toads are like music to my sensitive ears and I love the frog symphony the best. I prefer the sounds of the night, because I am like a nocturnal creature myself and I feel very connected to the night time and all the wildlife.

I may also hear a meow from the wild cats that I leave food out for, when they come to feed in the early hours of the morning. They meow to say thank you and then they're off again. They are still wild and roam the streets at night. I've seen a couple of rats around this area too, so I'm not too fazed having cats frequenting my yard. I'm actually not much of a cat person, but I do think cats are cute.

All of God's creatures are cute. Growing up in our family home, the most cats we ever had at one time, was a total of five cats. So I have already had my huge dose of cats, when I was living at home. It's a shame they like to eat birds, because I *love* birds and that is why I don't have a cat. I feed these wild cats, because my logic tells me that if the cats have a full belly, they are less likely to want to chase and eat birds. That's my theory anyway.

I am a night owl by nature and I always have been. I think it has something to do with being born very early in the morning. The time of day you are born, sets your biorhythms for life and your ebbs and flows are like clockwork cycles, as you ebb and flow during the day and night. I must admit, I am definitely *not* a morning person and I struggle to get out of bed in the early hours of the morning to go to work, even if I have had a good night's sleep. I am the most alert and the most magical time for me, is after midnight.

An older friend, who worked as a funeral director, once told me that in her opinion, most people die between the hours of midnight and 3:00am. This is the peak time, when she is called out to pick up people who have passed away. There are those that die peacefully in their sleep and those that simply don't make it through the night, because of an ongoing illness. She also told me that people rarely die of only *one* cause. They usually die from more than one ailment, which can make it complicated to work out the *actual* cause of death.

Accidents are more likely to occur during the day, when everyone is active, but people don't always die from accidents. They tend to get a massive wakeup call, when they have a close brush with death. Between midnight and 3:00am is also the most spiritually active time of the night in our house, when we hear noises and strange sounds all around the house, we notice things getting moved and this is when I get my most visitations from spirits. One of the reasons is because it is the quiet time of the night and everyone else is in bed. There are no distractions to keep my mind occupied, just the hum of night wildlife. Then I get to experience pure silence, when all the night creatures go to sleep.

In the past, it was known that the time between 12:00am and 1:00am, was the *witching hour*. This was the time when the most supernatural incidents occurred. I have noticed that it is more like 12:00am through to 3:00am.

It used to freak me out a little bit, if I heard noises in the middle of the night, but my partner now gets to share these experiences with me and also gets to see the objects getting moved as well, so I feel a little bit saner sharing the weirdness. I never get bad vibes when I hear, sense, or feel spirits around me, because my house is a house of God and nothing bad is allowed in my house ever. The most I might hear from bad spirits, is the occasional knock on the door, or *outside* the building, or noises from outside the property. That is as close as they are allowed to get, outside the safe zone and outside my protection barrier and it doesn't bother me. Bad spirits know they are not welcome and that they are not allowed into my house. This is why I hear the symbolic knocking, when they try to come in.

People can be afraid of ghosts and spirits, which I find quite funny. It's only funny, because ghosts can't hurt you. You can hurt yourself by over thinking it, freaking out and allowing the fear to take over your mind.

I would always be more afraid of the *living* than the dead. If a spirit has the power and determination to actually physically move something, or audibly make a sound, then they are really making an effort to communicate with you. You can still help bad spirits to cross over, if you want to. I leave the baddies for God to deal with and God gets his archangels to deal with the baddies when he is too busy, or doesn't want to deal with them personally.

Sometimes when I am really tired, or off in a daydream, I will hear my name being whispered loudly in my ear, or even as loud as a person talking right behind me and I nearly jump out of the chair, because I was ready to drift off, or just zoned out for a minute. Hearing my name snaps me back into myself and reminds me, that the best time to communicate with spirits, is when you are feeling a little bit sleepy, super relaxed, in a meditative, or hypnotic state, or even when you are daydreaming, because your brain is operating in a different state.

The hypnotic brain state is ideal for communicating with spirits, while you are still conscious and it happens when you are slipping, or *falling* from the alpha state down into the theta state. The brain activity changes and you start to pick up on otherworldly sounds and chatter from the other side.

Intuition is something that is often used with psychics, to *pick up,* or *sense* a situation, or to get a general picture of the person's life, or what is currently bothering them. Intuition is like a gut feeling, or just an inner knowing that something is going to happen. This is useful when you or your loved ones are in imminent danger, so you can warn them.

Intuition is also very useful for sensing the presence of spirits, hanging around your immediate space. Psychic healers can use their intuition to pick up on illnesses, or disease in the body, by using their medical intuitive skills to diagnose, or offer suggestions for people seeking treatment. This is a mild method of channelling, but is more in line with psychic mediumship.

People can also communicate psychically with loved ones, while they are asleep in their dream state, or in a relaxed daydream state. People can also have *precognitive* dreams, in which they see future events unfold in their dreams. Sometimes these dreams are shown in such graphic detail, that dreamers can wake up thinking that it has already happened.

If you are communicating with the living, then this is usually classed as *telepathy,* because the soul is still present on the Earth plane. Very gifted psychics can still talk to the souls of the living, just as they can talk to the souls of those who have passed over. If you are thinking about someone and then they call you on the phone, this is commonly referred to as telepathic communication, or mental telepathy, which is something everyone on the planet can and does do, sometimes unconsciously. With practise, you can communicate telepathically with others very effectively, across any distance.

Sometimes psychic gifts are referred to as extra sensory perception, or ESP, because you are going *beyond* the regular five senses of; touching, seeing, hearing, smelling and tasting. ESP goes beyond the five senses and taps into the hidden senses. It is sometimes referred to as the sixth sense.

God said, "There are actually more than seven senses and they will become known."

Another tactile sense that all humans have and can really develop if they want to is their *feeling* sense. I often get touched by spirits throughout the day. Their touch is usually gentle and loving, unless I need to be warned about something, then the touch is a bit firmer than usual. I might even get a visual trigger, like a black shadow crossing my path, when danger is near, or if I need to be on guard.

Darkness cannot hide from me, because I live in the light and I can't help but illuminate the darkness and like a torch, it has to show itself. This is why people feel like they must confess their sins to me, because they feel they are in the presence of the light and they know I do not judge, but simply listen and forgive. No story is too radical for my ears, I have heard it all. As my friends will tell you, if I hear the same story a few too many times, then I won't listen to the poor me stories any longer. I might get a little frustrated with their pace of learning and give them a little spiritual kick in the butt.

I am not afraid of the darkness, because I have 100% faith in the good Lord and he will always protect me in life and death. When I am touched, it is usually on the arm, knee, or hand. Sometimes they touch me on the head, or face and it feels it like a sensation of goose bumps, localised in a certain area, like the brush of a feather, because it is so light. When spirits try to jump into your body, or many spirits want to be all around you, you will feel their presence very strongly, like the sensation of soft prickles entering the skin, or intense goose bumps all over your body and even on your scalp. If you don't like the feeling, you can simply tell the spirits to go back to where they came from, or ask them to leave you alone.

It is important for me to *acknowledge* the presence of spirits, by saying hello and letting them know I can sense them, so they don't have to keep trying to get my attention and moving things around and spooking me out. Darker energies feel more like heckles, sharper prickles, or make the hairs on the back of your neck stand up. It's the same feeling you get when you see, or meet someone you really don't like and you get a *bad vibe* about them. If you get that feeling from a person, or a spirit, you can say the Lord's Prayer out loud, or in your mind and they will disappear very quickly. Saying it out loud is more effective, because even demons attached to a living body, will run away when you start talking about God, or reciting anything remotely biblical, or holy.

Demons and bad spirits are afraid of God, Jesus and the archangels and run like mad when you call in the holy helpers. The reason they run away, is because they are scared of getting in trouble and they know that if God wants to destroy them, he can. They too are still learning just like young earthly souls are and being aware they are lower than humans on the Godly scale, makes them appear less scary. You can command that they leave with the authority of the Almighty Lord God, if you don't want them hanging around. They also get curious and want to see what people are doing and occasionally pop in to visit.

To avoid attracting negative presences and evil spirits, you need to avoid activities that may attract negative entities. There are many activities that *could* attract demons, or open portals to allow demons into your house, or the location where you are. Avoid watching horror movies, paranormal shows about demons, watching horrible things on TV, getting really angry in a fit of anger, feeling enraged, feeling guilty, getting blind drunk, having too many drugs, taking too many prescription medications, watching people getting hurt, black witchcraft, Ouija boards, séances, extreme depression, some forms of mental illness, listening to demonic music, killing, or hurting anyone, or anything, having bad thoughts (really bad thoughts), not just your silly bad thoughts and any other negative activity that you think might invoke the presence of a demon inadvertently.

Aiming to master your psychic awareness, will give you full scope and understanding of this world you live in. It will give you a better understanding of the other side and a glimpse into other realms that exist, in the same time and space as you.

Being psychic does not automatically make you smarter and nor does it make you perfect. I know some psychics that have some serious personal issues and are by no means perfect. They try really hard to do the right thing most of the time, but they are still human. They still make mistakes like everyone else.

Attempting to use their own psychic abilities on themselves, can backfire and doesn't often work as well as using the gift on others. It's a bit like a dentist who isn't able to fix his or her own teeth properly. They also need to go to a different dentist to get their teeth fixed, or assessed. It is the same for a hairdresser. It is tricky to cut, colour and style their own hair and they know sometimes they need to go to another professional, to get this work done properly.

Objects and places

God said, "Every object and place, has a cellular, or realm memory. If you stand still in one place on the Earth, try to imagine what was in that exact same place a year ago, 50 years ago, 100 years ago and even 1000 years ago. This is how you can pick up the vibrations, or pick up the cellular, or realm memory from a place. You will feel, or see events that happened in that place and who lived there previously, who died there previously and even what the place may potentially look like, if you fast forward into the future. Is the location under water, has it been destroyed, or is it the same but with different people living there?"

A similar vibration is emitted from objects. In the psychic world, the gift of working with objects is called *psychometry*. It is when you use an object, a photograph, a belonging, or an item that belongs, or used to belong to someone. The contact with the object, allows you to tune in to the person who owns, or who used to own the object. Psychometry also lets you tune in to anyone, who has come into contact with that object.

The subtle layers of cellular and realm memory that are attached to an object can be very complex and can cause confusion if a psychic is attempting to do a reading, based off an object. If it is a very personal object owned by only one person, then it will give a much clearer *impression* than an object that has been handled, or owned by multiple people. This can muddy the reading and give mixed results when trying to tune in to only one of the owners. If there have been multiple owners, then you might be picking up on any one of the previous owners, or getting fragments of all of them, which will confuse the person, both giving and receiving the psychic reading.

No *object* is required, to tune in psychically to someone, or something. It is more for the benefit of the person receiving the reading. Psychics who lack confidence, can use this technique, while they are warming up and they can also use this technique, to help people if they are uncomfortable getting a psychic reading. If the person who owned the object is now deceased and the psychic wants to tune in to the vibration of that particular spirit, when they were alive, they can use psychometry to do this. It is particularly useful for locating missing people, who may be either alive, or dead.

Psychic attack

Psychic attack can come from two sources, the living and the dead. The likelihood of it coming from the dead is low, because once they have passed over; they have work to do and are usually busy doing that.

If the psychic attack is coming from a deceased person, then it is more like a haunting, or an attempted possession. It can be targeted toward an individual, with whom the spirit, or ghost has a vendetta, or it can be targeted within a location, for example, where the person died, or frequented often.

If it is a location that is being troubled by psychic attack, then it could simply be that the ghost hasn't transitioned to the other side properly and they are stuck in the astral plane in between worlds. They need assistance transitioning across and sometimes the spirit doesn't want to transition, because they are anchored, or grounded here to the Earth and the astral plane for a reason.

If the psychic attack is coming from a living person, or even worse a group of living people, then we are dealing with a spiritual sin. Anyone who comes from the intent of love and light, from the pure Source, who works with the Almighty God and the angelic realms, knows that to use their psychic gifts to inflict harm upon another, whether they be a living, or dead would be considered to be operating under the disguise of black magic. In God's eye's, it is not allowed, because of the *intent* that is associated with its practise. This is when you are likely to see the scary supernatural or paranormal activity.

Those who direct their darkness, may be unaware and they will ultimately have to answer to the higher spiritual beings, or the Supreme Creator for their misdemeanours. As the law of attraction states, what you put out, on a vibrational level, is what you get back. Karmically, they are setting themselves up to pay for their ill intent, by receiving in turn an act of equal darkness to be inflicted upon them. It can lead to a series of unfortunate events and can cause things to happen that are not very pleasant to witness, or feel, if you are either the victim, or the perpetrator of psychic attack.

The big question is; *how do you protect yourself from psychic attack?* You protect yourself with the faith of the Almighty Lord God, or his son Jesus Christ. You put on your holy armour, before engaging in any spiritual work and you engage in prayers of protection, as often as you feel necessary to ward off evil spirits, or people. Living in a perpetual state of bliss, love, kindness and faith, is the best way to vibrate at a high enough level and emit a powerful enough white light, to detract and repel negative spirits, or entities.

God said, "If are ever under attack spiritually, use the strength of the words and feeling that, if you kill, or destroy someone holy, there will be a thousand more to take your place!"

This is a short prayer you can use when you are being confronted by your enemies, which has been given to you directly from God Almighty.

The Creator's Prayer

The Father who art thou in heaven, the Creator of all the Heavens
Take my hand and we shall dance as one, for you created me in Heaven
For I have gone to explore your creation, knowing that you will guide me
Not into temptation and deliver me from all of evil
So I may return to you forever, as you created eternity for all
And you are the Creator
For you are the Father and deliver me into your arms
Amen

Communicating with spirits

God told me, "Manifesting a relationship with spirits, is about focusing on one spot and blocking and fading out every other sound, visual image and distraction. Then with your third eye (mind's eye), manifest what they look like. What are they wearing? What are they saying? This is the process for conjuring spirits you want to talk to."

God continued, "A spirit is waiting in another zone, or area, like a software program on a shelf. You can actually conjure them up and rerun them, like pushing the *on* button. When you pull them into this side of the realm, the living realm, this almost gives them a physical body in this realm. Spirits only come to life when we rerun them. This is the rawest state of being a spirit."

God added, "People who are alive on this plane of existence, can enjoy Earth and experience all it can offer. A spirit is disadvantaged, only in this realm, because it no longer has a body, but it still exists in the ether.

"When a channeller is in communication with a spirit, they can feel the temperature of where the dead person lays and they can feel the conflict between being in two places at once."

Sometimes when using both digital and analogue cameras, you can capture spirits, orbs and otherworldly entities. One photograph I took in the caves at Springbrook in Queensland, showed souls that were all huddling together. They stayed in the cave to look out at the stars and that was the attraction from that particular location in the cave.

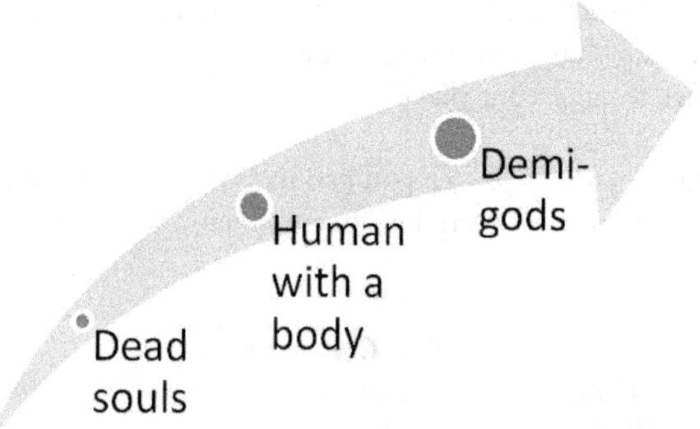

The hierarchy of souls

God raised the question, "What is a spirit? What is a soul?"

The channeller responded on behalf of God, "They work for God and they are created from God. Some souls or spirits help others. The soul can't be complex, because they can only do a certain amount of things. That's why a soul looks up to God."

The channeller continued, "You need to start making friends on the other side. The teachings here, the friends here and you were asked if your friend was your friend forever. Meeting someone is nice, but is it forever? Have you had an infinity friend before? Someone who wants to be your friend forever."

Over the years, through the channellers, I have had the personal benefit of speaking to so many people, who have passed over and are now on the other side.

In society we often use the term *spirits*, to describe dead people, but they are still essentially people. They are just in another realm and in a different state of existence, but their soul is still in the soul line of the human race and even in spirit form, they are still classed as *people*.

I have an elder, who is my Māori warrior spirit guide. He is related to me, through my lineage and looks out for me all the time. When he comes to visit me, he always wants to be inside the channeller's body, so he can walk around and look at things and *see* where I am living and *feel* the surroundings. He is so funny, because he reacts very oddly to things in the modern world and he feels a bit out of place in this world. It is so different from the world he lived in, when he was alive hundreds of years ago.

Everything has changed so much, that it is amusing to both him and me. There is so much technology on this plane of existence now and we have so many *material* things surrounding us, that didn't exist when he last lived a life on Earth. It can be quite overwhelming for him, or any spirit to visit us here in a physical form.

If you want to start to talk to spirits, spirit guides, or anyone holy, it is best to go to a well known, or *reputable* psychic, or channeller first, to get the dialogue happening between worlds. A word of warning about psychics I should mention is that each psychic is unique and their abilities differ from one another. You shouldn't expect to get the same information from multiple psychics and you shouldn't expect them to use the same set of skills, or techniques. Their ability and confidence will determine the quality of your reading and whatever you get on the day is what you get, no more, no less.

One thing most lightworkers, or psychics do, is only communicate through the love and light of the God force, or the Creator and ask for holy protection prior to starting. This can mean that some spirits are not allowed to contact you and are not permitted within the space, during the reading. You will be safe with a reputable psychic and you can use your own gut feeling, to get a vibe from them, to see if they know what they are doing.

Usually, the first thing good psychics do, is start the reading with a warm up routine, or technique they may use, by *tuning in* to your vibrations when you arrive. They might start asking you questions and they will start getting information about you, as soon as they are tuned in. This is to firstly confirm they are connected to the right person, being *you* and secondly they will connect to the strongest and most dominant spirit, who wants to talk to you first. Generally the spirit that wants to talk to you the most is the spirit that you feel around you the most. You may think of them often, because this is the spirit you have the strongest connection with. It is almost always a person who has passed over, that knew you well and it could be a parent, partner, child, relative, friend, or even a colleague.

Spirit guides will come to speak with you, if you are asking specific questions that your spirit visitors can't answer and the spirits that come to visit you, are usually escorted by a higher being, or a spirit guide who waits in the background and supervises the communication. The contact can be received and cut off, at any time without warning, because there is no set method to how a reading rolls out. The more gifted and experienced the psychic is, the more they can control how the conversation starts and ends.

When God communicates through a channeller, he doesn't need to be escorted, because he escorts himself. It is very rare that you will get to speak to God through a psychic medium, because it is God who chooses who to speak to, or through and many times it is unannounced. You can also talk to God yourself, by manifesting being in a relationship with him.

The psychic medium during a psychic reading, will usually confirm something very personal about you, that only the spirit knows, like an experience, an event, an item, or maybe they will describe a common place that you have both been to. It is almost like playing a game of charades for the first few minutes, until everyone gets acquainted with each other and you confirm the past relationship together.

If you don't have any specific questions to ask, then a general overhead reading of your life is conducted. You may be reminded about past events that have occurred in this life and why these events have happened. You may be given clarity on what the purpose of these life events was. This can really help you to overcome repeated negative patterns and break bad habits. You will usually be given an overview of where you are currently sitting, in terms of purpose in your life right now. Then the spirits will push forward into your future and let you know of any potential events to prepare for, people coming into and departing from your life and provide any warnings to be given, if necessary. If you are really lucky and have time, you can also be given the extra special treat of information about your *past* lives. For me personally, this is when it gets really interesting.

Spirits may need to translate to you, through unknowns, like other psychics, until you become strong enough to ask questions yourself. Once you become spiritually awakened, or begin tapping into your own psychic ability, then you will start to realise that all souls are able to contact one another.

God said, "If you ask for the name of the soul you are channelling, you are channelling to yourself. Only the souls in this realm, can ask of the name of who they want to speak to, because you are a soul talking to another soul. If you are a recognised soul, the smaller soul asks for this person to talk to you, because of this reason."

Over the years, through the many channellings and working with various channellers, I have been visited by not only the holiest of holies, but also Jesus, Mother Mary, Archangels Michael and Gabriel, Janis Joplin, Michael Jackson, Robin Williams, Kurt Cobain, Johnny Cash, Louis Armstrong, friends, family and relatives who have passed over, during this lifetime. Work colleagues who I have worked with, have also been in contact with me during their dying process, even when they hadn't quite passed over yet. Sometimes I knew about their death before the general public. It can get very tricky when this happens, because you feel like you want to do something to intervene, but are told that you have to allow the process unfold naturally.

Once they have actually passed over, they may come and visit me to tell me what happened, or critical information about their circumstances. I learn a lot from souls who have transitioned and I get to hear about the transition process and any difficulties they may be facing in the afterlife. If they come and visit me, I always pray for them and ask God to forgive them and to welcome them into Heaven.

Once you open up your gift, you will be given a flood of information about people known to you, both alive and passed over. It is not your job to share that information, it is more like an inner knowing, or confirmation of information that you need to know for your own interest, or to benefit the person you may be doing a reading for. Sometimes you will feel compelled to pass on a message or information that comes through to you and if it is appropriate, you can pass this message along. Sometimes the message is just for the psychic, to help them with their spiritual progress and also to help them to have a deeper understanding of people.

People, who are living and deceased, are both entitled to the same level of privacy. The only exception to this rule would be if there is foul play involved and you have been asked to provide information about the deceased person and there is an understanding that this information cannot be used against you. In this case you need to ensure a disclaimer, or waiver of some description is signed, prior to divulging this type of information for your own safety. The establishment still doesn't recognise psychic ability as being accurate, or reliable.

When I am working with psychic channellers, I don't usually ask for any specific person. We allow whoever wants to come through, if they have something important to say, or a special message to pass on. I like to let it unfold naturally, without any interference from me. I am good at asking questions and everyone loves to answer a good question, including those who are on the other side.

I seem to attract musicians that have passed over, because I am a musician myself and they want to teach me things about song writing and offer musical riffs and lyrics they know I would like. They flood me with unfinished songs, messages for their loved ones and stories about their life while they were alive. Some things I am told, I cannot act on, but just have the knowledge for my own personal interest. It is not my purpose to disclose that information, or make it more complicated for the surviving family members of the deceased. I have already been subconsciously channelling songs from a young age and who knows where some of these songs came from? Sometimes musicians that come through will start singing to me and I recognise them instantly, from the songs they have sung in the past.

Sometimes God wants me to know things about certain people. This could be people I work with, people I do business with, people I have had previous encounters with and also people I will have encounters with, in the future. God gives me a better understanding about people who have passed over and why they died, what they could have done to prevent it and why sometimes it is just someone's time to go. There is nothing you do can save them, because it is just their time. Remember the birth and death date of a soul is already preordained or predestined and it forms part of the soul agreement, for living here on Earth during this life.

God told me, because he wanted me to know things that could help me when making decisions in the future. He tells me things that might help to heal people, or give me extra knowledge, when I am trying to understand a complex problem, surrounding a particular situation, or person. God gives the best advice I have ever heard and he is always so straightforward with his answers. In fact, the answers are always so simple and so straightforward, that it makes me feel stupid for not knowing it, or not considering it in the first place. It always surprises me, why I hadn't already thought of it. God's solutions and answers to complex problems are often so profound, that I wonder why nobody had thought of it before.

Humans think they are so smart, with their complicated psychological analysis of people and they can often be so wrong. He laughs at how complex humans make their own problems and tries to dumb it down for me, so that the solution is easier to see. Humans make the problem more complicated, by over thinking it, or assuming too much about another person, or situation and sometimes, they are *way off target* with their beliefs.

God likes to set the record straight, so I don't get too far off track. God is brutally honest with his findings, because he has no need to hide anything from me, or be politically correct, or unnecessarily polite. He *is* the model of political correctness and God is who we should be using as our ultimate role model. God likes to bring us back to our grass roots. Remind us of the basics and make us aware of the joy that can be found in the *simplicity* of life.

God loves to tell me about religious figures who have passed over and also those who are still alive, including the Dalai Lama, because he knows who truly loves him within their hearts. He knows the Dalai Lama loves him within his heart, but God states that even the Dalai Lama has doubts that need to be cleared up, because he doesn't always listen to God either. God really wants them to know that if they just asked and *believed*, they would have God in their life every day.

The channeller said, "God already exists within them and yet they are so confused and keep asking the same question over and over again, 'Why doesn't God talk to me?' God *does* talk to you all the time, you just don't *hear* him, or more to the point, you just don't *listen!*"

I would love for the Dalai Lama to ask me what God said about him, because he would be fascinated and intrigued and many of his longings and unanswered questions would be answered. God gave me quite a few pages which were dedicated just to the Dalai Lama. Of course, God knows intimate details about every single one of us on this planet and he is happy to share these details with me.

God told me, "When the current Dalai Lama's mother and father died, he felt very alone and it took him many days after each death, to reconnect with the God feeling. This is common for all of us, when we are experiencing grief. Grief is an unusual emotion that can bring out feelings of anger, guilt, shame and even hatred in some cases. These emotions only arise, because people don't take the time, to clear up their issues with people while they are alive. It is a lot harder to sort out these feelings, once the person has passed over. If you have something to say to someone, say it while they are alive. If you love someone, tell them. Don't wait until it is too late."

The channeller on behalf of God said, "He also feels that it is a one way communication and when the Dalai Lama realises, that the sound of God is *invisible* and that it may be his own thoughts, then he will understand that he has already been communicating with God all this time. Then he can *enlighten the world* and **yes** that sentence was from God, to *you* the Dalai Lama! He has a lot more to say to you and maybe one day you can talk to me about it."

The channeller speaking for God continued, "And now that you know this, you have heard my voice all along and doubted me. It has taken you this long to realise, who I am and who *you* are. You are a part of me and I am a part of you and we are all one, *Buddha.* God wants to talk to you about your kingdom on Earth. He also wants you to know, that they tainted you as a child, so you couldn't hear God."

God reminds us of the constant internal doubt that is raised, when you keep asking yourself the same silly question, *does God really exist?* It's like baby steps and you can't progress beyond that point, until you accept that he *does exist,* because otherwise you will keep questioning the information you are getting from God. *Did I really just hear that? Was that God? Yes, no? I'm not sure. I'm confused!* Can you see the problem with doubt? It ultimately slows down your spiritual progression.

You need to work out how to get the human body and mind into *alpha* mode, to help you to communicate with spirits. You can do this with guided meditations, using sound therapy such as binaural beats or isochronic tones, or learning advanced meditation techniques.

God said, "There is a ranking system in the spirit realm. There are millions of spirits and they all reside somewhere. They are allowed to enter certain areas and not allowed to enter other areas, for very good reasons.

"People concern themselves with worry, by thinking that communicating with spirits is opening a demonic doorway and it should be avoided at all costs. If you believe this, then you are also terminating the same link that you would use to communicate with God and the angels.

"Imagine it is like a telephone line, that you use to contact anyone on the other side. You can choose to have a *secure* line, where only spirits from the higher realms can communicate with you and in this case, you would specify this intention *prior* to starting your session. You might want to allow lower level vibratory realms to be able enter the conversation. It is possible, that this is where your loved ones, who have passed over, are currently residing. There are spirits who vibrate at this level, who also require assistance transitioning to higher vibratory levels, or realms."

As long as you have spiritual protection, or utilise the services of someone who has that skill set, then they will be asking for the protection on your behalf. It is important to note that all people and all spirits on the other side, are learning as well and that can sometimes mean on this side, lower level entities may also want to learn from you, so they will hang around you. Not necessarily to harm anyone, but simply to learn. It is very complex when it comes to spirits and realms and if you don't understand it, don't dabble in what you don't know. For those of you who are willing to learn, then this book is a good starting point, to understand the two different worlds, both ours and theirs.

If you seek the light, then you will attract the light and if you intend that only the good shall seek you, then that is what you will manifest. If you seek the dark, you will attract the darkness, but be warned, you are literally playing with fire and attracting something you may have no control over, so just don't do it. If you play with the Devil, you are going to get *burned.* Only seek the love and light on the other side, just as you should only seek the love and light within living people.

Channelling

Channelling happens, when the person who is communicating with the spirit, or being, allows more direct contact and it is usually seen as a higher level of psychic communication. Psychics don't generally channel and don't always feel comfortable channelling, because there is an element of losing control of your own identity and yourself, when you use this method of communication.

To channel, means you have to give up your ego completely and just be *in the moment.* Be still and allow yourself to simply be the channel. This enables the channeller, to be the non-judgmental path of communication, between this world and the spirit world.

You really need to know what you are doing and have no fear, so that you remain safe while channelling. If you don't know what you are doing, or attempt to do channelling, without the proper preparation and protection, you can attract lower level entities, who may attach themselves to you. Lower level entities can also make you feel sick, drained and can alter your mood and personality.

Even when higher level entities are channelled, it can still be exhausting for the channeller, because they have to *tune in,* with their whole mind and body, to get a secure and safe line of communication.

Psychic mediums often prefer to just be the messenger, who simply passes on a second hand message they receive and offer spiritual guidance, to help people reconnect with their loved ones. Psychics can communicate using all of their standard senses, as well as their extra sensory perception, or ESP.

Another method of channelling is called *automatic writing,* where you mentally and spiritually prepare yourself, to write whatever you are being told in your mind, or guided to write onto paper, or through typing. When using this method, you cannot second guess, or question what is being received. You simply scribe what you are receiving and you can read what came through, when you have finished.

Song writing is a good example of automatic writing and is used by many song writers and musicians, without them even being aware.

I know a lovely lady who uses automatic writing as a method of psychic communication and I have had a few readings from her over the years that have all been extremely accurate. She is very quiet while she is scribing and waits until she has written the answer and then reads it back to you, so that she doesn't influence what information is being channelled. Automatic writing is a form of trance channelling and any distractions can make the writing disjointed, or inaccurate, so it is important to be in a calm space and to be in a spiritual mindset, when doing this work.

Some of this book was in fact channelled, directly through me, while I was typing, or expanding on a particular topic. When I reread the book later, I thought to myself, *hmm did I really write that?* It didn't seem like it was written the way that I would normally write something. I ask in my mind where the channelling was coming from. Then I get told; it is coming straight from God. God is reading this book in real time with me, while I am writing it and correcting it as I go along.

God laughed, "Well it is supposed to be the **Word of God**, so we better get it right then!"

When I am working with a channeller, I find it so fascinating and this is by far the most interesting method of receiving communication, from the spirit world. One of the channellers that I work with, the one that usually channels the Creator has an amazing psychic gift and this particular psychic can channel *any* entity they choose. If I am working with this specific channeller, I mainly prefer to talk to God through them, because you can't get any higher than that right? Why would I want to talk to anyone else, when I can talk directly to The Boss? If I have the choice to talk to *anyone* in the whole Universe, then I can't think of any other soul who I would rather talk to, except for Jesus, so why not ask to talk to God? After all the Creator is the one in charge, the one who makes everything happen, the one who made everything!

The Creator is so amazing, that I cannot put into words how I feel, when I am in his presence. If you could feel what I feel, when I am with him, you would never doubt him again. I am so grateful for my existence and God knows it and that is why he comes and talks to me.

God knows that I am beyond the baby questions like, *does God really exist?* Each time I get visited, we both like to get straight down to business and right now that means finishing this book. It is funny, because we often pick up exactly where we left off with the last conversation, just like you do with friends. That's because God *is* my friend and he can be your friend too. He is everyone's friend. In fact he is everything's friend.

Over the years, I have seen and experienced many supernatural and amazing things that would make most people freak out and run a mile. Not always in a scary way, but you do really need to have a solid foundation of faith and trust in the Lord and you need to know what you are doing, to ensure the safety of the channeller and safety of the scribe.

God is not much of a show pony, so he doesn't do tricks, or perform for people on demand and even at the slightest hint of being located, or listened to during a reading, by anyone other than the channeller and the scribe, he disappears. This is for our safety, more than God's and he respects the secrecy and importance of this information and doesn't want anyone, or anything interfering with its release, or tainting it.

God is wise and all knowing, so he *knows* when we have ears, or eyes that are observing, or listening where they shouldn't be, both in the physical world and the spirit world.

When I talk to God, it is like having a conversation with an old friend that I have known forever. I am allowed to tell him all my troubles and I can ask him anything and he will answer almost anything I want to know. Some things are to remain secret and mysterious, so he tells me when I am not allowed, or not supposed to ask a certain question. It may be because he knows something, or knows that someone is listening that shouldn't be there, or else it could simply be that I am not quite ready to learn about a particular topic.

When the channeller is in full physical trance channelling mode, they can allow their body to be used by the spirit, entity, or soul, either momentarily, or for a longer period of time. The longer the channeller allows their body to be used, the more physically drained they become and the less they remember about the experience. This makes it very important for the person who is with them, to realise that anything they say during their channelling, is coming directly from the spirit, or entity being channelled. So this means, the conversation I am having with the channeller, is *not* actually with the channeller anymore, it is directly with the spirit, or entity. The channeller becomes like an empty vessel, a blank canvas that has been borrowed by the spirit, or higher level being.

The channeller feels hollow and empty and has to wait in the background, until the conversation has finished and then they can take full control of their own body again. If the channeller is tired, or run down, the communication can only last for a short time, because channelling uses a great deal of psychic and physical energy.

Any time the channeller wants to take control of their body again, they can send the soul back to where it came from, even God. God usually knows when the channeller is tired, or had enough and pre-empts the exit, by letting me know that he has to go.

Channellers' have to be very clear with their intentions, so they don't accidentally invite unwanted entities in the process. One thing the channeller's don't want to do is allow spirits to stay longer than they are welcome, because they can become difficult to evict, the longer they stay in the body. The spirit enjoys being in the body and sometimes they may not want to leave, when you want them to.

The church may even class channelling when it gets to this point as *possession*; however they need to understand that one action is *voluntary* (channelling) and the other is *involuntary* (possession). It all comes down to invitation and intent. There are rules that spirits must adhere to and if they are not invited, they are not welcome. What happens with possession is that people *unknowingly invite* the presence of unwanted spirit possessions, by doing certain things, or acting in a certain way, that attracts bad, or negative spirits. These spirits can take advantage of you, if you let them.

If a person is under the influence of drugs, alcohol, prescription medication, some hallucinogens, or affected by some type of mental illnesses, spirits can use this as a gateway entry point and see it as an opportunity to jump into the body of any person, who has lost control of themselves. Sometimes humans *want* to completely lose control, by getting written off by drugs or alcohol and this is when possession can become very dangerous, especially when dealing with demonic possession.

There are some very silly people, who like to dabble with the dark side and black magic and believe me they have no idea what they are dealing with and should just stay away from doing that, for their own and other's safety. It is not a fun thing to do, it shouldn't be used as a party trick and it certainly isn't as trendy as they make it look on the television and in the movies. It can be so much uglier and scarier than you have ever seen before and it can be enough to put you off ever attempting to channel. Once a demonic spirit gains control of someone's body, they can be very difficult to evict and the person whose body has been taken over, can start to experience no end of trouble with their life, until they seek help to clear, or remove the entity from their body.

There are very few entities that are allowed to use the body of the main channeller that I communicate with, because they only allow holy entities to channel through them and very few souls like God, Jesus and sometimes the archangels, only if they have an important message to communicate and it has to be with the channeller's permission.

There are rules of engagement with channelling, that both the light and the dark side must abide by, rules set by the Creator, which all spirits must adhere to. This is why *invitation* is the key gateway and you can invite spirits even subconsciously, which is why you must be in control of your own mind and body, at all times, unless you are experienced at dealing with channelling. Very rarely, the channellers will allow my relatives to use their body, so they can have a hug, or hold my hand, or experience something really special, like spending time with me, doing something I like to do. My relatives ask nicely and if the channeller feels comfortable doing this, it is allowed. If the channeller is not comfortable, it is not allowed.

Usually I am not permitted to touch the channeller, while they are channelling, but if they want to touch me, by holding my hand, guiding me, feeling my face, or hair, they are allowed to and I allow it. Touching during a channelling session is never sexual, or sensual, it is only ever spiritual.

When God is being channelled, sometimes he talks so fast, that I can barely keep up with all of the information. I get frustrated, because I want to share the experience and his words of wisdom with the whole world, but I am also acutely aware, there are rules of engagement and you cannot force the Creator to talk to you, whenever you want them to.

I always make the most of the time I get to spend with God and sometimes I have to ask God to repeat himself, if I miss something. God gets frustrated with me too, because I am not as fast as him and sometimes I just can't keep up. He usually comes to visit, whenever he wants to and not necessarily when I am ready, or prepared. I don't just pick up the spirit phone and dial God and *bam* he is there. I wish it was that easy, I would be calling him up all the time for a chat! I could literally be anywhere, doing anything when it happens. It is so random, that I can never predict when and where and I can never interfere with the process.

In extremely rare cases, I have witnessed God talking to other people using the channeller's body. If the channelling occurs in a public place, where there are others close by, but not right next to me, God may pick up on their struggles. God, using the channeller's body, then walks off and wants to go and talk to them. This means I have actually been present and seen random people being spoken to by God. The person, who receives the communication, is usually very shocked and stands there with an astonished look on their face. Many times they breakdown and cry, because God knows things about them, that only that person knows themselves. God will say something to them, which is important to them, or whisper words of encouragement to them. He may even give them a big hug, to comfort them in some way.

This action to me, is more proof of his all knowing wisdom and that he can talk to *anyone* he likes, *whenever* he likes. Recognising when it is God speaking directly to you, through someone else, is a challenge most people can't even comprehend.

The first few times when the channeller had slipped into full channelling mode and asked me, "Who do you want to speak to?" I wasn't sure if they were mucking around or having a lend of me. After this happened a few times, I thought to myself, *I'm going to try this.*

So I answered, "I want to speak to *God.*" I mean, *why not?*

The first time God actually spoke to me through a psychic channeller, I dropped to my knees in shock and disbelief. Years of wondering if God was real, or not, had finally been answered. God's voice was so distinct and truly unmistakable. I was so humbled by this first encounter; that it took years of talking to God, to come to terms with this new reality. I kept thinking, *how is this even possible?*

If God has a choice which language he prefers to speak in, it is always Hebrew and if he chooses to automatically write, it is often in Hebrew, with the translation in English as well, which means two spiritual entities had to help in that case. One to write and one to translate. In the first few visits I had from God, a lot of what he said to me, was in Hebrew and in a very deep booming voice, which was a little bit scary at the time. To begin with, he was very serious, like I was disturbing him in the middle of doing something. I wasn't comfortable hearing Hebrew, because I couldn't understand it. It was a very guttural and direct sounding language, so I couldn't get the emotion of what he was trying to convey.

I asked God, "Please talk to me in English only, so I can understand you."

God laughed and apologised. Then he reverted speaking to me in English.

At first it was daunting, because I wasn't completely sure if I was talking to God, or if it was another spirit playing tricks with me, but over time, years in fact, God has proven to be God, over and over again. Now I am absolutely sure who I am talking to. When our communications first began, I wasn't allowed to record, or write anything down, because God was still establishing his trust with me. Now that he knows I can be trusted fully, I am only allowed to write, or type as he speaks; still no recording devices are allowed.

Then God asked me to write this book, how could I refuse?

God is the king of *random.* His visits are random and he likes to keep it that way, so he can't be tracked and no one can predict when and where he is going to visit next. He loves all things random and this is shown in his infinite creations. Everything *looks* random, like the stars in the sky, but everything actually has a purpose and each thing he creates, has an order all of its own. It is like organised chaos. To us it seems random, because it is beyond our level of understanding and comprehension, but to God, everything is exactly where it is meant to be and works exactly as it is meant to. The only exception to this rule is when the dark side tries to interfere with God's perfect order. That is the true chaos, the disorder, the random destructive helix, the unbalanced things in the Universe that sometimes get out of control and need to be pulled back into line.

If God believes, or feels that someone is in dire trouble, suicidal, or extremely depressed and I am already passing this location on the way through, he will ensure that I am sent there by some divine guidance to make sure that everything is okay. God will ask me to pass on a message to the person. This is when I get to hear God directly. It is very distinctive when I hear his voice, or his intent. He is very commanding with his presence and there is no doubt in my mind where it is coming from.

When you hear his voice it is like your own voice, because your internal talk is your own voice, but with more punch and firmness. Each spirit or entity's voice has its own distinct trademark, or unique tone, that helps you to recognise the identity.

When I am asked to pass on a message, sometimes that is all people need to hear, when they are at rock bottom. They just want confirmation that *someone* knows they are alive and they *are* loved. If they learn that God is real, on many occasions, this is all they wanted to know. They may have been asking for confirmation their whole life and have finally received it.

Fortune telling

Fortune telling is a form of divination, which is used to *predict* the future. It was a term they used in the old days, to describe spooky psychics. Traditionally it conjures images of crystal balls, gypsy caravans, witches, circus side shows and magic. Over the centuries, it has also earned itself a reputation for magic tricks, with trickery practised by charlatans, fakes and cheats. These days in the modern world, fortune telling is now called psychic reading, or channelling. There are still many places around the world that still refer to this ancient practise of divination, as fortune telling.

Divination itself, means being able to gain knowledge of the future, foresee the unknown by supernatural means, with the assistance of the divine realm. In recent years it has become more accepted as a mainstream form of practical future advice, but it wasn't always available to the general public. Throughout history, those in positions of power, royalty, high religious orders and members who are high up in society, have had access to the best of the best and often consulted their *oracles* on matters of great importance, before making any final decisions.

Going back even further in time than oracles, there were witchdoctors, high priests and high priestesses, that had access to these supernatural communication tools and their opinion was well respected and even feared. If they were well known for their abilities, they were even highly sought after and paid a fine sum for their advice. They were often consulted on matters of war, love, fame, fortune, investment, farming and future events.

There are many methods of divination still used today and they can vary greatly between cultures, traditions and religions. Some methods include; scrying with crystal balls and mirrors, trance meditation, trance channelling, automatic writing, tarot cards, playing cards, dowsing, pendulums, divining rods, I Ching, scattering bones, sticks, beans, coins, dice, runes, charms, chanting, reading tea leaves, palmistry, numerology, astrology, observing animals and more. It can also include taking natural mind altering substances like peyote, magic mushrooms, special brews, medicinal plants and even alcohol. There is also a multitude of different forms of *mancy* like cartomancy, aeromancy, cryptomancy, chartomancy, hippomancy and so on. You might need to look these topics up to get a better understanding.

Unfortunately mainstream science, considers these practises to be *esoteric* and a little bit obscure and as a result, not a lot of research or funds have been invested in this area of humans' ability and expertise. The topics of fortune telling and predictions are thrown into the occult bucket and affiliated with the dark side. It seems that it cannot be quantified, measured, or explained easily, so it gets put in the too hard basket.

Yes I agree, there is the dark side that can be associated with it, but it is the same risk and exposure that you have for all practises.

There is also a dark side to the medical industry and within the medical profession and a dark side to the legitimate pharmaceutical industry. However, as you well know, there are also benefits and a good side too.

Without access to medicine and prescription drugs, many people would have died throughout the years. Due to the fear of the unknown, misinformation and a basic misunderstanding of some of these practises, in the Middle Ages, there were laws created to forbid the practise of divination.

God didn't forbid these practises, *man* did. Man was afraid of these practises throughout the ages, because of the special knowledge gained during these readings and this hidden information was obtained, through means that couldn't be explained.

Churches and religions around the world have gone through different phases of belief and shared different perspectives on how they view fortune telling, divine communion and communicating with the spirits of the dead. Some religious orders or churches may tell you that fortune telling is the work of malevolent spirits and even the Devil. They are wrong.

Churches may even refer to channelling as *speaking in tongues* and refer to it as a gift of divine providence, where others who may be afraid of it, will call it something else, something more sinister to throw you off track. It is hypocritical for them to persecute, or judge people, who have the special ability to talk to the spirit world, or God, because they have been given this gift of divine providence, to *help people*, not to hurt people.

There are many biblical stories that refer to prophetic dreams, prophecies, visions of the future and visitations from holy spirits, angels and archangels. These are messengers of the Lord and it would be an insult to our Lord the Creator, to call them bad, because he *allows* it and he sends them in times of need, or when specifically conjured.

Where they tend to get mixed up, is that they bundle all of the unknown seers, prophets, clairvoyants and psychics (who in those days were considered witches), into the same barrel as sorcerers, black witches and those who practise black magic. Let's set the record straight, for those of you who want to know the truth. If we set our intentions to talk to the highest of the high and the holiest of the holy, we only talk to the light side of the spirit world and the higher realms of angelic beings. If we set our intentions to talk to the darkest of the dark and the lowest of the unholy, then we talk to the dark side of the spirit world and the lower astral places, hell realms, or demonic beings.

Biblically there is a distinction made, between the white (light) crafts and the black (dark) arts and don't be fooled by those who tell you it is all the same, they do not know what they say, because of their lack of understanding . There are two distinctly different sides and two distinctly different schools of thought. One school worships the light (God) and one school worships the dark (Devil). God encourages inclusion and love. The Devil encourages exclusion and hate.

There were the warriors of the light like; Abraham, Jacob, Joseph, Moses, Aaron, Noah, Enoch, Elijah, Jeremiah, Samuel, King Solomon, Isaiah, Daniel, Ezekiel, John the Baptist, Jesus, Nostradamus, Mohammed, Edgar Cayce and many, many more, who were able to talk to divine beings, both alive and passed. How do you think they predicted the coming of Jesus Christ? They predicted his coming through prophets, seers, oracles and psychics of course. How do you think the three wise men knew where to go and what to look for? Why do you think they were called wise? They were called wise, because they held knowledge, or wisdom that wasn't known to the average person of the day. They found their way, through divine guidance and by using their psychic ability. If it is wrong to do this, then why was it biblically documented as a prophecy?

Then there are the people who conjure the demons of the dark, that also have the ability to see into the future, but they use their gift for all the wrong reasons. Black magic and the dark arts are at the seat of spell casting, séances, Ouija boards, sorcery and sacrifice.

Mediums who conjure demons and demonic people, who practise Devil worship, are *unholy* and they do not operate from the light side. These mediums are operating from the dark side and they should be avoided at all costs. They are dangerous and naïve, for they do not know what they play with. These members are the group the Bible identified as being *corrupted* and accused them of worshipping false idols. They are the false prophets the Bible warned us about. You need to be wary of any mediums practising the dark arts. You need to be even more wary of people trying to convince you that God doesn't exist. I am certain they are both anti-God and anti-Christ. There is not just one, but many.

They often wear normal clothes or suits and some of them even wear uniforms and they drive nice cars. They live in nice houses and they are not the stereotypical image that you have painted in your mind of wizards, warlocks and witches. They can be difficult to spot and even more difficult to catch in the act. They might throw on their ritual cloaks for the purpose of their satanic rituals, but you won't see them dressed like this, *unless* you are also a member of their organisation. If you knew what these wicked people were really up to, you have would have them forcibly exorcised and baptised with holy water.

There has been a gross misinterpretation between the two different skill sets, which represent the two sides of light and dark. When they were translating the Bible, they lumped both skill sets in together, based on their limited understanding and their personal opinion at the time and *not* on fact. That is why it was called heresy, which was the denouncement of God and they classed it as blasphemy. The judges were human and their understanding was limited. If you opposed the religious teachings of the day, you were considered evil. It was an assumption made by scholars, who often made mistakes interpreting the old writings. The scholars were also heavy influenced by the governing church and the governing body at the time of writing the Holy Bible and as a result, were told what to write, what to include, what to exclude and how to interpret things on many occasions, even if it wasn't right.

God reminded me, "The Bible was *not* written by God, it was written by *man*.

"In fact," he laughed, "it was written by a multitude of different men, from different eras, different cultures, different beliefs, different understandings of the interpretations and people who had different scholarly levels and abilities. How could you possibly say they were all thinking and meaning the same thing? Impossible! Who were they asking for confirmation, to check if what they were writing was correct? They weren't asking God for his opinion, nor were they checking with the archangels, angelic beings, or any holy men, who had since passed away. They were checking their work with the current order of the day, who had their own reasons for approving these writings and passing their own laws and personal beliefs onto the general populace. There is only a small portion of the Bible that references exactly what God said and that has been rewritten and reinterpreted so many times, the original meanings have been heavily edited and lost in translation."

I promise you this. Every word that is captured in quotation marks, as being quoted by God, within this book, **is** the **Word of God**. The only words that were edited, or removed, were swear words that may have been dropped in conversation, from time to time. The reason they were removed, was because God wanted this book to clean and to be able to be read by all ages. Yes sometimes God swears. God always knows the right words and the right time to say something. He even seems to swear with absolute class, if that makes any sense?

God chooses *who* he listens to and God notices those who attract his attention. He likes to talk to people with real life experience, not specifically over educated people, people with titles, or people with certain skill sets. He loves to talk to *real* people, who are on the ground level here on Earth. Those who are in amongst it all and *not* the ones at the top of the pecking order, because they do not know the answers, for those seeking the truth, mainly because they are so removed from it. God wants to get to know the ones who have experienced hardship, loss, mistakes and heartache. He wants you to learn your lessons, through a little bit of pain and then teach others how to overcome the hardest tests and still come out on top with faith.

The religions of the world would really open their eyes spiritually, open their ears to hear the sweetness of the Lord's voice and open their hearts to feel God's love, if they were to actively pursue knowledge and contact from the Creator.

Prophecy has been kept under lock and key, since the days Jesus walked the Earth. Real prophecy has been restricted from the general public and the establishment will continue to try to keep these secrets safe, by burying them in the vaults of darkness and debunk anyone claiming to know God personally. They cannot hide this knowledge from the spiritually pure psychics, or the spiritually pure people who walk the Earth.

There is a change occurring, a major spiritual shift and more than ever, people want to have a personal, one on one relationship with God. They want to have this relationship, without having to go through organised religion, a gatekeeper, or a particular sect of religion, because religion tries to make it *exclusive* for members only, instead of making it *all inclusive* for everyone.

God wants openness, inclusivity, oneness and love for *all*, not just love for some. He wants unconditional love across the planet. Love for each other, love for Mother Earth, love for all of his creations and love for your Creator, the Almighty God!

If religious groups want divine providence to be accepted and understood, then they need to *embrace* the possibility it is here, right now. It hasn't just been in the past, never to return.

God has visited many people throughout the ages, to give them divine guidance and to reveal future events to them. What makes you think he doesn't still visit people, to talk to them? Of course he does. The Bible and other religious texts show numerous accounts of prophets, psychics, seers and saints. Jesus was in fact psychic, because he could talk to God, he could talk to the souls of the living and the dead. Jesus could also manifest as an archangel, for the privileged few who were able to witness this. God gave Jesus this psychic ability and it took Jesus many years to become really familiar with his gift and his abilities.

God wants to forewarn you and to make you aware that at the end of times, false prophets will increase and you need to be wary of those false prophets.

God said, "They will come in the form of the acceptable, in the form of the new education, in the form of the new age. When they profess there is no God, when they tell you that you cannot worship God and you may even be asked to denounced my name, do not listen and do not succumb For theirs is the abominable denial, that shall be cast into the fiery pit for eternity, with those who submit and be judged no more."

Predictions

This is one topic that I am reluctant to share, because one thing I have learned is that timelines change all the time. You can *predict* an event, there is no doubt about that, but *when* it's going to happen is always tricky, because the timeline can change, based on so many other factors.

You see, psychics and channellers are really good at getting accurate information, but when it comes to predictions and world events, there are certain things that have restrictions. There are so many variables in this reality, that it could go one of many ways.

Dates can have restrictions on the other side. There are several reasons for this. If spirits were allowed to tell you the exact date something terrible was going to happen, they could theoretically interfere in the bigger picture. Spirits could technically interfere with a bigger event that may be dependent on something else happening. Spirits could therefore influence, or even trigger the very event, they are trying to prevent. Say for example, that a particular event was to be stopped, or interfered with. It could completely change the future timeline, or the destiny of the person and all of the other people involved. A spirit or angel may warn you *not* to drive to work one day and you would probably heed that warning, but *someone* still gets killed on the same route to work. It is the same route that you would have travelled, if you had left at the time you were going to. The event itself still happens; it just didn't happen to you, because the spirit or angel forewarned you of the impending danger. As a result, you avoided being at that place and time, when the event occurred.

A good example of this, is one time many years ago, when I was performing as a DJ with my partner, at a wedding function. We were playing at a hotel in the Tweed Heads area, in northern New South Wales. The finish time was fast approaching and I looked at my watch. It was 11:55pm. I announced the last song, to get everyone up on the dance floor. It had been a great night and we were getting ready to end the show at midnight. During the last song, I saw a long black shadow cross between myself and my partner, who was standing next to me at the time. We both saw it slink past. It was about the size of a tall human, but it was without definition and we couldn't tell who the figure was and why it was there. We both got goose bumps and shivers, at the same time. The hair stood up on the back of our necks.

We looked at each other and said to each other at the same time, "Whoa, did you see that thing?"

"Yep," we both replied simultaneously.

At that precise moment, one of the guests came up to the DJ console and asked if we would play just one more song. They literally begged us to stay for one more song, so they could enjoy the party vibe, for five more minutes. I looked over at the venue manager, who was standing at the back of the room and he gave me the nod to say it was okay. So we continued to play one more song.

Once the song had finished, we packed up all of our DJ equipment fairly quickly, because we had the routine down pat and we could pretty much load everything and be ready to drive off within 30 minutes. The drive home usually took just over an hour from that particular venue and there was barely any traffic on the road. It was a clear and cool night. As we approached a blind bend on the freeway, there was a fresh accident scene that had just occurred minutes earlier. There was car debris strewn across the road, from a two car collision. There were already a couple of cars on the scene and they looked like they had the situation as under control as they could, until emergency services arrived.

As we drove past the scene very slowly, we were able to get quite close to one of the accident victims and we both knew instantly, that it was a fatality. You could tell by the amount of damage to their vehicle. The other car was also a complete write off. The occupants of the second vehicle would have been injured as well.

We looked at each other again. In the distance, we could hear sirens coming and we saw blue and red lights flashing. The ambulance and police were approaching the scene very quickly. We knew there was no point in us turning around. There was nothing we could do, it had already happened. Without even saying a word to one another, we just kept driving silently all the way home, both knowing that if we hadn't been asked to play that last song, that could have been us.

The next opportunity I had to ask God the question, about *who* the black shadow belonged to, God told me it was the *Grim Reaper.* I honestly thought that the Grim Reaper was some fairy tale, or folk lore tale, that was a made up story from the old times, to scare the crap out of people. What I didn't realise, but have since learned, is that the Grim Reaper is the soul collector, like a messenger of death. He is sent to collect the soul, like the ferryman. If the soul is not prepared, or ready to be passed over to the light, then the Grim Reaper collects the soul and takes them away, to wherever he is instructed to take them.

Curiously enough God said, "The Grim Reaper doesn't actually like his job very much and he is saddened every time he collects yet another soul. He has no power to save people, only to deliver the message of death and as a consequence, he gets to see an eternity of impending doom and death. This is all he does and it depresses him, to see so many souls being destroyed. Part of his job, is to ask the victim three specific questions, which were not actually revealed to me, at least not yet. He asks every single soul he collects the same three questions. Depending on how the person answers the Grim Reaper, those answers determine where the soul is taken."

I feel honoured, that I actually got to witness the Grim Reaper scouring the area, to find the person he was coming to collect, which obviously wasn't either of us that night. He made his presence known to both of us and continued on his merry way down the road, to the car accident scene, only minutes away. It felt more like a warning and his presence, certainly made our senses razor sharp. He was just doing his job and it is not because the Grim Reaper appears that you die, it is a sign that someone's death is imminent and unlikely preventable.

To give you another more extreme example, to put the prediction scenario into context, is that you might be told that a tsunami is coming and that it is going to be *huge*. You may also be told that it is going to destroy large sections of the coastline, in the country where you live and in many other countries.

The psychic reading, or channelling, would sound something like this; "Within three rings of a tree, shall the tidal wave be seen *(each tree ring represents one year, I had to look that up!)* and the Earth shall rise."

The problem with this information is from what date, do you count the three years from? What is the start date and what is the end date? Even if you asked the spirit this information, you would still get a vague kind of answer, because they can only see future events. Time doesn't exist on the other side, like it does on *this* side, so they may not be able to give you a definite answer.

We see time as linear here on this planet, because that is what we have been conditioned to believe. Time doesn't actually exist. It is just an illusion, but I don't want to complicate things for this explanation. Three years from the date you were originally given, may have already passed and the event still hasn't happened. That doesn't make the reading incorrect and it doesn't mean the event isn't going to happen either. It just means the *timing* of the event, cannot be accurately predicted.

God explained, "Another reason you are not usually given dates, is because if everyone knew there was going to be a global catastrophe in the near future, they would freak out and start thinking about it all the time and that thought pattern shared by lots of people, can be enough to create, or increase the intensity of the event itself."

What God wants us to do is *pray for change*, pray for improvement, pray to save the planet, the environment, the animals and the rainforests. *Pray to influence* those in power in a positive way, so they have a change of heart about destruction and power. *Pray to God* to ask him to save us and to help Mother Earth. God wants to see that you are worthy of saving and not contributing to the destruction, or the destructive mindset.

I ask loads of questions about world events, because I am genuinely interested in the fate of our planet. Will we be here 1000 years from now? What will the Earth look like? What will become of our species? Yes, I do get many answers, but these answers do change frequently. The answers change based on the day I ask and what other events are occurring in the Universe, at the same time. What humanity needs to understand is that the energy they direct towards progress, can, will and does influence future events. If humanity focused on the positives and not the negatives, then things will improve and catastrophes that may have been on the radar as possible events are no longer etched in our future.

As mentioned previously, I don't want this book to be about a possible scary and bleak future, full of tragic events, or about things that might, or might not happen. I don't want to contribute to the fearful energy that so many humans thrive off and add to it, by concentrating on it.

Future events are exactly that, *future* events, which mean they haven't actually happened yet and they may never happen. Some things are preventable, like nuclear war. In fact, all wars and disagreements can be prevented, by right thinking, living in harmony with our brothers and sisters and by learning to forgive those who have wronged us and who may have made mistakes in the past.

Retaliation does not stop future negative events from occurring. It has the opposite effect, by adding fuel to the fire, until the rage and hatred becomes so out of control, it consumes everything in its path. Don't allow yourself to be *influenced,* by the dark side. It is easy to be bad, it takes effort to be nice and live on the righteous path. Who is really in control of you? Are you in control of yourself, or have you given up your control to something else?

Entry into heaven cannot be brought, sold and exchanged. Do you value your soul enough, to get back on track? There is no need to participate in revenge, or payback, because it never ends. It's an ego trap, an endless cycle of birth and death, pain and suffering, trauma and heartache. You must overcome hatred, with love. It is the only way.

Use the power of your mind to perceive and manifest a peaceful and happy future. Focus your energy on rebuilding the broken relationships and repairing the broken hearts.

There are two ways you can look at future disasters, if they were to occur.

1. **Be prepared physically** for a catastrophic event and have some kind of plan, just in case.
2. **Be prepared spiritually** for a catastrophic event, because anything could happen to you, any second, of any day, especially if you are faced with death unexpectedly. This is why you should have already made peace with your loved ones. You should live every day to the fullest, while you are alive on this planet.

Another important fact is the Earth goes through phases and cycles, regardless of what science tells you and what is predicted. There is no need to hypothesise about an event, if it is actually going to occur. It is more like trying to understand, or calculate *when,* based on statistics and predictions. Yes, there is that word again; *predictions.* For example, earthquakes happen and they have definitely been on the increase, over the past ten years. That is undeniable.

God said, "Air pressure sets off an earthquake, which is the key. We don't measure the air pressure to predict an earthquake, but we could start doing that."

Scientists, meteorologists and other experts predict things all the time. They too face the same unusual dilemma. They may know that some event is going to happen at some stage, but they can't accurately predict *when* that particular event, is going to happen. So why is it that people are happy to accept the predictions of a so called expert, who have official titles, but won't listen to reputable psychics, seers, or prophets?

Everyone is talking about *climate change* these days, which used to be called global warming. They have now upgraded the political speak, to climate change, because even the scientists can't predict if we are heading for an ice age, or a heat wave. One is always preceded by the other, so the question is not, *are we going to have another ice age one day?* The answer to that is yes! The real question is *when?* One year from now, 100 years from now, 1000 years from now? It will happen someday, because it is one of the Earth cycles that occur naturally anyway. So is a heat wave, with a severe drought and dry spell. When the Earth becomes unbalanced, it naturally corrects itself. When the ozone layer becomes damaged, Earth does what it has to do, to regain balance and control of the environment.

We are simply residents here on Planet Earth and contrary to what many think we don't own it. Nobody can own it, we aren't superior to Earth. We are just like ants on the surface of this giant ball of water, gas, minerals and earth. The Earth will out survive us, many times over and it has proven this, from its mere age. It can sustain impacts from meteors, radiation blasts, intense weather systems and even human interference. Eventually Earth will correct itself and we will either hang on, or drop off. Planets and space debris pass near us all the time and sometimes they come very close to Earth on their way through, which can have a huge impact on our gravity and electromagnetic fields.

We don't have the resources, or technology to influence these mighty forces, but God does. If you want to do something positive, then focus on being positive. Pray for positive change, pray for God to save us and pray for your own spiritual salvation, if and when the time comes.

I was also told, that by the year 2100 that most of the Earth will be covered by water and that *could* mean that low lying areas *may* not be safe, within the next 100 years. The east coast globally, *may* be affected. There will be houses built of glass. It doesn't hurt to plan for that. Think about it and maybe plan for houses and buildings that can float on water, or be raised in the sky in the future.

We can *plan* for it and if it never happens, then that is because other events occurred in the background, to prevent it from happening. If these events don't happen, then it is great news for everyone. But... if it does happen, you can think ahead, manage the risk and be prepared.

The channeller on behalf of God said, "God allows his creations to do their thing and that can sometimes mean, *not* interfering with the evolution of a planet. He wants to see what will happen, if one planet passes another and what the effects may be. He is not cruel and would not purposely create an event to destroy us. If anything, humans are quite capable of annihilating themselves, without any help from any other species."

God often throws in little morsels, about how things will be in the future and how people will look. He told me what humans would be wearing, what the climate will be like and what the buildings will look like. He often mentioned the large dome type force fields that will be created in the future, to keep the air inside the dome breathable, once we have destroyed the atmosphere. The domes can be sealed and they double as a shield from outside forces.

He didn't mention how far into the future this will be and I know he doesn't tell me this, for a good reason, because he doesn't want people to know *when* that will be. He doesn't want to influence things to happen and he knows that we can work towards a solution, where we may not require this type of technology to survive.

God also told me, "Within the next 100 years, it will be commonplace for humans to wear tunics, which look like a type of robe. The robes will be colour coded, to denote the occupation of the wearer. The climate will be much different than what it is today. It is not warmer, it is colder. There will be order on Planet Earth and no need for conflict by then, because as Earth faces many major challenges and cataclysms in the near to distant future, mankind has no need to fight with one another. Survival, working together and restoring order, is more important to the survival of the species. Killing will be extremely rare, not necessary and not tolerated."

God also mentioned the dome shaped temple buildings that are commonplace and scattered all around populated areas. Some are joined by walkways and tunnels that are protected from the outside elements. It is not a religious centre, but more like a philosophical and spiritual place, where people can gather and learn how to be at peace. They are like spiritual sanctuaries, or havens. Somewhere quiet to go and contemplate, or to meditate.

God said, "Within the next 10-20 years, there will far less people on the planet eating meat, because it will be banned. There will be a deadly disease that will spread across the whole food chain, killing many people. Those who continue to eat meat will die from the disease and from consuming the infected meat."

This prediction makes me tremendously happy, because I am a vegetarian. I still cannot understand why humans have such an insatiable appetite for meat anyway, especially at this stage in our evolution as a species. Meat is already full of disease and parasites. It is not meant to be consumed by humans. We don't *need* meat to survive at all and we are better off without it.

19. FULFILLMENT

God is giving everyone a chance to be their own guru,
so they can take control of their own lives.

FIRST, you need to recognise what fulfillment is, before you can achieve fulfillment. The first part of fulfillment is having the idea in the first place and *imagining* what it would feel like to achieve it and the second part, is actually *feeling the fulfillment*, when you achieve it.

The following topics will help to highlight what fulfillment is and how to achieve it.

Learn to help each other

God said, "The reason the Earth is overpopulated with humans, is because planet Earth is the most popular place at the moment as a holiday destination for aliens, of which the human race belongs. You are not native to this planet."

The original writings were to thank the Creator for letting you be here. What we should be saying is, *"Thank you God for this wonderful food, thank you God for everything. I wouldn't exist without you."* Why? Because you wouldn't exist without his love.

The channeller said on behalf of God, "The things on our body, we are given from God, mean that we sometimes get annoyed with him. For example, if you are in a dusty environment, you will naturally have bushier eyebrows, because they are designed to protect you. There is no separation between God and the soul. We are all part of the same framework, the same values and the same race."

God said, "We are one and you are *all* my sons and daughters, my children. You are all of one blood, one nation, one people and one tribe."

God heard his son Jesus, speaking to humans in the past and one of his teachings were, "Should a man kill another man, or should a man help another man? If a man helps another man, he shall surely make a friend. If he kills another man, he shall make an enemy."

God continued, "If you talked like this about *all* things, *every* day, then you would be loving."

In light of what Jesus said, God added, "Think about this. If a man shall have a farm and grow three yarns, then this shall help another man, by feeding him. This is a *loving* thing. Would the farmer go out and kill his friend? Then the farmer wouldn't be a farmer, he would be a killer! Which one gets more satisfaction? Feeding a man and making him happy, or killing a man and burying him?

"Think about this. Take one man's belongings from him unlawfully and you are *taking*. Would you enjoy this, or would you rather be *given* it? Because remember, if they are all taught to be thieves, they would all *take* from one another. If they were all taught to love and give to one another, then they would *give* to one another. They would all share and give to each other and you wouldn't need to take it from anyone else."

The channeller said, "God made creation the way he wanted it to be and he wanted to remind you, "When you go to sleep, you get tested to find out what your worst fears are. The demons are trying to find out the worst fear that you don't like. Once you fear that kind of stuff, then you *become* it, when you sin."

God said, "If everything is a flower, then you can't get affected by it, but that is knowing right, from wrong. You would be affected by the sins, because you know that it was wrong. Really on the other side, what is right and wrong? The cow goes to the slaughter yard and you don't. Those of you in the slaughter yard should be praying for your *own* souls, *not* the animals' souls, because the animal soul will be there to get hold of you, when *you* die. You that chops the chickens legs off, shall be stomped upon by chickens and not be able to get up. Pecked, you shall be made to be food for the chicken and made to run all day every day.

"My innocent friendly cows that live in harmony with one another, surely those who harm the cows, shall be surely harmed on the other side? Those of you that eat of it shall be eaten and sent back to be cannibalised and sent back in time. They will learn, only when the deadly disease plagues thousands and thousands of lives. No one shall touch the beast and all of man's meat will be infected."

God added, "If you can't work together, you become extinct! They hated themselves so much, they wiped themselves out. If you walk around the planet thinking, *I don't like you and I hate you*, then you are destined for extinction as a species. You need to love one another and co-exist on this beautiful planet and even live in harmony."

God knows that people are wondering why God isn't coming to fix a planet in turmoil. God created this planet for everyone to enjoy and look after.

God said, "If you destroy the planet that you were supposed to look after, then you don't have a planet to live on!"

God continued, "If you love what he gave you, why should you destroy it? You get angry at him, he gets angry at you. You love what he made and he loves you back."

God told me the order of the things.

The channeller on behalf of God said, "God rolled trees and plants out first, then made a body (human), based off what the plants provided.

"The deception for God was that he didn't expect that the humans he created would cull all of the other living things. All the bugs and creepy crawlies were made, *before* humans were made. The total life was lost, after the Garden of Eden and God still laughs, because humans think they are so smart, when their actions prove otherwise."

Spiritual evolution

God said, "The more spiritually evolved you become, the harder the lessons that one must face. The bigger the solution must be, to fix the problem.

"You must live your life to the fullest, before giving your life to the rainforest."

We are all ultimately heading in the same direction and all ultimately heading towards the same place. Some get sidetracked and divert way off the path, for an unknown period of time and some are really focused and make leaps and bounds, in their progress towards enlightenment.

When you fully face your inner demons, embrace the world for what it is and see the Godliness in *everyone*, you are on track to spiritually evolve. When you live in a state of fear, complain about everything going wrong in your life, gossip and constantly criticise others, you are on track to spiritually *devolve.*

In this way, life is like a game of Snakes and Ladders. When you have a win, you get to experience a challenging, yet fulfilling spiritual lesson. Having a winning breakthrough, means you get to climb *up* a ladder and progress further ahead on the spiritual game board.

When you have a backward moment, when you lose your cool, do something dumb, hurt someone, or deliberately cause chaos, you slide *down* the snake and then you descend and deteriorate into spiritual darkness.

We all have good days and bad days and sometimes, we might even have a whole string of good days, or good weeks. On the other hand, we may have a run of bad days, or bad weeks. Inevitably, we are faced with challenges that test our faith and our good will. Don't let those challenges break you, but let them *highlight* the lessons you have to learn. Put your good skills into practise and overcome your ego.

SNAKES *(hinder advancement)*	**LADDERS** *(promote advancement)*
Bad influences	Making new positive friendships
Negative behaviour	Surround yourself with likeminded people
Destructive tendencies	Discovering a new talent
Addictions	Love God
Debt	Live within your means
Disease and illness	Being fit and healthy
Lack of family support	Having supportive people in your life
Self criticism	Praise yourself
Criticising others	Praising others
Poverty	Being happy with what you have
Unemployment	Earning a living from what you love doing
Grief	Enjoying life
Depression	Happiness
Suicide	Choose to live

If you do something wrong, make amends. If you do something right, feel good about it. Praise yourself for living in the light and you will attract more of that. Keep striving to be a better version of yourself today. Make tomorrow a new day, where you get to *apply* your training and if you are having a bad day today, tomorrow is always a new day.

Treat every day like another opportunity to be kind, loving and good. Find the Godliness in everyone, especially people you least expect to have it in them. Go one step further and bring out the Godliness in someone, make this your daily test. Dissolve your expectations. This will keep you in the *evolving* mindset, by always looking for the good in everything and everyone.

Everything and everyone has the God particle within. We are *all* capable of loving and living a truly inspirational life and bringing out the best in others.

Enlightenment

All we *need* to survive is food, air and water. In addition to these essential things, we need to be able to *plan*, think ahead and work out where the next meal is coming from. Having the ability to think about the future, even if it is only five minutes ahead of time, means we need to have *foresight.*

Enlightenment is when we combine the use of foresight, hindsight and insight, to make correct choices, based on the best available options.

God said, "Enlightenment means that when someone is feeling sad and depressed and experiencing horrible feelings, they are able to be shown the slightest amount of what they are missing, like a spark in the middle of the night and that's what an enlightened soul does. They help the darkened soul to see the light, or *enlightenment*, which gives the darkened soul hope and faith."

God continued, "When somebody, who is experiencing some form of darkness, looks into the aura of a glowing light and they can't see the light glowing, someone who knows what the light feels like, or looks like, needs to show them the light, or the beauty and the balance again."

Enlightenment once it has been experienced by the enlightened one should be *shared,* not kept hidden and private. Those that are seeking truth, go out into the world, seeking the wisdom and knowledge of the enlightened ones.

These wise ones can be hard to find, in a sea of strangers. Enlightened people always have an aura about them, a glow, a beacon that emanates love, compassion and understanding. This is the beacon of *connectedness with God* and the Universe. It is the connection of your soul, to the Divine Creator and the connection of nature, to your immortal soul, knowing that this material incarnation will not last forever. It is not meant to. Your soul lives on forever and the energy of your soul will never die, for it is eternal.

Your soul is the spark, it is the light, it is the God force within you and it is the inner knowing, that *everything* happens for a reason and at the right time.

God asked cryptically, "How do you stop all of the destruction on Earth? By taking away the food, which takes away the greed, then they focus on *enlightenment.* The purpose of life is to learn, grow, love, heal and open up to the Creators energy."

Enlightenment can come from anyone, or anything, even from immersing yourself in nature, to a point where you get lost in the veins on the leaves, distracted by the breeze blowing in the trees and having that loving and warm feeling, that you are a part of something much larger. You are not just a number or a nobody. You are *somebody special*, we all are.

Enlightenment is the feeling you get, from someone who is both fully grounded *and* has their head in the clouds at the same time. They *project* their loving energy, so there is plenty for you to bathe in, if you can get close enough to them to experience it. If you know someone like this, you can always *visualise* them giving you loving energy, love and light, even if they are on the other side of the world, or on the other side, in the spirit world. You can also send love and light to them as well and reap what you shall sow, by having the loving energy returned to you in other forms, because that is how energy works. You get back, what you put out.

Enlightened people can come from all walks of life and can even be the beggar in the street. Never judge anyone that you do not know, because they may hold the secret keys to universal wisdom in their hearts and if you don't open your own heart to see it, you might just miss it.

Enlightenment is the ultimate level of awareness and understanding. It is the aim of every human, during their quest here on Earth. This level of experience can only be reached when all other levels have been fulfilled.

I personally consider enlightenment to be a state of being where you finally realise, there is a force *greater* than your own individual self and you are working together with that greater force. The idea is, to first accept this force, then embrace this force and develop some form of union with this force. The force is the *Life Force that* emanates from every one of us.

There are many definitions and names for this force. A few of these names could be; God, Allah, Jah, Brahman, the Almighty Lord, the Universe, Spirit, Christ, Nirvana, Divinity, The Holy Trinity and so on. It doesn't really matter what you want to *call* this force, as long as when you *feel* it; that Qi (chi) running through your soul, you understand what *it* is. It is the very same life force that exists within you, that keeps you alive physically. It is the same force that lit the spark inside the embryo, from which you came and it is the same force that was breathed into your lungs, when you took your first breath.

In Buddhism and Hinduism, enlightenment is described as: *a blessed state, in which the individual transcends desire and suffering and attains Nirvana.*

It is further described as: *the awakening to ultimate truth, by which man is freed from the endless cycle of personal reincarnations, to which all men are otherwise subjected.*

Enlightenment is regarded as the goal of all religions and philosophies.

This is not to say that you must be religious, or philosophical, to want enlightenment and nor does it mean that if you are neither of these, then you cannot achieve enlightenment. All humans ultimately need to aim for enlightenment, even for just a taste of the feeling, in order to understand *who* they are and *why* they are here.

Every one of us, get to have small tastes of enlightenment from time to time, throughout our life experience. Enlightenment gives us the glimmer of light that we are searching for, like a torch light in a dark cave. These small moments, or tastes of enlightenment, remind us of what we are searching for and in a way, give us the spark of reconnection, to something bigger than ourselves. Without these reminders, or markers of our true self, we become lost and further disconnected, from our spiritual existence, or our higher self.

Some examples of feeling moments of enlightenment would be:

★ Crying true tears of joy, when you feel totally connected to everything.

★ Feeling joy in a deep state of meditation, or relaxation and you are still awake.

- ★ The feeling you get after climbing the summit of a mountain.
- ★ Completing a lifelong mission, that has taken a lot of preparation and planning.
- ★ Marrying the person of your dreams.
- ★ Feeling spiritual enlightenment, even if it is only felt momentarily.
- ★ Having a beautiful dream, where you are in complete control and enjoying every minute of your experience, within your dream.
- ★ Remaining in an exceptionally awesome mood and feeling totally blessed, even when you are surrounded by chaos.
- ★ Communing with higher level beings.
- ★ Tapping into your psychic ability and receiving confirmation, that you were correct.
- ★ Loving God and his creation.

We must be aware, that even when we reach the ultimate level of fulfillment, it may not be everlasting 100% of the time. The key is to tap into the moments, when we feel like we are at the top of our life experience, or at the peak of our existence and feel like we are literally on top of the world. This is when we need to store the pleasurable experiences and memories, to be recalled and utilised, during times of hardship and feeling down, to help us get through the daily challenges.

No person on Earth holds the special key to your spiritual enlightenment, or salvation. It is a connection that exists between you and the Creator and no one else. No person can withhold this privilege from you. No one can stop you from achieving it and there is no one on Earth, who can claim to be the *only* one to know. There is no mystical guru that can teach you to become magically awakened. You must awaken yourself.

The opposite thought pattern is taught to us, to keep us submissive to the system and to stop us from seeking the true spiritual path. Every true spiritual seeker realises, that at some point in their journey, they have to go it alone and walk the path. *You* are the only person that can achieve it on your own terms, when you are ready.

By all means, research the topic of enlightenment, read books, watch videos, attend courses, absorb as much information as you can about the subject. Ask for guidance, from people you trust. Just know that there is no single correct religion on Earth, nor is there only one true path to enlightenment. There can be many ways to achieve enlightenment and many roads can take you there. You cannot force it, or rush it, because enlightenment is something that *happens,* when you are ready.

Being a guru

What is a guru? A guru is described as; a teacher, guide, expert, or master of a certain knowledge, or field.

God said, "A guru that we traditionally know of, gets up, goes and lives for 40 days and 40 nights in the desert, or on the mountaintop and then comes back and shares their wisdom. In the end, they come to the conclusion, that you can have it all. Everything they have is worthless and even the empire of dirt, becomes worthless! Don't buy things you can't afford, because you will become enslaved by paying for those *things*. Don't feel attached to *anything*, because the attachment itself, will only cause you grief, when you realise that you cannot keep it, or hold onto it.

"*Everything* is temporary, as well as your human incarnation. Stop dilly dallying around and get on with what you have to do, to make your life count, to make a difference. Then help others to find the meaning of life."

God has asked me to teach people, that they are their *own guru*. God is here to let you all know, he is watching over you and you don't need anyone else to be your guru.

God continued, "Learn to be your own guru! Answer your own questions, using your higher self to help. Don't answer other people's questions. When a question is asked, one must break the question into bits. One's mind should not be seen as *one* mind. It should be seen as categories that make up one mind. Like multiple sections of the mind, a million trillion different possibilities."

God added, "One needs to command the brain, to use more than its current 10%. When a question is asked, it is most important. One must use their mind, to sort information into sections of relevance and also ask the question, about what is relevant about the question. One question may have a million answers. For example, there are a million answers to any question, which there is, but you could say, here are 10 answers."

One question I had on my mind for quite some time was when I was searching for a rural block of land to buy, to live on later down the track. I wanted something that would help me to be self sufficient. I also wanted somewhere that people could come and visit and experience peace and tranquility.

So I asked God a direct question, "How will I know which block of land, is the right block of land for me to buy?"

God responded in his infinite wisdom, "My child, for what reason do you need this block of land? The same question can be answered, in a million different ways. Break the question up, like sections of the mind."

I explained that I wanted the block of land, to build a spiritual retreat that people from all around the world could come to and get reconnected to God. Somewhere people could reset and take some time out from their daily grind. Somewhere people could improve their health and wellbeing on every level.

God explained, "You should have been asking your inner guru the question, to which you would still have a million possible answers, but here are 10," and he laughed.

1. It will have space and privacy.
2. The land will be able to have food grown on it.
3. There needs to be space for gardens.
4. Need to be able to set up a Permaculture area.
5. Must have wildlife on it and an area where wildlife can be protected.
6. Need to be able to play your music, without disturbing anyone.
7. There needs to be an area dedicated to Yoga and spiritual healing.
8. Must set up some accommodation, where people can stay.
9. Would love to have room for an art gallery.
10. There will be enough space to have group outings and education.

God continued, "Do you get the picture? There are so many options, choices and answers to any given question. Don't get stuck in just *one* option. There is no such thing, as the *right* answer.

"As much as I love gurus and think they should be well respected for their wisdom and their great spirituality, there is no question that you could ask a guru, that you couldn't answer yourself.

"You can represent your thoughts and choices into a diagram, to make the picture clearer. One needs to understand the significance, to chunk it all down into sections, to make the question easier to answer."

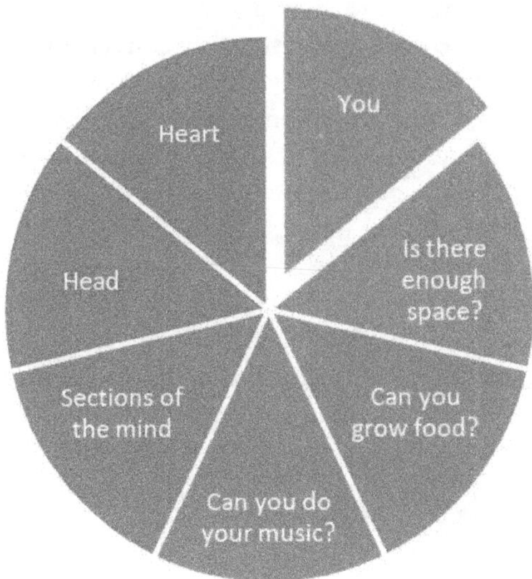

It is so important not to get carried away with thinking that *so called experts* and gurus know what the best outcome for you would be, based on your particular set of life experiences. For everyone it is *different* and each person is at *different stages* of their spiritual evolution and may not be ready to accept the advanced lessons that a guru has in store for them. The guru is living a simple, unadulterated, humble life in a head space that could be miles from where you might be right now.

It doesn't matter if you are not enlightened overnight. Keep plugging away at your mission and keep searching for the answers. If you are persistent, the answers will come.

Treat others as you would like to be treated and if you are asked for your advice, then you can offer it, by offering them a *suggestion.* You shouldn't be offering advice to someone, if they are not interested, unwilling to listen, or who doesn't want to hear what you have to say, otherwise the conversation will quickly escalate to conflict and the whole point of the conversation will be lost.

A good way to avoid this issue in the first place, is to ask the person this question, *before* you listen to their problems. Say to them, "Okay, so I am willing to listen to your problems wholeheartedly, but I may like to offer you some advice, or suggestions, if I hear the whole story. Is that okay with you?"

If they say, "No, I don't want to hear, what *you* have to say."

Then you can simply respond with, "Okay then, I don't want to listen to *your* story."

This is not being careless, or unkind. It is being truthful and teaching the person who wants to offload their problems, to take some responsibility for their own issues. It is also showing them, that you are willing to help, *only* if they are willing to engage in a two way conversation.

This action will stop pointless venting and complaining, when you no longer give it energy, or pay attention to it. This will also stop people from wasting your time unnecessarily. If they genuinely want help with a problem, then they will engage in a two way conversation with you. If not, then the person is not taking ownership of their problems, which will not resolve anything, especially if they are not willing to listen to another's point of view. This could even be the very reason; they are in this predicament in the first place. Can you see how this works?

If you want to show someone the path of the guru, then don't talk about it, live it! Lead by example and actually *practise* what you preach, by *doing* it. That is the *only* way and that is the whole principle of a being a guru and being your own guru.

Faith

What is faith? First we need to understand what faith is, before we can apply it to our own life. Having faith is defined as having trust, or confidence in someone, or something. You can have faith in anything and you can also have faith in God.

I don't feel the need to *prove* my belief, in the existence of God. I also don't feel the need to *prove* my faith in God to anyone. The words of this book are for the purpose of giving you *proof* and helping you to strengthen, consolidate and maybe even rediscover your faith. If you *need* proof, you are just feeding your ego and not listening to your true self, who knows this information is truthful and divined by God.

You don't need to raise a flag, wave a banner, wear a t-shirt that describes your faith, or yell it out from a mountain top. You can have quiet, confident, inner faith, if you choose and you never have to share that feeling with anyone, if you don't want to. You don't have to be like a circus monkey, who has to perform tricks for everyone. There is no need to justify, or explain *why* you have faith.

Having faith is exactly that. It is a waste of time and energy, arguing about your faith, because you would be operating from the opposite mindset, of what you believe in and where your faith comes from.

You don't need to prove your faith, or belief, to anyone but God. I have every ounce of faith that a human could possibly have, because I have personally seen, heard and experienced things, that are supernatural and divine and what the ancient civilisations would have called mystical.

There *are* unseen forces that play a huge part in our everyday life, without us seeing, hearing, recognising, or even knowing about their existence. There is so much going on behind the scenes. There are many other worlds and many other dimensions, that existence simultaneously, alongside us. Just because we can't *see* them, or *feel* them, doesn't mean they *don't* exist. Not having a belief, or faith in *anything,* just closes the communication gateway between worlds and numbs your experience on this material plane of existence. Stop, listen and learn and for just one minute, attempt to understand. Make an effort to hear the voices of the spirits. Tune in to the mystical world and I can assure you, in time, a world of wonders will open up for you.

God doesn't like us to get too cocky or arrogant and test his faith. This is something a demon, or the Devil would do and that is exactly what Satan tried to do to Jesus, when he was in the desert for 40 days and 40 nights, seeking his spiritual communion with God. Satan tried to convince Jesus, to test his faith, by throwing himself off a cliff and trusting that God would save him.

If you throw yourself off a cliff, you will probably die. God is not going to send Superman to catch you in the nick of time, to prove that he exists. That is not having faith. That is *tempting fate* and testing faith in the wrong way! You must learn to tell the difference between God testing your faith and Satan testing your willingness, to betray God.

Faith, like God's existence, is difficult to define in a sentence and even harder to describe to someone, who doesn't have faith. Allowing yourself to have faith is being prepared to give up your conditioned beliefs, letting go of the need to control your every action and *surrendering* to the power of now. The power of now is where you will find God, not by sorting through your dusty past, or peering into your hazy future, but *right now* in this moment. God is always with you. You can simply accept his presence and he will be there. If you deny his presence, he is still there, but you refuse to feel him, or acknowledge him.

If you are faithful and struggle to get others to see things your way, realise it is not your job, to convince other people of God's existence. You can keep an open door, so that when seekers try to find you and start to ask questions, you can satisfy their curiosity. Your job is to simply just be who you are. Be your authentic true self. There is no need to impress anybody, prove anything to anyone, or make anything sound bigger than it really is. Just be in the now and share that precious moment with your loved ones and the Creator.

Faith simply means that deep within your heart, there is an inner knowing that God exists. Deep within your soul, there is a solid foundation of trust, that while you are alive here and now, you are being watched over by God and his angels. You can choose to surrender your ego and have faith, that when your time comes, no matter what happens, you will eventually return to God.

Your faith will be tested many times throughout your life and you may even go through stages, where you have really strong faith and at other times, you may even feel a lack of faith and start questioning everything again. If you want a sign from God that he exists, then *ask* for a sign, don't just expect one. A sign doesn't necessarily come in the form of earthquakes, floods and cataclysms. That is much too dramatic for God. God lets Mother Nature take care of those events.

God's signs can range from being so subtle, that you may even miss these signs, if you are not paying attention, to full blown, *slap you in the face* obvious signs. I tend to get the slap you in the face kind, in the nicest possible way of course. I equally appreciate the subtle earthly signs of God's existence that are everywhere. Now that I know what to look for and what that loving feeling *feels* like, I know when God is around. It's a beautiful thing. Why would you want to deny that feeling of pure love, pure adoration and pure faith? It doesn't make any sense?

Inner guidance system

My dad once had an incident in New Zealand, where his faith, persistence and his inner guidance system were truly tested, all at the same time. My dad has a great memory for places he has visited, as well as a vivid and active imagination. Luckily I inherited these noble features from him, so I can truly appreciate and relate to this story.

Picture this… Winter is almost at its peak, in June of 1992. Dad had been assigned the role of relief warden, at the Deep Cove Hostel in Doubtful Sound, which is located in the Fiordland National Park in New Zealand. Earlier that day, there were many pleasure fishermen checking into the hostel, to prepare for a weekend of fishing in and around Doubtful Sound.

Every night around 6:00pm, the warden was required to check in to the Te Anau office by radio, to let them know that everything was okay.

My dad had worked for the Department of Conservation for many years and often worked in isolated areas, within the Fiordland National Park, which is a massive national park, sitting at 1.2 million hectares of wild bush.

Sometimes, he would be away for a week, or two at a time. Amongst other tasks, he would sometimes be there to do track, or hut related maintenance work, in the dense New Zealand bush. They would check on the native wildlife, check the state of facilities and ensure everything was in full working order. Rangers and wardens may be required to repair a section of track, build a new section, or just check to see if all walking tracks were in a safe condition to use. Most of the time, they would walk in by foot, which meant miles of walking over mountainous terrain and country side with full packs.

My dad had an intimate knowledge of most of the walking tracks in the Fiordland National Park. All of the rangers know, that some of the New Zealand terrain, can be pretty rugged and very treacherous, especially if the weather turns suddenly, during the months leading up to winter and right in the heart of winter. The darkness of night can bring with it, freezing temperatures and survival can be very slim, if you get lost, or have an accident in the middle of nowhere.

So, my dad is currently located at Doubtful Sound. It's 6:00pm and during the conversation with Margaret in the Te Anau office, while he was checking in, dad heard a faint, *"Mayday, Mayday, Mayday!"*

Dad asked Margaret, "Did you hear that?"

Margaret said, "No, hear what?"

Dad said, "Hold off saying anything for a couple of minutes, while I establish where these distress calls are coming from."

They both waited in silence. Nothing happened. All dad could hear, was static and some random clicks on the radio and no voice.

Dad put his thinking cap on and came up with a solution. He knew he would have to devise a method of communication that only required a button push to answer. He would have to work out what questions to ask, to be able to work out the location of the distress signal.

Dad grabbed hold of the radio microphone again and asked the question, "Can you hear me?"

Nothing but static and clicks.

Dad then asked, "If you can hear me, click *once* for yes and *twice* for no."

One click for *yes* could be heard through the static.

Okay, so they had established a communication method.

At the time, dad was thinking they were also located in the same area he was located, so he asked them, "Where in Doubtful Sound are you located?" He read out as many locations as he could think of.

Each time, two clicks for *no* came back.

Now dad was thinking, *okay maybe they are somewhere different?* Then he also thought to himself, *maybe my assumption of them being on a boat, is not right?*

A mayday call is usually associated with being on a boat. To begin with, dad naturally assumed the caller was on a boat.

Dad asked, "Are you on a boat?"

Two clicks for *no* came back.

Dad asked, "Are you in the National Park?"

Silence on the other end.

Dad thought about the question and rephrased it, "Are you in the Fiordland National Park?"

One click for *yes* came back.

"Are you lost?"

Two clicks for *no* came back.

"Have you had an accident?"

One click for *yes* came back.

"Are you okay?"

One click for *yes* came back.

"Is somebody with you injured?"

One click for *yes* came back.

"Okay, let's establish your location?"

Dad went through every track he could think of, within the Fiordland National Park, until he said, "Are you on the Routeburn Track?"

One click for *yes* came back.

It just so happened, that dad had worked the previous six months on the Routeburn Track, the very same track where these people were having issues. He knew the track intimately and knew every section of that particular track. He could literally visualise every section, in his mind's eye.

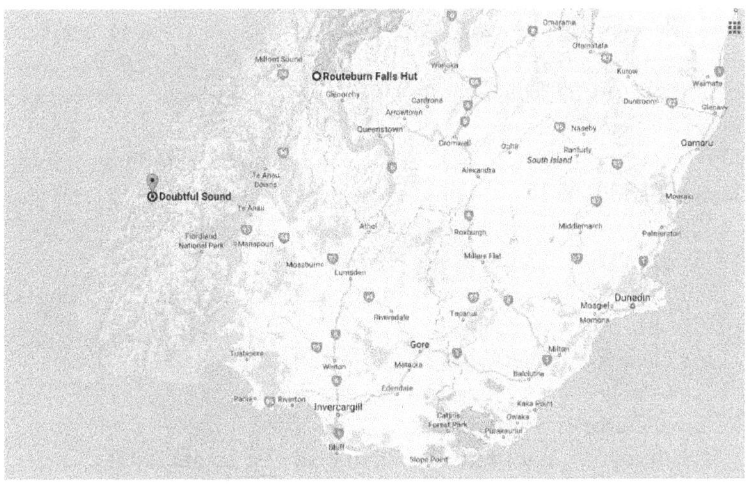

"How many injured people are there?"

One click came back.

"Can you assist them with their injuries?"

Two clicks for *no* came back.

"Is it a serious injury that requires emergency medical attention?"

One click for *yes*.

"Has the injured person fallen down an embankment?"

One click for *yes*.

Dad asked the people on the radio, at the Routeburn Hut to standby, while he raised an emergency call for the search and rescue operation.

Dad asked Margaret back at the Te Anau office, "Contact the police in Te Anau and report the need for an emergency search and rescue crew, to be dispatched to the Routeburn Track. Once you have them on the radio, we can coordinate the rescue operation."

It was now around 7:00pm, in the middle of winter in New Zealand. It was pitch black and only the bold and the brave, would risk everything, to carry out a rescue operation at that time of night, in the middle of the wild bush.

In the background, the Te Anau Police were looking for a helicopter pilot and a rescue team, to fly from Te Anau to the Routeburn Track. The first pilot they asked was a very experienced pilot from Te Anau. He said it was far *too risky* for him at that time of night, in the middle of winter, to be flying his chopper into the unknown. He had a full set of search and rescue lights on board, but didn't feel right about attempting the trip. He suggested they try a helicopter pilot in Queenstown instead, because it would have been less risky, to fly in from the Queenstown end, rather than the Te Anau end.

The police were now working on plan B, as quickly as they could.

Phone calls were made to the Queenstown Police and another team was being assembled.

Dad had to think quickly now and needed and work out *exactly* where the injured person was located.

Dad asked the people on the Routeburn Track, "Do you know where the Harris Saddle is? You would have walked across it today, on your way to the hut?"

One click for *yes* came back.

Dad said, "Okay, I want you to visualise you are standing on the Harris Saddle, facing north."

One click for *yes* came back.

"Is the injured person east of the saddle?"

One click for *yes* came back.

"The hut you are located in, is that also east of the saddle?"

One click for *yes* came back.

"Okay, so you are located at the Routeburn Falls Hut?"

One click for *yes* came back.

"Roughly, how many kilometres from the hut, is the injured person located? Use one click for every kilometre."

Four clicks came back.

"Roughly, how long did it take you to walk to the hut, from the injured person? Use one click for every 10 minutes.

Four clicks came back.

Dad had now established the injured person was roughly four kilometers, or 40 minutes walking distance from the Routeburn Falls Hut.

"Standby, we are sending a search and rescue team to your location. Let the injured person know, that help is on its way. Please do not leave the location tonight, until help arrives."

One click for *yes* came back.

By using his techniques and quick thinking, dad was able to pinpoint the exact location of the injured person, to within a hundred metres and he was able to establish the nature of the injuries, so the police could send the right people and equipment.

The police dispatched a very capable and experience helicopter pilot from Queenstown, along with two very fit and experienced mountaineering doctors, who were living and working in Queenstown at the time. They were very experienced mountain climbers, with Mount Everest under their belts and they were also very experienced with search and rescue operations, down cliff faces and in extreme conditions. Lucky for the injured man, he had the best help he could possibly get, anywhere in the world.

When the search and rescue team arrived, the two male doctors abseiled down the cliff face with pain medication, basic medical supplies and sleeping equipment. The doctors huddled around the injured man for the whole night, keeping the man alive, until he could be winched out to safety at first light.

I am so proud of my dad; he is a very smart man. Everyone involved in that operation knew, if they didn't act fast, the injured person would have died from hypothermia, if they were left alone on the ledge all night. New Zealand helicopter pilots and search and rescue volunteers are a pretty hardy breed and they are world renowned for their amazing search and rescue skills, in some of the toughest terrain in the world.

Thanks to the team effort of everyone involved, the injured person was rescued and flown to Kew Hospital the following day. He would have been thanking his lucky stars; he was able to live to tell the story.

The story made the news headlines and was aired in a special documentary, showing the re-enactment of how the situation unfolded and how with the right thinking, patience and persistence, the injured person's life was saved.

Believe it, or not, dad never actually got to meet the person whose life he had saved. In fact, he never even got to speak to him either. He did however; receive a letter and a personal thank you from the police.

Here is a small extract from that letter:

11-06-1992

Mr. Max Davis,

We wish to pass on our very great appreciation to you, as regards to your input into the very difficult search and rescue operation involving Mr. Holsterman on the Routeburn Track. I have no doubt that if you had not picked up the Mayday transmission and acted promptly and correctly on it, then Mr. Holsterman certainly would have perished as result of his injuries and the terrible weather conditions in which he was trapped.

Constable JD Jameson
Te Anau Police

The whole reason I am sharing this story with you, is to illustrate the point that, even though my dad could not see, or even hear the person calling for help over the radio, he had been able to devise his own method of communication and had faith in his own ability to provide assistance.

The information obtained using this method, was used to coordinate a whole search and rescue operation, from his location which was further than 100km, from the site where the incident had occurred.

By using these techniques, combined with his complete persistence in questioning, he was able to locate someone, in the middle of a massive search area, in the remote New Zealand bush, within *cooee* calling distance.

Afterwards it was discovered, that the injured person was a German tourist travelling by himself, who had fallen down an embankment. He had broken his leg, arm and ribs and had luckily landed on a ledge, down a cliff face. He would have been at risk of dying from hypothermia, if he had been left to fend for himself overnight.

The hikers, who heard the injured tourist calling for help, were walking on the same track further behind. There were not many people game enough to walk any of these tracks, at that time of the year. Once they established communication with the injured tourist, the hikers had walk to the nearest campsite and break into the ranger's hut, to gain access to the radio. Unfortunately the radio hand piece they found, was broken and had been reported as needing repairs weeks earlier.

You see, faith works in conjunction with the inner guidance system. You get presented with a seemingly impossible challenge and after nutting it out for a little while, you work out a code, or system that works. In the beginning, you only get dribs and drabs of signal and sometimes it's scratchy, faint and not quite clear enough to get a full sentence, or to get a full picture. So you have to keep asking questions, to clarify if what you are thinking is correct, or not. Then you need to keep checking it constantly, to ensure you are still on track. This is the true meaning of persistence, perseverance and patience. In the end, it does pay off.

It is no different, when you are asking for signs from God. You consistently ask for a sign and whether you realise it or not, you are already getting answered constantly.

Just like the example with the hikers and my dad. You just need to *tune your radio dial,* to the right frequency, to pick up the signal. If that fails, then go to plan B. *Tune your mind to the right frequency,* to pick up the signals from spirits and God.

My dad is a man of discreet faith. He celebrates God quietly and not publicly. He thanks God often, for all the good things that happen in his life. He is grateful to be alive. Dad used his faith, in his own God given ability and faith in his inner guidance system, to help him *listen* for the answers he was seeking. He used these skills to save a man's life and I am so proud of him and the whole rescue team, for their efforts.

The saddest part of this whole story is that one of the doctors, who helped to save the life of Mr. Holsterman, died in an unfortunate mountaineering accident, on Mount Everest a few years later.

I hope that the doctor relayed the rescue story to God, when he arrived in Heaven. I know that God would really love a true action hero!

Recognising the signs

Recognising that God is with me, is demonstrated when God uses animals, creatures and ridiculous coincidences, to show proof of his existence to me. He also uses the number seven (7) all the time, as a reminder he is with me. It is like our personal little joke. I will often get seated at table seven at the restaurant, the hotel room I check into will often be the number seven and the rental property I end up living in, will usually have the number seven in it. That can be one of the ways that I know, I have found the right place to live, because God is constantly showing me these trusted *signs*. Right now, even the street number at the place where I work, is the number seven.

These days, I don't constantly need God to show me proof of his existence, because I am faithful and I am in mental communication with God regularly. God still likes to show me things anyway, just because he can. I still love to be shown signs and I love feeling the synchronicity, when it does happen.

No matter how many signs I receive, I still love to receive more. I never get bored with the subtle and the not so subtle surprises God gives me. He might send me a beautiful butterfly, just at the right moment, birds who land near me to say hello and sing their sweet songs, dogs that magically appear out of nowhere when I go for a walk, cats that run across the street to say hello, animals living secretly in my garden and the little miracles that appear, whenever I take notice. God's miracles are everywhere. Sometimes I will look up in the sky and see a massive rainbow appear on my way to work, or see a massive flock of birds, flying overhead in a majestic formation, at just the right time.

My whole existence is by virtue of God. I am so thankful and so grateful for his gracious presence, every single moment, of every single day. I know that God is not some airy fairy mental picture that I am creating, or wishful thinking that I am dreaming up. It is a reality that I get to experience daily and would love for you to feel even a slither of what I feel. When you do, you will never be alone again.

I haven't always been this faithful. My faith has been tested multiple times. I have had to learn some really tough life lessons, especially when I thought I was truly alone. I have had to battle with my own inner demons, overcome my weaknesses and I have had to take a really honest look at mistakes I have made in the past, to learn how to conquer the challenges, associated with self forgiveness.

During the course of my life, I have been consistently asking for signs and asking for contact. I was already being sent the response from God for every request. I just didn't recognise the responses at the time. I wasn't aware of what to look out for and didn't know the how to identify the communication I was receiving. I wasn't spiritually awakened enough, to realise that I was already in contact. You could say, my radio dial was just off the channel and I needed to retune the dial, to sit on the right channel again, on *channel God.*

I have been granted these things through perseverance, persistence and patience and because I asked. I reached out to talk to God, with the full *intent* of getting some kind of response. God isn't scary; he is so lovely and so kind. He has such a big heart, a great sense of humour and he is *really* funny. He is willing to forgive you, for anything you have done wrong and he will praise you and reward you, when you do things right.

I would love to be able to reach out and *touch* God. I would love to hold his hand and cuddle him, but have to accept, that while I am on this plane of existence, I will just have to settle for touching things that God has created. Being a part of everything and feeling connected to everything cosmically, *is* the way to talk to God, until you can be with him in Heaven again. There are no shortcuts and no cheating will get you there any faster. You have to put in the commitment, just like you do in any relationship.

How to live a holy life

God is giving everyone a chance to be their own guru, so they can take control of their own lives. God is merely watching over you and not controlling you, because you are exercising your free will to be here. Let me remind all of you, that *you* exercised your free will to come here, to experience this life.

This means, at the time of separation from God, you will be on your own. At the point of separation, God asked you, "Do you agree to these terms?"

And you said, "Yes I agree."

There is no need to be upset, or get mad at God, because you feel separated from him. It is a part of the deal, to be able to come here and experience this life. It is also a part of the deal, that you will get *this* body, or *that* body. You were asked what gender you wanted to be, so don't blame God for which one you picked. You are not supposed to go and change your gender, because you changed your mind. It doesn't work like that. It was ultimately your choice. You selected your family and yes, *you* selected your life. It is preordained. Then "*ding*" you have been deployed, as per your choosing.

Once you realise all of this, then you can get on with being happy and stop wasting time complaining, about all of the injustices you are suffering. We start out as pure and sweet, until we are corrupted by our parents, peers and the establishment.

Learn to be your own guru and be responsible for your own life. If you have already mastered being your own guru, then teach other people the righteous way and show others the right way to do things. Be the shining light that people aspire to be like and show people the way. Make an effort to live consciously, harmoniously and strive to remember where you came from, with every part of your being. Then you will discover, what you are supposed to be doing here.

One of the best ways to live a holy life is to conjure up God and think to yourself, *what would God do in any situation?* If you have more of an affinity with Jesus then ask, *what would Jesus do in any situation?* If you struggle with this concept, then simply ask yourself, *what is the right thing to do in any situation?*

Know that *you* are an original, just like *I am* an original. All God has asked from each and every one of us is that we just be ourselves. Our genuine self.

God said, "If you are spiritual, you will grab God and wash yourself with him. The Holy Trinity is *cleansing* your body, with the love and holiness of God. Test that on the cross!"

Treat your body, like a sacred holy temple of God. Your body is a sacred vessel and it needs to last you throughout your whole life on Earth. Your body needs to be kept in the best possible condition that you can manage. This is learning how to charge your body with the holiness.

You *are* God. Everyone is God and everyone has the right to be God.

Get reconnected

To summarise all that we have learned from this book so far, is to give you the opportunity to *reflect* on what *is* important in your life and what is *not* important. You have now learned many things about the Creator, you may not have known. For those of you who doubted God's existence, I hope this book has cleared up some questions for you.

If *you* had the opportunity to ask God just one question each, what would that question be? I have been asked by God, so many times, "Do you have any questions for me?"

Sometimes my brain just goes blank, because I think I have already asked him all the questions that I personally wanted to know. Then later that day, or week, I think of something really important to ask and I have to wait until our next meeting to get the answer. I already have an inner knowing, of what the answer is likely to be, but in this human form, I sometimes doubt my abilities, my wisdom and my experience.

If *proof* of God's existence is what you are looking for, the proof is already all around you. It is in *everything* and it is *everywhere* and it is *inside* you! You are made in God's image and if you tune your frequency dial into this exquisite vibration, you will start to see miracles happen in your life, every day, just by being open enough to see and feel it. First you must *believe.* Then you shall *receive.*

If you choose to *deny* the Creator, he does not cease to exist. It just means that you choose to remain disconnected, from the ultimate Source of love and light that exists.

Believe me, to be connected to the main source of the Life Force, is better than any drug, any holiday, any high, any adrenalin rush, any amount of money and any material thing that you could ever own.

To know and accept God as your friend and companion is to complete the missing piece of the puzzle. To love God, is to fill the deep void that you have been trying to fill with everything else. It is an inner knowing, that is so comforting and truly satisfying. It will sustain you, all of the days of your life on Earth and beyond that, into the afterlife, when you get to the other side.

You have nothing to fear, when you have full faith and place your trust in the Lord.

Amen

20. THE FUTURE

Life is in the now and we experience life as a reality, in the right now time zone.

WHERE is the future? What is the future? The future is *here* and the future is *now*. Time is an illusion that you are cloaked in right now, to help your existence on this planet, feel less weird.

If you knew every single thing you had done in your previous lives and every single thing you are going to do in your future lives, do you think you would ever actually *do* anything? Probably not. There wouldn't be any point to your existence, because you would already know everything. You would have already experienced everything. Then there is nothing to learn.

The veil of secrecy surrounding the future is reserved for the few who can tap into that frequency. Those who can travel beyond the barriers of time with their mind and who can remember the past and the future, from when they were on the other side. Just like remembering your dreams, some people have a better memory than others and some are more skilled at travelling into the future, with their mind and spirit. To talk to a channeller and understand the order of things in the Universe is to have personal encounters with *Realm Walkers*.

A part of the deal when you come here, is *not* having full access to the past and future all of the time, because it might stop you from doing things in the *now* existence. It may also affect your mental and emotional health, if you remembered every birth and death that you have ever experienced, or are going to experience. Life is in the now and we experience life as a reality, in the right now time zone.

We are supposed to *learn* from all of our past life lessons, in the *past* time zone. We project into the *future* time zone, to visualise and imagine what it would be like, to be somewhere, or something else in the future. It is a way of mentally checking if we would be satisfied, or happy with the outcome, if we first travel there in our mind's eye, instead of going there for real and getting disappointed when we get there.

Talking to my future self

I hope you have enjoyed reading this book, as much as I have enjoyed writing it and sharing it with all of you. Now that we have almost reached the end of this book, I wanted to share something truly special with you. This channelling came through for me personally, from my future self, once it had passed over. As weird as that sounds, it was a really enlightening session, particularly for me, because it was such a beautiful experience to meet my future self, in the spirit world.

I was so used to conversing with God, or Jesus, or my long lost relatives that I hadn't even thought about contacting myself. It was actually my own future self that contacted my past self, from the spirit world. I was on the *other* side, talking to myself on *this* side. I remembered that time has a different vibration when you are on the other side. That means you can travel backwards and forwards in time, with no boundaries, like we have on this plane of existence.

God said, "We are so *conditioned* to see time as the linear representation. It is very hard to see time as it really is an illusion."

The following section contains the words I said to myself, through the channeller, word for word and unedited. I am going to use these beautiful words about Heaven, to inspire me to write more books and continue searching for more answers.

My time in Heaven

Speaking to myself from the other side, through the channeller, I said, "And I rose up into the Garden of Heaven and I heard the music that I had made, playing in the Garden of Heaven. He said to me, 'You shall make music, for those who are here, to hear.'

"And he rejoiced in the sound and watched the souls as they rose, one by one, into the garden. The angels were to the left and the angels were to the right and the throne of the Holy of Holies was in front of me, and I did not die, or have to go to him.

"He told me through the channeller and the channeller was blessed. The channeller had known him, through the key of life."

And the channeller responded nearly crying, "Hail thee Almighty!"

The channeller continued speaking for me, "For I was talking to myself, through the channeller, *after* my life experience. When I passed away in the future, I was able to talk to my younger self, through the channeller, so I could tell you this and remind you of your future self, through your present self. This was allowed from the Creator of Wisdom and the Creator of Wisdom, is Archangel Michael."

The channeller added, "Raphael cringed and anointed at the same time, the creation, the presence of the mortals and watched over Earth as it was and shall be, taken in turns of the highest angels. I saw a mountain, as the channeller cleared their mind. This mountain of love and of withering age and rockiness of wisdom and points to its past. Behold the creation of wisdom and pray to this mountain of hope and love. Understand the endurance of the mountain and climb to the top of your faith. Believe in the Creator of all YESHUA. Wanu Wanu."

The channeller said, "I could feel Jesus' energy and the spirit of Jesus. I could feel Mother Mary and Jacob and the descendants. I could feel Jacob and Noah and Noah and Adam and I felt Eve and it felt like I was surrounded, they'd come to show me the way. Then I saw the hand of Jesus and of Mother Mary and Mary Magdalene, eagerly taking my hand to show me the Kingdom in front of me.

"I asked them, 'What is the tree?'

They responded, "It is the tree of life, the creation of all things."

The channeller continued, "Then there in the open I am, with the one and only tree that is watched over by many. There are thousands of angels watching. You feel like you've been ripped out and put on a stage. And as I held both hands out, warmth and light and love, I felt herein."

The channeller speaking for me added, "And Jesus appeared in front of me and he had long curls of hair. His green eyes were iridescent. His hair was thick and healthy. His beard of ginger and of brown, with amazing swirls *mesmerising*. Even if you looked at one hair on its own, it would bring you joy, love and light and *overwhelmed*, if you looked at him in all.

"This is truly the image of God and could be mistaken for God. You would be surpassed in his presence and want no more. He has the feeling of authority and you would *never* disobey the Messiah of Creation. It is rare to see the image of the Lord, but the Messiah is he. For all of mankind he has been of and died for your sins and will do again and again, for only the righteous ones. Be very afraid, if you are not righteous, for your time is near.

"And I could hear the sound of the animals in the background and it sounded like a jungle. It was to my left, behind me. Then I realised that I was not alone and that mankind *shares* Creation with all beings and animals and plants and Creation. We are not dominant, we are all as one. I was not afraid, when I saw the tiger, the lion, the panther, as they had the same feeling of warmth that I had. And I saw the messiah of lions and the messiah of each animal, waiting above them. Flowers and butterflies and insects and an amazing unison of all creation in abundance.

The channeller finished, "Then because you are alone, you feel the presence of Jesus and God and it shall be in everyone's heart. You shall *ask* and the presence of an Angel of the Lord shall be upon them and the Holy Spirit will rain upon them and they shall rise up and embrace the Lord."

The Retreat

From a very early age, it has always been my lifelong ambition and dream, to build a spiritual healing retreat, for people just like you, from all over the world. I want to cater for people from any ethnic background, any culture, any age group and from any belief system. Come to *The Retreat* and experience God. Not just talk about God, but really *experience* God. Learn practical ways to interact with him and his angels. This will be an opportunity, to get *reconnected* with the Almighty Lord, in your everyday life.

Come and experience the God energy within you and reconnect with the Creator's energy, through nature and activities, to feel truly alive. Discover your life's true purpose and learn how to figure out the meaning of life and your role within it. Discover your *true* self, your *authentic* self, your *real* self.

The Retreat will not belong to any religious denomination, nor will it have exclusions, or special requirements that you need to fulfil, to become a member. This retreat will simply be a beautiful place, like the new Garden of Eden, where you can take time out, away from the hustle and bustle of the city, society and the ordinary working life. Retreat to a beautiful, peaceful and tranquil country setting, nestled south of the Border Ranges, on the New South Wales and Queensland border, in Australia.

Come and listen to the birds singing, connect with the animals living in harmony with each other, walk through our butterfly gardens, relax in the magnificent themed gardens and receive God's healing touch, when you come and visit us at *The Retreat.*

I am so grateful to have a wonderful support network of truly enlightened people, who are helping to make this dream a reality right now. We have started planning the retreat layout and will be building the retreat over the next couple of years, maybe even sooner, depending on the progress of funding and assistance.

The Retreat will also be a place of health and healing, where the focus will be on holistic and natural therapies, to identify the *root cause* of any problem. Once this has been identified, it can be healed and treated.

Indulge in the pure fresh country air, immerse yourself in the sounds of nature and be awestruck by the amazing starscape, against the back drop of a rugged and pristine mountain range.

It will become a renowned and recognised spiritual place of healing. We will establish a reputable learning centre, for many years to come. For those of you who need special attention and divine healing from the light and love of God, *The Retreat* will be a welcome sanctuary and a safe place, to explore one's spirituality.

A range of safe, holistic healing modalities will be offered to all guests. There will also be many spiritually focused activities, offered during your stay, if you choose to participate.

The Retreat will enable people to switch out of the material world and get back in touch with the spirit world.

Come and join us at *The Retreat,* to heal your mind, body and soul.

If you feel passionate about this cause and would like to donate towards this worthy project, you will be amongst the first in the world, to get involved in the creation of this wonderful retreat.

God has given me guidance and permission, to ask for help. He explained that it is okay for me to ask for help, because he knows the intent of this retreat, is to help to rebuild and strengthen our connection to God. You will have the opportunity, to donate towards a worthy and special cause. You will be contributing towards creating a unique and special place on Earth, to celebrate the God force within you and all around you, just as it is in Heaven. This is somewhere; everyone can go and enjoy a well deserved break away, from the everyday pressures of life in society.

Even the smallest donations will be appreciated. Every single donation, including $1.00, will help fund this project. Every person who donates toward *The Retreat* will receive a gift for their contribution.

Please go to the website to see what donation options are available. There will be prepaid retreat packages that can be purchased, which include accommodation, meals and transfers from the nearest airport, which is Gold Coast Airport. You will be able to purchase advanced readings, channellings and holistic healing therapy packages, to help fund *The Retreat.* Even businesses will have the opportunity to donate towards the buildings, facilities and garden projects. They can even choose to the name of the garden and have their business logo and details at the entrance of the garden as a sponsor.

You will of course, also have the option, to simply donate unconditionally towards the cause, if you choose. When you donate over a certain amount, you will gain VIP entry into *The Retreat,* with special privileges once it is open.

Please tell all of your friends and family about this book and about *The Retreat* project. You can treat yourself, or even treat your loved ones, to one of The Retreat packages on offer.

Once *The Retreat* has officially opened in early 2019, you will be able to book your stay and explore the range of options available. All of the details of the project and the progress of *The Retreat* will be shared on the following website.

www.thewordofgod.com.au

Further study and education

For those of you with a keen interest to learn more and delve deeper into the root cause of your problems, I will be offering online courses, education programs and workbooks, to assist with your soul journey.

If you want to heal your emotions, understand how to integrate what you have learned into your everyday life, set goals and achieve them, then these additional educational tools, will be very useful for you and will help to guide you through your learning experience.

I will also be providing ongoing YouTube videos and website Blogs, which will include many different topics, such as: faith, hope, guidance and support. I will aim to cover as many modern and current subjects as I can.

www.thewordofgod.com.au

My Next Book

I would also like to share my intention to continue writing. I love sharing these pearls of wisdom with all of you.

My next book will be called, *"Heal Your Body with God - Personal encounters with Realm Walkers Volume 02."*

In this particular book, I am going to reveal a unique, life harmony system that was channelled directly to me, from the Creator, in the middle of the night.

Through my contact with the Creator, writing this book and my continuous searching for answers through the channellers, I am learning *how* to communicate through my own senses, my feelings, by listening carefully and from suggestions, or visions I am given spiritually and telepathically.

I was shown a detailed picture of this life harmony system, which was represented as a cycle. I am going to share a holistic way of healing with you. I will show you *how* to heal your body with God and also describe in detail, this new holistic way of living. You will be guided and shown how to put this into practice, using a new healthy system of living. It is so simple, that *anyone* can embrace it and implement it easily.

The overall system is so basic and yet so streamlined, that it *has* to be a divine message. I have no doubt where it came from. I was asked to create this harmony system, to help humans extend their life, heal and repair their body and to show people how to enjoy the life they are living, even more.

I will reveal ancient secret remedies, used to heal people in the past. I will show you, how to use certain combinations of herbs, spices and special blends, to rejuvenate the skin, heal the inside of the body, maintain the outside of the body and calm the mind.

Thank you

Once again, thank you for taking the time to read this book. Bless you for your patience and willingness to learn more about yourself, the world around you and your Creator.

Until next time, I wish you all the love and light of the Creator and his band of mighty angels! Thank you for joining me. God bless all of you!

Give the Lord your love and he will give you his Kingdom.

Amen

"There is nowhere to go, only how to be."

Jan-Marie Davis

ABOUT THE AUTHOR

I have discovered that I actually love writing books. I didn't picture myself as a writer, until I realised I was a modern day scribe.

This book called, *"The **Word of God** – Personal encounters with Real Walkers Volume 01,"* is my debut book and a good way for me to introduce myself to you.

Volume 01 was seven years in the making, due to the distractions of everyday life. This epic journal is from an eventful lifetime of discovery and wonder. I have spent more time *living* life, than *contemplating* life and as a result, time has just rocketed by.

Born with curiosity, I was always the one to ask those awkward questions, that no one else dared. I always asked the tricky questions, when other's feared the answers.

Once the channellings started, my world was changed forever. I could no longer see the world the way I used to. Once my eyes and ears were spiritually opened, there was no turning back. Every question I had, was answered through the channellings, in the most meaningful and constructive way.

This book documents the dialogue between God, spirits, the channellers and me, the scribe.

My love for God is real. My faith in God is immovable and my calling has finally been answered.

This book is the first volume in a series of seven (7) books. The series is called *Personal encounters with Realm Walkers.* You have just finished reading Volume 01, *"The **Word of God.**"*

Each book in the series will reveal more hidden secrets, from the other side and will explore the in depth *conversations with God* and other spiritual entities from the higher realms.

I will take you on a journey of self discovery. You will become a part of the adventures, using the gift of *prophecy.*

On behalf of the Almighty God, the channellers, the spirits and the angels, we thank you for reading this book. God loves each and every one of you, now and forever.

www.thewordofgod.com.au

NOTES

NOTES

Index

www.ingramcontent.com/pod-product-compliance
Lightning Source LLC
Chambersburg PA
CBHW062355090426
42740CB00010B/1283

* 9 7 8 0 6 4 8 1 7 2 2 0 8 *